Library of
Davidson College

VOID

Pitt Latin American Series

Pitt Latin American Series
James M. Malloy, Editor

RECENT TITLES

Argentina

Argentina Between the Great Powers, 1936–1946
Guido di Tella and D. Cameron Watt, Editors

Argentina: Political Culture and Instability
Susan Calvert and Peter Calvert

Argentine Workers: Peronism and Contemporary Class Consciousness
Peter Ranis

The Life, Music, and Times of Carlos Gardel
Simon Collier

The Political Economy of Argentina, 1946–1983
Guido di Tella and Rudiger Dornbusch, Editors

Brazil

Capital Markets in the Development Process: The Case of Brazil
John H. Welch

External Constraints on Economic Policy in Brazil, 1899–1930
Winston Fritsch

Kingdoms Come: Religion and Politics in Brazil
Rowan Ireland

The Manipulation of Consent: The State and Working-Class Consciousness in Brazil
Youssef Cohen

Politics Within the State: Elite Bureaucrats and Industrial Policy in Authoritarian Brazil
Ben Ross Schneider

Unequal Giants: Diplomatic Relations Between the United States and Brazil, 1889–1930
Joseph Smith

Frondizi and the Politics of Developmentalism in Argentina, 1955–62

Celia Szusterman

University of Pittsburgh Press

Published in the USA by the University of Pittsburgh Press,
Pittsburgh, Pa. 15260

Published in Great Britain by The Macmillan Press Ltd, in
association with St Antony's College, Oxford

© Celia Szusterman 1993

All rights reserved

Printed in Great Britain

ISBN 0-8229-1181-7
LC 93-60339

To my mother and father
in Memoriam

and to Daniel
for the infinite joy he brings to my life

Contents

Preface   x

Acknowledgements   xiii

1   The *Revolución Libertadora*, 1955–58: Liberalism Restored?   1
1. Introduction   1
2. The Decline of the Peronist Regime   3
3. The *Revolución Libertadora*, 16–21 September 1955: An Account   11
4. The State of the Armed Forces   13
5. General Lonardi and his Foiled 'National Revolution'   16
6. General Aramburu's Objective of a 'Democracy for Democrats'   19
7. Conclusions   30

2   The Split of the *Unión Cívica Radical*   32
1. Introduction   32
2. A Background of Internal Strife   33
3. The UCR in the 1930s   35
4. The UCR in the 1940s: The Youth Movement and the *Intransigencia*   38
5. The *Intransigencia* during the Peronist Decade   44
6. The Internal Structure of the UCR   47
7. The 1956 UCR National Convention in Tucumán   49
8. The UCR Splits – the UCRI is Born   51

3   The Elections for the Constituent Assembly, the Perón–Frondizi Pact and the Failure of the *Revolución Libertadora*   54
1. Introduction   54
2. The *Libertadora*: 'Caretaker' or 'Revolutionary'?   54
3. Perón in Exile and Peronism in the *Resistencia*   62
4. The Constituent Assembly, July–November 1957   64
5. The Aftermath of the 28 July Elections: the Perón–Frondizi Pact   70
6. Conclusions   73

4	**The Ideology of Developmentalism and the Development of the Ideology**	**75**
1.	Introduction	75
2.	Developmentalism as an Ideology	75
3.	The Intellectual Atmosphere in the Aftermath of the Second World War	79
4.	The Premises of Developmentalism	83
5.	The Role of the Developmentalist Ideology	89
6.	The Electoral Campaign and its Organisation	91
7.	Arturo Frondizi – from Radicalism to Developmentalism	97
5	**The Implementation of the Developmentalist Economic Programme. The First Aim: 'Development'**	**108**
1.	Introduction	108
2.	From 23 February to 1 May 1958	109
3.	Frondizi's Inaugural Address	111
4.	The Cabinet	113
5.	A 'Revolutionary' 1958?	116
6.	The Stabilisation Plan of 1959–60	120
7.	The Evaluation of the Developmentalist Economic Policies	122
6	**The Develpmentalist Strategy: the Internal Constraints. The Second Aim: 'Legality'**	**131**
1.	Introduction	131
2.	Composition of the Legislative Power	131
3.	Frondizi and Congress	133
4.	Frondizi and the Judiciary	143
5.	Conclusions	145
7	**Frondizi's Relations with the Political Parties**	**147**
1.	Frondizi and the UCRI	147
2.	Frondizi and the Legal Opposition	164
8	**Government and Society: the External Constraints. The Third Aim: 'Social Peace'**	**168**
1.	Introduction	168
2.	Developmentalism and Intellectuals	168
3.	Developmentalism and Entrepreneurs	176

4.	Developmentalism and Labour	179
5.	Developmentalism and the Military	192

9 A Gamble Too Many: The Elections of March 1962 and the Fall of Frondizi — 208

1.	Introduction	208
2.	The 1961 Elections	208
3.	The March 1962 Elections	210
4.	The Fall	215

Epilogue 220

Notes 225

Bibliography 293

Index 306

Preface

> The last temptation is the greatest treason:
> To do the right deed for the wrong reason.
>
> T. S. Eliot's Thomas à Becket

Latin America's poor performance in recent decades was not caused by failing to get policies or prices *right*, but rather by not getting *politics* right, in the words of James Dietz and Dilmus James.[1] It will be my contention that Argentina's predicament has been the result of just such failure, and although I have chosen Frondizi's thwarted government to explore the reasons why this should have been so, I do not believe he was the only, nor the main culprit in an irritatingly long process during which Argentina appeared resolutely to have left a brilliant future behind her. The dilemma facing Argentina was the centuries-old one that so many countries are facing today – how to consolidate a new, democratic republic after a sudden rupture of the old corporatist regime lacking the necessary values and traditions of the desired republic. Perhaps the answer lies in doing what needs to be done rather than by dreaming of what ought to be done. What the Frondizi experience revealed was that the task of institution-building towards the consolidation of a liberal-democratic type of government and society which had been the hope of those who overthrew Perón in 1955 could not be carried out by sheer voluntarism and utilising undemocratic behaviour. The principles of corporatism, State dirigisme and xenophobic nationalism had to be discarded if a free, democratic, and just system could flourish on a sound economic base. With the benefit of hindsight, Frondizi can be regarded as a pioneer in terms of his economic policies. Alas, that was not how his contemporaries judged him.

Argentina in 1958 had not yet learnt the hard lesson of politics, that is to say the contrast between expectations and fulfilment. Finer has noted that 'when a government sets out to be faithful, it is frequently unwise; and when it has learned to be wise, it is frequently unfaithful'.[2] Frondizi acquired his wisdom just before taking over the presidency, thus his unfaithfulness was more readily seens as duplicitous and, given the passions arisen by Perón and Peronism, treacherous. The developmentalist experiment can be studied under a double focus: (a) as a developmentalist (economic) project, and (b) as a political project, and as such known as *integracionismo*. The fact that it is remembered as developmentalism rather than integrationism reflects the fact that it was relatively more successful in the economic than in the political arena.

The aftermath of Perón's overthrow, including the government resulting from the elections held in 1958, seemed a promising period from the point of view of the revelation of clues to understand Argentina's predicament. Certain elements of a typically Argentine political tradition [and political culture, to use a term in vogue once again] can be traced back to that period (others, to even earlier ones). All in all, I hope this study of the years 1955–62 will contribute to an understanding of the reasons why Argentina only recently appears to have been able to place its future ahead, rather than behind.

When I submitted my thesis in 1986, the Public Records at Kew had just been made available for 1955. I have been able to consult the records up to and including 1961, and the Washington National Archives on Argentina for the years 1954–59. Regrettably the Foreign Office still sees fit to keep from historical scrutiny some documents that are over 30 years old. It is to be hoped that in the present world context, such secrecy will soon become obsolete.

The fact that 30 years after Frondzi's overthrow *the Unión Cívica Radical* – its division in 1956 obliterated as a passing aberration – is still struggling between a populist strand and a more modernising one highlights the difficulty of the task Frondizi faced. It took Alfonsín's victory in 1983 finally to prove to the whole country – and not just the Peronists – that they were not the whole people and thus representatives of the 'interests of the Nation'. The fact that only 30 years after Frondizi's presidency the country as a whole (including the military, business community, labour and politicians) seems to have learnt the harsh lessons of intolerance and ideological fundamentalism (of whichever sign) – and that this required the horror and traumas of thousands of deaths, political, ideological and State terrorism as well as of hyperinflation – exerts a humbling influence when looking at the country's past history. Perhaps all the horror, the pain and the misunderstandings were necessary to achieve that state of maturity Sir John Ward so sadly saw lacking in the whole of South America. A good friend of Argentina, whose despatches were always thorough, always fair, he despondently wrote what many would find insulting even today and yet rings so true. Shortly before leaving his posting he remarked that 'a complete and perfect solution of Argentina's economic problems can however hardly be expected in the foreseeable future, given the prevailing political conditions and the low levels of intelligence, morality and competence which are endemic to South America at this immature stage of its development'.³ At least two of the indictments in the case of Argentina seem to have been overcome.

CELIA SZUSTERMAN

Acknowledgements

My former supervisor at St Antony's and present friend, Alan Angell, was able to remain constant and unfailing in his support and encouragement throughout the years. The editor and the publisher of the present series, Rosemary Thorp and Tim Farmiloe, showed remarkable patience and faith each time a deadline came and went. This book started as a D.Phil thesis at the University of Oxford. My examiners, Sir Raymond Carr and Guido Di Tella, made comments and suggestions that guided me during the process of rewriting.

There are two people to whom I owe a special debt of gratitude. One is Ezequiel Gallo, with whom, in Essex, Oxford, London and Buenos Aires, I have shared for twenty years worries, irritations and hopes in relation to our compatriots. The other is Juan Carlos Torre, who first suggested that the period 1955–58 could provide interesting clues in the understanding of contemporary Argentina. My colleague and good friend generously read several chapters to my great benefit. Throughout the years, be it in Oxford or in Buenos Aires, he patiently and critically read the first chapters offering comments that were consistently thought-provoking. Alas, the Atlantic Ocean made its presence felt, and for the last chapters I was regrettably unable to benefit from Juan Carlos Torre's views.

I owe a special debt of gratitude to those men and women who had supported Frondizi, and shared with me their memories of hopes and disenchantments. I have benefited from their personal recollections. Amongst them, my stepfather, Isak Radunsky and Juan Lozano. Nicolás Babini not only devoted hours to reminisce, but he shared with me his comprehensive collection of cuttings, short-lived publications, etc. My conversations with Ezequiel Gallo, Guido Di Tella, Natalio Botana, Tulio Halperín Donghi, Gustavo Ferrari, Félix Luna, Ernesto Laclau, Ismael Viñas, Ricardo Rojo and Silvia Sigal, in Oxford, London, Buenos Aires and Paris, were invaluable in helping me build a picture and recreate a feeling for the period.

My thanks go to all those protagonists of the events told here, even though not one will be able to share all the views contained herein, who were willing to devote hours to help me. Although I hesitate to pick certain individuals, Roberto Alemann, Alvaro Alsogaray, Rogelio Frigerio, Rodolfo Martínez and Alejandro Agustín Lanusse were especially generous with their time.

Finally, many friends offered different kinds of support throughout the years. Foremost amongst them, the late Matilde and Manuel Madanes, and Jorge Garfunkel. And my gratitude to all those friends who shared preoccupations, miseries and joys: Malcolm Deas, Ana María Mustapic, Ignacio Klich, and Andrew Graham-Yooll. I am indebted to my colleagues at the University of Westminster: Ana de Otaola, Roger Bell and Hilary Footitt. Deirdre Gallagher spent a whole week at the Public Record Office in Kew photocopying the files for 1961. The Library staff at the School of Languages were always willing and efficient in providing help.

It is customary to thank one's spouse for her/his patience. In my case it is inappropriate to do so: my husband, Tono Masoliver, has none. But he did have something more important to offer, something which helped me enormously through the years: the example of what dedication to, and love for one's work is all about. Without such a companion, the solitary task of book-writing would have been much more difficult to fulfil.

1 The *Revolución Libertadora*, 1955–58: Liberalism Restored?

1 INTRODUCTION

The *Revolución Libertadora* is still clouded by passions, resentments and partisanship, notwithstanding the embrace of President Menem and an ailing Admiral Rojas in 1991 symbolising the end of thirty-six years of mutual hatred and misunderstanding. Were the military in Argentina in 1955 acting as the Praetorian guard of the oligarchy, wishing to turn the clock back to 1943, or 1930, or even 1912? Was it the reaction of the propertied classes to halt the inexorable advance of the working class, advance that would have threatened the capitalist system and the unequal distribution of privileges it guaranteed? Or, if the capitalist system as such was never really under threat, was it a means of putting workers 'in their place' after almost a decade of demagogically-created uncontrol? Was it the attempt to fight the unfinished battle of democracy against tyranny on Argentine soil dating back to February 1946, when Perón was first elected to the presidency? Was it perhaps the reaction of one half of the population of Argentina resenting the fact that not only their needs and wishes were ignored, but that they were even dismissed as anti-Argentine and anti-popular simply because they were anti-Peronist?

It is necessary to answer the above questions to understand the significance of Dr Arturo Frondizi's victory at the polls on 23 February 1958 on a platform advocating 'national reconciliation'. This propitiatory view of Peronism would break the anti-Peronist front with long-standing consequences for the development of political life in the country. The events of 16–21 September 1955 illustrated once more the close links that civilians and military had established since the early days of the nation. In this sense, the *Libertadora* continued a tradition of cooperation dating at least back to 1890 and the frustrated *Revolución del Parque* which marked the birth of the *Unión Cívica Radical* (UCR). If in 1890 – and subsequent uprisings until 1912 – civilians and military had opposed 'the oligarchy', in 1930 civilians and military joined forces to overthrow President Yrigoyen, who until his victory at the polls in 1916 had been an expert in civil-military conspiracies. Throughout the 1930s *yrigoyenistas* had repeatedly tried to overthrow the conservatives who in turn maintained their control by means of rigging elections. And again between 1940 and 1943 civilian politicians tried to forge links with military men to stop President Castillo's attempts at manipulating the army to guarantee his own non-democratic project. This time a group of officers decided they had had enough of civilian manipulation and they felt it was their turn in 1943 to place the Nation on the road to its long-awaited greatness. Thus, when in 1955 a motley group of civilians and uniformed men put their differences aside to overthrow Perón, their actions were inscribed in a long-standing tradition.

The relative ease with which Perón was toppled and the weakness of a regime which fell almost without a fight, has bewildered many an observer of the Argentine situation. On 5 September 1955, an official at the Foreign Office remarked: 'The absence of reaction from the army [to Perón's withdrawal of his earlier offer to resign] or from any other potential sources of opposition lead me to think that he is likely to remain in power for as far ahead as we can now see.'[1] Although with hindsight it would be easy to dismiss such a comment as revelatory of an extraordinarily short sight, Mr Wilde's remark is more easily justified once the actual picture of the opposition at the time is understood. Indeed, Mr Wilde had been correct when he had observed, three weeks earlier, that 'the disquieting thought [. . .] is that we have heard no rumours about what is to replace the Perón regime. It is all very well to go throwing bombs and beating up policemen, but someone will have to provide an alternative government; and of this there is no sign'.[2] When Perón's downfall did occur, it was not as a result of a coup d'état carried out by the armed forces as an institution, but rather a patched-up work made up of a series of *pronunciamientos* by officers in the higher ranks of the Army and the Navy, not all of them in active service (as in the case of General Eduardo Lonardi, head of the Revolution) nor with command over troops (as was the case with General Pedro Eugenio Aramburu, Director of the *Escuela Nacional de Guerra*, the National Military Academy).

The lack of homogeneity in the rebel groups was soon to be highlighted by the removal of General Lonardi on the night of 13 November 1955, and his replacement as Provisional President by General Aramburu. Radicals and Conservatives, Socialists and Catholics, Liberals and Nationalists illustrated the diversity in motivations, political beliefs, and intentions of men who shared one feeling, that of moral indignation, and one purpose: the overthrow of Perón. Not only was there no ideological homogeneity, but as one participant reported, 'the uncertainty as to who were in fact our fellow revolutionaries was complete ... if indeed the revolution was to take place'.³ So how did it come about? And why did Peronism – and Perón especially – produce such antagonism?

2 THE DECLINE OF THE PERONIST REGIME

Peronism had secured in Argentina, and for the first time in Latin America as a whole, the active and massive political participation of workers and women. It had done so using an anti-establishment form of rhetorics that, although not totally knew in Argentina – Yrigoyen had claimed to represent the cause of the Nation against 'the regime'⁴ – encouraged a relationship between the *Caudillo* and the masses which gave a vernacular appearance to schemes that had been defeated in Europe at the end of World War II. There were many reasons to oppose Perón, but the men of the *Libertadora* chose to explain his removal using a manner of rhetorics emphasising moral overtones rather than reasoned explanations. The report published by the government of the *Libertadora* on its own achievements was rife with references to the need 'to reestablish the ethical and juridical order' and 'to dismantle the apparatus of totalitarianism', the latter being described in a strongly qualified list of evils: 'impertinent proselytism', 'irredeemable sectarianism', 'wilful ambition', 'impenitent syndicalism', etc.⁵ The danger of such language was that instead of clarifying the real wrongs of the regime, it underlined its outer, demagogic manifestations, all the time couching its criticisms behind an obscure rhetoric, most probably inaccessible to a majority of the population.

Back in 1946 Perón had realised the power of language when he turned the opposition's insistence on 'democracy' on its head and declared that what was at stake in the forthcoming elections was not a confrontation between 'liberty or tyranny, democracy or totalitarianism', but 'a championship match between social justice and social injustice'.⁶ The message had been repeated oft enough for the language of the *Libertadora* not to carry disquieting resonances. The *Libertadora*'s effort to 'elevate' the tone of the debate seemed to justify fears amongst Peronists that social hatred was the motive behind Perón's deposition. Far from producing the much desired 'de-Peronisation' of the masses, the *Libertadora* induced the 're-Peronisation' of popular sectors whose fervour for their leader had not been enough to provoke spontaneous mobilisations in his support.⁷ The labour leaders' complacency, coupled with senior Peronist officers' reluctance to share power with the former, provides a reasonable explanation for the inaction immediately following Perón's overthrow.[8]

The Economic Context and Relations with the United States

Even though recent analyses of Perón's economic policies have offered a revisionist perspective endeavouring to rid those years of the widespread negative appraisal they have received, the fact remains that Perón's decision to reallocate resources from agriculture to industry resulted in a drastic reduction in Argentina's exports, while the indefinite protection awarded to the manufacturing sector resulted in the long run in high costs and inefficiency – what economists have dubbed 'the Argentine cost'. If this is taken together with the hostility towards Argentina in the US and the UK, one is in a better position to understand the reasons behind the country's retreat from the world market.[9] The exacerbation of State interventionism in the economy that had started for pragmatic rather than ideological reasons during the previous decade via the implementation of protectionist tariffs, was compounded by Perón's corporatist practices and resulted in an inward-looking economic structure that would reveal its limitations as early as 1951.

The assessment of Argentina's economic performance as disastrous during the Peronist decade has been largely based on Raúl Prebisch's 1956 damning Report,[10] as well as on the late Carlos Díaz Alejandro's detailed study published in 1970. The latter's conclusions were that the belated attention – post-1953 – that Perón's government had devoted to agriculture and cattle-rearing activities, coupled with the disastrous harvests of 1950–2 following prolonged droughts, meant that exports were only sufficient to pay for 50 per cent of imports.[11] Moreover, the country's dependence on the world market for primary products had remained unaltered, especially since the import-substituting activities encouraged by Perón's industrialising effort had increased the demand for foreign reserves. The result was a growing external indebtedness while the 1952 deficit reached US $800 million. Rampant inflation soon made itself felt, and the cost of living index, taking 1943 as base, soared to 607.5 in 1954 and 682.3 in 1955.[12]

The pace of industrialisation had already started to slow down, affected by electricity shortages back in 1948–53. But the stagnation of the manufacturing sector was largely provoked by the failure of governmental policy to recognise that any future industrial growth had to come either from the expansion of manufactured exports or from the more complex import-substituting activities. This was partly the result of Perón's preoccupation with the labour market (reflected in the impetus received by small-scale light manufacturing and construction activities, the main sources of employment in those years) which made very difficult the transition to a higher phase of industrialisation.[13]

Contradictions and inconsistencies in economic management give credence to the conclusion that there was no unified Peronist economic policy, much less a long-term development strategy, but there was instead a single goal and guiding principle behind all decisions: to achieve a redistribution of income in favour of urban workers.[14] But by 1955, in the face of mounting inflation and a fall in real wages,[15] the mood amongst trade unionists who could neither claim notable successes in the domain of social conquests nor in that of wage claims, was subdued. As an observer at the US State Department noted:

> [. . .] Why the labour unions were not mobilised when the crisis came is still a mystery and was part of the paralysis which seemed to grip Peronista leadership during the revolution. [. . .] the answer may lie in the fact that the labour movement seemed to have lost much of its vitality with time and as a result of imposition of leadership and control from above [. . .].[16]

Such lack of response had been evident earlier, at the time of Perón's shifting position towards foreign investment. In the hazy realm of the Peronist doctrine, 'economic independence' was equated with 'anti-imperialism', that is, an anti-US stand dating from US ambassador Spruille Braden's intervention against Perón in the February 1946 presidential elections. The new, favourable approach, would be highlighted by the oil concessions negotiated by Perón in favour of the California Petrol Company, a subsidiary of the American based Standard Oil.

As early as 1953, at the time of Milton Eisenhower's visit to Buenos Aires ('To say that I was amazed at the reception Perón staged is a gross understatement. Red carpets, colorful bands, military honor guards, were everywhere')[17] Perón had been making overtures towards the Americans and by 1955, negotiations to secure closer economic relations were well advanced.[18] The US administration had first shown signs of its willingness to repair the damage done by Braden's disastrous interference as early as April of 1946.[19] In 1955 three issues dominated exchanges between Ambassador Nufer, Perón, and Assistant Secretary of State for Inter-American Affairs Henry Holland. The first was a loan for US $61 million from the Export-Import Bank to Sociedad Mixta Siderúrgica Argentina

(SOMISA) to finance, in participation with American suppliers, a portion of the US costs of steel producing facilities in Argentina.[20] The second was the contract with the Standard Oil Company of California signed on 25 April 1955,[21] and last, but by no means least, the issue of profit remittances abroad.

The Americans placed the utmost importance on this latter issue, and if agreement was never reached before Perón's downfall, it was not due to the president's unwillingness, but to his Economy Minister Gómez Morales's insistence that such remittances could not be allowed to begin until the calendar year 1956.[22] The Americans were deeply disappointed at this delay, given Perón's personal assurances to Ambassador Nufer on 15 April 1955 that he would approve the remittance of profits to old established US investors and his letter to Henry Holland explaining the Argentine position.[23] The Argentine ambassador in Washington explained to Holland that Gómez Morales's 'shortsighted opposition to a fully satisfactory solution' remained the main obstacle.[24]

In the event, none of the three issues would be resolved before Perón's downfall, nor would other questions that were of interest to Perón on the one hand – military aid – or the Americans on the other – the devolution of the expropriated *La Prensa* newspaper to its former owner, Alberto Gainza Paz, seen by the State Department as a prerequisite to change the attitude of the virulently anti-Peronist US press, and thus ensure a change in public opinion. In a letter to the US ambassador in Buenos Aires, Holland stated this forcefully:

> If, because of the present state of public opinion in the US we have to cool off in our relations with Perón, then we get, first, a state of concern in his mind, then one of resentment and, finally, a resumption of the unfriendly and uncooperative actions that created so much trouble for us a few years ago. [. . .] We are not going to get a more favorable public opinion unless the press adopts a more favorable attitude. The press is not going to do that unless the *La Prensa* problem is solved.[25]

Perón himself was not impervious to US public opinion, and his ambassador proudly informed Holland that 'he [Paz] had been responsible in some measure for the viewpoint of this particular story', in reference to a *Wall Street Journal* article of 27 June 1955 reporting on the events of June, and headed 'US Officials Favor Perón – But Largely for Business Reasons'. Holland agreed that it was 'a useful article'.[26]

While Díaz Alejandro notes that investment in industry was hampered by the government's policy of either hostility or indifference towards foreign capital in general, and direct foreign investment in particular, recent analyses have shown that the alleged 'extreme nationalism' of Perón's policies was more a 'myth' than a 'reality'.[27] Some have even challenged the idea that there was a clear difference between the two periods into which Peronist economic policies have been divided – 1946–52 and 1952–55. While the first would reflect the more exaggerated interventionist and nationalist policies, the second, more pragmatic and less xenophobic, had taken into account the bitter lessons learnt from the first. As State Department papers recently released show, Perón was keenly seeking US goodwill and investment. The Foreign Office documents also highlight what was seen as a distinct – and favourable – change in Perón's attitude towards US investment.[28]

On 25 June 1955, in reply to a request from the American Department at the Foreign Office, the British Ambassador in Washington provided an account of US reactions to the 16 June military rebellion led by General Menéndez against Perón. The ambassador, David Muirhead, pointed out that although the US press generally regretted the failure of the rebellion, the State Department was more worried that 'the seizure of power by the Army [. . .] may well endanger the new Standard Oil of California oil concession in Argentina, which was regarded as the first real break in the exclusively nationalist Argentine economic policy'.[29] The press report that Muirhead quoted was the same *Wall Street Journal* article of which Paz – unbeknownst to the UK ambassador – had boasted to Holland, and in which it was said that:

> A growing flock of US businesses have a dollar-and-cents stake in the political fortunes of Argentina's Juan Domingo Perón. Reason: Whatever else US officials may think about the Argentine strong man, they rate him a powerful advocate of bigger US investments in Argentina and of more US-Argentine trade. [. . .] they've spotted no challengers in the power struggle who would be likely to match Mr. Perón on this score.

The report went on to say that in 1953 American firms had some US $406 million tied up in Argentine enterprises, 'only about US $100 million less than the US stake in much nearer and more populous Mexico'.[30] A later communication from the British Embassy in Washington quoted a *New York Herald Tribune* article stating that 'while the US holds no brief for Perón, concern was expressed [in Washington] that a government dominated by [the opposition to Perón] would be strongly nationalistic and anti-American [. . .] and dedicated to opposing foreign investments in any form'.[31] This uncertainty as to who or what would replace Perón was a constant worry in both the US and UK diplomatic correspondence.[32]

The Standard Oil contract not only raised the clamour of the opposition, allowing UCR deputy Arturo Frondizi to deliver one of his most impassioned and admired speeches in July 1955, but it hurt the nationalism of the military establishment to such an extent as to make some people claim this as an overriding motive for the September revolution.[33] Although the American Embassy in Buenos Aires dismissed this as a motive, and mentioned that 'at least some of the higher military officers favoured the contract'[34] rumours in Buenos Aires had reached such a peak that less than ten days after overthrowing Perón, General Lonardi publicly rejected the contract between the previous administration and the Standard Oil Company. When reporting the news to Washington Ambassador Nufer remarked:

> It is unfortunate that Lonardi thought it necessary to commit himself about the contract so early in the game. I can only assume that pressure from nationalist elements and perhaps even from his associates in the armed forces, must have been very strong [. . .] I am afraid for the time being petroleum is a dead issue and I doubt the provisional government will be inclined to revive it even in the event it should later on consider itself strong enough to do so.[35]

The ambassador was right, and it would take three years and the about-turn of the fiercest critic of the contract – Arturo Frondizi – before oil and the issue of concessions to foreign firms again came to dominate the political scene in Argentina.

The Religious Front

The Roman Catholic hierarchy had stood behind Perón since 15 November 1945, the date of publication of a pastoral letter forbidding Catholics to vote in the forthcoming presidential elections for candidates supporting 'anti-Catholic' principles, lay education being foremost amongst these. The military government had introduced compulsory religious education in schools by decree in December 1943 and Perón was seen as a guarantee that this would be maintained. Indeed, in March 1947 a Peronist-dominated Congress legalised religious education.[36] Monsignor Copello, Argentina's primate cardinal, left little doubt of his support for Perón against the lay candidate of the *Unión Democrática*. Nevertheless, Perón's attitude towards the Church became increasingly ambivalent,³⁷ and by 1950 the distancing between Perón and the Church was reflected in the manifestations of the 'Peronisation' of Argentine society: the total control over the media, the profusion of Peronist symbolism. Indeed, by 1950 all totalitarian trappings were everywhere in evidence.

The disquiet in Catholic circles was further exacerbated by the unfolding of the rivalry with the intervention of the State in areas that the powerful Catholic Church in Argentina had traditionally considered its domain: social welfare, education and the unity of the family. The impingement in the area of social welfare was reflected in the State's newly acquired monopoly over social aid through the workings of the Eva Perón Foundation.³⁸ The political mobilisation by the Peronist Party of women and youth (major components of the Church clientele) made matters worse; the younger priests came increasingly to share the aversion of the middle classes for Peronism.

Catholics did not give the impression of being keen to create Christian trade unions nor a Christian Democratic Party,³⁹ although a series of articles published in *La Prensa* – in trade union hands since its expropriation by Perón – in November 1954 attacked what it deemed as Church interference in the labour organisations. Perón, for his part, interfered in what the Church considered its territory when he set up the UES (Union of Secondary School Students).⁴⁰ Catholics in general were anxious to extricate their children from the Peronist indoctrination at schools, from Peronist organisations and Peronist cult. Eva Perón's ghosted 'autobiography', *La razón de mi vida*, was compulsory reading in schools, part of the attempt at replacing the Catholic Doctrine with a 'national doctrine' that would provide the country with a 'unity of conception' that the Peronist State believed it had the right to demand from its citizens.⁴¹

Perón slowly unfolded his strategy against the Church albeit stopping short of declaring open war. The 1947 law establishing compulsory religious instruction in schools was abolished, in 1954 divorce was legalised and in May 1955 a Peronist-dominated Congress passed a motion, as an amendment to the Constitution, directed towards the separation of Church and State.⁴² These liberal measures that the Church had come to expect from the Radical Party but certainly not from the Peronists, were little more than politically motivated vindictive decisions, and seen as such, revealing in the eyes of many the true nature of the regime and proving the argument of Perón's mere utilisation of the religious issue.⁴³

The Church retaliated. On 11 June 1955, on the occasion of the Corpus Christi celebrations, a giant demonstration was organised in which many more people than merely fervent Catholics participated. The police reported that opposite the Congress building an Argentine flag had been burnt and replaced by the Vatican flag. Official reaction was one of outrage, and in a speech delivered on 17 June Perón accused the demonstrators of having joined the ranks of the *antipatria* [enemies of the fatherland] – by then already engrossed by Radicals, Conservatives, Communists, Freemasons and a host of 'foreign agents'.

The protection of the national symbols was a military prerogative, and thus the latter set up an enquiry on the flag-burning incident. The findings submitted to the president on 10 July indicated that the burning of the flag had in fact been carried out by *agents provocateurs* from the Federal Police. Those directly responsible were to be found in the government's own ranks; they were Perón's chief of police and his Interior minister. Fortunately for him they had tended their resignations, but the incident would not be forgotten, and Perón himself would not be forgiven.[44] The Vatican's reaction to the incidents was swift. Following the expulsion from Argentina of Monsignori Tato and Novoa, blamed by the government for the unauthorised 11 June act, the members of the administration directly responsible for their expulsion were excommunicated on 16 June. It was the first time since 1850 that a Catholic government had been chastised by the Vatican. In the eyes of many the embodiment of the anti-Christ,[45] for a group of naval officers led by Admiral Toranzo Calderón, this time Perón had gone too far. That same day they launched their almost suicidal air-raid on the Casa Rosada, the seat of government, and the War Ministry building, where Perón had taken refuge from the attack. The *Confederación General del Trabajo* (CGT), the labour federation, firmly controlled by the Peronists, appealed to workers to gather opposite its headquarters to defend the government. Since the CGT's headquarters were in the vicinity of the War Ministry, those who had responded to the appeal became the victims of the naval aviation's bombs and submachine guns. There were around one thousand casualties, two hundred of them fatal. It was the worst single episode of violence in Argentina this century.[46]

The assault on the churches carried out on the night of 16 June was a retaliation for the naval aviation's attack, and part of the escalade against the Church. Although Perón broadcast a message on the evening of 16 June declaring that 'the fight was among soldiers', a group of men in civilian clothes led an assault on a dozen churches in the centre of Buenos Aires, plundering and then setting fire to them. Perón, a supreme tactician, seemed to realise that the situation needed defusing, and the 'liberalisation' of the regime was reported. He not only dismissed the most obviously anti-clerical members of his Cabinet (including the Interior and Education ministers) but even attempted a *rapprochement* with the opposition. Lord Reading, for one, was not impressed, and he commented: 'I doubt whether any Dictator can successfully "liberalise" himself. When he ceases to dictate, the reason for his supremacy vanishes.'[47] Perhaps Lord Reading was nearer the truth than he realised, since it is very possible that US Ambassador Nufer, whose predicament on Perón had not gone unnoticed by some of the latter's collaborators,[48] had transmitted to Perón Hoover's message on learning of the 16 June events. Hoover's telegram indicated that Nufer might 'wish to seek informal opportunities' to make 'Argentine officials' aware that:

> [. . .] demonstrations religious tolerance, punishment looters and church incendiaries, announcement Government reconstruct churches, and further constructive progress in principal economic problems now under discussion US will all be helpful in countering severe reaction already felt among US press and public.[49]

On 15 July Perón made his most conciliatory speech, promising that henceforth he would be the 'president of all Argentines', and announcing that existing restrictions on the opposition would be lifted although the state of war would not. Perón even allowed the opposition leaders to make radio broadcasts for the first time in ten years. Arturo Frondizi was one of only two politicians who accepted the offer, and he made no concessions to Perón in his speech.[50] From then on, events moved fast. Only two months earlier *The New York Times* had carried an article stating that Perón could not be brought down.[51]

3 THE *REVOLUCIÓN LIBERTADORA*, 16–21 SEPTEMBER 1955: AN ACCOUNT

The events of 16 June marked the point of no return for the conspirators. Perón would never be forgiven for such effrontery. At the same time, Perón's punitive measures for the air raid – the dismantling of the naval aviation paramount amongst them – gave rise to fears and suspicion in military circles. The civilian opposition, for its part, took advantage of the June events. Officers were overwhelmed by pamphlets and letters urging them to act against 'the tyrant', and even chicken feathers and grains of maize were thrown through letter-boxes in a none too subtle allusion to their alleged cowardice in not coming forth against Perón.[52]

On 31 August the CGT declared a strike in support of Perón, after his speech that morning offering to resign. That evening, facing for the last time the multitude gathered in Plaza de Mayo, opposite the Casa Rosada, Perón forsook any attempt at conciliation and overtures towards the opposition made on 15 July. He delivered a violent speech, almost a provocation: 'for each one of us that may fall, five of them will die', his infamous *cinco por uno*.[53] At that time there existed a mosaic of conspiracies, but no overall plan. In the eyes of some Foreign Office officials, little could be expected from the ranks of the civilian opposition, whose leaders 'unfortunately [lacked] political "nous"' and 'constructive thought'.[54] On the military side, the Navy was at the vanguard of conspirators, and even before 31 August it had achieved a unified command for the rebellion. But on her own the Navy had little chance of success – the inclusion of Army rebels was deemed essential for victory.

At the time of the June rebellion General Aramburu had stood by General Lucero, Perón's loyal War minister, and against the rebels, but on 31 August he was approached by many of the conspirators seeking someone to lead the revolutionary movement. When General Aramburu did not respond promptly enough to their appeals, the young army officers stationed in the Province of Córdoba grew impatient, and Colonel Ossorio Arana offered the leadership of the revolutionary movement to retired General Eduardo Lonardi for reasons of seniority.[55] The decision to act taken by the Córdoba garrison was prompted by two circumstances: firstly, because the period of military conscription was due to end in September, leaving a gap before the new recruits would be available as 'operational troops'; secondly, rumours abounded in the sense that the CGT, with Perón's acquiescence, was about to arm civilian militias.[56] Washington listed this as one of the motives of the revolution, stating that:

> Perón's projection of labor into the arena with intimations in August that labor organizations might be made into a sort of civilian army, prompted even some of the higher echelon officers still in the service to the conclusion that they had had enough. Thus even they were ready to defect to the rebels, which more than anything else determined the final outcome after the revolt had been set in motion by numerically inferior forces.[57]

The rebellion broke out in Córdoba, but its outcome remained far from clear until Perón hinted at his possible resignation. On 19 September, newspapers published a letter signed by the president addressed 'to the Army and the people of the Nation' in which he stated:

> ... if we fought, it was against our will, forced by the reactionary forces. I tried to leave power a few days ago, and I insist on offering

this as a solution. The vice-president's and the legislators' decision to follow my example thwarts a constitutional solution. The Army can take charge.[58]

A military Junta was formed, presided by General Molina, Army Commander-in-Chief, and the truce declared gave new strength to the dying rebellion. The insurgents were taken totally by surprise by such peace offering; they were in a clear minority position, short of supplies and surrounded by loyalist troops. It would appear that Perón had hoped that his letter would unleash widespread popular indignation leading to a massive mobilisation in his support that would allow him to carry on the fight – perhaps a replica of 17 October 1945. This time nobody asked Perón to withdraw his implicit resignation. The CGT remained silent, and when it eventually made its voice heard, it offered the image of an institution more concerned with its own interests than those of the *First Worker*. The CGT's General Secretary, Hugo di Pietro, in a message broadcast on 24 September, made what was effectively an appeal for demobilisation, repeating the guarantees he had received from the then President Lonardi 'to respect the social justice achieved by the workers, to respect the CGT and the unions that are part of it. The government does not plan to intervene them'.[59] The message was clear: it was time to trust the Army – as Perón himself had implied – and forget Perón.

The dice had been cast on the 20th when Perón took refuge in the Paraguayan Embassy, and the Junta accepted rebel Admiral Rojas's demands: Perón's resignation, and the naming of General Lonardi as *Jefe de la Revolución* and head of a provisional government.

4 THE STATE OF THE ARMED FORCES

One explanation for the relative ease with which Perón was toppled must be found in the predicament of the armed forces. Peronist non commissioned officers were a majority in the army, but these loyalist forces were not prepared to crush the rebels – even when they did not approve of them, they understood them. Moreover, they remained loyal to their War minister rather than to Perón. Therefore the repression of the rebels was carried out with little conviction, supplies never seemed to get to the loyalist troops, which in turn seemed to take far too long to reach their destinations. If most of the generals did not join the rebellion, neither were they prepared to fight for Perón.[60]

The army as a force was hopelessly divided, and the divisory line was drawn by the different attitudes towards Perón and Peronism, impeding any strong consensus nor unity of behaviour that would allow a reference to 'the army's point of view' without incurring in serious misconceptions.[61] Even after the purge that followed Lonardi's replacement by Aramburu on 13 November 1955, several groups were still very much in evidence within the army – there was a tiny number of Peronist officers; a majority of 'neutrals' led by General Bengoa, the newly appointed War minister; a small group of revolutionaries unwilling to persecute the Peronists within their ranks and who were in close contact with the Catholic Nationalists in Lonardi's administration. These were officers more preoccupied by the trappings of the Peronist government than with the fundamentals of its corporatist design, and who accepted Lonardi's slogan (borrowed from Urquiza's 1853 declaration after defeating Rosas) of *ni vencedores ni vencidos*; finally, there were those who had taken part in the 1951 uprisings, and as a result had been forcibly withdrawn from active service and in some cases suffered terms of imprisonment. These were deemed the unwavering anti-Peronists, popularly known as *gorilas*, although Lanusse disputes such attribution, indicating that men like Rojas and Turolo, 'turned anti-Peronist at the umpteenth hour' were the true vengeful zealots.[62]

Not only was the army divided in 1955, but the Peronist decade had marked the beginning of overt competition inter-forces, each endeavouring to modernise its equipment at the expense of the others, contributing in this manner to augment the deep suspicions in which the Navy (at the head of the June 1951 and June 1955 uprisings) held the Army (which had remained loyal to Perón until the last minute and had greatly expanded and modernised its equipment during the Peronist decade).[63] Furthermore, the Navy had picked the spoils in September 1955: for the first time, the Federal Police would be under its direct control, as would be six provinces, including the rich agricultural province of Santa Fe, in the littoral region. The Air Force, on their part, close to the Catholic and nationalist Right, mistrusted the liberal Navy, the more so since the development of the naval aviation fostered by Perón, and the refusal by President Aramburu's government (of which Admiral Rojas was vice-president) to buy new fighter bombers for the aviators. Each force seemed more concerned with strengthening its hold on the State, carving a fief, than with matters of national defence. Inter-service rivalry sometimes reached almost farcical proportions, as on the occasion of the visit of Undersecretary of State Holland at the end of November 1956. Rojas (then vice-president) sought a private meeting with Holland and Nufer to indicate the Argentine Navy's desire to purchase equipment from the US, particularly an aircraft carrier.

To allay President's Aramburu's surprise at the Rojas-Holland-Nufer meeting when these three emerged from a private hotel room to join the President for lunch, [Holland] found it advisable to refer to the general tenor of his conversation [with Rojas]. Aramburu [. . .] interrupted [Holland's] explanation at the mention of an aircraft carrier to say that this was not needed, since what Argentina basically required was assistance of a financial nature.[64]

The Air Force chiefs also took the opportunity of this same visit to point out to the military representative in the visiting delegation that Argentina was 'desperately in need of equipment, particularly planes, necessary to carry out obligations under the Rio Pact and adequately perform its mission of assisting and maintaining internal order'.[65] General Douglass, Chairman of the US Delegation at the Inter-American Defense Board, suggested that the Argentines pursue their requests through formal channels.

The divisions in the military institution deepened after the deposition of Perón. Amidst the divergences and ideological confusion there were some distinct positions. On the one hand, there were those who justified, and wanted to strengthen even more, the political involvement of the military corps. War minister Ossorio Arana, who replaced General Bengoa on 9 November 1955 because of the latter's leniency towards Peronist officers, declared that officers had to receive 'a solid knowledge of politics'.[66] Those who stood for apoliticism were left in an isolated position. But a majority of officers were particularly sensitive to the prevailing ideological climate and were imbued by the Manichean view of the world resulting from the Cold War.

On the other hand, the staunch anti-Peronists demanded an ideological rather than organisational unity of the military institution. They upheld the notion of 'guardianship' – the Army's role was to be the interpreter and guardian of the national interest.[67] They proved to be the strongest, and Ossorio Arana undertook one of the most dramatic purges in the Army in November 1956, relieving seventeen generals from their commanding posts, replacing them with young colonels. One of these, Colonel Arribau, who was Aramburu's Secretary at the Presidency, justified the purge stating that 'there are generals who believe the highest position in the hierarchy is that offered by the military establishment, while we believe that it is the one achieved by those who fought in defence of liberty'.[68]

Another development that marked the post-1955 army was the subversion of military values, and the ensuing indiscipline, resulting from the newly acquired influence of young officers over their superiors, whom they accused of misleading them or of being too patient and even cowardly *vis-à-vis* Perón. Furthermore, the dossiers of the officers that had been ousted before 1955 as a result of their conspiratorial activities against Perón, would have to be inspected by their former subordinates before they could be reincorporated to active service. Some refused to undergo such treatment, even if it meant they would not be reincorporated, on the grounds that it violated important institutional principles. Moreover, the 'commissions of enquiry' set up to examine the financial activities of Perón and his associates further eroded military discipline, enticing young officers into extra-military interests at a time when internal cohesion was at a low ebb.[69] The issue of the purges as well as that of the manner of the reintegration of the officers who had been forced to retire by Perón, fostered personal rivalries and jealousies and remained a source of rancour and discord within military society for years to come. At no other time in the history of the military institution had discipline been so undermined.

The execution on 9 June 1956 of General Valle and others, accused of attempting to lead a Peronist revolt against the government, would mark the *non plus ultra* for the *Libertadora*, and would cut an unbridgeable gap between Peronists and 'liberators', victors and vanquished, closed a quarter of a century later in the symbolic embrace between President Menem and Admiral Rojas in 1991.[70] In an unprecedented move in Argentine politico-military history,[71] the killings of 9 June underlined the audacity of the *Libertadora* in punishing dissent with a brutality that Perón never dared apply to his enemies.

5   GENERAL LONARDI AND HIS FOILED 'NATIONAL REVOLUTION'

Less than a week after the September uprisings it was evident to a US correspondent that 'there was no central revolutionary leadership in Argentina', while Ambassador Nufer's telegram to the State Department reported that 'revolution was in no sense uprising of civilians against government [. . .] It was a military split'.[72] But the few civilians who had been involved felt 'amazed and worried' on finding out that the newly sworn-in Provisional President had already decided on the composition of his Cabinet without consulting them. Bonifacio Del Carril noted that this lack of consultation with the other revolutionary groups 'produced a clash of tendencies and opinions that was not a good presage'.[73] In his *Proclama de la Libertad*, issued on 23 September, General Lonardi justified the renewed intervention of the military in the political arena as 'surging from the love of freedom and honour of a subjected people who want to live in accordance with their traditions', ending with an invocation to the Virgin.[74] But which traditions did this self-proclaimed rescuer of the nation have in mind?

General Lonardi surrounded himself by men who thought it possible to place the *Libertadora* under one doctrine, and perhaps bring about the national revolution that Perón had promised but failed to deliver. Most prominent amongst such men were Mario Amadeo, Juan Carlos Goyeneche, and Lonardi's brother-in-law, Clemente Villada Achával (respectively Foreign Affairs minister, Press Secretary and Private Secretary). They belonged to a Catholic and ultranationalist tradition that in Argentina can be traced back to the 1920s and the influence of Maurras. After a series of failures, they believed their opportunity had finally arrived. This motley group of nationalists, corporativists and Catholic integralists, who suffered from an acute nostalgia for authoritarian regimes, were not worried about an electoral denouement to the revolution, as most other groups were. Their aims sounded far from reassuring to those who had fought Perón in defence of liberal principles. Mario Amadeo had written a pamphlet reproaching Perón for having misappropriated the 1943 revolution, but insisting that this should not 'imply the absolute rejection of the themes that brought him to power'.[75] Goyeneche, on his part, had been 'an important source of information on the inner councils of Castillo's administration' for the Nazi Party Security Service (SD-*Sicherheitsdienst*) in Argentina, and while on a tour of Germany in 1942 had met Himmler and Ribbentrop. To the latter he expressed his [Goyeneche's] misgivings concerning Nazi ecclesiastical policies, in an effort to reassure Catholic nationalists back in Argentina.[76]

Peronism without Perón had found its first expression in a group of men keen on ascribing to the *Libertadora* an ideological unity that given its mixed origins, it could not have. To carry out the conciliatory policy towards Peronism that Lonardi intended, the revolutionary forces should have had a cohesion and consistency of purpose that they lacked. The intolerable arrogance and arbitrariness of Perón had led people to set aside political realism and the effort to understand what Peronism had meant. Instead, while one group hoped the nationalist ideals of the 1943 revolution could be restored and carried forth, another believed that the democratic ideals thwarted by that same uprising could now be put to practice. The former wanted to breath new life into the illiberal principles that had originally nurtured Perón, while the latter wished to obliterate the memory of what they saw as an aberration in the struggle for democracy in Argentina.

Relations with Labour

A report in *The New York Times* on 27 September noted that exiles from the Peronist regime who were still in Uruguay had shown signs of being 'less enthusiastic' about the provisional government, which 'they doubted [. . .] would come anywhere near their minimum hopes'. Not only did they fear the influence of men whose anti-liberalism made them automatically suspicious of being pro-Fascist, but they were concerned about Lonardi's decision to accept 'such Peronist bulwarks as the CGT'. The *Proclama de la Libertad* had pledged to 'our brethren workers' that their 'legitimate conquests would not only be maintained, but bettered'. To stress such promises, Lonardi met the CGT's General Secretary, Hugo di Pietro repeating that the workers' social advantages would be respected, that the CGT would not be dissolved, neither would it be intervened nor its assets confiscated. He ended the meeting 'daring to request the workers to appeal [to him] with the same trust that they approached the former government', and if they would certainly not 'find the demagogue', they could be 'certain to find a brother or a father'. Di Pietro himself transmitted such news on the radio.[77] A further reassurance for the workers, and further reason for misgivings amidst diehard anti-Peronists, was the presence as Labour minister of Dr Luis Cerrutti Costa, legal adviser to the powerful metalworkers union (UOM), and who had been one of Perón's supporters and collaborators during the latter's early days in 1943 at the head of the Labour Department (the *Secretaría de Trabajo y Previsión*).[78]

While the president was taking pains to gain the confidence of workers and union leaders, others were keen to remind them that in Argentina in 1955 there indeed had been *victors* and there were *vanquished*. On 24, 25 and 26 September military aeroplanes overflew the city of Rosario in an intimidatory gesture, while union offices were taken over by non-Peronist trade unionists calling themselves *sindicalistas libres* (free trade unionists), together with armed groups of civilians backed by the Army and the Navy. The appeals made by the Labour minister to stop such actions remained unheeded. In an effort to counteract the increasing pressures on the government to move against the CGT, Cerrutti Costa negotiated the resignation of the CGT's steering committee and their replacement by other less well-known – and thus hopefully less irritating – Peronists. In exchange, the minister offered guarantees that the unions would remain in Peronist hands.

A delegation of Socialists who, having been displaced by Perón from their dominating position in the labour field pre-1945, had hoped to be the main beneficiaries of the expected de-Peronisation of the unions, went to see Lonardi on 21 October to express their worries about Cerrutti Costa's attitude towards the CGT, adding their 'alarm at the dark dealings in favour of the setting up of a kind of neo-Fascism . . . with the help of public officials who seek to manipulate the labour movement with political ends'.[79] What were indeed at stake were contrasting visions of the role the unions should play and their mode of integration in the State, that is, whether the integration encouraged by Perón should be maintained – apparently Cerrutti Costa's and Lonardi's position – or abolished – the view of the *sindicalistas libres*.[80] Feelings on this matter ran so deep that they dominated the political scene, outshining all other issues, including the economy and the functioning of the political parties, in a state of chaos after the decade in the wilderness to which Perón had relegated them.

While the revolutionaries displaced by Lonardi were pressing him to act against the CGT, unrest was also mounting in the armed forces, where the War minister, General Bengoa, was accused of refusing to press investigations into alleged Army graft during the Peronist regime.[81] His replacement by retired Colonel Arturo Ossorio Arana was hailed by *The New York Times* on 11 November as a 'major victory' for the liberal elements in the armed forces. The following day Lonardi appeared bent on redressing the balance once more in favour of the anti-liberal elements: he declared that the Interior and Justice Ministry would be divided in two. To this end he demanded the resignation of the much respected Dr Busso, who headed the joint ministry, and appointed two well-known nationalists to the restructured bodies: Amadeo and de Pablo Pardo. This proved too much, and on 13 November Lonardi was forced to go, being replaced as provisional president by General Aramburu. The end of the *Libertadora* Mark I, in Potash's terminology, signalled the end of Argentine nationalism as an independent political force, but not as a dominant ideological trend.[82]

6 GENERAL ARAMBURU'S OBJECTIVE OF A 'DEMOCRACY FOR DEMOCRATS'

Inaugurating the *Libertadora* Mark II,[83] General Aramburu undertook the governmental task from the standpoint of the victors. The deeply felt hostility towards the 'enemies of liberty', as Peronists were referred to, was seen as thinly disguised social resentment. But Aramburu and the men who displaced Lonardi embodied that attitude of perplexed equilibrium that Halperín Donghi has remarked existed between the authoritarian stances imposed by their predicament, and the liberal-democratic traditions in whose name they claimed to be acting.[84] They saw their role as that of 'restoring the political parties to a centre from where Perón had removed them'.[85] Their vision was forward-looking – it was that of a free, democratic country, open to the world after a decade of isolation. As all visions, it could be open to challenge, but at least it hoped, albeit clumsily, to guarantee an *ordre politique* in which it would be possible to hold and pursue contrasting and competing visions within a constitutional framework – as long as such visions were not of Peronism, since it had disqualified itself by not respecting the rules of the liberal-democratic political game. Thus Peronists were out, and Socialists were in. A document issued by Aramburu's government underlined the provisional character of the new administration:

> The first and essential aim of the *Revolución Libertadora* has been to overthrow the dictatorial regime. We have triumphed in the armed struggle. Our task is now to eliminate all traces of totalitarianism in order to reestablish the rule of morals, of justice, of law, of freedom and of democracy. Once this aim is achieved, [Argentine] citizens will be able to express their authentic will, they will decide their own destiny. And the solution to the formidable Argentine problems that are not part of the essence of the revolution's objectives, will lie in the hands of the constitutional governments that will follow after this Provisional Government.[86]

Whatever else one might read into the *Libertadora* Mark II, its aim was to restore democratic politics and an institutional set-up that would allow its development. And that, if any, was its historical justification. In the words of the correspondent from *Le Monde*, 'the real tragedy of the Argentine government is that it only represents a liberal centre, probably a minority one', while the dominant view is a '*criollo* version of nationalism and anti-imperialism'.[87]

The main beneficiaries of the *Libertadora* were not expected to be the much-abused 'oligarchs' – allegedly at the centre of a permanently unfolding and truculent conspiracy spanning decades – but those middle sectors whom the 1912 Sáenz Peña Law had hailed into the political arena from where Perón had so effectively banished them once again.

The *Junta Consultiva Nacional* (JCN)

In setting himself up as the only representative of 'the people', Perón had succeeded in 'emptying the political space'.[88] The *Libertadora* now intended to fill that void with the political parties. Accordingly, it set up a *Junta Consultiva Nacional*, (National Consultative Board), in which all 'democratic' parties had an equal number of representatives. This meant the smaller parties – Socialist, Conservative, Progressive Democratic – were over-represented in the twenty-member JCN, much to the chagrin of the *Unión Cívica Radical* (UCR). The JCN would act as an advisory body on political matters of the government's choosing. General Lonardi had emphasised this point when he commented on the JCN's collective decision to present its resignation as part of the pressures exerted on him on 12 November:

> It [wouldn't] bother me in the least to continue governing without them, since they dare pass judgement on the government when they had the honour of being convoked to give their opinion exclusively on those matters presented to them.[89]

It was never more than a token of political activity. For most of the time, it was engaged in useless debates that reflected the disarray into which politicians had been thrown by Perón's distinction between *pueblo* and *anti-pueblo*. Thus the Radicals, who until 1946 had little doubt that they were the true representatives of the people, in 1955 were struggling to retrieve that role. But Perón's displacement had been very effective, and they found themselves unwittingly in the camp of the anti-people. The manner in which some of them tried to solve this dilemma was by anachronistically reviving the historical confrontation between Radicals and Conservatives.

The Electoral Issue

If in September 1955 the *Libertadora* had been able to take advantage of the moral prestige that the military profession carried, a year later its lack of legitimacy, that is to say, its lack of moral title to rule, was becoming increasingly clear. The time had arrived to start thinking about the future. In June 1956 Aramburu announced that the revolution would disappear 'with the same patriotism with which it took over power'.[90] But the real momentum came during the traditional 'comradeship dinner' of the armed forces to celebrate Independence Day on 9 July, when Aramburu announced the political schedule. The latter included provisions for general elections to be held in the last quarter of 1957, the future sanctioning of a statute establishing the rules by which political parties were to operate, and an undertaking to draw new electoral legislation. He also stated that the government was considering the possibility of summoning a Constituent

Assembly to amend the 1853 Charter, reinstated by decree on 1 May 1956, ignoring the 1949 Peronist amendments. The statute of the political parties and the electoral law, brought to the foreground two burning questions: one had to do with the internal cleavages in the UCR, while the other impinged on inter-party rivalries and disputes.

(a) The Statute of the Political Parties

The statute, sanctioned on 16 October, was a straightforward document. It included provisions for the recognition of parties (with the Peronists in mind, the use of personal names in the title of a party was not allowed), the requirement to submit annual accounts, to be independent of foreign organisations and to publish lists of party members. 'It may well be asked why it has taken the Government three months of arduous negotiation to produce such an anodyne document', remarked the British ambassador.[91] The answer lay in the fact that during that period discussions focused on a single issue: whether the party registers should be renewed, or whether nominations for the future elections should be based on the old registers.

The gist of the matter was Dr Arturo Frondizi, leading member of the *Intransigencia* faction of the UCR, whose increasingly oppositionist stand *vis-à-vis* the *Libertadora* arose deep misgivings in military circles.[92] Ricardo Balbín, Frondizi's senior in the *Intransigencia*, and the UCR's presidential candidate in the 1951 elections, together with *unionista* members of the UCR[93] was actively seeking the government's intervention to hinder Frondizi's possible candidacy in the promised elections. Something the government itself was keen on impeding, not just because Frondizi would be breaking the anti-Peronist front, something he was already doing by adopting an oppositionist stand against the government, but because there was evidence that some of his close associates were in contact with the exiled Perón.[94] The Navy, where the staunchest *gorilas* were to be found, concentrated its efforts in preventing Frondizi from becoming a candidate, while the Interior minister, Laureano Landaburu, was adamant that the statute should reflect the government's *prescindencia* in internal party matters.[95]

The Navy put forward a draft proposal that was determinedly opposed by Landaburu. The controversy centred on article 18, which established that the legitimate party authorities were the ones existing before 16 September 1955, and that in those districts where more than one body claimed to represent the same party, the respective registers should be amalgamated and internal elections carried out within 120 days. This in fact favoured the *unionistas*, closest to the *Libertadora*, since the UCR registers were old and contained a majority of *unionista* party affiliates. Landaburu persuaded

Aramburu to support his *prescindente* project, embodied in Decree-Law No. 19,044/56 of 16 October. It included a *cláusula de aditamentos* which established that in those cases where more than one faction lay claim to the party's name, such factions would have to be distinguished by an addition to the name. This clause made possible the split of the UCR into *Unión Cívica Radical del Pueblo* (UCRP) and *Unión Cívica Radical Intransigente* (UCRI). As will be seen in the next chapter, this paved the way for the breaking of the anti-Peronist front, and for Frondizi's future presidency.

(b) The Electoral Law
For the first time since the debate of 1911 on the legislation to extend citizenship rights, the role of the political parties as mediators between the State and society became the focus of attention.[96] The challenge that *radicalismo* had posed since 1891 to the conservative governments, a challenge based on a single tactic – electoral abstentionism – pointed at a single issue: the rules of political succession, rules which had been misconstrued by fraud. The actual consequences of the Sáenz Peña Law of 1912 went far beyond disencumbering the vote. The idea had been to incorporate *radicalismo* – which did not propose to upset the socio-economic system, but to widen participation in the unfolding of national prosperity – in the capacity of an honourable opposition. The attempt backfired when the first UCR government was elected in 1916 – the Conservative élite had grossly misjudged the attraction that the allegedly anti-establishment UCR posed for that section of the population recently invested with the attributes of citizenship.

The electoral system sanctioned by the Sáenz Peña law was the 'incomplete list', favouring the first-past-the-post party with two thirds of the contested positions, while the party which came in second place took up the remaining third. The 'incomplete list' system discriminated against small parties, discouraged the formation of new ones, favoured the established interests and furthermore, it created a paradoxical principle: the greater the degree of competition, particularly multi-party competition, the less representative the delegation sent to Congress.

As part of the revitalisation of the republican-democratic aims and a tradition that went back a century, the government of the *Libertadora* undertook to replace the system of the 'incomplete list', which encouraged the polarisation of the political spectrum and discriminated against those same small parties that were now the government's firmest supporters. Introducing the debate in the JCN, the vice-president, Admiral Rojas, chairman of the JCN, declared that the stability of Argentine democracy required a law that would exert its influence in 'the future political development of the country'.[97] No such transcendental law would emerge. Because the minority parties were over-represented in the JCN, a resolution was adopted favouring proportional representation. Radicals of all allegiances denounced the replacement of the Sáenz Peña Law as a renewed expression of *antirradicalismo*. Proportional representation, in Radical eyes, could amount to nothing less than an anti-Radical conspiracy:

> [. . .] once again in the history of our country [anti-Radicals] get together and coincide in seemingly innocent and democratic ideas, forgetting their deep doctrinaire and programmatic differences, since their overwhelming aim is [. . .] to prevent a Radical government.[98]

A compromise was reached, and while elections for a Constituent Assembly were held on 28 July 1957 on the basis of proportional representation, the Sáenz Peña Law was reintroduced for the 23 February 1958 general elections.[99]

Relations with Labour

Aramburu carried out what Lonardi had promised he would not do: the intervention of the CGT. Decree-Law No. 3,032/55 of 16 November justified the measure since the Peronist government had

> used the CGT to corrupt its essential mission as a representative body whose aim was to safeguard the working masses, and had instead transformed it into an instrument to dominate the workers, forcing them to serve the ends of the totalitarianism implanted in [the] country.[100]

The CGT had become a symbol of all the evils of Peronism, signalling as well the different attitudes of the *Libertadora* Marks I and II. Lonardi's attempt at continuing with some form of 'Peronism without Perón' was superseded by the determination to wipe Peronism out. As part of this effort a naval officer was placed at the head of the CGT, its recently appointed authorities were arrested, and the secretaries of all trade unions ceased in their functions. By the end of November both the dissolution of the Peronist Party and of the CGT was announced. Socialists and Communists, who promptly took over the unions cleared of Peronists by the military, would henceforth be irretrievably discredited in the eyes of the working class. The displaced labour leaders who had developed under the protection of the State during the Peronist decade, would soon learn to operate in an antagonistic relationship *vis-à-vis* the State, and the potential of the working class for social and political disruption would be constantly expressed during the Provisional Government's life. Despite frequent political repression, strikes became a common feature of urban life: in the Federal Capital alone there were 52 disputes in 1956 involving 853,994 workers, amounting to 5,167,294 days lost. The figures for the previous year had been 21 disputes and 11,990 workers involved, and 144,120 working days lost.[101]

The multiplication of labour conflicts had its origins both in strikes to defend union rights, and in thinly concealed political motivations. Some entrepreneurs acting arbitrarily, since Peronist legislation was still in force, applied sanctions to shop floor stewards and rendered null some social benefits acquired during the past decade, and this climate of what was felt as social vengeance encouraged armed resistance by Peronists. The campaign of social unrest and sabotage undertaken in those years was invested with heroic traits, and became known in Peronist mythology as *La Resistencia*. Although one such episode was serious enough to require the brief reimposition of the state of siege, 'what caused the [Government] most anxiety was that many politicians sought to turn the troubled situation to their own advantage by wooing the trouble makers with an eye to catching votes . . . '.[102]

The intended *desperonización* proved a far from easy task. That the labour organisations were not totally destroyed was lamented years later by Dr Zavala Ortiz, who said that the failure of the *Libertadora* had been 'its lack of determination. Peronism should have been deprived of its union organisation and its methods of struggle, which reflected the will of a *caudillo* and not the will of the people'.[103] The fact that the government was unable to articulate a coherent policy in the labour front was exploited by the labour movement. Seriously diminished at first, the Peronist unions began to take advantage of the differences amongst its adversaries. The reconstitution of Peronist unionism began in 1957, when the government called for elections in the unions. Although from his exile in the Dominican Republic Perón sent orders to boycott the elections, and insist instead in the recognition of the pre-September 1955 union authorities as the only legitimate ones, the new generation of unionists, eager to take over control, took no heed and won the elections in a majority of industrial unions.[104] Indeed, it was they who guaranteed the survival of Peronism as a political force. Believing that in their debilitated position confronted by an antagonistic State they would be able to obtain little round the negotiating table in terms of wage claims, they concentrated instead on long-term, political aims such as the return of Perón and of the CGT and intervened unions to Peronist hands.[105] Such a strategy would help to unite the rank and file simultaneously articulating an opposition to a society which found it difficult to interpret the significance of Peronism and assimilate the changes introduced since 1945. Therefore union leaders increased their isolation while gathering moral strength from the demands to rehabilitate Peronism.[106]

The Economic Issue

The men of the *Libertadora* were not strong in economics and in this field Aramburu preferred to avoid shock tactics that could risk tearing apart the fabric of a weakened society. Aramburu had extended his *prescindente* attitude to the economic arena, and felt the provisional character of the administration he headed did not warrant the undertaking of dramatic changes. Thus the recommendations of Industry Minister Alsogaray to press forward with the dismantling of the system of quasi-monopolistic protection installed by the corporatist-State inclinations of the previous regime, went unheeded. This was the subject of a debate lasting for six months, at the end of which both Alsogaray and Alizón García, another member of the Cabinet, tended their resignations. Both men were adamant that for the *Libertadora* to have any meaning beyond the imperative of Perón's deposition, it was a matter of urgency to alter drastically the existing protectionist, State-directed economic structure and create in its place 'a modern, free-market economy'.[107] Its failure to do this, according to Alsogaray, marked the caducity of the revolution. With the State continuing with the import-substitution industrialisation policies of Perón, the *Libertadora* failed to promote the regeneration of the process of capital accumulation that had begun its downward path in 1952, and which Perón had belatedly tried to check.

In his eagerness to seek expert advice, Lonardi had consulted Raúl Prebisch, then head of the United Nations Economic Commission for Latin America (ECLA). Perón had originally sought Prebisch's advice – although this never materialised – and Lonardi now named him adviser, a role in which he was confirmed by Aramburu. Prebisch produced a dramatic report, his *Preliminary Report on the Economic Situation in Argentina*. Its conclusions had been made public by President Lonardi on 27 October 1955. The next day national newspapers echoed the denunciations on the calamitous economic condition in which the Peronist government had left the country. The report analysed the situation rather narrowly focusing on the size of foreign reserves (which had effectively dropped from US \$1,682 million in 1946 to US \$450 million in 1955, as a result of the fall in exports and the energy deficit). The ensuing inflation was blamed on massive wage increases and state interventionism in the economy. While productivity had expanded 3.5 per cent in ten years, real industrial wages had been raised by 37 per cent. The conclusion was predictable – other social groups had experienced an inevitable fall in their standard of living, and among the latter Prebisch sympathetically pointed towards agricultural producers.[108] A quarter of a century later, Prebisch acknowledged publicly that his report had reflected a readiness to exaggerate the seriousness of the situation.[109]

Implementing in part the recommendations in the report, the *peso* was devalued in order to improve the terms of trade. Since in the short run agricultural activities have a low supply elasticity, and taken together with the fact that in Argentina agricultural output is a crucial component of wage goods, the ensuing pressures for increased money wages did not come as a surprise. Aramburu's government proved unwilling to restrain such pressures, and consequently the inflationary process remained unchecked, and agriculture's early gains were soon wiped out. In spite of the positive steps that Aramburu's government took to convey a favourable attitude towards foreign investment, its actions appeared indecisive and, as the British ambassador reported, they 'typified the failure to resolve the conflict between nationalistic political pressure and the country's economic needs'.[110] In his valedictory despatch, Sir Francis Evans underlined that nationalism was what 'prevented the country from taking those steps which alone could lead it into the path of recovery'. A mixture of irritation and sadness was evident in the ambassador's remarks on the 'fierce emotional reactions, unthinking, unreasoning, and destructive' that were aroused whenever there was 'any hint of encouragement to foreign interests' to take a share in the development of national resources and utilities, the latter being invested with a 'precious sanctity'.[111]

Perhaps, as a Foreign Office official noted, the problem lay in the fact that 'the mass of voters haven't yet been hit hard enough economically to know what a mess the country is in and how much sacrifice is necessary to pull it through'.[112]

Aramburu's Efforts to Secure US Financial Aid

While the country remained oblivious to sacrifices, the Argentine government, with the full support of the US ambassador, hoped the State Department would rush to offer generous aid and soft loans. But the latter, together with the US Treasury, needed a lot of convincing. Anticipating that the Argentines would be making specific requests for aid from the US, on 26 January 1956 Henry Holland sent a lengthy memorandum to Deputy

Under Secretary of State Murphy, enticing him to 'understand the general nature and dimensions of the Argentine problem'. He recalled how under Perón, the US had followed 'the same policy of economic assistance and friendship which [it had] pursued with all the American states regardless of the degree of dictatorship of the government', and how the fall of Perón had placed in power 'a number of people who harbor deep resentments against the United States'. The need to create 'a completely new relationship of mutual understanding, confidence and friendship' so as to make Argentina 'an aggressive partner in our war against Communist subversion in this hemisphere' meant that the US should help Argentina to 'solve her urgent problems' and offer a policy of 'generous aid'.[113]

The Treasury was not moved, and stated that it would be concerned 'strictly with objective economic criteria and not with political considerations'.[114] The ABC Working Group set up to consider aid to Argentina, Brazil and Chile, issued a report spelling out the steps Argentina would have to take to 'reverse the policies which brought about present difficulties'. Such measures included bringing inflation under control; developing a long-range agricultural and livestock programme that would give adequate consideration to the country's productive opportunities and export possibilities; rehabilitating and overhauling the railway system ('a sine qua non for genuine progress'); increasing electric generating capacity ('assured fair treatment, private capital could do a considerable part or all the job'); seeking to earn foreign exchange by exploring new products such as forestry and minerals, 'eliminating excessive government control that hampered activity and increasing petroleum production as rapidly as possible'.[115] It concluded that:

> It is clear that Argentina commands neither the necessary domestic savings nor [foreign exchange] to undertake all these projects . . . ; [. . .] she will need large amounts of external financing. The figure of 1.2 billion dollars mentioned by Prebisch has no known firm basis. The actual amount 'needed' depends on the specific plans and programs of the Government, about which we know practically nothing. The amount she will seek from foreign governments or international institutions will depend upon her willingness to accept private foreign investment and the extent to which she obtains capital goods by contracting short and medium term equipment obligations abroad.[116]

This would mark the beginning of protracted negotiations between Aramburu's government, represented by a financial mission headed by Dr Carlos Coll Benegas who spent the best part of July, August and September

1956 in Washington and New York, and several Eximbank, World Bank, IBRD, US Treasury and State Department officials. The US $1,200 million figure was never taken seriously in the US, nor was the later one of US $500 million that kept cropping up. Treasury Secretary Humphrey insisted that the Argentine government was 'entirely unrealistic in the amount of borrowing they want to do', and suggested US $20 to US $30 million 'as the order of magnitude' the US should be considering. He was adamant that the US president 'should not commit the US Government to make any loans to Argentina', and adduced as the 'main trouble' Argentina's 'little dollar earning capacity'[117] as well as US existing commitments to Brazil and Chile. Secretary Dulles agreed but asked Holland what would happen if Argentina did not get some assistance from the US, extracting the doom-laden response that 'the present government would fall and the Radicals and Socialists, who don't like the US, would probably take over'.[118]

Henry Holland was in an invidious position. On the one hand he used all the arguments he could muster to incline the State Department, and then the Treasury, to assist Argentina financially, insisting on the primacy of political arguments over straightforward financial considerations.[119] On the other, he did his best to convey to the Argentines the principles sustaining the economic policies of the US Government.[120] He explained these policies were based on the concept that:

> the primary burden for the economic development of any country was on that country's private investors, [whose efforts] could be supplemented by the very important contributions of foreign private investors, and that Government financing could play a most important but nevertheless relatively minor role. [. . .] accordingly [he] was somewhat disturbed over indications that the Argentine Government was planning to expropriate CADE and to apply for Government loans to expand its operations.[121]

The Eximbank, Holland explained, would find it very difficult to 'permit the extension of a loan to a government for an expropriated property for which private capital was readily available'. Coll Benegas referred to the 'extremely bad reputation' that CADE had in Argentina 'owing to fraudulent practices in the past', and said that government intervention was only intended as 'an intermediate step in the eventual taking over of the firm by private Argentine capital'.[122] The Americans remained unconvinced, and CADE was eventually nationalised.

The two main issues at the centre of the US position were the need for convertibility, and the lack of loans for projects where private capital was available. This was a question of principle, but on a more pragmatic level the US was concerned by Argentina's lack of dollar reserves, and thus the issue of convertibility was frequently raised.[123] When the Eximbank line of credit for US $100 million was finally approved on 6 September 1956 at a meeting of the National Advisory Council on International Monetary and Financial Problems, private capital was explicitly mentioned.[124] The line of credit was to assist in financing the purchase of US equipment and services, and in making specific loans under it the Bank would give 'due consideration to the progress which Argentina continues to make in attaining monetary and financial stability and in according satisfactory treatment to private investors . . . '. The figure of US $15 million was earmarked to be utilised in the private sector.[125] When the Argentine ambassador conveyed his government's disappointment at the final figure, remarking also on the disproportion with the assistance rendered other countries, especially Brazil, and requesting Dulles' help to raise the figure to US $112 million as well as lift the US $15 million requirement, Dulles retorted that he thought US $100 million 'far exceeded earlier expectations' and that the figure represented 'a distinct achievement for the Argentine Financial Mission'.[126]

While the state of the economy continued to dominate US–Argentine relations, in Argentina the matter tended to be dismissed rashly by people who continued to regard economic issues in terms of national independence versus foreign domination and dogmatically upheld – without actually using his words – Perón's banner of 'economic independence'. Foremost in the defense of this position were the Intransigent Radicals, who were not orphaned of support within the government, as the case of admiral Rial's resignation would illustrate. In the end, the *Libertadora* paid but lip-service to liberalisation.[127] The task of bringing about the structural changes that inaugurated a new stage in Argentine post-war economic policies would be left to Frondizi. The intransigent leader would, surprisingly, yield in matters the *Libertadora* felt unable or unwilling to tackle.

7 CONCLUSIONS

The *Revolución Libertadora* had been ostensibly carried out to restore the rule of law and democratic values: both aims would prove difficult to achieve when confronted with a Peronist opposition that, stripped of all legal political means, resorted to sabotage to challenge the first, while its leaders attributed different interpretations to the second. While the supporters of the *Libertadora* believed that the quality of democracy lay in the goodness of the doctrines being upheld, this view was contested by those who thought sheer numbers provided sufficient legitimation for their actions.

By calling itself a 'revolution', the September 1955 insurrection was bound to disillusion those who expected it to be 'revolutionary'. But 'revolutionary' it could not possibly be given its origin in a variety of groups which had only been united in their abhorrence of Perón. Thus whenever controversial issues arose, be it in the field of the economy or of education, military and civilians were divided as to how far back the boundaries of State interventionism ought to be drawn. And looming above all this was what the British ambassador had described as the 'nationalism, individualism, intolerance, and lack of co-operative capacity which are unfortunate elements in the Argentine character', ensuring that a short-term answer to the country's pressing economic problems could not be achieved.[128]

Faced with this reality, General Aramburu opted for the expectation of solidarity with the *Libertadora* – which could be invoked – rather than for an ideological commitment – which could not. The awareness in government circles of the secret contacts between representatives of Perón and Frondizi understandably offended deeply that sense of the supremacy of 'revolutionary solidarity'. Hence the more admirable General Aramburu's resolution to ensure the peaceful transference of the government on 1 May 1958 to a man he neither liked nor trusted.

The *Libertadora* failed not because it was insufficiently revolutionary (that is, 'surgical'), but because instead of enhancing society's recovery of its freedom, it took up the mirror image of Perón's discourse. The latter had been dependent on an image that portrayed Perón as the embodiment of 'the people', thus his enemies were the enemies of 'the people'. Society after Perón should have been able to recover its independence at every level, including the expression of passions and interests. But this was not to be. Accepting the other side of the Manichean imagery with which Perón had replaced politics, the *Libertadora* turned out to be neither 'liberal' nor truly 'liberating'.

2 The Split of the *Unión Cívica Radical*

1 INTRODUCTION

General Aramburu is reported to have said, a decade after handing over power to Frondizi on 1 May 1958, that he 'should never have taken the nails off the coffin in which Perón had buried the political parties'.[1] Notwithstanding, throughout the thirty-nine months of his provisional presidency he endeavoured, and to a limited extent succeeded in establishing political (as opposed to military) rule. If political rule is a consequence of acknowledging the problem of diversity in society and of the belief that conciliation is the most desirable way of tackling such diversity (which reflects the existence of differing interests) by definition it does not, and cannot reduce all things to a single unity. This last attitude must, on the contrary, be attributed to those who oppose politics – the believers in 'fundamentals' on which everybody must of necessity agree.

But this fact (that one cannot be 'political' while insisting on basic, necessary 'fundamentals') was overseen by many of the actors both within and without the *Revolución Libertadora*. These – be they *gorilas* or Catholic nationalists – made up the ranks of those who saw society as a natural unity which politics divided and disturbed. This was a view that prevailed in Argentina since at least the 1920s, when Maurras was a key influence on *criollo* nationalists, and can be traced back to Hipólito Yrigoyen and his idiosyncratic ways of blurring the distinction between party – his own, the UCR – and Nation.[2] It was this distrust, disbelief in, and impatience with politics that could arguably be singled out as one of the greater ills afflicting the Argentine body politic. If politics is 'an activity – lively, adaptive, flexible, and conciliatory . . . the way in which free societies are governed',[3] then before searching for the causes behind the failure of democratic consolidation in post-Peronist Argentina it may be pertinent to begin by looking at the peculiar features that the political activity took in the country. To this end it will be relevant to focus on the party that could first lay claim in Argentina to the adjective 'popular' – the *Unión Cívica Radical*.

The UCR had expected to be the main beneficiary of the *Libertadora*'s 'cleansing' operation. It alone among Argentine political parties could contend to represent – or at least to have represented until Perón's arrival – a majority of the electorate.[4] The people who had firstly been fraudulently deprived of their majority by the 6 September 1930 coup, and latterly had been 'fooled and misled' by Perón's demagogy, were now expected to 'return to the fold' and to their true representatives. However much some Radicals believed or hoped that the political clock could be set back to 1943 – if not 1930 – it was clear to others that the future could not be sought in the past. In the 'unhealthy state of Argentine domestic politics',[5] only a small group of people thought they knew the way forward. Some of them were members of the UCR, most of them were not. From different backgrounds they all embraced a new creed, developmentalism, and they did so with an obstinacy that only faith can engender. In the process of their teleological quest they introduced a new style of politics the essence of which lay in the alteration of the rules of liberal-democratic political behaviour. This change would rebound in the negligence of party politics by those in government, and a parallel emphasis on individual rather than collective protagonists. In order to explain this shift, it may help to recall certain dominant features of the UCR, as well as the unfolding of the specific events that eventually led to the split of the party and the election of Arturo Frondizi as President of Argentina on 23 February 1958.

2 A BACKGROUND OF INTERNAL STRIFE

If parties are divided in times of crises, it is not because they have suddenly lost a previously maintained cohesion, but rather because crises exacerbate pre-existing divisions.[6] Indeed, the emergence of factions within the UCR – a healthy sign in itself – had more than once in the first half century of its existence led either to personal or collective withdrawals from the party.[7] Some authors have pointed out that it was the lack of homogeneity in the UCR which was conducive to ruptures every time a programme had to be agreed upon.[8] The contradictory interests represented in the party, traditionally expressed with more emotion than logic (Yrigoyen being the utmost exponent of this trait) resulted in the emergence of a series of factions and in five major splits in its history; these occurred in 1891, 1897, 1924, 1956 and 1963.

In 1891 and 1897 the schisms reflected the principled position of some Radicals, who would not enter into any kind of pact or agreement with other political forces, both inside or outside the conservative administration, defending the widening of the electoral franchise as sole programmatic declaration while lifting the banner of morality. The fact that a programme was never adopted during the formative years of the UCR (1890–1916) has been attributed by some authors to the Radicals' peculiar predicament. They had to oppose a ruling elite which presented itself as modernising and in favour of progress and economic advancement.[9] To find a distinguishing identity, the UCR had to appeal to traditional, almost metaphysical values with strong moral overtones – *la Causa, la reparación nacional, la moralización* – despising anything even remotely resembling concrete policies, and more specifically, economic policies.[10] Ezequiel Gallo has remarked on the contrast between the virulence of the rhetoric of the opposition and the moderation of its proposals. The conservative government would seize on such rhetoric – as well as the UCR's tendency to resort to armed insurrection – to support their contention that anarchy and chaos would follow an UCR government.[11]

This is how a Radical who has written the most detailed study of the UCR up to date has defined the issues at stake both in 1891 and in 1897, simultaneously providing an example of the rhetorical style so dear to *Yrigoyenistas*,[12]

> What was at stake, in both opportunities, was the politico-institutional orientation of *la Causa*, whose intransigence, in thought and in attitude, was determined by the need to proceed with a firmness of behaviour as definitive as the expression 'radical'. Since the *Unión Cívica Radical* was The Cause aimed at the salvation of the prostrated or offended nationality, no concession nor agreement could be legitimised, given that it was not a question of specific and circumstantial, governmental or electoral political interests of a mere party, but the permanent custody of the interests of a national, moral and institutional order, the most general and permanent interests of the Argentine people.[13]

The vagaries dictated by the intransigent espousal of the Cause would taint Radical behaviour for years to come. The split of 1924 which gave rise to *personalistas* (supporters of Yrigoyen) and *antipersonalistas* (those opposed to him) was the result of Vicente Gallo's atempt to put an end to Yrigoyen's control over the party, but it also reflected the existence of contradictory interests. Among the latter were the long-standing interregional rivalries between the city of Buenos Aires and the rest of the country, episodes in a much longer historical tradition of regional squabbles for control over the country's natural resources.[14] This was evident in the three tendencies into which the UCR was divided in the 1920s:

- *Yrigoyenismo*, supporters of Yrigoyen's populist, rhetorically nationalist style, favouring government spending and responding to the urban sectors of Buenos Aires;[15]
- *antipersonalismo*, in favour of the same policies, but this time on behalf of the urban sectors of the Province of Santa Fe, and
- *Alvearismo*, opposed to government spending, and echoing the exporting interests of the agricultural sector in the Province of Buenos Aires.[16]

In a sense, as Peter Smith has remarked, the Radical movement failed as a party because it failed to overcome the fundamental and historic cleavage in Argentine society, that between the Federal Capital and the provinces.[17]

3 THE UCR IN THE 1930s

The 'Infamous Decade' of the 1930s, characterised by fraudulent electoral practices to ensure a Conservative majority, appears to have been much less iniquitous – except on the issue of election rigging, albeit not in the City of Buenos Aires – than is generally accepted. Not only was there very little unemployment, but Argentina withstood better than any other country the effects of the Depression – real wages during the decade were higher than in the previous one, while GDP grew steadily from 1932 onwards encouraged by the industrialising zeal of the Pinedo Plan.[18] On the political front, deputies in Congress 'argued and struggled over some prominent issues': political amnesty, taxes, mortgage regulations, unemployment, the state of siege, the meat trade and electricity concessions.[19]

The 1930s marked the culminating moments in the development of the UCR. The correlation between party abstentionism and revolutionary attempts at seizing power which in January 1935 marked the preeminence of the former,[20] meant that as from that date the party took over the role of parliamentary opposition. Marcelo T. de Alvear had succeeded Yrigoyen to the presidency of the country in 1922.[21] A sincere believer in the rules of the democratic game, something that cannot be maintained of his predecessor with his insistence on the supremacy of movement over party and of the Executive over the Legislative power, Alvear became the leader of the UCR after Yrigoyen's death in 1933. He remained head of the party until his own death in 1942. His task was not made easier by the *de facto* or fraudulently elected administrations ruling the country after 1930. Throughout this period Alvear had been either imprisoned or banished. He also had to contend with the belligerence of some of his own partisans, adamant that the only path to power left to the UCR to fight electoral fraud and reinstate universal suffrage, was a revolutionary one.

But Alvear, who had spent a third of his life in Paris, showed little enthusiasm for revolution and opposed all violent attempts encouraged by UCR members throughout the 1930s. His would be a conciliatory leadership, accepting the almost unavoidable return to electoral abstentionism, but greeting with relief the decision of the UCR convention of 1935 to abandon the abstentionist banner. As a direct result of this decision, as well as of a failed revolutionary attempt led by the UCR at Paso de los Libres in December 1933, a group of UCR members – mainly university students – set up a faction known as FORJA (*Fuerza de Orientación Radical de la Joven Argentina*).

FORJA regarded the lifting of abstentionism as an abandonment of the UCR's principled position. Moreover, it described Alvear's disavowal of the 1933 insurrection as 'coincidental with the British plan which demanded the legality of Radicalism and its conversion into the Party of Order'.[22] FORJA's manifesto was entitled *The Revolutionary Vocation of Radicalism*, and it reflected the reaction of its younger members against the accommodating attitudes favoured by Alvear, and against government policies defined as corrupt and damaging to the interests of the country, because they favoured foreign capital. Alvear and the 'old' leadership were accused of conniving with the government in economic matters, particularly those referred to concessions of electric power monopolies to foreign firms, in an accord known as the *Concordancia*.

FORJA acknowledged its debt to the ideological movement of the 1918 *Reforma Universitaria*, adopting its rallying cries for a Latin American revolution and, at a more modest level, an end to private (namely religious) education, especially at the tertiary level. It also placed itself firmly in the *Yrigoyenista* tradition, denouncing 'the weakening of the moral values that should define the historic movement of Radicalism'.[23] With the purpose of rescuing the UCR from the 'old gentlemen' controlling it, FORJA called for a change in the internal structure of the party. The way to do this was twofold; internally, it required the direct vote of party affiliates in the election of party authorities, and externally, it was necessary 'to pinpoint the causes and responsibilities for Argentine indebtedness to the privileged foreign monopolies'.[24]

Throughout the decade of its existence, FORJA endeavoured to rescue the allegedly nationalist tradition of the UCR, defending its secular origins and raising the banner of 'the people' against what it saw as an oligarchic government chiefly interested in making deals with foreign capital. The decisive ideological impact of FORJA within the UCR, and especially on its Intransigent faction, lingered on after its self-dissolution in December 1945. More nationalist than leftist – indeed, there were many 'extreme right-wingers and anti-Semites in FORJA' – FORJA's dissolution in 1945 was 'Jauretche's personal decision in the face of Braden's campaign against Perón'.[25] It was from FORJA that Perón borrowed his three banners of 'economic freedom', 'political sovereignty' and 'social justice', banners upheld since the early 1930s by *Yrigoyenistas* within the Alvear-dominated UCR.[26] FORJA explained, in the ornate language favoured in those days, that in 1945 it no longer had a purpose, since

> the ideas and aims sought with the creation of FORJA have been achieved with the establishment of a popular movement in political and social conditions that are the collective expression of the national will for self-fulfilment; FORJA's birth was the result of the absence of such a will, abandoned by Radicalism.[27]

When the UCR's Federal Capital convention met in 1936 it voted, among other things, in favour of the 'nationalisation of all sources of energy', shortly before the elected UCR councillors in the municipal administration voted in favour of extending the electricity concessions to CHADE amidst cries of corruption. This decision resulted in a new split in the party which overcame the divisions confronting *Yrigoyenistas* and *Alvearistas* (since supporters of both camps had voted in favour of the concessions) and giving rise to an 'Opposition Bloc' instigated by Oscar López Serrot. Together with Arturo Frondizi, a 29-year-old lawyer and a UCR member since his student days in 1930, and at the time 1st Vice-President of the National Convention of the UCR, they launched a debate within the party on the role of the State and foreign capital in the economy.[28]

País Libre was a new short-lived – April to September 1937 – weekly publication that played a critical role in the wording of the manifesto voted by the UCR national convention in 1937. In contrast to the Bloc, directed towards the internal party struggle, *País Libre* was launched to foster an ideological debate. It wanted the UCR to provide clear programmatic definitions 'underlining its character as a popular movement dedicated to the political, economic, social and moral liberation of the country'.[29] The 1937 convention was to prepare the party for the elections that were to take place in 1938. While some favoured a joint formula agreed with General Justo – elected president from 1932–8 in fraudulent elections where, moreover, the UCR had abstained[30] – the convention was carried by those obstinate defenders of the party's traditional stand against any form of electoral pacts, first established when Alem rejected the agreement between

Roca and Mitre in 1891.[31] In the event, *País Libre* backed an 'all Radical' formula headed by Alvear, criticising the Bloc's attempts at dividing the party. But it was Roberto Ortiz who became president in 1938, and he started a campaign against electoral fraud, but his efforts were reversed when he fell ill and was succeeded by his vice-president, Castillo.[32] In the context of the present work, *País Libre* has a special significance since one of its editors was Arturo Frondizi. Frondizi's appeal to party members to fight for a new Radicalism, firmly rooted in the principled *Yrigoyenista* tradition, added a novel element: the need to think about the means of political action, not just its ends. Frondizi wrote in *País Libre*:

> We must not tell the people that we must govern because we are the majority; let us tell them specifically why we want to govern. [. . .] It is not enough to repeat that electoral freedom and the respect for the Constitution will be guaranteed, but it is necessary to announce what we intend to do about land ownership, since the land should be in the hands of those who work on it; what attitude will be adopted to counteract the action of the large imperialist capital that kills all endeavours to secure a national economy; what steps will be taken to improve the predicament of the proletariat [. . .] lastly, [it is necessary] to explain . . . whether one is in favour of the oligarchy or truly in favour of the people's cause.[33]

Twenty years later Frondizi still appeared to be asking the same questions, and when his turn came to provide the answers, they were totally unexpected by his voters as much as by his party colleagues.

FORJA had also instilled amidst the party ranks an impetus for change which was first evident in the electoral platform of Amadeo Sabattini, whose term as governor of the Province of Córdoba (1936–40) secured the predominance of *Yrigoyenistas* in that province at a time when the party machinery was in *Alvearista* hands. Although vague in the best Radical style, Sabattini's programme foresaw progressive inheritance taxation, the acquisition of land by the State for its distribution amongst 'authentic farmers', and the setting aside of land for 'collective State-owned farms'.[34]

4 THE UCR IN THE 1940s: THE YOUTH MOVEMENT AND THE *INTRANSIGENCIA*

By 1945, other signs of restlessness had emerged within the UCR, and FORJA's aims and principles were reasserted in the party's Youth Congresses organised by Moisés Lebensohn in the Province of Buenos Aires in 1938 and 1942–6, leading to the emergence of a new faction, the Movement for Intransigence and Renovation (MIR or *Intransigencia*) led, among others, by Arturo Frondizi. The Youth Movement gathered all the anti-*Alvearista* UCR members in a new, more vigorous, more articulate wave. Its efforts were still centred on what they saw as the opportunist appropriation of the party machinery by more conservative members, stifling any chances of bringing new breath into Radicalism. Under Lebensohn's guidance, the Radical Youth Congresses of the Province of Buenos Aires caused the greater impact on the party. In his opening speech at the Fifth Congress in May 1942 in the provincial town of Chivilcoy, Lebensohn referred to the internal crisis of the UCR describing it as part of a deeper crisis in Argentine politics. He began by demanding the direct vote of each party member in internal elections to counteract what Lebensohn saw as the excessive importance of the *punteros,* pivots of an internal party structure based on the granting of personal favours instead of representing the aims and ideas of party affiliates. He concluded with an exhortation delivered in the best Radical style:

> The Argentine people will fight passionately when they feel that from their efforts a new restructuring of the country will be born, based on true justice; when they feel that from their sacrifices profound transformations will emerge, justifying them, and they will feel this way only when, from the internal life and actions of the party, a halo of moral grandeur and the impassioned impulse of justice will emerge.[35]

The issue of the internal voting mechanism – which would be crucial in splitting the party in 1956 – had first appeared in 1931 when it was included in the Organic Charter (*Carta Orgánica*) of the UCR. It was taken over by the Youth Movement, and then by the MIR. They finally succeeded in 1948, when the direct vote was adopted, and as a result the MIR gained control of most of the UCR's ruling bodies. The MIR's explicit purpose was to fight the *unionistas,* who were at the time actively seeking an electoral agreement with the UCR's long-standing enemies – the Conservatives, Progressive Democrats, Socialists and Communists – with the purpose of confronting Perón with a *Unión Democrática* in the February 1946 elections.

The *Avellaneda Charter*

The MIR was launched in 1945 with a document known as the *Avellaneda Declaration* which followed closely in the spirit of the many statements

issued by the Youth Movement – in turn influenced by FORJA. It therefore began with a reference to the predicament of the party, insisting on the need to recover its 'characteristic principled positions in search of the popular and historical plenitude of its impaired function'.[36] The Avellaneda Declaration, together with two documents known as *Profesión de Fe Doctrinaria* and *Bases de acción política*, issued at the end of the MIR's 1947 congress, also held in Avellaneda, were jointly known as the *Carta de Avellaneda* (*Avellaneda* from now on). *Avellaneda* remained the undisputed manifesto of both parties that emerged from the division of the UCR in 1956. Given Frondizi's active role in drafting it, and the fact that it was the official platform on which he fought – and won – the February 1958 presidential elections, it merits quoting at some length. The main paragraphs in *Avellaneda* were the following:

(a) 'The history of Radicalism is inextricably bound with the history of the country.'

The history of our country is the result of the struggle of progressive popular currents, propelled by a deeply-felt pursuit of excellence, against backward looking oligarchies hindering the great achievements that should have made the Argentine man a free man. The doctrine of Radicalism was not the result of theoretical ramblings, but of the long and painful struggle to set up a political, economic and social democracy [. . .] that will serve as a guide for the future development of the Nation.

(b) 'The economy as a means of achieving higher ends.'

The economy, in the life of men and of the Nation, is not an end in itself but a means that allows the achievement of individual as well as collective ideals; its importance . . . is directly related to the need to ensure the material bases for the free development of the personality of the country and its inhabitants: the economic liberation of the Argentine man and of the Argentine Nation.

(c) 'The agrarian question.'

The land will be for those who toil it, be it individually or on a cooperative basis [. . .]; it will cease to be used for speculative ventures, [. . .] and agrarian production will be defended from the activities of monopolies and hoarders, its circulation and marketing will be in the hands of large cooperatives of producers and consumers under State control and participation.

(d) 'The nationalisation of natural resources.'

All natural energy sources, public utilities and foreign and domestic monopolies that hinder the economic progress of the country, will be nationalised, handing its management to the Nation, to the provinces, to the municipalities or cooperatives [. . .].

(e) 'The defence of small, independent enterprises.'

All economic activities not included in the process of nationalisation will be assured the widest economic freedom, without artificial barriers created by the government, by speculative interests or by large capital concerns.

(f) 'Industrial development.'

[The UCR shall seek] comprehensive industrial development, as long as it is not founded on low wages [. . .].

(g) 'Internal party problems.'

The main problem is to unite Radicalism, for which purpose it will suffice to spread its doctrine and appeal to those men whose conduct guarantees that they will be able to serve it. Since if it is true that parties need ideals and platforms, they also require worthy members that will offer guarantees for the moral reparation that the Republic demands. The Radical doctrine and people are intact and thus the only thing that remains to be done is to purge some leading members and nurture, from the midst of the new generations, those leaders able to confront the great problems looming over the country.

(h) 'A statement of intransigence: the rejection of any electoral pacts.'

We are opposed to the UCR entering any electoral pacts, because in the normal running of the institutions, the country must be governed by organic parties and Radicalism as such aspires to face alone the responsibility for structuring a new Argentina.[37]

The responsibility for the three documents that made up *Avellaneda* was as follows: the *Profesión de Fe* was written by Arturo Frondizi, Antonio Sobral and Gabriel del Mazo; the *Bases* by Frondizi, Lebensohn and del Mazo; the *Declaración* (quoted above) by Lebensohn. The *Profesión de Fe* spelt out the great *Yrigoyenista* themes, underlining the principles of social justice and man's spiritual (as opposed to material) essence, as well as the meaning and role of the UCR:

> Radicalism is the historical current of the emancipation of the Argentine people, of the authentic fulfilment of their life in the nurturing of their moral goods and in the avowal of the great ideals born in their entrails. . . . it is a guarantee against all materialistic philosophies of human life.
>
> [. . .] Radicalism is the organic and social current of what is popular, of federalism and of freedom, close to the soil and interpreter of our emotional and humane authenticity . . . it is the people itself in its heroic deed to constitute itself as a Nation, in possession of its wealth and its spirit.
>
> [. . .] The UCR is not merely a party . . . but the patriotic mandate of our native national solidarity, and the intransigence with which it must be fulfilled . . .
>
> This is why Radicalism is a conception of life, of the whole life of the people; and the Radical revolution, taking man and his freedom as its starting point, turns politics into an ethical creation . . . [38]

The third document, the *Bases*, charted in eleven points the future path for Radicalism. Point III posed the 'democratisation of culture. [. . .] Radicalism will reinstate the 1918 University Reform'. This was a *crie de guerre* against what were seen as advances of the Catholic Church in the field of education, especially after the introduction of compulsory religious education in schools after the 1943 military coup. Point IV was titled 'Organisation of an economic democracy', and it recommended 'control of the economy according to the plans established by the representative organs of the popular will . . . to build a regime that will subordinate the economy to the ends and rights of Man and will mobilise his resources, not in the limited benefit of the propertied classes, but of national development and social welfare'. The notion of a centrally-planned economy was reinforced in Point V which stated as an aim 'the nationalisation of public utilities, energy, transport, fuel, and of those capitalist concentrations that constitute cartels or monopolies', but this was rather bewilderingly intended to 'safeguard private initiative in its creative reality'. The collectivist ideal reappeared in the management structure of the enterprises to be nationalised, made up of 'autarchic entities [. . .] with the participation of consumers, producers, technicians and workers'. The following point (VI) extended this concept to the industrial field. Under 'Industrial democratisation' the objective was the 'participation of technicians, employees and workers in management and profits'. Trade union freedom and the right to strike were guaranteed. In the agricultural field, the proposal was for 'an immediate and profound agrarian reform' since land should not be regarded as a 'merchandise' and should be placed 'at the service of society and labour'. In the arena of foreign affairs, the *Yrigoyenista* tradition was recalled to ensure non-participation in political, economic or military alignments.[39] The vagaries of Yrigoyen's alleged nationalism were put forward as policy objectives, thus when Perón continued Argentina's hemispheric isolation through his refusal to sign the Bretton Woods agreements, he would encounter no opposition from the UCR.[40]

The Intransigence was being confronted by a new phenomenon – the presence of Perón. *Avellaneda* must be seen in the light of a double confrontation, the internal dispute with the *unionistas* on the one hand, and Perón's social policies on the other. After Perón's victory in the 1946 elections, the Radicals had to reconcile themselves with the previously unthinkable fact of not embodying the majority of the electorate.[41] The Intransigents blamed this on the Unionists' decision to join the Democratic Union, abandoning the 'cause of the people'. If in 1945 the Intransigents sought to define their position by confronting the Unionists, once Perón was in power they had to define their identity in contrast with Peronism. And they did this by attempting to outmanoeuvre Perón, position they maintained throughout the Peronist decade.[42]

When in 1962, during the course of a series of conversations with Félix Luna, Frondizi looked back on *Avellaneda*, he said that it had never 'pleased' him totally, since it was a 'catalogue of recipes', while 'the main thing had been to uphold a truly revolutionary position and, once in power, to carry out . . . everything that had to be done within the basic orientations of Radicalism'.[43] Moreover, he remarked defensively that the *Profesión de Fe* made a distinction between ends and means, when it stated that 'for Radicalism ends are unchangeable: those of freedom and democracy for the integration of man; but means can vary because they are tools, and the social conditions for national fulfilment are changeable'.[44]

One of the leitmotivs of the UCR, its avowal never to enter into any kind of agreement with other parties or forces (the *antiacuerdista* principle) was again endorsed by the 1947 UCR Convention, which issued a resolution stating that

> No party authority nor body can produce statements, or documents, or organise acts that may imply an alliance, pact or union with other parties

or political forces alien to the UCR. Any such acts must be considered to be absolutely null and void.[45]

This was the true spirit of intransigence, refusing to compromise, obstinately hostile to any kind of political agreement in itself regarded as morally reprehensible. Few, if any, of the delegates at the convention seemed to realise that the term 'intransigent' itself evoked the negation of politics.[46]

The Intransigent documents would have far-reaching consequences. If on the one hand their 'radicalism' attracted vast numbers of young people who refused to accept that the opposition to Perón's government had of necessity to be identified with anti-popular and reactionary positions, on the other hand they would prove the source of many a future misunderstanding. As Halperín Donghi has remarked, Radicalism's programme 'has always been the opposite of what its electoral clientele would have wished for',[47] the latter being mostly found amongst the middle classes.

5 INTRANSIGENCE DURING THE PERONIST DECADE

As a result of the elections held on 24 February 1946, the UCR had 44 representatives in the national Chamber of Deputies, a majority of whom identified with the *Intransigencia*. The Radical Bloc of the 44, as it became known, constituted the only congressional opposition to the Peronist regime, albeit seeking to outdo it in its own territory. On 17 December 1946, Crisólogo Larralde, Antonio Sobral and Arturo Frondizi, the three Intransigent members of the UCR's National Executive Board who had been charged with the reorganisation of the party after the February defeat, issued a document known as the Manifesto of the Three. After a lengthy evaluation of internal dissent regarded as a reflection of deep and substantial differences on the 'idea of what is Radical, and on the meaning, significance and mission of this civic force', there was a paragraph in the manifesto which was an exercise in one-upmanship. It read in part that 'the [Peronist] government . . . shows that it does not interpret the revolutionary meaning that the UCR posed, promoted, and started to carry out as the path of the Argentine people. Revolution and government are thus . . . terms inexorably opposed'.[48] Ten years later, after Perón's downfall, Frondizi remarked:

> the Radical Party embraced the cause of social and economic justice many years before Perón. What Perón did was to steal our programme

and our slogans [. . .]. Today we have regained our traditional position as interpreters of the progressive, democratic aspirations of the people.[49]

In the course of 1946 the Radical deputies tabled bills proposing the nationalisation of the railways, of the telephone network, and of the electricity supplies, in an attempt to reverse the 1936 decision to extend the concessions to the CHADE electricity company.[50] While in the economic and foreign policy areas the Radicals were able to maintain a 'holier-than-thou' attitude, in the arena of social policy the government was firmly in control. There was little left for the opposition to do but to remark sullenly:

> [. . .] labour legislation by itself will not solve the colossal economic and social problems of Argentina, such as the problem of the land, and of private monopolies, although it is evident that it mitigates unfair situations and allows for the tackling of economic and social issues in a peaceful manner.[51]

The single issue that sparked off the nationalist fervour of the Radicals was the one concerning the country's oil resources. On 3 July 1947 a group of ten Radical deputies – Calcagno, Frondizi, Balbín, del Carril, del Mazo, Dellepiane, MacKay, Peña Guzmán, Pomar and Sobral – tabled a bill on the nationalisation of oil which was not passed. When in February 1954 the newspapers reported the government's intention to sign contracts with a group of private foreign companies for the exploration of untapped oil sources and their eventual exploitation, the newly-elected president and secretary of the UCR's National Committee – Frondizi and Monjardín respectively – launched an impassioned campaign in defence of the State monopoly over oil resources, and against the proposed contracts. The statement they released on 19 February read in part:

> With reference to the negotiations that [. . .] hurt national sovereignty and jeopardise the present and future of Argentine economic and spiritual development, the UCR cannot remain expectant nor be an accomplice if it remains silent, since one of the most honourable chapters of our economic history is the one that refers to the constant action in defence of our oil, against the voracity of international monopolies.[52]

It concluded with a four-point resolution:

1. To denounce to the Argentine people the purpose of the regime of reaching oil agreements that compromised [Argentine] sovereignty and the future of the Republic.
2. To tell all Radical members to undertake an active campaign to clarify the regime's designs in order to provoke the popular resistance that will put an end to them.
3. In case such warnings went unheeded, and any agreement was reached that handed out [Argentine] oil sources to foreign companies, *the UCR would declare it null and void.*
4. To undertake the forthcoming electoral campaign under the banner of the defence of Argentine oil.[53]

When the contract with the California Standard Oil Co. was signed by Perón on 25 April 1955,[54] Frondizi and Monjardín issued a detailed statement in defence of the State oil corporation, *Yacimientos Petrolíferos Fiscales* (YPF) which in its final part stressed the resolve of the UCR's governing bodies 'to support and express their solidarity with YPF, a company that illustrates Argentine ability to carry out its great national tasks', to repeat their 'repudiation of any agreement that involves the handing out to foreign firms, be it directly or indirectly, of all or part of Argentine oil', and

> to point out that our country's predicament shows once more that international oil monopolies support and are supported by dictatorial governments that suppress freedoms and sell out the country's wealth . . . To denounce that the oil contracts that are being negotiated are part of a plan to subject our country economically, politically, and militarily to foreign powers that do not fight for the ideals nor interests of the Argentine people.[55]

But the *Intransigencia* was not the whole of the UCR. The Unionists still had considerable clout in the party and they were far from pleased with the 'radical' zeal of the Intransigents. Their concern was to limit the party to an oppositionist role that focused on the government's 'totalitarian' features, in this way keeping alive the spirit of the Democratic Union. Two events caused considerable concern amidst the Unionist ranks; the first referred to the participation of the party in the 1949 Constituent Assembly entrusted with amending the 1853 Charter (the main purpose of the former had been to remove the clause forbidding the re-election of the president). When the amended constitution was promulgated, the Unionists had refused to take the oath of loyalty, while the Intransigents had acquiesced.

The second took place in 1951, when the MIR-controlled UCR decided to take part in the 1952 general elections notwithstanding the ever-increasing hurdles the government was putting in place to impede the activities of the opposition. The UCR's candidates to the presidency and vice-presidency were two leading Intransigents, Ricardo Balbín and Arturo Frondizi respectively. Their platform was *Avellaneda*. The Unionists, feeling threatened from without by the Peronist incitement of the working class, and from within almost equally uncomfortable by the daring tone of *Avellaneda*[56] and the sectarian practices of the Intransigents, were in fact more faithful representatives of the original Radicalism with its reluctance to make choices that might have cost them votes.

The upholding by Intransigence of a doctrinaire populism was seen as a dangerous form of dissent and would indeed prove totally inadequate to quell the growing fears of the middle classes, neglected and aggrieved by Perón.

6 THE INTERNAL STRUCTURE OF THE UCR

The revolutionary movement launched by General Lonardi from Córdoba in September 1955 mustered civilian support chiefly from the Unionist ranks in that province,[57] but Unionists were also foremost amongst those who pressed General Aramburu and Admiral Rojas to get rid of the nationalist and 'totalitarian' grip over the *Libertadora* during Lonardi's short administration.[58] But the change in direction of the *Libertadora* as from 13 November 1955 did not appease those avowedly liberal middle classes worried by the fact that the UCR – the only party that could challenge the dismembered Peronism – was then under the leadership of the Intransigents, amongst whom Frondizi, president of the UCR's National Committee since 1954, played a dominant role.

The internal structure of Radicalism had been established by the 1892 Organic Charter. Grass-roots 'clubs' were organised into committees (one for each province and one for the Federal Capital) which in turn chose delegates to the National Convention which met every six years. The purpose of the convention was to nominate candidates to the presidency and vice-presidency in the national elections contested every six years. The number of delegates per province was the same as those they were entitled to send to the national Congress. Jorge Wehbe, Radical militant since 1933 in his native province of Córdoba, recalled how machine politics in the 1950s was still the exclusive political style in the party. The only people who went to the local committees were officials and party members, 'whose number was more or less constant'. The only activity in those committees was the struggle between the different petty *caudillos* who used to 'sell' their votes (that is, those of the members of the committee they controlled) to the candidates for elective office (at party, municipal, provincial, or national level).[59]

The next body in the party hierarchy was the National Committee which met once a year. It was a federal body constituted by four delegates from each province and four from the Federal Capital. Its functions included the sanctioning of a 'declaration of principles' and of the programme for the forthcoming presidential term. The direct vote of party members to elect candidates had been established since the MIR gained control in the 1948 National Convention. Nevertheless, there was one exception – the nomination of candidates to the presidency and vice-presidency remained the responsibility of the National Convention so as to preserve unblemished the federal ideal. This was because the direct vote would have meant the overwhelming predominance of the most heavily-populated districts: chiefly the Federal Capital and the Province of Buenos Aires. Notwithstanding this explicit clause, the committee of the Province of Buenos Aires, chaired by Ricardo Balbín, had resolved on 18 October 1953 that there should also be a direct vote for electing presidential candidates.

The minority groups in the UCR (Unionists and Sabattini's National Intransigence) had been demanding the reorganisation of the party machinery to include their participation at all levels. But the MIR was not prepared to relinquish its control, and as a result, when the National Committee met on 8–9 March 1955, Frondizi was re-elected as its president.[60] In his speech accepting his renewed appointment, Frondizi took the opportunity to remind the *Libertadora* of its commitment to re-establish democratic rule. Balbín, a member of the committee, rose to applaud Frondizi, yet stressing the need to support the government unambiguously. In this, although an Intransigent himself, he was closer to non-Intransigents like Zavala Ortiz who were less enthusiastic about the urgency of elections. Zavala Ortiz had declared that the more fearsome prospect was 'the failure of the Revolution rather than the Revolution itself' and that they would support 'an unconditional legality when the hour of legality arrives: we do not want a premature legality when it is still time for revolution'.[61] Zavala Ortiz was deeply and sincerely worried by the faltering support that the *Libertadora* was receiving in civilian quarters, mainly in the Intransigence.[62] In a radio broadcast he spoke 'in defence of the Revolution', declaring:

> If this revolution fails or is defeated, what will have failed is the democratic intention itself, and anti-democracy will have triumphed

[. . .]. That is why it is a national duty to look after it, improve it, defend it. But this defence demands everybody's synchronic effort – military and civilians alike [. . .]; the concurrence in the actions of the revolution therefore demands the concurrence in the defence of the revolution.63

As early as 31 October 1955 *La Nación* was quoting UCR members who accused Frondizi of pursuing a 'divisive policy' and of being 'the obstacle to the party's unity'. In the course of a visit to the Province of San Juan, Frondizi publicly began to distance Radicalism from the government, stating that support for the *Libertadora* could only be conditional, 'as long as it remains true to the objective of reestablishing the rule of morals and of liberty', but 'Radicalism is not part of the government and in many decisions, mainly the economic ones, we do not agree'.64 The anti-Peronist front was revealing publicly its fissures. Frondizi had dared challenge the government of the *Libertadora*. Some were scathing in their attack. Anticipating the actual split, *The New York Times* correspondent reported that '[the UCR] was split this week by the presidential ambitions of Dr Arturo Frondizi. [. . .] In committee meetings it was angrily charged that Dr Frondizi, who represents the extreme left in the party, was attempting to become its "dictator"'.65

7 THE 1956 UCR NATIONAL CONVENTION HELD IN TUCUMÁN

The National Committee of the UCR had met in San Juan on 12 September 1956 and passed a resolution summoning a special session of the National Convention to be held in Tucumán on 9 November. The representatives of a group of the smaller provinces – Tucumán, Jujuy, Neuquén, and Santa Cruz – all of them in their thirties, representing the 'new generation' of party cadres, had been meeting for some time to devise a strategy that would ensure their control over the party, traditionally in the hands of the larger provinces and the City of Buenos Aires. Tucumán was chosen as site of the convention because it was Intransigent Celestino Gelsi's territory, and he knew he 'could control things there'.66

Out of the eight points on the agenda the seventh was 'the appointment of candidates for the presidency and vice-presidency of the Republic'. On 5 November *La Nación* reported a meeting of the MIR in which it was claimed that among others Balbín, Larralde and Illia (Intransigents from the provinces of Buenos Aires, the two former, and Córdoba, the latter) raised with Frondizi the advisability of postponing the date of the convention, to delay any decisions on the issue of nominations. They argued that the presidential formula should emerge from the direct vote of all party affiliates, as the Buenos Aires committee had proposed, and not of the convention.

According to the newspaper report, the postponement was presented as the 'last attempt to stop the splitting of Intransigence'. The Unionists, meanwhile, were adding pressure from outside the MIR. That same day Zavala Ortiz went on radio to declare that there were factions within the UCR 'that have become virtual parties within the nominal party . . . there are party leaders who, in order to stress their ideological differences with us, have resorted to doctrines or ideas which are not Radical'.[67] Furthermore, he made the first public accusation, in a thinly disguised reference to Frondizi, of the alleged evidence of a 'materialistic interpretation of history' and of the 'Leninist interpretation of imperialism' within the UCR.[68]

What lay behind such ominous warnings? It would seem that, at least in the case of the Intransigent dissidents, a prosaic personal rivalry between three men who each believed he had a right to be the UCR's presidential candidate.[69] The three men were Ricardo Balbín, Arturo Frondizi and Amadeo Sabattini. The latter believed that as the head of the National Intransigence and governor of Córdoba Province (1936–43) and given his seniority within the party, he had a stronger claim than either the younger Balbín or Frondizi.[70] Sabattini's support for the *Libertadora* was, in contrast to Frondizi's, unconditional, and so was his insistence on party unity, a concern he shared with Balbín, but which was not at the forefront of Frondizi's preoccupations.

Balbín, who had shared the presidential ticket with Frondizi when they were defeated by Perón in the 1952 elections – the party convention had made the nominations – now insisted this time that the nominations should be the result of the direct vote of party members. This would almost certainly secure him the nomination, since he controlled the party machinery in the Province of Buenos Aires, where the majority of UCR members were to be found. Frondizi was the candidate of the 'Gelsi group': after 'a lot of adding and subtracting' they had finally decided that Frondizi was the most suitable candidate since he could be expected to 'add' votes, while Balbín's staunch support for the *Libertadora* was sure to 'subtract votes from the popular sectors'.[71]

Feelings were running high when 204 delegates of the UCR met in the northern province of Tucumán in November. Balbín insisted again on the direct vote when he met Frondizi in the provincial capital in an effort to reach an agreement. This was not forthcoming. On 8 November *La Nación* carried an account of the estimates being made by Frondizi's supporters. According to such calculations, the allegiances of the delegates to the convention were: 163 for the MIR, 20 for Sabattini's National Intransigence, 13 for Larralde's Unified Movement of the Province of Buenos Aires, and 8 for Zavala Ortiz's *Unidad Radical*.[72] The number required to have quorum was 103. Referring to rumours that several Radical leaders had suggested – in an attempt to achieve a compromise – that the supporters of the direct vote be allowed to choose the vice-presidential candidate, the reporter from *La Nación* remarked that such rumours 'underline the fact that the issue of the nominations is seen as the crucial one in the convention, and the direct vote and the party's reorganisation are excuses to stop Frondizi's nomination'.[73]

The MIR delegates met on the first day of the convention, and by a majority of 63 voted that the item on the agenda referred to the direct vote should be examined by a special commission. This effectively meant that the issue would not receive an airing during the convention. To show their opposition to this decision, the dissenting delegates did not attend the meetings of the convention in the hope of undercutting the necessary quorum. Finally, on the night of 11 November, the 136 delegates present cast their secret ballots in favour of Frondizi's presidential nomination, and of Alejandro Gómez, a little-known teacher from the Province of Santa Fe, as vice-presidential candidate.[74] *The New York Times* reported on 13 November that Frondizi had won his nomination 'as a result of what some of his colleagues described as "a steamroller technique"'.

8 THE UCR SPLITS – THE UCRI IS BORN

The reactions to the nominations were swift to come, even though public opinion had to await the end of a national newspaper strike to learn about the convention's vicissitudes and their outcome. To underline their distaste at the proceedings, Balbín and Illia had departed abruptly from Tucumán. Larralde, on his part, issued a statement on 16 November accepting the nominations, but appealing simultaneously to Frondizi to turn them down so that the reorganisation of the party could be undertaken. For his part, Zavala Ortiz announced that Unionism would demand the constitution of a new national committee of the UCR, and his statement was followed by similar ones from the party machinery in several provinces under Unionist control.

The *Mesa Directiva* (steering group) of the national committee promptly intervened the rebel districts: the provinces of Buenos Aires, San Juan,

Córdoba and Santiago del Estero.[75] Statements from one group were followed by counter-statements from another, while frantic meetings took place during the usually inert summer months. The actual sanctioning of the UCR's split was first revealed on 9 February 1957, after a meeting in the Province of Buenos Aires in which Balbín, Sabattini, Zavala Ortiz, Santiago Nudelman and Crisólogo Larralde decided to reorganise the party. In a radio broadcast that same day Frondizi said that the 'segregation' of some sectors of the party, was 'final and irrevocable'. Although endeavouring to blame his opponents for the split, the possibility of dividing the party had been considered by Frondizi's supporters before the Convention. On 2 October 1956 *Le Monde* had carried a report indicating that 'Frondizi's friends advised him to leave the old cadres behind and create his own party. But this is of course, a risky adventure'. In an impassioned radio broadcast which marked the launching of his electoral campaign, Frondizi said:

> The country will now understand why this crisis is final – we are two different things. We speak two languages, we feel different passions. What for them was the *gauchaje*, the rabble, the zoological torrent, today is, with the same pejorative sense, the electoral scum. For us, it was and always will be the Argentine people.[76]

Frondizi had dared utter the ultimate heresy – the dividing line was not that separating democrats (that is, anti-Peronists) from supporters of 'totalitarianism' (that is, Peronists), but the one confronting 'the people' and the anti-national 'oligarchs'. Furthermore, that same 'liberating revolution' which Frondizi himself had contributed to bring about was now being accused of dictatorial practices:[77]

> Had I so wished, I could have been the candidate of all [. . .] factions. It would have been enough to support the government unconditionally and postpone the discussion of its economic and social policies with their evident oligarchical and anti-national results. It would have been enough not to have demanded an amnesty [for political prisoners] and not to have criticised the repressive and anti-democratic measures of certain revolutionary sectors . . . In other words, I should have had to betray the party's programme and should have rebelled against the mandate of the Radical people.[78]

On 16 March 1957 Frondizi's supporters in the UCR added the term Intransigent to the name of the party in accordance with the new political parties statute, creating the *Unión Cívica Radical Intransigente* (UCRI, Intransigent Radical Civic Union). The dissident factions joined forces disregarding their previous confrontations and personal animosities, and under the chairmanship of Larralde lay their claim to the UCR's popular tradition by adding *del Pueblo*, becoming the Popular Radical Civic Union (UCRP) on 20 March 1957. Both parties retained *Avellaneda* as their respective platforms. The differentiating factor had a name: Arturo Frondizi. A year later, celebrating Frondizi's victory at the polls, Rogelio Frigerio, editor of the weekly *Qué sucedió en siete días* (known as *Qué*) blamed the oligarchy for the UCR split, which it denounced as part of the 'machinations to atomise and confound the national front'.[79] Frigerio's version was rather different in 1977, when he recognised that Frondizi had been responsible for splitting the party, although not as a result of the issue of the nominations, 'but with the aim of rebuilding the national movement' which had to include Peronism in its midst.[80]

The anti-Peronist front in which the *Libertadora* had placed its hopes for the future, was definitively broken, and in the forthcoming elections the UCRP and the UCRI would be competing with each other for the anti-Peronist as well as the non-Peronist votes. At least, this was what everything seemed to indicate at the time, and the reason for considerable disquiet within the armed forces. Indeed, a confrontation of 'unprecedented proportions' in military circles erupted in the aftermath of the UCR Tucumán Convention.[81]

3 The Elections for the Constituent Assembly: The Perón–Frondizi Pact and the Failure of the *Revolución Libertadora*

1 INTRODUCTION

In the interpretation of Intransigent historian Gabriel del Mazo, the division of the UCR was 'inevitable'. Setting aside the discussion on ex post facto admission of historical inevitability, the desirability of the UCR split in the context of Argentine politics at that time, taken in conjunction with the dissolution of the UCRI in 1962, a mere six years after its creation, remains arguable. Revealing once more Radical preference for 'movements' rather than parties, del Mazo wrote in 1957 that the opportunity lay open for the UCRI to transcend the narrow limits of a political party to become what the old UCR had always purported to be, 'a national and popular cause'.[1] The political implications of dismissing as 'anti-national' and 'anti-popular' those who disagreed with such a vaguely defined 'cause', were lost to those whose personal ambition and obdurate ideological outlook led them to attempt a redefinition of the rules of the political game. The present chapter will analyse the repercussions in the military and political fronts of the split in the UCR leading up to the general elections of 23 February 1958.

2 THE *LIBERTADORA*: 'CARETAKER' OR 'REVOLUTIONARY'?

The Reorganisation of the Government, 25 January 1957

On 26 October 1956, while on an official visit to Tucumán Province, President Aramburu announced the electoral calendar that would restore democracy to Argentina. The first event, due in July 1957, were elections for a Constituent Assembly which would be charged with amending the 1853 Constitution. This would be followed by general elections 'in the third quarter of 1957'. The provisional character of the government was reaffirmed and a tentative date was set for the end of the *Libertadora*. While such a public commitment sealed the fate of Aramburu's presidency, the divisions and divisiveness in the official camp shook the fragile anti-Peronist side.

The Cabinet reshuffle undertaken by Aramburu on 25 January provided further evidence both of his independence (or arbitrariness, given that he had not discussed the issue in the Junta)[2] and of his personal quandry, torn between his promise to hold elections and his abhorrence of Peronism. Demanding the resignation of all his civilian ministers, Aramburu replaced five of the ten. The most significant changes were the removal of Dr Eugenio Blanco from the Economy Ministry, where he was replaced by Dr Roberto Verrier, and of Dr Laureano Landaburu from Interior, his replacement being Alconada Aramburú. The only – unofficial – explanation provided for the changes was that the first stage of the revolution ('the destruction of the dictatorship') had been accomplished, the second stage ('democratic reorganisation') required 'a faster tempo and different men'.[3] Dr Blanco's 'obtuse nationalism' had proved a hindrance for Aramburu's and Rojas' public pleas in favour of foreign investment in oil and electricity.[4] Furthermore, his indecisive handling of the economy coupled with wage and labour demands had resulted in a bleak economic outlook.

It was widely known that while he was head of the political ministry Dr Landaburu had pressed for the government's *prescindencia* (non-intervention) in internal party politics, and he had opposed – as Frondizi did – the holding of elections for a Constituent Assembly before the general elections. His replacement led inevitably to renewed charges of *continuista* intentions of the government. The British ambassador reported to the Foreign Office that the general policy of the government was 'to encourage the growth of opposition to the Frondizi-dominated National Committee of the Radical Party'.[5] What were the reasons behind the preference for the UCRP and the dislike for Frondizi?

The men of the UCRP – Unionists and non-Frondizi Intransigents alike – believed that the military intervention of September 1955 had to have a truly 'liberating' objective to obliterate any remnants of the Peronist 'aberration'. In this they coincided with the military, albeit they were equally at a loss as to the way to achieve it. The manner in which the UCRP assembled motley factions whose chief unifying axis was their mistrust of Frondizi and their support for the government, made the party vulnerable to accusations of backing *continuismo* and *quedantismo*. While the former referred to government actions to secure an official candidate for the elections, the latter was the name given to the alleged intentions of groups within the military – especially the Navy – to stay in power by means of delaying the call for general elections. Balbín was accused of intending to be the 'heir' to the *Libertadora* when he declared that it was 'necessary to save this revolution to ensure that it will be the last one'.[6] Frondizi's position was the exact opposite:

> Those who left Radicalism [that is, the UCRP] ask the government not to call for elections, using as a pretext the people's lack of political preparation. Those of us who have always shown our faith in the people, simply ask that the commitments undertaken by the armed forces be respected – that general elections take place at the end of the year [. . .] We want fair play. And when we say *we,* we are speaking in the name of the people who are not prepared to tolerate that a minority decide what their destiny ought to be.[7]

It is difficult to ascertain whose advise the president finally followed when he included in the Cabinet three radicals of the anti-Frondizi groupings. Potash has suggested that Aramburu had sought Balbín's advice through General Leguizamón Martínez, son-in-law of Eduardo Laurencena, member of a traditional UCR family from the Province of Entre Ríos.[8] Carlos Alconada Aramburú maintains that his appointment as Interior minister to replace Landaburu had come through General Ossorio Arana on the advice of Zavala Ortiz.[9] But the fact remains that in a highly-charged political atmosphere, the president chose to name as political minister a man of the anti-Frondizi forces of Radicalism. The British ambassador remarked that 'the eventual objective seems to be to create a central group of moderate political parties (i.e. all the anti-Frondizi Radicals, the Progressive Democrats and the Christian Democrats) which could offer effective and united opposition to Frondizi'.[10] This was a reflection of the growing misgivings that Frondizi's oppositionist stances were provoking in official ranks, as well as of the support he was receiving from Frigerio and his magazine *Qué,* in which well-known Peronists were writing.[11] *Qué*'s indictment of the UCRP left little room for compromise. It accused the UCRP of embodying 'the definitive alliance of anti-popular forces to frustrate the fulfilment of a programme imbued with a national sense'.[12]

At this stage, albeit masked in veiled language, *Qué* was beginning to suggest publicly the possibility of an electoral alliance of the 'popular' forces. The identification of 'popular' with Peronist was sure to irritate both military and civilian who regarded Peronism as little more than a vernacular version of Fascism. Decree-Law No. 4161 even forbade the use of the word Perón and its derivations.

Confrontations within the Armed Forces, March–May 1957

The lack of either political or ideological cohesion in the government, compounded by the constant bickering of politicians in the *Junta Consultiva Nacional*[13] offered the opportunity to groups of officers to see themselves in the role of advisors to the government. The two issues that were at the focus of constant attention were oil – and any decision which could be suspected of compromising Argentine sovereignty over her resources – and the electoral calendar.[14] The latter was at the core of intra-service apprehensions and inter-service rivalries.[15] The first tremor occurred a fortnight after the UCR Tucumán Convention, and it resulted in the forced retirement of seventeen Army generals.

A group of nationalist staff officers at the Army Ministry felt that the decision to hold elections for a Constituent Assembly on the basis of the system of a new electoral law based on proportional representation was a dilatory tactic. The view in the nationalist sectors displaced at the time of Lonardi's removal in 1955, a view shared in the Frondizi camp, was that the government would take the final decision as to the advisability of holding general elections once the results for the July 1957 Constituent Assembly elections were known, using them as a test of public opinion. Frondizi's supporters believed the electoral schedule revealed the government's intention to remain in power by means of postponing the general elections. The rival UCRP was equally incensed by the replacement of the Sáenz Peña Law by proportional representation.

The deliberations within the Army unleashed by the announcement of the electoral schedule were serious enough for a group of officers to start plotting against Aramburu. When a group of senior officers demanded the resignation of Army minister Ossorio Arana, accused of not defending the Army's interests when the UCRP Arturo Mathov publicly denounced the permanence in the Army of 'Nazis and neo-Fascists',[16] Aramburu stood by the minister being questioned by his subordinates, and Ossorio Arana took the opportunity offered by the fact that the end of the calendar year was the time for deciding promotions and retirements in the Army, to dismiss its Commander-in-Chief, General Zerda, and order the unprecedented retirement of seventeen generals. This decision put an end to a series of intra-Army confrontations that originated in opposing political and ideological outlooks – the ousted officers were all nationalists, some suspected of Peronist sympathies.[17] A further consequence of the November events was the consolidation in power of the president, who would have to await another seven months and a new shuffle in the Army hierarchy before he could have a team capable of restoring some form of discipline in the force.

Inter-service relations (uneasy at the best of times) deteriorated as a result of these rumblings of discontent within the Army, since on several occasions one or another group of officers would blame the Navy for its alleged intentions of blocking the electoral process.[18] Potash has emphasised the concern of Navy minister Admiral Hartung at the contrast between what he saw as the prevailing perceptions of the Navy as 'an aggressive force' set out to dominate the government, and the 'self-image of Navy leaders, who saw themselves in a defensive posture trying hard to retain a hard-won share in the decision-making process'.[19] The Navy's misgivings in this sense were reinforced by the fact that President Aramburu's firmer grip over the Army after the November purges resulted in a parallel diminution of the power of the military Junta that had been established after Lonardi's ouster in November 1955. The enhancement of the president's powers over those of the Junta impaired the Navy's chances of exercising its political clout. Vice-president Admiral Rojas was quick to acknowledge this, and to resent the fact that Aramburu was increasingly heeding his civilian advisers – in this case, Interior minister Landaburu – in detriment of the proposals put forth by Rojas and the Navy.

The peak of the Army-Navy confrontation occurred in March and was resolved by the simultaneous resignation of Trade and Industry minister Rodolfo Martínez, and Under-Secretary at the Navy Ministry, Rear-Admiral Arturo Rial. In personal letters to Aramburu which it was widely believed Rial himself had passed on to the Frondizi news-sheet *Resistencia Popular*, Rial had accused Martínez of incompetence in handling the electricity monopolies.[20] Their publication and peremptory tone were seen as 'such a flagrant act of insubordination that it at once became a question of whether Rial or the President himself should go'.[21] Rial's personal ambitions had led him to seek support amongst those most openly opposing the government – the UCRI and nationalist sectors for whom Vice-President Rojas was the worst enemy. The outcome of the episode was to show the Navy as rife with discontent and internal divisions as the Army and 'the authority and efficiency of the Provisional Government [. . .] questioned'. As the British ambassador somberly remarked, 'at a moment when the maximum of unity and confidence is needed this country seems more divided and the Government less representative and stable than ever'.[22] For his part, Frigerio wrote in *Qué* that the president had lost 'the confidence of the armed forces and of the Nation', and that as the government faltered, 'the revolution has irretrievably lost its cohesion and spirit'.[23]

A further blow would be struck at the unity of the armed forces, the government's only true basis of support. This time it would be the turn of the Air Force to vent its discontent at the time of the publication of the definitive electoral calendar prepared by Interior minister Alconada Aramburú. On a national radio broadcast on 30 March, five months after his original announcement, President Aramburu notified the country of the new dates. The general elections were now scheduled to take place in February 1958, and not at the end of 1957, as Aramburu had originally promised. Almost immediately the Air Ministry issued a communiqué disassociating itself from Aramburu on the grounds that the honour of the Armed Forces was at stake since they had promised the elections in the last quarter of 1957. The Air Force minister, Air Commodore Julio Krause, stated that as a matter of principle the ministry he headed would withdraw from membership of the ruling Junta.[24] The other two forces would not give in and after several days of mutual recriminations Krause was replaced in a compromise solution in which his successor was chosen by the Air Force rather than by Aramburu.

Six weeks later the continuing state of indiscipline and political ferment in the Army, the president's own force, would be revealed. The latest crisis to shake the Army concluded on 16 May 1957 with the resignations of the Army Minister General Ossorio Arana, and his Under-Secretary, General Leguizamón Martínez. The crisis had been brought about by Ossorio Arana's high-handed treatment of another officer, General Solanas Pacheco, who had been offered the post of head of the Military College and wanted to appoint his own nominees as personal collaborators, a plea that Ossorio Arana rejected, placing Solanas Pacheco *en disponibilité*. This provoked an uproar amongst the generals, who decided to back Solanas. But, as the British ambassador remarked, 'the generals would hardly have made such a concerted and effective effort to oust their Minister for love of General Solanas Pacheco'. The latest of these 'games of military musical chairs' was brought about by a combination of 'internal service causes, [. . .] personal ambitions and [. . .] political manoeuvring'.[25]

The Economy

With his support base constantly weakened and narrowed Aramburu did succeed in fulfilling his promise of handing over the presidency to his elected successor on 1st May 1958. He proved less able – or willing – to alter the economic model pursued by Perón. Faced with a deteriorating economic situation, with inflation climbing to 17 per cent and a balance of payments deficit of US $75 million that would increase in 1957 to US $100 million owing to higher petroleum import prices resulting from the Suez crisis plus a severe drought that damaged the maize crop, Economy Minister Verrier proposed an austerity programme to reverse the situation. As a way of adopting a 'decisive policy of free enterprise',[26] the measures included the elimination of subsidies on transport, fuel and electric power, a reduction in government expenditure via forced redundancies in the public sector, the postponement of half of agreed pay increases for all ministries, heavier taxation, the abolition of a fixed exchange rate, the lifting of all restrictions on imports of capital goods and machinery, and the removal of price controls and imposition of a wage freeze.

Although Aramburu backed the programme, half his cabinet threatened to resign if it were to be implemented. Hoping to gain the support of the political parties, the president asked the leaders of twelve parties to meet Dr Verrier and hear his appraisal of the situation but, as the Americans reported, 'these leaders showed no sympathy for any belt-tightening programme with general elections scheduled for the end of [the] year'.[27] Dr Verrier resigned and Adalbert Krieger Vasena was appointed in his stead.[28] Although Krieger's appointment indicated no change in the overall economic philosophy, by accepting Verrier's resignation the president conceded the watering down of the austerity programme, in this way subordinating 'desirable solutions' to 'a politically volatile climate'.[29] The point was reinforced by the Argentine ambassador to Washington in a conversation with Acting Assistant Secretary of State for Inter-American Affairs Rubottom, when pleading for economic assistance. Ambassador Vicchi said that the US had 'a great opportunity' to consolidate in Argentina those elements which were advocating 'democracy, free enterprise and international cooperation' by 'lending a helping hand', since the Argentine government 'could not be expected to do the politically impossible even if it was economically desirable'.[30] Six months later, disheartened by the results of his second visit to Washington in search of financial aid, the President of the *Banco de la Nación* of Argentina despondently mused to a State Department official that it was very difficult 'to be treated like a schoolboy with the school master saying you did fine on that problem but you forgot the comma over here, so let's see how you do next term and maybe you will get a better mark'.

What the Argentines saw as a mere detail was for the Americans a fundamental question of principle. It referred to the unresolved issue of compensation for the expropriation by Perón of meatpacking and energy-supplying plants. Coll Benegas left Washington at the end of October 1957 pleading 'if only the US could say that [they] are interested in Argentina . . . '.[31] But the abyss could not be bridged. While the Americans – at least the State Department – insisted that they *were* interested in Argentina, the Treasury was not persuaded that political considerations should override economic ones. Throughout 1956 and 1957 the Provisional Government sent high level emissaries to plea with the US: following Coll Benegas' mission in 1956, Gainza Paz, the editor of *La Prensa* newspaper which Perón had expropriated and the *Libertadora* had given back, had made a similar request to President Eisenhower.[32] The Argentine ambassador did not miss an opportunity to press the point, while Coll Benegas returned in 1957 still insisting for aid and an increase in the US $100 million in lines of credit granted by the Eximbank a year earlier.

The Argentines, with that mixture of 'egocentrism and naïvety' that so baffled the Americans and perturbed the British, could not see that there was a matter of fundamental principle that divided US and Argentine perceptions.[33] While the latter considered that her good will towards the US should be rewarded financially, the former insisted that no aid would be forthcoming where private capital was available and willing to invest and only barred from doing so because of lack of confidence in the political willingness or commitment of the Argentine government to encourage free enterprise. In this context, the matter of compensation for individuals against the arbitrary actions of governments was crucial.[34] But even then Bernbaum – Director of the Office of South American Affairs in Washington – noted that 'all Eximbank loans to the Government for power and petroleum are out of the question in view of the availability of private enterprise. This would apply regardless of Argentine action on the claims of US companies'. He added that 'it is not clear that Argentine officials understand this distinction'.[35] In his confidential memorandum to Rubottom, Bernbaum went on to spell out 'the three obstacles impeding the extension to Argentina of additional credits'. Besides 'the Argentine Government's failure [. . .] to honor its moral commitment' to satisfy the legitimate claims of American businesses, the other two were its 'insistence on Government ownership of electric power in the Greater Buenos Aires area despite the availability of private capital', and 'its refusal to allow private capital to participate with YPF in the petroleum industry, as well as the Eximbank's general policy not to make loans to anyone in this field'.[36]

3 PERÓN IN EXILE AND PERONISM IN THE *RESISTENCIA*

The crumbling of the Peronist Party's feeble structure as a result of the events of September 1955 meant that the Peronist opposition to the *Libertadora* would be embodied in Perón (for most of this period in exile in Caracas, until Pérez Jiménez's overthrow, when Perón sought asylum in Trujillo's Dominican Republic), in John William Cooke, his personal representative, and in the new generation of union leaders. In 1956 Perón still trusted that a sympathetic military coup would overthrow the government of the *Libertadora*, and therefore was opposed to any attempts at 'normalising' the intervened unions.[37] But a new generation of union leaders were keen to take advantage of the fact that according to Decree-Law 4161 about 60,000 former Peronist officials, including unionists, had been proscribed from holding official posts.[38] Their strategy was one of 'opposition and negotiation', tactics that were a better reflection of working class methods than the revolutionist tactics preferred by Cooke.[39] In a letter to Cooke, Perón, forever the skilful manipulator, understandably regretted any actions which could lead to the weakening of his grip over the movement:

> It is unquestionable that the dictatorship has . . . its allies to exert influence over our Peronist masses through leaders who, forgetting their mission, go for personal, rather than national and popular solutions; the masses can be influenced in an opposite direction to our *justicialista* designs through deceit, fatigue, or simply because they desire a solution to their terrible ills.[40]

Perón – if not Cooke – realised at this stage that he could not, from abroad, control his followers' every movement. Moreover, the fact that Perón had either neglected or purposefully hindered the formation of political leaders, preferring instead to surround himself with '*yes* men'[41] meant that the only Peronist cadres left in Argentina capable of mobilising supporters were the trade union leaders.

The process of redefinition of the types of action of the trade unions had begun when Aramburu took over from Lonardi on 13 November 1955. This marked the beginning of a learning process for the unions, accustomed to act under the protective arm of the State. Furthermore, union leaders had now to contend with the presence in many unions, not just of the military interventionists, but of Socialists, Communists and Radicals who had entered the unions under the protection of the *Libertadora*.[42] Such learning process ran parallel to the one undergone by the other participants in the political scenario: the parties and the Provisional Government itself. If the latter had at first shown a certain timidity in dealing with labour problems, by mid-1957 it felt confident enough to pursue a firmer, when not repressive, policy. It had decreed that existing wage agreements should be valid for another year to keep inflation down, and notwithstanding a series of strikes to protest against such measures, the government remained firm.

Strikes and mobilisations had manifestly political aims, and in June 1957 there was a general strike to secure 'the freedom of trade union prisoners, the normalisation of the CGT, the derogation of the repressive legislation, and of the decree that extends the date of expiry of wage negotiations'.[43] Through such openly political aims – the only specifically to do with labour came at the end of the list – the labour leaders sought to capitalise on the feelings of isolation prevailing in the working classes and to acquire the moral force needed to confront the government's repressive policies. A decree ('punitive and offensive')[44] strictly limiting legal strikes and providing severe sanctions in case of failure to resume work when strikes were declared illegal, aroused resentment amongst trade unions whose leaders were obliged to act as both agents for workers' claims and as key political actors in an unstable political situation. Elections for union officials had been held in most unions, and the government had convened a congress of union delegates in August 1957 to end the intervention of the CGT, but it ended in a fiasco after two weeks, with delegates divided between the '32 Group' of 'democratic unions', with a membership of 857,000, and the '62 Group' of Peronist and Communist-dominated unions, with a membership of 226,000.[45]

Since the conflict unfolded in the political arena, it was easier for Cooke and his radicalised version of Peronism to achieve, if not an agreement with the union leadership, at least the possibility of concerted action. Cooke's dream of a 'final insurrection' brought about by a 'revolutionary strike' was boosted simultaneously by the acts of sabotage and terrorism undertaken by the *Resistencia*,[46] and by Perón's ambiguous letters from exile, encouraging Cooke to ensure that 'everybody, everywhere and in every circumstance, will carry out a war without mercy against the dictatorial rabble, in such a manner that it will succumb, overwhelmed by millions of small actions, be they individual or collective'.[47] As long as he succeeded in unsettling whosoever was in office, Perón did not mind whom he supported, and Cooke fitted his destabilising intentions ideally with his revolutionary rhetoric.[48] As Cooke would find out in 1961, Perón's backing was not based on shared principles and Socialist utopias, but on matters of political expediency.

On 17 May, while beginning his letter 'we are heading towards the *justicialista* revolution in all its consequences', Perón replied to Cooke's pressures to prepare an insurrectional schedule saying that 'to establish in a preconceived way a path for action, setting dates and circumstances, is to move haphazardly'.[49] In any event Cooke was not dismissing political action within the restrictions set by the government's banning of Peronism. The first big opportunity to test the proscribed movement's political clout arose with the elections for the Constituent Assembly on 28 July 1957.

4 THE CONSTITUENT ASSEMBLY, JULY–NOVEMBER 1957

The Position of the Parties

Although most political parties agreed on the need to amend the 1853 Constitution reinstated by a Provisional Government's decree of 27 April 1956, they disagreed on the timing of the summoning. The legality of the abolition by presidential 'proclamation' of the amendments sanctioned by a Constituent Assembly in 1949 – with a majority of Peronist delegates[50] – had been timidly queried at the time, given that the individuals and parties that backed the *Libertadora* believed their first duty was to stand by its decisions. This explained the cautious remarks of politicians who were reluctant to draw attention to the lack of legitimacy of the revolutionary government to call for such an assembly. Horacio Thedy of the Progressive Democratic Party declared that the only valid constitution was the 1949 amended one, and that therefore it was this version that had to be changed, and not the original 1853 one.[51] Thedy was acknowledging tacitly that the government was setting a bad precedent, since for the first time in Argentine history a *de facto* government was placing itself above the constitution.

For its part, the UCRP National Convention, consistent in its unconditional support for the government, issued a declaration on 9 July 1957 backing the derogation of the 1949 Constitution, rejecting the validity of the latter on two counts: firstly, that it was 'the pseudo-legal basis of the totalitarian system implanted in our country', and secondly, that it 'violated the 1853 Charter and was an expression of electoral fraud', since it allowed for the re-election of the president and vice-president, something expressly forbidden in 1853 unless a whole presidential period had elapsed.[52]

While aware that the government of the *Libertadora* was not legally entitled to convene such an assembly, the UCRP had agreed to place it above the constitution.[53] Balbín declared that although the UCRP had opposed the idea of a Constituent Assembly prior to the election of a constitutional government, 'the Revolution has seen it as a necessity to carry out its programme, and the citizens of our country must accept its call'.[54] Balbín's statement coincided with a document issued by the UCRP listing the amendments it would submit to the Assembly. The most noteworthy were those where the party showed its coincidence with the government in the need to curb the power of the Executive[55] simultaneously strengthening the Legislature. There was a firm belief that the restitution of constitutional checks and balances would prevent the repetition of a dictatorial experience. None the less, the UCRP was adamant that a section on workers' rights should stay. Together with the clause allowing for the re-election of the president, this had been the outstanding amendments introduced in 1949. The UCRP list of amendments to be discussed included aims long cherished and embodied in *Avellaneda*:

- The maintenance of the Sáenz Peña electoral law;
- State exploitation of oil resources;
- The social function of property;
- Agrarian reform;
- Job security for public employees;
- Encouragement of the cooperative movement;
- The study of measures to protect the middle classes.[56]

The UCRI had opposed the call for the Assembly since the party believed that in accordance with the need to uphold the rule of law, any amendments to the constitution should be left to the future elected Congress. It proposed that 'the battle for the *Constituyente*' be based on three premises with the aim of defeating 'the oligarchy':

- To take part in the elections, since 'each vote of the people will be a place won over from the oligarchy';
- To declare the Assembly null and void, demanding immediate general elections;
- To undertake that once in government, the UCRI would appeal to the Argentine people to decide, 'without restrictions to its liberty' nor 'proscriptions', which Constitution should be in force.[57]

Leaders of all parties were offered access to the radio on the day the campaign was declared officially closed (24 July). While the other politicians took the opportunity to reaffirm their support for the government,[58] Frondizi's speech left little doubt that he was campaigning *against* it, and it provided as well an excellent illustration of the main tone and themes in which Frondizi would fight not just the 1957 elections, but the February 1958 ones, too. He said that the elections for a Constituent Assembly were

> a trap set for the people to ensure the domination of a minority which . . . is carrying out an economic and social programme against the interests of the people [. . .].
> What is needed, . . . is the belligerent ballot. Not just the ballot that repudiates, but the one that can triumph, that can overwhelm, that can prevent the government of the motherland staying in the hands of politicians who are enemies of the people and of the Nation . . .
> It is essential to understand that this is not a struggle between parties, but of the people against its enemies.
> [. . .] everybody must know that on Sunday the 28th . . . a new struggle between two historical forces is being fought. On the one hand, the forces of the oligarchy represented by *continuismo*, by the parties that have official backing and by those who speculate with the absence of the [Peronist] people. On the other, the popular forces . . . parties which, like the UCRI, defend the national and popular cause, and also those who in good faith believe that casting a blank ballot will be a better way of expressing their rejection [of the government] or their discontent.[59]

Frigerio had launched an attack along similar lines, denouncing in *Qué* that the reformist zeal was a façade to 'safeguard the oligarchic government and the continuation of its anti-national economic policies'.[60] Such barrage of abuse against the government, plus the hardly veiled attempts at opening leeways in the Peronist rank-and-file, where the tactic of casting blank ballots was gaining momentum, caused bewilderment and deep concern in government circles. *The Manchester Guardian* did not fail to recognise the style that had left its imprint on Frondizi's campaign:

> In both political and economic sectors of the current crisis the most extreme views are clearly those of the Left-wing Radicals, led by Dr Arturo Frondizi . . . and they probably reflect the majority opinion in the country – because their policies come nearest to those of Perón and so have the workers' support.[61]

The Guardian then went on to note that Frondizi's 'demagogy and apparently unlimited personal ambitions have alarmed both the Navy and the Right-wing Radicals and the *Continuistas*', and concluded that these sectors had to choose between two perils, 'one is that Dr Frondizi will win the coming elections, the other that civil war would be an almost certain result of any attempt to prevent his victory'.[62] Had the paper's correspondent been aware of the content of the letters that Perón was sending to Cooke, he would have concluded that there was now relatively little cause for alarm, given that Perón himself was beginning to worry about Peronist votes going to Frondizi. Aramburu on his part did not seem to be over-concerned with Peronism when on 13 June he denounced those carrying out 'a war without mercy against the government', and

> who through lack of vision or through deceit, [or] calculation, are playing in favour of anti-democracy, repeating, wittingly or unwittingly, knowing it or without knowing it, the same attitudes and words that led our people as well as others to end up under the dictatorship of providential men.[63]

Decree No 3838 of 12 April 1956 limited the terms of reference of the Constituent Assembly to (a) the establishment of a new electoral system; (b) the reinforcement of individual liberties; (c) the strengthening of the federal system and municipal autonomy; (d) the reinforcement of the independence of Congress and the limiting of the attributions of the Presidency and (e) the introduction of adequate arrangements for the ownership and exploitation of natural energy sources. Indeed, however hopeful Aramburu may have been as to the outcome of the Assembly, to all and sundry the overriding purpose of such preliminary elections was to find out voters' preferences, thereby providing an idea of what to expect in the forthcoming general elections.

The Position of Peronism

Perón and Cooke were as aware as everybody else that the July elections would provide the first real test of the extent of Peronist influence in the country. The threat posed by Frondizi was indirectly acknowledged by Cooke when he wrote to Perón about 'a matter of great importance', referring to fears in government circles that Peronist votes could go to Frondizi and thus their main objective was to prevent this happening.[64] So desperate were in fact some groups in government circles, that Cooke was secretly offered the chance to reopen his magazine *De Frente* which the *Libertadora* had banned in September 1955. Since Cooke would be campaigning for blank ballots, the objective was to 'stop our [Peronist] votes going to *frondicismo*' thereby neutralising it.[65] But there was no agreement and the ban remained.

Perón himself appeared nonplussed as to the best destination of the Peronist votes given the proscription of the Peronist Party. At first he had been reluctant even to take seriously the 28 July elections. But Cooke's analysis, in the sense that the conditions for an insurrectional strike were not given, coupled with reports that there were '*peronistas sin Perón*' who were increasingly attracted by Frondizi's appeals, inclined the exiled former president to accept the political reality of the elections. In fact ever since 1955 Cooke had begun discussing a possible alliance between Perón and Frondizi. The idea had been the brainchild of Intransigent activist Ricardo Rojo, who took up Cooke's defence when the Provisional Government imprisoned him. In Rojo's account, when he first suggested a *rapprochement* Frondizi told him it had to be an absolute secret and that if anything transpired, Rojo would be 'on his own'.[66] The contacts continued throughout 1956. As Cooke's defending counsel, Rojo had access to him in prison. This was interrupted when Cooke was transferred to Rio Gallegos in the far south, from where he staged a spectacular escape in March 1957 together with fellow inmates Héctor Cámpora, Jorge Antonio, Patricio Kelly, José Espejo and Pedro Andrés Gómez.[67] Rojo went to Chile to resume daily discussions with Cooke from 3 p.m. to 7 p.m. while Cámpora brewed maté for them. At that time, only Cooke, Rojo and Frondizi were involved. According to Rojo, 'Cooke coincided with the Intransigent movement in general lines' and believed Peronism had to forge an alliance with Frondizi.

Throughout 1956 the issues discussed included Peronist support for Frondizi's candidacy, the future of the CGT, the defence of Peronist social conquests, the legalisation of Peronism, the question of oil exploitation along the nationalist lines expressed by Frondizi in his book *Política y Petróleo* and against contracts with foreign firms, although economic policies were never discussed in any detail. The conversations had a central theme: legalisation of Perón's movement in exchange for backing Frondizi at the elections. Rojo insisted with Frondizi that he had to offer a real and honest integration of Peronism into democratic life, and the latter specified the limit should be the legislature. This meant that while Peronists would be allowed in Congress, they should not expect any role in the Executive Power. Cooke agreed and his wife, Alicia Eguren, was entrusted with the task of taking the draft proposal to Caracas where Perón was exiled. Perón sent it back with just two amendments: he had crossed out participation in Congress, and added a demand that his military grade as well as the properties of the Eva Perón Foundation be restituted. Frondizi refused the second demand, and Perón accepted this. Years later Rojo asked Perón why he had rejected the offer of a Peronist presence in the Legislative Power, and his reply was straightforward, 'you [Frondizi and Rojo] wanted the whole kit and boodle'.[68] In any event, in mid-1957 Rogelio Frigerio arrived in Santiago de Chile with a personal letter from Frondizi and Rojo realised that his arrival meant the end of Rojo's mediation.[69]

Perón took into consideration three possible actions he could recommend his followers in the July elections. The first was electoral abstentionism – bound to be unpopular and probably unviable since it was penalised by law; the second was blank balloting; and the last the defacement of ballots to render them invalid. Perón's shifting position from one tactic to the other was a reflection of what came to typify his actions during his long years in exile. Faced with the need to make decisions thousands of miles away, ignorant of internal conditions, he would agree to the different – and often contradictory – suggestions of his visitors, who tended to favour whatever course they saw as most favourable to themselves.[70] Perón's aim was always the same: to remain in control of what he deemed to be *his* movement. In relation to the July elections he shifted from considering that 'Peronist traitors' were a greater threat than 'actual enemies',[71] to recognising that Frondizi – 'undoubtedly the most astute' – was 'the most dangerous of all', while the 'traitors' (that is, the *peronistas sin Perón*) were 'not really dangerous as soon as we find them out'.[72] Therefore five weeks before the elections he was still recommending abstention *and* blank balloting, until Cooke sent him a letter listing twenty long reasons why it was essential to simplify the order (*directiva*), and recommended blank balloting.

Frigerio, meanwhile, was vigorously campaigning against blank ballots and abstentionism from the pages of *Qué*, denouncing both tactics as 'an oligarchic plot'. In an extraordinary demonstration of rhetorical gymnastics which purported to assimilate the 1957 situation to that of the 1930s when the UCR had been in favour of abstentionism, he went on to write:

> The oligarchy hopes to repeat its earlier experience of making the people abandon the elections on a principled stand, knowing that the future certainty of the impossibility of any other solution will lead the people to apathy, indifference and breakdown. It aspires to repeat the manoeuvre that allowed the consolidation of the regime of the Infamous Decade, when popular disenchantment rendered trade unionism so sickly that it fell prey to the docile strikebreakers of the theoretical Left, and politics was embodied in the professionals of foul play, picked up from the dustbins of fraud.[73]

To counteract such arguments which had the backing of reputed Peronists as Arturo Jauretche,[74] Cooke told Perón that he had issued 'directives' explaining to Peronist supporters that any apparent coincidence between 'the Movement' and the government of the *Libertadora* was purely spurious and that only those with a 'limited political vision' could feel confused:

> Peronism has its tactics and strategic aims that transcend the mean political ploys of the government or the parties . . . Since we are heading towards a popular insurrection to put an end to Tyranny and return the government to the legitimate President of the Argentine people, we shall continue with all relevant actions, even though they may coincide with the partial interests of *gorila* groups; we do not care if the government is *gorila*, *frondicista*, *bengoísta* or *neoperonista* : our objective is to overthrow it, whatever its name.[75]

5 THE AFTERMATH OF THE 28 JULY ELECTIONS: THE PERÓN–FRONDIZI PACT

Three days after the elections *The New York Times* hailed them as

> a fine demonstration of Latin American democracy at work . . . President Aramburu . . . has reason for pride and satisfaction . . . for one thing, [the elections] could have gone terribly wrong with a victory either for Peronism or for the extreme nationalist wing of the Radical Party led by the demagogic Arturo Frondizi.[76]

The results showed a majority of 'pro-reform' votes: 4,043,989 (equivalent to 118 seats), figure which included all minor parties that had expressed their support for the Assembly (including Socialists and Communists, together with Conservatives and the UCRP). The 'anti-reform' ones only mustered 2,360,167 (or 87 seats) and this figure included the ballots cast for the UCRI as well as for several provincial neo-Peronist groupings, for the Popular Conservatives and the Liberal Democrats. In terms of political allegiances, what the results revealed was a non- or anti-Peronist majority in the country. Blank votes (Peronist) were 2,080,121; the UCRP obtained 2,117,161 votes, while the UCRI came third with 1,821,459.

The elected delegates had met for the first time on 30 August, and on that same day the 75 UCRI *convencionales*, true to their campaign pledge, contested the legality of the assembly and walked out, leaving it with a precarious quorum. The remaining delegates spent the next three weeks in 'quibbling debates about the past',[77] in order to decide whether the 1953 or the 1949 Constitution was in force. With the sole opposition of the two Communist delegates, the decision was in favour of the 1853 Charter, thereby legitimising the Provisional Government's decree of 1 May 1956. By 15 November, ten weeks after the start of its deliberations, the withdrawal of the Democratic Party delegates and of the *Sabattinista* faction of the UCRP marked the end of the ill-fated assembly. No voices were raised to lament its demise. If the assembly came to nothing, the 28 July results proved of the utmost importance in subsequent events leading to the 23 February 1958 general elections. The main consequence was that Frigerio saw further confirmation of the need to secure an agreement with Perón if Frondizi was to have any chance of success.

The UCRP had carried the most populous districts: the City of Buenos Aires and the Provinces of Buenos Aires and Córdoba, while the UCRI had come first (that is, ahead of the UCRP *and* of blank ballots) in eleven districts, which included the most geographically marginal and least populated provinces.[78] Cooke's analysis of the results revealed a certain discomfort. He acknowledged, not lacking in sarcasm, the influence that Jauretche and Scalabrini Ortiz – both writing in *Qué* – had in swinging the middle-class voters towards Frondizi in the City of Buenos Aires, where the UCRI had come second with 299,178 votes, behind the UCRP's 405,637, while blank ballots (284,569) had ended in third place. Cooke wrote that the '*porteños*, as soon as they reach a certain comfortable economic position, begin to regard themselves as "*pensantes*", and are vulnerable to the preachings of *Qué*, *forjistas*, etc.'[79]

Behind the apparent triumphalism of the expression 'the votes belong to Perón',[80] the fastidiousness with which he included as a measure of Peronist support, not only blank ballots, abstentions, annulled ballots and exclusions (former Peronist officials who were not allowed to vote) but even 'the votes that are now Frondizi's or other parties', that is to say, everybody, indicated that the results had fallen short of expectations.[81] So much so that Cooke ended his analysis by underlining that all efforts to legalise the Peronist struggle had to be resisted – 'we must search for organisational ways that will check the attempts . . . to lead us away from the insurrectional path and transfer our struggle to "legality"' given that from the mass of Peronist supporters there existed 'in excess those required to take active part in an insurrection'.[82]

He was right about the renewed efforts to lead Peronism away from the insurrectional path, but he soon realised he was wrong in thinking he could commit Perón in that direction. He had written to Perón that the 'hardcore of two million men and women' who had cast a blank ballot, were 'a sure base either for an electoral triumph or for armed struggle, once the necessary conditions are given'.[83] Not only did Perón reply in an increasingly evasive tone to Cooke's insistence that Peronism's 'ideological potential' should be utilised to strengthen its 'combatant outfit' and avoid the 'deviationist infiltration' of the *blandos* ('doves') who wanted to veer the Peronist Movement towards the 'fictitious legality manipulated by the government', but albeit reluctantly, he had begun to consider the possibility of some kind of arrangement with Frondizi for the forthcoming presidential elections. Perón wrote to Cooke:

> It is undoubtable that . . . if one could trust Frondizi, something I rule out, the offer transmitted by the emissaries who visited you would not be totally preposterous . . . Political pacts between opposed factions are always in bad faith, even though they may be convenient. In Frondizi's case, moreover, it happens that the votes are ours . . . Nevertheless, considering the possible advantages, it is better not to give a negative answer prematurely, but to bid our time in order to make them believe in the possibility of an agreement . . . [84]

Cooke himself was increasingly inclined towards reaching an agreement with Frondizi, in whom he had started to recognise a potential threat to the survival of Peronism. He remarked that Frondizi's 'renewed attempts to capture Peronist wills' might prove 'very attractive to the masses which will have to opt between that solution [Frondizi], or a Balbín government or worse'.[85] Furthermore, dropping his continual references to an insurrection, he described the forthcoming elections as a 'matter of life and death', since it was necessary to bear in mind that 'amongst the Peronist majority there are gradations in fervour that do not allow to predetermine that everybody will follow no-matter-what order'.[86]

This coincided with the views of those UCRI members who were taken by surprise when Perón disclosed in 1959 that there had been an agreement between himself and Frondizi, agreement which Frondizi had violated once in power. In their view, the elections could have been won by the UCRI even without Perón's order to his followers to vote for Frondizi,[87] while the order itself proved disastrous inasmuch as Frondizi's government would be unable to rid itself of this 'original sin' in the eyes of the armed forces.[88] According to this interpretation, the military's dissatisfaction with Frondizi – *in crescendo* until 1962 – was grounded on this agreement with Perón, regarded as the ultimate betrayal.

Frondizi has always argued, with a degree of disingenuousness, that he never put his signature on a piece of paper that would in any way bind him to Perón,[89] what a former supporter described as a typical example of 'lawyer's chicanery',[90] since nobody has denied that meetings did in fact take place between Perón, Cooke and several Frondizi emissaries. The *frigerista* version depicts Frigerio explaining his thesis on the 'alliance of classes and social sectors' to Perón, the role that the latter and the Peronist movement would play, concluding that there was a mutual 'commitment determined not by the electoral circumstances, but by loyalty to the doctrinaire and strategic conception of developmentalism'.[91] The outcome of this meeting was a written *order* signed by Perón, and clandestinely introduced and reproduced in Argentina,[92] in which the exiled leader told his followers to vote for Frondizi and the UCRI on 23 February, and that 'those who do not obey [this order] must be denounced as traitors to the Movement'.[93] Moreover, the editor of the daily newspaper *Clarín* promised Frondizi that if a reliable international news agency sent a cable to Buenos Aires with Perón's directive, he would publish it. France Presse duly sent news of an interview with Perón in Ciudad Trujillo and it made the headlines in *Clarín*, '*El pueblo en la pomada: Frondizi en la Rosada*'.[94]

In exchange for Perón's 'order' to his supporters to vote for Frondizi, the latter undertook to 'reinstate all social, economic and political conquests of the people' by means of revising all economic decisions 'taken since 16 September 1955' which infringed national sovereignty, the end to 'political persecution', including the lifting of proscriptions, and the return of all confiscated properties and goods (including those of the Eva Perón Foundation), the normalisation of the unions and of the CGT within 120 days, the replacement of all members of the Supreme Court of Justice and the elimination of all magistrates that had taken part in acts of political persecution. With the exception of the requirement that within two years a Constituent Assembly be convened to declare the lapsing of all authorities and calling for general elections, all other steps had to be implemented 'within ninety days as from [1 May 1958]'.[95]

6 CONCLUSIONS

Frigerio remains convinced that an agreement between Frondizi and Perón was essential, since, whatever else one might think of Perón, 'he had not failed in his historic mission of organising the working class'. Since Frondizi 'represented the middle class', an UCRI electoral triumph without Peronist support would have amounted to 'the middle class trampling underfoot the working class'.[96] In the event the UCRI triumph represented the trampling underfoot of the *Revolución Libertadora*. Instead of the desired victory of the democratic, anti-Peronist forces which a united UCR would have secured, President Aramburu found himself handing over the government to the man who had led a virulent campaign against the *Libertadora* with the support of those same anti-democratic elements the September revolution had hoped to obliterate.

The extremes to which Frondizi went to deny the existence of the *pacto*[97] must be understood in the light of two traditions that were being violated by such an agreement. One went back to 1891 and Alem's declaration of the 'radical' and 'intransigent' character of what was then the *Unión Cívica*, rejecting any agreement between political leaders that made a mockery of universal suffrage. The second tradition was more recent and went back to 1955 and the belief, implicit in ones, explicit in others, that Perón was the vernacular version of the totalitarian regimes defeated in World War II. In this climate of hatred (and fear) a pact with Perón was tantamount to a pact with the devil. The possibility cannot be altogether dismissed that had Frondizi chosen instead the option of openness and explained the 'need' for such an agreement in the name of national reconciliation, he could have carried with him part of that public opinion which instead became constantly suspicious of the president and of his motives.

4 The Ideology of Developmentalism and the Development of the Ideology

1 INTRODUCTION

The secret agreement with Perón, as well as the manner in which the oil contracts with foreign companies would be negotiated, revealed the neglect of politics understood as an activity directed to reaching compromises amongst competing views and interests, and in which political parties are key actors representing the existing diversity in society. After more than a quarter century in which politics had meant vote rigging, deals amongst leaders disregarding Congress, appeals to the military to 'save the Nation', censorship and repression, and the violation of the independence of the judiciary, the style of decision-making preferred by Frondizi and Frigerio did not contribute to heal the wounds in the body politic. The deception and double-dealing, quickly labelled as 'Machiavellian', continued the long-standing tradition of transgression of the rules of the political game. The ensuing disillusionment contributed to foster an atmosphere of moral vacuum – deepened by future crises – , an atmosphere in which messianic military governments as well as illegal armed groups would thrive, holding the country for the next quarter of a century in a limbo of arbitrariness, authoritarianism, and sheer hopelessness.

What were Frondizi's and Frigerio's motivations? They have been accused of setting out 'to break the government and destroy the UCRI',[1] of being led by a ruthless ambition for power in Frigerio's case, or of a congenital inability to make up his mind in Frondizi's. More sinisterly, were the President of Argentina and his *éminence grise* working relentlessly to push the country towards the Soviet sphere of influence, as some politicians in the UCRP believed?[2] Or were they 'militants in a national movement', as they claimed, labouring for the aggrandisement of Argentina and to secure her rightful place in the concert of nations?

Frondizi never failed to make an impression. A former collaborator described him as 'the most brilliant politician of his generation',[3] a view shared by military men like Castro de Nevares and Solanas Pacheco,[4] while when Frondizi visited the US at the beginning of 1959 American officials remarked on his 'calm, dignified approach', while the British described him as having a reputation for 'being cold-blooded, calculating and unscrupulous' but 'certainly a man of outstanding ability' although the caveat was added – 'by South American standards'.[5] The fact is that in the three years up to 1957 he had instilled fresh ideas into a languishing Radicalism, organising a new party, the UCRI, which many believed would lead the country along the path of national reconstruction. A 'solitary personality', he was surrounded by supporters whose esteem bordered on 'veneration'.[6] With hindsight, this solitary man, imbued with fleeting messianic feelings[7] could not but drift away from a party where internal squabbles were rife and ideas were 'opaque, vague or abstract'.[8]

With military and politicians bickering endlessly over the political calendar, the economic debate was overlooked other than by the occasional generalisation attributing almost sacrosanct features to a natural resource such as oil. Until Frondizi introduced the issue of industrialisation in his campaign, economic policy had been a 'taboo subject' in the UCR because, in Babini's unkind but probably accurate words, 'one does not dwell on things one ignores'.[9] There are indications that Frondizi was acutely aware of the inadequate grasp of economic matters by his party colleagues, but although several of his close collaborators remember his pleas 'to change the party',[10] the manner in which he embraced Frigerio and neglected his party shows that he felt either unable or unwilling to press for the changes he deemed necessary. In fact, the body of ideas that would become known as *desarrollismo* (developmentalism), would only begin to take a precise, almost dogmatic shape after the 1958 electoral victory.

There was a lag, therefore, between ideas and reality. The ideas that presumably had been behind government policies between 1958–62 were only expressed *ex post facto*. Frigerio justified this by a reference to the demands of the 'day-to-day struggle', which meant that the experience of government was not 'articulated in a national and popular doctrine, coherent and profound, based on the rigorous analysis of the objective conditions of the country'.[11] With the exception of Frigerio's editorials in *Qué*, where the fundamentals of developmentalism – such as the need for foreign capital to create heavy industries and, at the political level, the need to integrate Peronism in a class alliance or 'national movement' – had been anticipated (albeit at the time the Frondizi–Frigerio collaboration was not public knowledge) prior to Frondizi's accession to the Presidency what would become the basic tenets of developmentalism were nowhere to be found. Developmentalism had therefore the traits of a 'delayed' ideology; it was a reflection on things done. Indeed, with the exception of the stress on heavy industry, voters were told what they had voted for when the government they had voted for was no more.

From a very different political background Frigerio had arrived at a set of economic ideas similar to Frondizi's, but while the latter's ascent to the political limelight had been open, Frigerio's was not, and his conduct had been far from principled. The description provided by the British ambassador reflected the widespread view of Frigerio as 'clever and a hard worker, but corrupt and unscrupulous and an unsavoury influence [on Frondizi]'.[12] Maintaining that to be active in politics one had to be 'violent and ruthless', Frigerio had pursued power with an ambition and a determination almost unparalleled in Argentine political circles.[13] But there was more than boundless ambition in Frigerio. He had a millenarian view. Frondizi's concern with economic matters would become, embodied in Frigerio, a grand design for economic development in which Frondizi – the messianic man – would lead a 'national movement' directed to ensuring the greatness of Argentina.

2 DEVELOPMENTALISM AS AN IDEOLOGY

When the world economic crisis of 1930 revealed the weaknesses of a model of economic growth centred on the export of commodities, the conservative agrarian élite ruling Argentina imaginatively encouraged the expansion of industry. Perón continued along the lines of import substitution industrialisation, adding to the model the organisation of workers subjected to State control. Half-way through his decade in power he had realised the constraints of the model and sought an accommodation with the United States in the hope of attracting foreign investment primarily in the oil field. He started negotiations with the Eximbank for a US $60 million loan to build a steel mill at San Nicolás, although the *Libertadora* had to conclude the process initiated by Perón. Given the rhetorical xenophobia favoured by Perón, such reversals of policy were never brought into the open, with the exception of the upheaval caused in Congress by Frondizi's denunciation of the Standard Oil contract. As in many instances, the *Libertadora* was confronted by a dilemma it could not – or would not – solve. In the Manichean political climate dominated by Good vs Evil, Liberty vs Peronism, Democracy vs Totalitarianism, it was extremely awkward for the Provisional Government to be seen as following in Perón's steps. With his fragile and shrinking basis of support Provisional

President Aramburu was probably wise to leave economic decisions to his successor, albeit he made sure that his Trade and Industry minister, Julio Cueto Rúa, briefed president-elect Frondizi on the state of negotiations with the US and the existing concerns about oil exploration and exploitation.[14]

It was firstly Frigerio, and then Frondizi, who offered a set of ideas that would have merited extensive debate, and yet they were never challenged at the intellectual level but succeeded instead in firing the imagination of a considerable sector of the electorate. Besides a set of ideas on the path Argentina had to follow to fulfil her alleged destiny of greatness, the manner in which such ideas were expressed implied a peculiar style of political action whose defining trait was the indifference towards the rules of the liberal-democratic political game. Frigerio's interpretation of society, which he claimed was based on a 'scientific analysis', did not admit alternative explanations. The core of the doctrine was economicist, and its roots could be traced back to Frigerio's reading of Marxian texts in his youth, from which he extracted a belief in the irrefutability of an economic science, in laws that govern all acts of men whose actions can only be understood as an expression of social forces, in the inexorable march of History towards a predetermined end, a path signalled by inevitable and necessary stages. And of course there was the Leninist contribution in terms of a vanguard group who would be the first to recognise the operation of such laws and the direction in which History was advancing, contributing to their fulfilment in order to hasten the pace of History. In Frigerio's interpretation, the organisational setup would be largely irrelevant – it could be a political party, or a technocratic group within a government, be it military or civilian. The developmentalists have been accused of élitism, dogmatism, schematism, economicism, and preferring secret dealings to open discussion.[15] This they have denied. However, these labels are not altogether inappropriate in the discussion of a cluster of notions said to constitute a 'scientific theory'.

The forms of literary expression used by Frigerio were basically two: the weekly magazine *Qué*, and books and pamphlets where he singlemindedly pursued the same theme. This was consistent with the division of labour agreed with Frondizi, according to which the latter would concentrate on political action while Frigerio would be in charge of the 'programmatic elaboration' centred round the idea that Argentina's problems were of an economic nature, resulting from the international division of labour imposed in the nineteenth century by Britain's colonial designs. To satisfy British needs Argentina had specialised in the export of temperate agricultural commodities. This arrangement was no longer feasible because of the external bottlenecks resulting from the deterioration in the terms of trade. Those who insisted on maintaining an economic structure geared to the export of meat and cereals were acting against the national interest. The latter was defined as depending on the setting up of heavy industry, which in turn would propel self-sustained growth. Prior to the establishment of heavy industry, it was essential to secure an energy-providing infrastructure: the urgency was to become self-sufficient in petroleum to eliminate the burden of its importation from the balance of trade. Foreign capital would bridge time lags in the process of accumulation, investment, production and distribution.

Although Frigerio's ideas can be found in *Qué*, he gathered them in a series of books which were published after Frondizi's overthrow in 1962. In his *Crecimiento económico y democracia* Frigerio offers a summing up of developmentalist ideas which, although in Argentina embodied in Frondizi and Frigerio, were prevalent in the 1950s and 1960s in what later became known as development economics. Its core was a 'dirigiste dogma' relying on anti-price mechanism, while being pro-planning, pro-government controls and intervention and pro-trade protection.[16] Thus Frigerio espoused the need for a national development plan which had to include – and he remarked that this was something 'on which there is not much disagreement' – an increase in the rate of accumulation of domestic capital; the encouragement of inflow of international capital and technology; import substitution; the direction of investment towards 'essential and most reproductive sectors'; and 'the regulation of consumption, trying to conciliate the increase in savings with the satisfaction of the needs of the population'.[17] The 'national movement' in the shape of a class alliance would carry out the plan whose end result would be 'liberation', or the 'national revolution'.

3 THE INTELLECTUAL ATMOSPHERE IN THE AFTERMATH OF WORLD WAR II

In the atmosphere created on the one hand by the remarkable economic growth experienced in the post-war years, and on the other, by the Cold War fears, the idea of transformation through economic growth soon gained widespread favour. The newly achieved independence of the former British Gold Coast, which in 1957 had become Ghana under the leadership of Kwame Nkrumah, fired the imagination of peoples not only in Africa but also across the seas. While Nkrumah talked persuasively about an era for a new Africa heralded by industrialisation,[18] across the Atlantic Juscelino Kubitschek had already been preaching a similar message.[19]

Developmentalists like Frigerio and Kubitschek were offering an answer to decades of soul-searching on the part of Latin American intellectuals, obsessed by the inability of their countries to follow in Europe's and the United States' steps. The answer lay in growth – measured in terms of an increase in GDP – which meant development, a word that did not necessarily mean the same to all who used it.[20]

For Frigerio it meant heavy industry that would secure for Argentina a place among the powerful nations of the world. For Kubitschek it meant the same for Brazil,[21] but he added a meaning neither Frigerio nor Frondizi would attach to it: this was security, that is, a means of keeping Communism outside the American hemisphere. For Nkrumah it meant, more modestly, the abolition from Ghana of 'poverty, ignorance and disease'.[22] Economists themselves had only recently been concerned with problems of growth in terms of explaining the behaviour of an economy over an extended period.[23] Events which characterised the world economy since the 1920s, such as the accumulated evidence that large-scale unemployment was a chronic problem (rather than a periodic nuisance), the realisation that a large part of the world's population lived in conditions of extreme economic poverty, and the rise of the Soviet Union as a world power, led to questions concerning rates of growth and prospects for growth in the future. Such diverse reasons for the widespread interest in growth economics had to produce a variety of explanations. Contrary to Frigerio's claims for a 'scientific economics', economists at the time were far less certain about its scientific status. In 1957 Henry Bruton dismissed the existence of a set of principles that could be 'confidently . . . called the modern theory of economic growth' but acknowledged there was a series of 'seminal ideas, revealing insights, penetrating bits and pieces of analysis, loose ends, and unrealistic assumptions'.[24]

If neither history nor economics can offer definite answers as to what causes economic growth, both disciplines suggest what the right questions might be.[25] Frigerio's version of a science of economics is one in which the answer – industrialisation – is the only possible one to the question he will pose as being the crucial one, 'What contributes more to our nationhood?' In Frigerio's thinking, a type of development based on the belief in the inevitable sameness of industrialisation is elevated to the rank of a dogma.[26]

Take-off and the Role of the State

In the late 1950s and early 1960s, W. W. Rostow's ideas on a model of sequential development in five stages were enthusiastically received,[27] although economic historians were sceptical about the notion of stages as a useful tool in analysing historical experience. They were particularly critical of the idea of a 'take off' which implied that change was discrete – that is, occurring in spurts – rather than continuous. But the political attractiveness of the proposition that 'in many senses, all nations concerned with economic growth at the present time are treading the path Britain first set foot on in the eighteenth century' ensured its widespread endorsement.[28]

The fundamental allure of the 'take off' (an industrial revolution tied directly to radical changes in methods of production)[29] was that it produced decisive results over a relatively short period of time. The essence of the take off is a sectoral expansion, a leading industry with sufficient forward and backward linkages and spread effects to influence the whole economy and to prepare the way for other industrial expansion before the impetus of this original sector fades. A crash programme of investment would provide the 'big push' and, as Kubitschek, Nkrumah and Frigerio insisted, capital in such amounts that would dispense with the need for a policy of forced savings – as had been applied by Stalin – could only come from abroad. And to make certain that it was adequately invested, the State would device the appropriate means, implementing planning mechanisms and generally playing an active role.

At an abstract level, the State had to instil the consciousness of development – the belief in the feasibility of the developmentalist project. At a concrete level, the State had to act to create favourable conditions for the expansion of the economy, investing in works of infrastructure, and generally setting priorities for investment. This required a quick pace; the issue of the 'rhythm' of development made a reference to the dilemma between distribution and accumulation. The pace was essential to shorten the gap between consumer aspirations and demands and what the economic effort was able to supply, and the State was to play the main role in ensuring the bridging of the gap between aspirations and their satisfaction.[30]

ECLA and Industrialisation

The idea that economic growth meant development and that it could only be brought about by industrialisation, had been put forward by Raúl Prebisch, head of the United Nations Economic Commission for Latin America in ECLA's '1949 Manifesto'.[31] The latter exercised considerable influence on Latin American economists formed in the post-war years. Industrialisation had got the advanced nations where they were: there was a subjacent idea of progress in its nineteenth-century version, which turned the idea of the slow, gradual, inexorable progress of mankind to higher status in knowledge, culture, and moral estate, into a dogma.

Prebisch and ECLA explained that historical backwardness could only be overcome by modern technology in industry to warrant the structural changes needed in the economy. Development could only mean technical progress linked with industrialisation. Economic growth and its inevitable consequence, social justice, were not possible within the context of a technically backward and economically static society. The creation and adaptation of technology through education was a primordial factor in the modernisation of society.[32] The basic precepts of the ideology of development as proposed by ECLA were: (a) an anti-dependence nationalism; (b) a modernising capitalism; (c) regional integration; (d) national effort; (e) expansion of the internal market; (f) absorption of the labour force; (g) raising of the technological level; (h) endogenous creation of technology.[33]

Nevertheless, there was a caveat to ECLA's proposal. A warning was duly made to those who thought that the most expedient way of introducing new technology was by means of industries associated with foreign capital. The danger lay in the disadvantaged position native entrepreneurs would be left in, and this mattered since the responsibility for development was placed by ECLA squarely on their shoulders.[34] Frondizi and Frigerio harboured no such fears since the State would implement planning mechanisms to direct those investments towards priority areas, simultaneously protecting the interests of the native entrepreneurs. Moreover, the people themselves would have control over the economy, 'via the enforcement of a democratic system with no traps'.[35] The 'democratic control of the economy' envisaged by *Avellaneda* was thus qualified, the control mechanisms being less direct than the principles in that document would lead one to expect. The scarcity of national savings, an inherited budget deficit and the deterioration in the terms of trade 'force us to ask for the help of foreign capital which, in the briefest period and with the strength of its high technical level, will collaborate in the creation of heavy industries'.[36] Foreign capital would not enter into direct competition with native capital but it would 'strengthen our ability for self-determination *vis-à-vis* the great powers'.[37]

But if Frigerio accepted ECLA's thesis on the deterioration in the terms of trade, plus what amounted to the myth of industrialisation, he rejected ECLA's nationalism as far as the role of foreign capital was concerned. Moreover, Frigerio dismissed the hopes ECLA placed in the setting up of a Latin American Common Market. Continental integration could only take place, in Frigerio's view, at a later stage, once regional integration at the national level had been secured.[38]

4 THE PREMISES OF DEVELOPMENTALISM

The Role of Science

A few months after being appointed by Frondizi in 1958 as his Secretary for Socio-Economic Relations, Frigerio was forced to hand in his resignation to a reluctant president, but he took the opportunity to bring together in a book the premises of the 'national and popular doctrine'. The result of his endeavours was published under the title *The Conditions for Victory*[39] in which the doctrine of developmentalism, 'coherent and profound, . . . [founded] on a rigorous analysis of the objective conditions of the country', was articulated. The technocratic blueprint for industrialisation was transformed into a doctrine for populist motivation, a veritable 'national theory' without which there could be no 'national struggle'.[40] In 1959 his aim in writing a book was to set 'a framework for the scientific interpretation of our reality' which would serve 'to distinguish the incidental from the principal' in order 'to find the path and the strategy of the struggle for the union and liberation of our people'.[41] Frigerio's constant references to the scientific method of interpreting reality must perforce be traced back to his intellectual background and his readings of Marxian literature in the 1930s and 1940s, when he was active in the left-wing group *Insurrexit*.[42] It is possible to trace two streams in Frigerio's references to science. The most frequent one is inscribed in the Marxian tradition of historical materialism. It is more abstract, and it is used as an epistemological tool. The application of the scientific method to an understanding of Argentine history will uncover the 'guiding strand' in the stages of economic progress which unfold dialectically until, inevitably and inexorably, the last stage ('development', 'liberation', 'national revolution') would be attained.

The other stream, derived from the first, enhances a particular economic theory as the 'science of economics'. This science will explain that the value of things is to be found in the amount of human labour needed to produce it (as Ricardo established and Marx adopted), that therefore added value can only be produced by (technological) ways of making human labour more efficient and productive and, as a result, economic growth can only be a consequence of increasing the intrinsic value of the goods being produced, and never as a result of trade.[43] By referring to science as the foundation for his ideas and actions, Frigerio endeavoured to present an integrated thought system in an attempt to establish relationships between phenomena that were not (and are not) necessarily related, while neglecting circumstances whose relevance was not taken into account.

Marxian Influences in Frigerio's Thinking

Frigerio has been accused of being a Marxist.[44] People like Babini, who cannot be suspected of an obsessive anti-communism, have also remarked on Frigerio's alleged Marxian beliefs, while others stressed his 'Stalinist approach and style'.[45] Certain guidelines in Frigerio's reasoning can easily be traced back to specific Marxian premises which had been the object of debate in left-wing circles in Argentina and in Latin America in the 1930s and 1940s, the years of Frigerio's youthful Marxist activism.[46]

Frigerio himself was perhaps over-expeditious when describing the intellectual tradition in which he was inscribed, preferring to cite Hegel rather than Marx.[47] Marxism was transplanted to Latin America in the version of the German Social-democracy as an ideology of development and modernisation in the midst of an unstoppable class struggle within which Socialism represented the party of progress. The paradigm of social democracy according to which the possibility of socialism rested on the development of the productive forces, was unquestionably accepted in Latin America. The Marxism of the Second International was an interpretation of Marxism claiming a scientific character for its notion of history as indicating the development of economic systems in a necessary sequence, in accordance with an evolutionist process that in its final stages contemplated a revolutionary rupture stemming from the unfolding of objective conditions. In Kautsky's view, Marx's merit was to offer a scientific basis for socialist politics. Frigerio had probably taken from Kautsky the idea that the study of history is necessary to furnish the proletariat with a memory of the past from its own perspective, and to show that only an historic memory could be the foundation of a political consciousness: that is to say, the awareness that action was not arbitrary.[48] The teleological element in Frigerio's and Frondizi's writings is always in evidence, as when Frigerio maintained that 'we are moving in the direction of history, in the direction of the emergence of the Nation and of the people. [. . .] Man [. . .] is endowed with a will directed towards an end'.[49] The meaning of History can only be uncovered by a scientific historical analysis such as the one offered by Frigerio, given that 'the analysis of our past is [. . .] indispensable to find answers, as well as to conceive of solutions that will assert our national condition'.[50]

But Frigerio's historical interpretations are better understood as ideological combat tools. Rather than questioning the present as a helpful guide in interpreting the past, what Frigerio in fact does is try to justify the present by the past, the hallmark of teleological history. Thus Argentine history is depicted as a series of crises which are links in an historically 'necessary' and 'inevitable' chain leading inexorably to a state defined variously as 'national development', 'national revolution' or 'national liberation'. Frondizi also attempts a dialectical interpretation of history, criticising 'liberal and revisionist historians' for their tendency to break the 'continuity' and 'totality' of history, noting contradictions but not 'the overcoming of the contradiction'.[51]

References to the actual shape of that final stage of 'economic independence', 'liberation' or 'revolution' where the historical struggle inevitably leads, are only found sporadically in Frigerio's writings. Many years later, when pressed to define the model of society the developmentalists had in mind, Frondizi stated that private property would have disappeared, since 'the historical trend is towards socialisation' and he quoted from the papal Encyclica *Mater et Magistra* in support of this belief.[52] The present stage is one of the struggle for national independence, but eventually, nations will be abolished since 'the Nation is an historical category' and it may not exist in the future although nations will disappear only when they have achieved their historical 'assignment'.[53] And the historical assignment or historical cycle they must fulfil before disappearing is to develop fully their productive forces, to industrialise. This view was derived from Marxian 'laws of capitalist development' according to which 'ultimately, bourgeois society brings the whole of mankind, . . . within the purview of a single social order, and is genuinely "world-historical"',[54] or, in Frigerio's terminology, 'mundo uno' (one world).[55]

An Economicist and Determinist Interpretation

Although when confronted with the accusation of 'economicism' Frigerio is always at pains to deny it, his attempts at refuting such accusations are openly contradicted by his political actions and writings. Indeed, his 1967 book, *The Statute of Underdevelopment*, was intended as a friendly warning to General Onganía's self-styled 'Argentine Revolution' not to succumb to pressures to call for elections before the 'revolutionary goals' were achieved, since 'absolutely everything else must be subordinated' to the 'deliberate development of productive forces'.[56] He went on to write that 'elections should be the result of the success, and not of the failure of the Armed Forces', reproducing almost to the word the arguments he had so virulently opposed a decade earlier.[57] His economicism leads him to conclude that the form of government is irrelevant given the prevalence of objective structures in which men are mere agents or 'bearers' (*träger*) of such structures, a central Marxian tenet.[58] The notion of individual responsibility fades insofar people are mere executors of the requirements of social forces over which they exercise no control.

Development and Underdevelopment

Development is not an 'economic model' but 'a political imperative of our peoples in this specific stage of their historical evolution'.[59] The stage Argentina was in during the late 1950s and early 1960s demanded the full development of productive forces, entailing 'the rejection of spontaneity and gradualism'.[60] Development therefore, takes place in great spurts; it is not linear, but it is 'inevitable', yet inevitability is intrinsic to a linear concept of progress. However, since development is not gradual, the State can and should act to accelerate the process of growth. Since domestic savings are insufficient to secure the desired rhythm given the high rates of investment demanded by the capital goods industries, foreign capital will be necessary. The importance attributed to foreign capital and, furthermore, the insistence that its destiny, and not its origin were the main consideration, blurred the character of nationalism claimed by the 'national and popular' doctrine of developmentalism. To conceal the fact that they were consciously adopting contradictory ideals and beliefs, the developmentalists proposed a distinction between a rational (technical) nationalism based on science, and an emotional one that could effectively operate against the national interest. If capital, 'be it national or foreign' is applied to 'the priorities and strategy of development as set by the national State', the result will be a 'profoundly revolutionary and national function, albeit performed by foreign capital'. Thus 'American dollars' will not be 'impregnated by an alien fluid', but what was needed was a clarity as to the ends sought and 'great flexibility in their execution'.[61] The 'national and popular' character of the developmentalist doctrine is justified in a 'nationalism of ends rather than means', and to justify the credentials of this position Frondizi wrote that 'no programme of authentic national liberation and social justice' could reject the necessary international financial and technical cooperation for development as shown by 'those nations which are struggling to liberate themselves from colonial dependence [. . .] from Nehru and Sukarno to Nasser and Nkrumah'.[62] The semantic confusion implicit in the conceptual references to 'national liberation' brought about by foreign capital did not seem to trouble either Frondizi or Frigerio.

That the outcome of a plan, however excellent, can hardly be expected to turn out exactly as it was originally devised, was not taken into account. The fact is that the struggle for the realisation of the plan becomes in itself a decisive factor in the historical process. The emphasis on ends, with its consequent disregard for the means employed, results in the latter shaping a form of society which was not necessarily the one intended.[63] The logic of the developmentalists' reasoning led them to conclude that Argentina was

> an underdeveloped country which cannot be differentiated qualitatively from other nations of the continent and from former Asian and African colonies. Underdevelopment is not a matter of degrees, nor can it be measured by per capita national income.[64]

While it is true that a single index such as per capita income, tells little about a country, Frigerio's suggestion to consider instead the existence or otherwise of an 'integrated industrial structure' as a determining feature, merely dismissed the comparison between Italy and Argentina in favour of a positive comparison between the latter and Bangla Desh. These arguments, he maintained, were not the result of either 'national masochism' or of an 'intellectual deficiency', but of the imperative necessity for 'structural change'. The usefulness of the comparisons proposed by the developmentalists could only be apparent to somebody who regarded heavy industry as the *Deus ex machina*. Industrialisation acquired a singular meaning; rather than an aspect of development, it became its essence, since it entailed the qualitative change of society. The comparison between India and Argentina was seen as outrageous in some Argentine sectors. A right-wing magazine, rejoicing at Frondizi's downfall in 1962 and making fun of the former president's allegedly sudden embrace of religious piety, remarked that it had not been sufficient to teach him that the Catholic Faith had rent Argentina from underdevelopment 'centuries ago'.[65]

Frigerio's vision was so 'holistic' that it left little room for disagreement. It rested on a fundamental belief that there was such a thing as a 'developed condition' rather than ways and manners of 'development'. Hence the 'ends' – imprecisely defined – become unquestioned, unquestionable and permanent, while the 'means' are forever changing in pursuit of those increasingly vaguer ends.

The Idea of Integration

The developmentalist *Weltanschauung* rested on two concepts, development and integration. While the former was identified with industrialisation, the latter also resulted (at a world level) from technology.[66] 'Integration' became a key concept in developmentalist thinking, gaining in scope until it acquired such comprehensiveness that it gave its name to a new political grouping after the fall of Frondizi in March 1962, when the UCRI split and Frigerio and Frondizi set up the shortlived Movement for Integration and

Development (MID). Before being elevated to the rank of a fundamental belief, the idea of integration had been applied to different fields. In the words of an observer, 'integration retains the political advantage of meaning many things to many people'.[67] Frigerio wrote about the 'ideal of the community' to turn economic development into the 'lever of the spiritual integration of the nation',[68] but more often, integration was used in a geographical and, more importantly, in a political sense.

At an immediate level, geographical integration referred to the extension and consolidation of an internal market, being thus a pre-requisite for industrialisation. At the same time, regional integration amounted to a redefinition of federalism: the former could only be achieved by means of industrialisation, while the latter had to be subordinated to the 'aims of the Nation'. Competition and confrontation between regions and provinces had to be avoided. There would be a National Development Centre which would set priorities and decide which regions should be favoured, and which would have to wait. When Frondizi listed the 'priority zones' for development, he left out about half the provinces in the country. Except for Patagonia, blessed with oil and coal, Mendoza and Salta with oil, and Córdoba, Buenos Aires and Santa Fe, seats of the automobile and steel-making industries, the rest of the country would have to await a later stage when industrial integration would be achieved as a result of linkages provided by those core activities which would act as poles or foci of development.[69]

However, the pressing task was to achieve political integration, in the shape of a 'national movement', 'national front' or 'class alliance' to bring about 'the fulfilment of the Nation itself'.[70] The 'national movement' had to unite the Nation above class, political, and ideological differences. Thus the principle of integration is derived from the myth of 'the people'. Frondizi wrote that 'all other contradictions and all ideological nuances or tactical differences give way when confronted with the great objective of national unity'.[71] The presence of the working class was of course essential since 'the working class is a most important part of the Nation', which is in its turn 'the whole whose fulfilment presupposes the inclusion of the totality of the social classes that constitute it'.[72] For Frigerio, Peronism's historic contribution had been the 'nationalisation' of the working class 'in breadth as well as in ideological depth' via the establishment of a single labour confederation (CGT) and the farmworker's statute.[73] Development is not then an ideology but a national doctrine, a 'national programme', synthesis and expression of the Nation's interests. Those who oppose it thereby oppose the interests of the Nation as a whole. Amongst such opponents are those who defend their narrow economic interests – linked to the export-import activities – or are misguided by a liberal ideology – and therefore unwittingly playing into the hands of the agrarian sector or even worse, of Great Britain. There are moreover those who misled by a spurious nationalism which dogmatically opposes them to everything foreign, oppose industrialisation or fail to realise its paramountcy for the prosperity and greatness of the Nation. A Manichean interpretation of Argentine history is proposed, unfolding in a dialectical process in which two contradictory forces are permanently at loggerheads: one national, the other anti-national. Even though Frigerio wrote that 'no party nor group of men or isolated individuals can claim to be the exclusive possessors of truth', only the enemies of the Nation could fail to recognise 'such a simple and explicit formula' as the programme for economic development proposed by the developmentalists.[74] Perón is hailed by Frigerio in his role as *caudillo*, as the man who inspired a national doctrine and who understood the strategic importance of the class alliance.[75] In 1946 Peronism had constituted 'the melting pot where the working class was integrated with all the other sectors of the population aspiring to reassert national sovereignty, strengthen economic independence and usher in social justice'.[76] This assessment implied a remarkable reversal in a man who a few years earlier had deemed Perón so insupportable as to travel successfully to Switzerland in search of funds to help bring him down.[77]

Frigerio's and Frondizi's historical accounts have resonances of the political discourse and practice invented by Marat during the French Revolution. At its centre was the notion that politics was a matter of establishing just *who* represented the people or the Nation. The conspiracy theory (the idea of an aristocratic plot) allowed for a constant interpretation and justification of events. 'Development' could be said to have no objective limits, only enemies. The Nation was defined by what it excluded, in the Argentine case the 'liberal, agro-exporting interests'.[78] But although the national movement had not yet crystallised, Frigerio claimed to belong to it. The national movement as 'subject' was prior to its existence as 'object' – it was Frigerio's as well as other people's will that would shape it and the doctrine would play a decisive role in this process.

5   THE ROLE OF THE DEVELOPMENTALIST IDEOLOGY

The Ideology as National Doctrine

The role of the developmentalist ideology or national doctrine is to clarify the terms of the contradiction between what is national and what is anti-national, since:

Argentine politics suffers the distortions and confusions created by the historical contradiction between what is national and what is anti-national. Different parties – Christian Democrats, Socialists, Communists and pseudo-nationalists – think they serve the interests of the Nation while, in practice, they rotate in the traditional orbit of the colonialist structure.[79]

In the period of political nation-building, when emerging nationhood is threatened by foreign encroachment, nationalism is functional inasmuch as it raises national consciousness, contributing to strengthen national frontiers. In Argentina in the late 1950s, far from being necessary, nationalism enhanced the paranoid xenophobia that Perón had fostered. Furthermore, the distinction between a nationalism of ends and another of means only contributed to the semantic confusion prevailing in Argentine political life. According to Frigerio, Britain was to blame for the sorry state of affairs in Argentina because with 'her allies in the agro-importing oligarchy' and 'her internal influence over formal, democratic liberalism, . . . she still controls the necessary resorts to maintain our dependent structure'.[80] Only 'popular pressure and popular control over the levers of power' could break 'once and for all that [dependent] relationship' and bring about 'the emancipation of the Nation'.[81]

The developmentalist 'national doctrine' would supply what Peronism had been lacking, that is a 'social strategy' to bring together the non-working class sectors and groups in a common struggle. The developmentalist language was progressive ('change', 'liberation', 'revolution', 'national struggle', etc., all figured prominently in their discourse), and so were their ideas. But their language was misleading since it is possible to argue that developmentalism was also conservative, since it endeavoured to maintain the system by means of giving more thrust to its dynamic elements. The tension between language and aims had not been evident during the electoral campaign, when language took pre-eminence, thus helping identify the UCRI with progressive, even 'revolutionary' ideas. It would only be once in government that their 'conservatism' became apparent.

By offering a picture of society in which all classes, sectors and groups shared a common interest in development, the ideology was in fact propitiating the unity of all members of society around the project of a small group of them. The irony would be that those groups attracted by the developmentalist style of conservatism remained suspicious of their intentions as a result of the language in which they were being expressed. The purpose of the doctrine was not just to provide a 'cement' that would bring together groups with contradictory interests, but it had to create the Nation.[82] Under Peronism the class alliance had been embodied in Perón. Frigerio had to rely on a group of men, with the result that a strong personal leader was replaced by an 'enlightened' vanguard of totally committed men and women.

The Role of Developmentalists as Vanguard

The militants in the 'national cause' would have the responsibility of helping the whole of the Argentine people to achieve this communion with the doctrine. The style of operation of these men and women would bring back to memory the style of revolutionary politics as represented by the Calvinist-Jacobin-Leninist tradition of enlightened vanguardism.[83] In Argentina the active, ideologically committed political radical had been relegated to the isolated existence of the *anarco-sindicalists* who had arrived from Europe at the turn of the century, and whose influence on Argentine trade unionism Perón had decisively crushed. Frigerio himself had practiced such activism in his *Insurrexit* days, but the UCRI provided Frigerio and his friends with the legitimacy they needed to become more than a mere sect. After 1962 and the dissolution of the UCRI, developmentalists became a group determined to implement their idea of development via whosoever had the means to gain power – constitutionally or otherwise. However frequent Frigerio's protestations that he was guided by science, his books, more than scientific treatises had the flavour of combat publications or manuals for developmentalist militants, seeking earnestly, energetically and systematically to transform their society.

Peronism had provided 'old certainties' based on hierarchy, personal loyalty, patronage and corporatism. Arriving on the political arena after Perón's fall, developmentalists were active in a period signed by changing expectations. They were imbued with a new and exhilarating sense of freedom and opportunity widespread in non-Peronist sectors after 1955. But in their keenness to bring about change as they saw it, they acted in ways that would prove self-defeating.

6 THE ELECTORAL CAMPAIGN AND ITS ORGANISATION

To all intents and purposes, *Avellaneda* remained the official platform of the UCRI, supporting the image of the party as a broadly left-wing, anti-imperialist body, an image backed by certain campaigners and campaign publications. Although Frondizi would subsequently dismiss *Avellaneda* as a 'declaration of principles' rather than a blueprint for action, as a campaign manifesto it conveyed a broad image of the party in the eyes of the electorate. Moreover, Frondizi did not seem to disclaim *Avellaneda* when during a campaign tour of La Pampa Province he said that 'on 23 February we shall go into the *Casa Rosada* to rule the country with a programme of love and human solidarity' since the UCRI's programme was that of 'an historical political organisation'.[84]

What follows is an attempt to analyse the unfolding of certain ideas and forms of action of a group of men and women embodying a new doctrine in the Argentine political spectrum, Developmentalism (*desarrollismo*), sometimes also known as Integrationism (*integracionismo*). This novel configuration began to take shape in 1957. The interest in this period lies not only in establishing the degree of Frondizi's *volte face* but in illustrating the manner in which the transition took place from a system of centralised political power under the *Libertadora*, to one of restricted competition, and the role played in this transition by new political actors imbued with new ideas and practising a novel political style.

Elections are endowed with emotional appeal; they provide the voter with an occasion to express his allegiance to, or disconformity with, present political performance, as well as to confirm his loyalty to a party with which he has long identified. From 1930 to 1946 fraudulent electoral practices and two military coups (1930 and 1943) had prevented Argentine citizens from expressing their views with any hopes of influencing events. From 1946 to 1958, the Argentine voter had cast his or her ballot to show either loyalty to, or abhorrence of, Perón. In 1958, with the Peronists banned from taking part in the political competition, non-Peronist voters had the chance of casting a positive vote, in favour of the party, platform, and candidate of their preference. For the first time since the 1912 Sáenz Peña Law an electoral campaign was fought around specific issues, albeit within an emotional atmosphere permeated by the exclusion of Peronism. Moreover, economic policy dominated the scene, introducing a change in the political imagery of the country, not used to the public debate of policies beyond 'them and us' issues. The stress on the economy, on the need to develop oil as a source of energy that would provide the infrastructure for heavy industry, gave the campaign a definitely 'modern' flavour. With the exception of Alvaro Alsogaray's tiny *Partido Cívico Independiente* (PCI), the UCRI was the only party to raise and debate specific issues, fighting its campaign – as opposed to the PCI – within an oppositionist stand against the *Libertadora*. The UCRI endeavoured to attract as many votes as possible on the strength of its programme. The problem was that it was not too clear what that programme was and as it happened, it turned out to be different things to different people. This would not have been very surprising were it not for the fact that these divergences were institutionalised in practice, given that the campaign was conducted from three separate headquarters – although subsequent events revealed that it had effectively been won from just one.

Three Headquarters, Three Programmes, Three Styles

The official UCRI headquarters had been set up in Rio Bamba Street, an unofficial think-tank was organised by Rogelio Frigerio in Luis María Campos Avenue, and a group of young, enthusiastic, left-wing UCRI collaborators of Frondizi had taken up position in Leandro N. Alem Avenue under a large banner that read *Alem por Frondizi Presidente*, linking themselves, via a pun, with the founding father of the old UCR. Young university graduates who had effective control over the students' federation (FUBA), amongst them Félix Luna, Nicolás Babini, Noé Jitrik and Ismael Viñas were given the task of organising the Alem headquarters along the lines of the 'committees for action' used in North American campaigns.[85] The fact that the 'anti-imperialist' wing of the campaign, instructed to attract that section of the electorate traditionally identified with the perpetual search for the millennium – the young and the intellectuals – was to be modelled on United States' practices was only seen as incongruous with hindsight.

The three groups were the prongs of one campaign strategy grounded on the need to add votes, although at the time they were unaware of the overall plan and regarded one another with suspicion. *Alem* (the groups were known by the name of the street where their respective headquarters were located)[86] was the embodiment of the left-wing romantic aura that had accompanied Frondizi throughout his political career. In 1954, on being elected president of the UCR's National Committee, Frondizi had declared that his appointment amounted to 'a symbol of trust for those of us who work in all fields towards the formation of a revolutionary consciousness'.[87] It was this language that persuaded a group of young graduates to accept Frondizi's offer of organising a Student Secretariat attached to the National Committee.[88] Among *Alem* activists there was deep mistrust towards *Luis M. Campos* since they knew contacts with Peronism were centred there but they were unaware of the details being negotiated.[89] On their part, *Luis M. Campos* were dismissive towards the romantic and ineffectual *Alem*, while they despised the old Intransigent circle at *Rio Bamba* (regarded as old-fashioned in their outlook and in their style of machine politics).[90] For their part, the party hands at *Rio Bamba*, following Frondizi's suggestion, had organised a Committee for Political Action headed by Alejandro Gómez, vice-presidential candidate. They were moderately satisfied that *Luis M. Campos* was chiefly a research unit and had no inkling of contacts with Peronism, while they were not altogether displeased to keep the younger *Alem* enthusiasts at a distance. *Alem*, meanwhile, regarded *Rio Bamba* as the '*zanahorias*' (dupes).[91]

The difference in approach between *Alem* and *Luis M.Campos* has particular relevance in the context of Frondizi's alleged *volte-face* once in government. In fact, Frondizi has remained adamant that he was faithful to his long-standing anti-oligarchic and anti-imperialist stance, insisting on the distinction between nationalism of ends and nationalism of means. For those in *Alem* the ends included such things as agrarian reform, worker participation in industry, nationalisations, curtailment of foreign monopolies and of the influence of the Catholic Church in education – in short, the *Avellaneda* principles. A favourite slogan hanging from a banner for all to see along Alem Avenue was 'struggling for an immediate and profound agrarian reform'.[92] Furthermore, *Alem* identified itself with the tradition of Radicalism, revealing an obsession with origins which *Luis M. Campos* definitely did not share, preferring instead to underline the novelty of their methods and approach to politics. *Programa Popular*, published by *Alem*, was true to the old UCR rhetorical style, maintaining in July 1957 that Frondizi's quest for the presidency was 'the consequence of an internal process of clarification and affirmation which aimed precisely at returning Radicalism to its ethical and doctrinal origins'. *Luis M. Campos* – its official denomination was *Centro de Investigaciones Nacionales* (CIN) – was more concerned with the future than with the past, and liked to compare itself to 'other private institutes in the most advanced countries', like the London School of Economics.[93] One hundred and fifty experts ('economists, sociologists, statisticians, jurists, writers') working in thirty committees, were in charge of 'classifying, systematising and elaborating all technical information on the fundamental issues affecting the country'. The stress on modernity, identified with technical expertise, was reflected in the account of the origins of the CIN provided in *Qué* on 29 April 1958, explaining that it was set up by 'a group of scholars' who realised that issues 'vital to the material and spiritual progress of the country', like self-sufficiency in oil, needed to be confronted 'with specialist criteria, leaving aside all improvisation', to be included in a national plan. In that same article *Qué* acknowledged publicly for the first time the close relationship between Frigerio and Frondizi, with the intention of paving the way for the prominent role that Frigerio – and his team – would be called to play only days later. CIN and *Qué* emerged *ex post facto* as the result of a strategy deviced jointly by Frondizi and Frigerio in January 1956, a strategy of which Frondizi's Intransigent colleagues were hardly aware. More importantly, the fact that *Qué* had been campaigning for Frondizi all along was also made public at the end of April 1958, after the magazine had taken great pains nine months earlier to deny any links with Frondizi. The denial, following an earlier one issued by *Rio Bamba*, confirmed the disclaimer contained in the latter in the sense that *Qué* was 'neither official nor unofficial organ of Radicalism' and that the magazine represented 'a national and popular thought which is not aligned with any party'.[94] In an authorised biography of Frondizi, Nelly Casas wrote many years later that 'Frondizi and Frigerio met daily with their collaborators to discuss the orientation of the magazine and its articles. *Qué* was the main weapon of the campaign'.[95] Isidro Odena, also close to both Frondizi and Frigerio, observed that Frigerio's decision to take over the editing of *Qué* was something both men agreed on their first meeting in January 1956.[96]

That meeting had been arranged by a common friend, Narciso Machinandiarena, at his sister's house, Delia Machinandiarena de Jaramillo. According to Narciso's widow, Blanca Stábile, the question of finding a political figure that would be 'acceptable to the Peronists' and thus able to gather a 'national movement' had arisen in the group of friends headed by Frigerio, who had been meeting systematically since the 1940s to study and discuss the predicament of the country. As a result of their 'analyses of the Argentine situation' they had come up with the idea of the need to prolong the existence of the 'national movement' after Perón's departure, and their problem had been to find a political figure to replace Perón. From that first meeting, the relationship between Frigerio and Frondizi would become almost symbiotic.[97] The full implications of the devised strategy would not be apparent until much later, when the developmentalist style revealed a disregard for political parties and their traditional forms of behaviour, preferring instead to rely on the performance (more often than not, *sub rosa*) of a relatively small group of men and women.[98]

Meanwhile the official UCRI publication, *Informativo Radical*, in a far cry from *Qué*, but more in tune with UCR idiosyncrasy, quoted Frondizi on the need to 'rule the country with a programme of love', while *País Unido*, a weekly edited by Celestino Gelsi, carried in its first issue an interview with Frondizi in which the latter spoke of the need to free all political prisoners, of the paramount value of freedom, and summed up his position saying 'we are at the service of what is national and popular'.[99] *Qué*, *Programa Popular*, *País Unido*, were Frondizi's campaign publications since he found no support in the national press, with the exception of *Clarín*.[100] *Qué* was undoubtedly the most ambitious – and successful – of the three, not only in terms of circulation figures, but in terms of sheer depth and range of coverage, discussing the matters that would dominate the campaign and, as it turned out, the future government's policies.[101]

The Role of *Qué* in Frondizi's Electoral Campaign

An analysis of the articles published during this period shows that *Qué* set out to draw the path the future government would follow. It is equally evident that Frondizi relied increasingly on Frigerio (and he, in turn, on the CIN) to provide what Frondizi came to consider a prerequisite of any 'modern' administration: blueprints for action based on research findings, a complete novelty in Argentine politics. Facts were set against intuition, prejudice, and self-interest in support of arguments, apparently ignoring that facts are liable to different interpretation. While the earnestness with which facts were sought provided a much-needed boost to academic activity and research, the claim to be in possession of the truth based on facts excluded argument and debate, in turn the very essence of political life.

Qué was to provide the medium for the dissemination of policy guidlines grounded on 'truths'. *Qué sucedió en siete días* was first published in February 1946[102] by Baltazar Jaramillo, who had been president of the federation of university students (FUA) in 1934–5. Scion of a landowning family from the Province of La Rioja, Jaramillo had founded and edited *Qué* from 1946 to 1951, year in which it was banned by Perón for carrying in its cover a picture of Libertad Lamarque, an actress against whom Eva Perón bore a long-standing grudge. It seemed fitting then that the magazine should reappear after Perón's downfall, when Frigerio became its editor.[103]

While *Qué*'s articles on oil, industry and education were lengthy pieces sometimes reflecting careful research, the editorial orientation was relentless in presenting Frigerio's Manichean view of the world ('from within and without the political parties, the Argentine people line up in two main tendencies, the national one and that addicted to colonialism').[104] Nor was there any doubt as to which side the Peronists on the one hand, and the *Libertadora* on the other, were placed. In *Qué*'s view, controlled by 'a minority which usurped power', the *Libertadora* aimed at 'reinstating a colonial economy [taking] the social situation of the country back to 1930'. There was a tacit acceptance of the symbiosis between Peronism and 'the people' who had been 'dispossessed on 16 September [1955]'.[105] *Qué* was in favour of a political force or 'national movement' which would correct such distortions by means of including in its midst all 'popular elements' whose interests were those 'of the Nation itself'. 'The deepest masses of Argentine society, the workers, the entrepreneurs, and together with them large sectors of the middle class' must 'find their political expression' in an 'organic force which, with sincerity and wisdom, will pursue the objectives of [. . .] sovereignty of the Nation, a just social order, and respect for those factors responsible for creating national wealth'.[106]

To help in this enterprise Frigerio had recruited nationalist ideologues Raúl Scalabrini Ortiz and Arturo Jauretche, who shared Frigerio's appraisal of the need to adapt Peronism to the current times, integrating it within a new synthesis: an historically 'superior' instance of the 'national movement' which had previously found expression in Yrigoyen and Perón.[107] Frigerio had not read Hegel and Marx in vain. *Qué*'s image was unmistakably identified with the opposition to the government of the *Libertadora* ('the oligarchy has returned to power: we must remove the material bases of its hegemony'),[108] with the definition of Peronism as 'the people' ('sovereignty, social justice and economic liberation [Peronism's three banners] [. . .] belong to the country as a whole'),[109] with a strong stance in favour of nationalised industries ('sovereignty is at stake in the battle for YPF'),[110] and against colonialism and imperialism ('colonialism cannot triumph: it will be swept away by the unstoppable movement of the people').[111] These were the ideas on which Frondizi fought his electoral campaign.

7 ARTURO FRONDIZI – FROM RADICALISM TO DEVELOPMENTALISM

Born in 1908, Arturo Frondizi was twenty-two and a lawyer when he decided to embrace political activism in reaction to the military coup that toppled Yrigoyen on 6 September 1930. In his biography of Frondizi, Pandolfi wrote that until that date, 'the eleventh of the twelve children of an Italian immigrant couple' had felt 'a remote commitment' towards the country, 'but when Yrigoyen fell, he felt directly, almost physically, the need to take part in politics'.[112] By the end of the year he had been a delegate to the Congress of Radical Youth, and he became a UCR card-carrying member in 1932, when the military authorities allowed the reopening of party registers. In the following years, and until events in Europe coloured the political atmosphere in Argentina inducing a shift in priorities, the young Frondizi embraced all popular causes, and in his professional capacity he took up the defence of political and trade union prisoners. The circles in which he moved – The Argentine League for Rights of Man, The Alliance of Intellectuals, Artists, Journalists and Writers, both surrogate Communist Party organisations – brought him into close contact with members of the CP and of the liberal Left. His opposition to the renewal of the electricity concessions to CADE during Justo's presidency reinforced his leftist image, and he was accused of being a communist.[113] Until 1943 he backed the idea of a Popular Front to combat Fascism and Nazism which had widespread support in Argentine intellectual and political circles. But the 1943 coup convinced him of the need to rethink the terms in which to define the Argentine political scene. Recalling the events of 1946, Frondizi remarked that 'the Intransigents had struggled against the nascent Peronism in its own grounds, that of popular nationalism', but he did not mention the fact that the rest of the UCR was increasingly coming to regard Perón as little more than an ersatz *führer*.[114]

It was perhaps Frondizi's speech of 28 July 1955 in response to Perón's offer of 'pacification' that revealed the Intransigent leader at his most Radical. In his vehement appeal Frondizi stressed the significance of the Constitution, reaffirmed moral principles and the value of personal freedom, all of which had to precede the deep changes the UCR believed the country demanded. Such changes had been impeded by 'the economic privileges represented by latifundia, monopolies and imperialist penetration'. The renewed economic base that 'national development' required would be achieved 'through the uprooting of privilege, of monopolies and through the sanctioning of a profound agrarian reform'.[115] Emphasising the UCR's principled tradition, he recorded the differences within the multifarious opposition to Perón in order to distance himself and his party from the conservative elements that now repudiated Perón. Future preoccupations that would signal his abandonment of the UCR tradition were only cursorily mentioned; a 'diversified industry' embracing 'from light to heavy industries' would have to be sustained on the 'development of the agrarian economy'. Frigerio would later convince Frondizi that for the equation to function, oil had to be added to it, producing the formula that was to guarantee the Argentine panacea: oil + meat = steel.

Two years later, what would become the most controversial decisions of his future administration were included in two main campaign speeches that had limited impact given Frondizi's restricted access to newspapers and radio. Since the government of the *Libertadora* was but too pleased to ensure that Frondizi got as little press coverage as possible, the UCRI candidate was restricted to personal appearances and even then his statements were barely reported in the national press. Therefore when Frondizi insists that his subsequent policy reversals were not such since he had anticipated them in the course of his campaign, a majority of the population could be excused from having failed to realise this. His first important speech, the 'Programme for Twenty Million Argentines', was delivered in July 1957 during the campaign for the Constituent Assembly elections and it did not depart from the *Avellaneda* principles. Although stressing the importance of heavy industry and economic development, it did not differ noticeably from previous statements, including the need for a sole labour confederation, and the democratisation of the economy via the participation of workers, technicians and entrepreneurs in the elaboration of policies. It was only in his 'Message to Twenty Million Argentines' of January 1958 that he mentioned what Babini has described as 'alarming innovations in the eyes of his long-suffering party colleagues'.[116] These innovations were the appeal to foreign investors, and freedom of education, and a redefinition of economic democracy in terms of workers' participation in the 'discussion' of their problems, a far cry from the 'control' promised in *Avellaneda*.

The polemical aspects challenged Radical beliefs grounded on a staunch rejection of foreign investment, especially in the area of basic resources, and an equally resolute opposition to private education and more specifically, to the presence of the Catholic Church in educational matters, principles sustained by the University Reform movement of 1918. State monopoly over the exploitation of natural resources and the provision of free education at all levels had an almost dogmatic status amongst traditional UCR supporters. Frondizi had been an articulate and vociferous champion of these principles throughout his political career and his reappraisal of them reflected the extent to which at the beginning of January 1958 he was no longer the same type of politician he had been until then, even though few seemed aware of this change at the time. Somebody who had noticed the change was Alvaro Alsogaray, who one week after Frondizi's electoral victory wrote that 'only Dr Frondizi's statements during the campaign . . . open a favourable question mark and allow us to hope for something constructive'.[117]

Frondizi and *Qué* on Education and the Church

The lay postulates of the 1918 University Reform were constantly invoked by the UCR and had been incorporated into *Avellaneda*. If there were two issues that forged the Radical identity after 1918, they were the Reform and oil nationalism. Gabriel del Mazo, active participant in the heady days of 1918 and relentless propagandist of the merits of Reformism,[118] wrote in *Raíz* a criticism of the Education Bill tabled in Congress in 1947 by the Peronist Government. The 'logic of the heart', 'an effectively national culture', the 'struggle for the reintegration of man' rather than 'professional expertise' were held in opposition to the Peronist project favouring 'an intellectual type of culture' when the pressing demands of the times were for 'moral perspectives in education . . . the perspectives of the heart'.[119]

In an interview published in *Qué* on 25 June 1957 under the heading 'Frondizi affirms Yrigoyen's stand', the UCR leader did exactly the opposite. Although he mentioned 'spiritual aspects', the emphasis was on the need to educate technicians and scientists who would contribute to development. This plea for a new direction in higher education had been forcefully made by Frigerio five months earlier in an editorial in *Qué*. In it he had stated that the University should become 'the lever of national progress' educating scientists and technicians 'imbued in the spirit of the country and ready to work in the practical solution to the thousands of problems affecting production'.[120] Frigerio had attacked the university which had only 'contributed to provide those professionals the oligarchy needed to enforce its domination'. The humanist tradition so dear to university students was condemned by Frigerio, mocking the notion that the university should not be 'a factory of technicians' but that its role was to 'develop spirits. The *homo universalis*!'[121] The study of the humanities if at all necessary, should be linked to the study of 'the lives and histories of our autochthonous cultures'.[122] Not having had a university education himself, Frigerio had little respect for an institution which saw itself as something more than just a workshop for mining engineers and agronomists. Frondizi was more cautious, declaring that he could even accept that the country needed more 'philosophers, sociologists, literary men', but he preferred to stress the shortage of technicians. Echoing Frigerio's misgivings, he depicted Argentine universities as 'factories of doctors [providing] the material for a ruling class which oppresses the people'.[123] And to produce a different type of graduate, a different type of university was needed.

The Reformist tradition was fundamentally lay – if not anti-clerical – emphasising student participation in the government of the universities. When the 25 June interview was published, it provoked an uproar and 'widespread dismay in *Alem*', where it had the effect of 'a nuclear explosion'.[124] A private meeting was arranged between Viñas, Rojo, Félix Luna, Ramón Alcalde, Babini, Jitrik and Frondizi, where they challenged him on the views expressed in *Qué*, 'reminding Frondizi that he was violating the party's platform'.[125] According to Rojo, Frondizi candidly admitted that 'he needed the backing of the Church' and although Rojo realised that the 'need to add votes' was paramount, the rest of the group found it a bit too much, and *Alem* was disbanded soon after.

What Frondizi had declared in *Qué* was that he was against one of the sacred principles of Radicalism – the State monopoly in education. Reacting to the ensuing scandal, *Qué* published an article entitled 'the Left defends lay education . . . just as the oligarchy does'. A parallel was drawn between the vernacular Left and the oligarchy, both seen as sharing a preference for foreign ideas. This was a veiled reference to the education policies of the *Libertadora* which, acknowledging student involvement in the fight against Perón, had offered the student movement the opportunity of choosing their own Rector for the University of Buenos Aires. This they did, and the Socialist José Luis Romero was their choice, and Ismael Viñas became his secretary.[126] There was no room for doubt – 'the *criollo* left', 'the oligarchy', 'the lay tradition', 'imperialism', they all backed 'irreligiosity'. The Left was accused of being incapable of understanding the religious feelings involved in popular cults such as those of *Pancho Sierra* or *Evita*.[127]

The magazine reminded its readers that Yrigoyen – 'not manifestly Catholic' – had opposed a Divorce Bill tabled by the Socialist opposition in 1922, and six years later had given official recognition to non-State schools. Old quotes from Frondizi were disinterred to justify his replies in the published interview and prove that he had been consistent in his favourable attitude towards the Church since, for instance, in 1956 he had said that the Catholic Church 'will not have any problems with a Radical government'. The *Qué* interview was based on extracts from a document latterly published by the Argentine Bishops' Conference. Frondizi had been asked to comment on the document, expressing his total agreement with it , excepting the Bishops' reference to the desirability of only one labour federation. The main ideas espoused by Frondizi were his belief in the family 'as the basic cell of society', his stand against divorce, against State monopoly in education, against the separation of Church and State and that 'religion [should play] a fundamental role in the moral recovery that all Argentines are prepared to undertake'. *Qué* followed the interview with articles favourable to the Church in its 23 and 26 July and 6 August issues. The reasons behind such conspicuous endorsement of the Catholic Church were twofold. On the one hand, political expediency dictated it. Frondizi and Frigerio knew how crucial the Church had been in creating the atmosphere that would eventually make Perón's downfall an imperative. Frigerio did not forget that Catholics had been prompted to organise politically as a reaction to Perón's attacks on the Church.[128]

Catholics in Argentina were divided into a nationalist, anti-liberal trend, and a liberal-reformist one. The Catholic nationalists had a longer history in the country. In the 1920s they became attracted to the extreme nationalist movements being formed in Europe. General Primo de Rivera's dictatorship in Spain (1923–30) and his son's (José Antonio) establishment of the *Falange*, provided the most noteworthy sources of inspiration. Outraged by the UCR's liberalism and laicism, in 1930 they placed their hopes in General Uriburu's coup, to be disappointed once more in his successors, until General Ramírez's coup in 1943 opened new perspectives. Most Catholic nationalists supported Perón during most of his presidency, impressed by his appeal to the Social Doctrine of the Church in his quest for legitimising sources. In 1954 his violent anti-clericalism revealed how vague and superficial his adherence to Catholicism had been, failing to recognise – or choosing to ignore – the centrality of education for the Church. The events of 1954 made Catholic support for Perón no longer viable. The more liberal Catholics organised themselves for the first time in July 1954 to fight against Perón and, after September 1955, against the influence of Catholic nationalists in Lonardi's short-lived administration. The Christian Democratic Party was formally established in December 1956 to take part in the July 1957 elections.[129] It secured 4.8 per cent of the total number of votes, achieving its highest percentage (13.4%) in the better-off quarters of the Federal Capital.[130] It would be from the ranks of Catholic nationalism that Frigerio and Frondizi would recruit collaborators, men like Mario Amadeo and de Pablo Pardo.

There was also an ideological explanation in the developmentalist appeal to Church support, explanation provided by Frigerio's grand design for a 'national movement' or 'alliance of social classes and sectors' in which the Church ranked as a 'social sector' of considerable magnitude, whose 'spiritual influence' was counted on 'to strengthen in the popular consciousness the postulates of the programme of national unity'.[131] More immediately, it was felt that Frondizi's image in the United States needed improvement, and who better than Monsignor Plaza, about to visit that country, to take to an American audience the message that Frondizi was not the extreme left-winger the American press had made him to be.[132] Frondizi had aroused American suspicions as a result of his stance in Congress in 1947 and 1950 when he had opposed the ratification of the Rio de Janeiro Treaty of joint defence of the countries in the Organisation of American States as 'compromising vital aspects of national defence'.[133] Furthermore, he had vehemently opposed the Standard Oil contract that Perón had proposed to sign in April 1955.

Another issue that would produce genuine dismay and not an inconsiderable amount of moral indignation was the part assigned to foreign capital in the developmentalist strategy. Frondizi's about-turn on this matter paved the way for the appointment of Alsogaray as Economy minister in June 1959.

Frondizi, *Qué* and Alsogaray on Oil

Findings of psephological studies point out that the electorate judges retrospectively, since voters appear to respond to events they have experienced and observed; proposals for the future, being vague and uncertain, do not grasp their imagination nor do they govern their actions.[134] In Argentina, voters' experience of Arturo Frondizi was grounded on his performance as leader of the opposition between 1947 and 1955, as well as on his outspoken criticism of the government of the *Revolución Libertadora*. Nothing ranked higher in the UCR demonology than the participation of foreign capital in the exploitation of natural resources. At the time of the congressional debate of Perón's proposed contract with the Standard Oil Company, Frondizi had rejected it because it meant 'the establishment of foreign bases' in Argentine territory, crossing 'the southern part of the territory of the motherland with a wide colonial strip whose sheer presence . . . would be the physical mark of serfdom'.[135]

Almost three years to the date, during a nationwide radio broadcast on 24 July 1958, the then President Frondizi assumed direct responsibility for signing oil contracts with foreign firms whose scope was much wider than the one Perón had proposed to sign. When the argument was put forward to Frondizi on several occasions that he had misled the voters who, one could reasonably argue, had been engaged by his long-standing record as a nationalist in economic matters, he replied that in his campaign speeches he had anticipated his new stand. He attributed his new views to a pragmatic appraisal of the situation, since he had realised that the country did not have the resources to attain self-sufficiency in oil in the short term, and that therefore foreign oil companies would have to be brought in to undertake the exploitation of resources that *Yacimientos Petrolíferos Fiscales* (YPF), could not hope to do by itself. With the exception of Alsogaray and *Tribuna Cívica*, nobody had dared voice what was essentially a sensible view.[136]

True to the UCR tradition and the principles of *Avellaneda*, in his 1954 book *Petróleo y Política*, Frondizi had argued persuasively in favour of the nationalisation of oil deposits and of the State monopoly over all exploration, extraction and commercialisation activities. In the rhetorical prose of the best anti-imperialist orthodoxy, the book gave an account of the 'abuses' and 'crimes' perpetrated as a result of the prevalent policy in the world of granting concessions to big private oil companies. Argentina had to become self-sufficient in oil to extricate itself from the tentacles of the 'international octopuses' and safeguard its national sovereignty. On 17 December 1957 an Intransigent publication, *País Unido*, referred to *Petróleo y Política* as 'a crucial stage . . . in Argentina's expression of its will'. The aim was self-sufficiency in oil production; the diagnosis, that this was prevented by means of depriving YPF of the necessary funds to develop and expand exploration and drilling.[137] Should public funds prove insufficient to back YPF's activities, Frondizi proposed that 'the Argentine people supply their *pesos*, their dollars and their gold to carry out the great task of finally liberating their motherland from all foreign economic submission'.[138] He denounced what he described as a campaign to discredit YPF while attacking those who maintained that the State was a bad administrator. He described the purpose of such a campaign as attempting to create an atmosphere propitious to the acceptance of 'concessions and contracts of surrender', and claimed that one of the 'deep motives' for the 1955 revolution against Perón had been 'to stop an oil concession that was going to inflict a mortal wound on national sovereignty'.[139] Finally, he unambiguously summed up the UCRI's position on the 'oil issue', which was 'to declare as a definitive national decision YPF's monopoly in everything related to the oil problem'.

There was no inkling that the position of either Frondizi or the UCRI had changed when five months later (and three months before the February 1958 elections) *Informativo Radical* was reproducing a speech Frondizi had made in the Province of La Pampa in which he had stressed that 'the UCRI would not look abroad for loans'. Nor was there any disclaimer when Gelsi's *País Unido* attacked a document presented by the Chamber of Commerce to President Aramburu on 19 December 1957 as a 'sell out of the Nation' since it recommended the concession of oil exploitation to foreign companies.[140] For its part, *Qué* 's denunciation of any attempts to grant concessions to foreign oil companies had been relentless, although there was a difference in tone between, on the one hand, Frigerio's editorial comments and the magazine's investigative articles and, on the other, Raúl Scalabrini Ortiz's virulent diatribes in his own column. Although far from renouncing the nationalist rhetoric, there were in the former cursory and vague references to the participation of foreign firms in the oil sector. Thus halfway down an article entitled 'Beware: Petroleum is the key to sovereignty!', *Qué* explained that when it was said that oil exploration and exploitation 'must be in YPF's hands' this did not mean that 'any collaboration should be rejected', since 'YPF can sign contracts with private firms, even foreign ones'.[141] There was a caveat, that 'all capital, wherever it may come from, will be welcome' as long as 'it fulfils the essential prerequisite of remaining under YPF, key to our sovereignty'.[142]

The belief that a contract with a foreign company could lead to alien enclaves in Argentine territory appealed to the kind of chauvinistic zeal that Scalabrini Ortiz urged in his column, denouncing all Argentine ills as resulting from British manoeuvrings. The government of the *Libertadora* ('the only thing that this revolution has liberated has been Great Britain's enslaving intentions') and Alsogaray were little else than *cipayos* [quislings] when they suggested that YPF did not have the financial resources nor the administrative efficiency to expand oil production.[143]

The severest indictment was reserved for Alsogaray; he was accused of being 'a propagandist for the surrender of our oil' and the Civic Independent Party's publication, *Tribuna Cívica* was 'a mouthpiece of the large monopolies to forward their own interests'.[144] This line of attack had been launched by *Qué* a fortnight earlier in a three-page article of an almost libellous content, implying that Alsogaray was on the payroll of foreign oil companies and challenging him to confess the precise amount of the sums he was allegedly receiving.[145] The article concluded that

> the foreign monopolies may pay handsomely, but not enough to bribe the national consciousness, nor to erase the lapidary judgement that everybody has formed on the former Industry minister and present adviser in high government circles [Alsogaray].[146]

However, when *Tribuna Cívica* was first published *Qué* hailed it as the expression of the PCI, drawing a positive parallel between the latter and the British Tories, both supporting 'popular capitalism', and it welcomed Alsogaray's defence of the 'weapons of neo-conservatism . . . in terms that facilitate the discussion'.[147] There was nothing disreputable about free competition so long as it was kept out of 'all those activities which guarantee the sovereignty of a genuinely free country'.[148] Even before Frigerio had negotiated successfully the oil contracts at the beginning of 1958, there were other coincidences with Alsogaray that the latter readily acknowledged, while Frigerio would continue to deny.[149] *Tribuna Cívica* sought to distance the PCI from 'the old-fashioned political parties' and 'their old-fashioned methods'.[150] If one omitted the references to the perils of interventionism in the economy, there was little that either Frondizi or Frigerio could have objected – after May 1958 – in a statement Alsogaray made during a press conference with foreign journalists, claiming that more than a new political party, the PCI represented 'a real ideological movement' aimed at changing public opinion and replace 'retrograde national and social-interventionist politics'.[151] Alsogaray's party could not have been further from Scalabrini Ortiz – and for that matter, from the deeply-rooted statist tradition of the UCR – when he pointed at State interventionism in the economy as the source of all problems. It was on this count that Alsogaray had resigned from Aramburu's government and openly criticised the *Libertadora*, declaring that its chief error had been 'the maintenance of State interventionism, excessive and ineffectual, which drowns the economy and irritates the productive forces'.[152]

The PCI's campaign, the contents of its publications, and Alsogaray's public statements, were single-minded: their battle was against what was variously condemned as 'totalitarian bureaucratism', 'dangerous economic dirigisme', 'totalitarian State monopoly' or 'national-social dirigisme'. The embodiment of such evils was YPF, and throughout 1957 and well into 1958, the PCI became an almost single-issue party, insisting on the need for foreign capital to achieve self-sufficiency in oil and to contribute to the modernisation of Argentine industry. In an argument that would oft be repeated by Frondizi and Frigerio, *Tribuna Cívica* also maintained that what were at stake were the means, rather than the ends.

Reading the pages of *Tribuna Cívica* it is very hard to disagree with Alsogaray when he maintains that in fact it was Frondizi who moved towards Alsogaray's point of view, and that this confluence led Frondizi to appoint Alsogaray to the Economy Ministry in June 1959. During February 1958 Alsogaray was publicly giving Frondizi the benefit of the doubt,[153] simultaneously warning against the 'grave danger facing the Republic' embodied in the 'national-social-statist' groups surrounding the UCRI candidate. While Frondizi's statements during the campaign had 'opened a favourable question mark and allow us to hope for something constructive',[154] warnings were sent about 'the irresponsibility, arrogance and self-satisfaction of the high chiefs of a preposterous and corrupt State bureaucracy' who, together with political leaders 'imbued of a socialising mentality' would encourage 'the abusive meddling of the State in the life of its citizens', resulting in the decadence of the country and the loss of personal freedoms.[155]

The day Frondizi was being sworn in as president *Tribuna Cívica* offered a dispassionate – and it would turn out, accurate – account of what the new government would have to do if it wanted 'to avoid a crisis: precisely the opposite of what the platform of the victorious party maintains'. The fundamental measures that would 'inevitably have to be implemented' were those that the PCI had been advocating all along, amongst them 'the extraction of oil with the participation of private capitals', 'elimination of State controls' and 'the elimination of bureaucracy and State monopolies'.[156] Frondizi's inaugural speech was welcomed as 'an echo of our own impassioned campaign', while it 'must have sounded ominous to many of his followers'.[157]

The New York Times, which on 24 February had announced on its front page 'Frondizi is victor in Argentine poll, backed by Perón', subtitled 'Leftist lawyer is elected president over Balbín, leader of the moderates', a week later carried an article by Tad Szulc reporting the president-elect's declaration that he would 'welcome government and private cooperation from the United States for Argentina's economic development', even in the 'sensitive and politically explosive areas of petroleum and electric power'.[158] When the American correspondent asked Frondizi whether he 'could be considered an economic nationalist in view of his Leftist politics' the reply had been that he was 'an economic nationalist in the sense that [he placed] the national interest of Argentina above all else', and that moreover:

> he would not oppose the presence in Argentina of US or other foreign oil companies provided that this presence was arranged under contracts for the performance of specific tasks and did not infringe on the integrity of Argentina's national oil monopoly.[159]

Since the 1920s the UCR and all manner of nationalist groupings, from FORJA to the more extreme xenophobic characters, had presented the 'national interest' and foreign investment as irreconcilable: if one had the former at heart, the latter was anathema, and vice versa. Instead of attempting to educate Argentine public opinion, Frondizi and Frigerio chose to impose the oil contracts with foreign firms as a *fait accompli* on an unsuspecting country, thereby sowing the seeds of the mistrust in politics and politicians which in the long run contributed to erode the basis of democratic stability.

5 The Implementation of the Developmentalist Economic Programme. The First Aim: 'Development'

1 INTRODUCTION

When the results of the 23 February 1958 elections became known, Frigerio had reason to congratulate himself on his efforts: the Peronist masses had followed the 'directive' sent by Perón a few days earlier, and with the exception of 405,816 blank ballots, Peronists had now voted for the UCRI. Overall the party obtained 44.90 per cent of the votes, followed by the UCR with 28.90 per cent, the rest of the parties trailing far behind. The recently created Christian Democratic Party received 3.16 per cent of the votes, while the Socialists received the approval of only 2.92 per cent of the electorate, their best results being in the Federal Capital, their usual stronghold, where they obtained 5.64 per cent. Three small conservative parties managed to secure less than 1.5 per cent each, while Alsogaray's PCI received 0.44 per cent. The UCRI had triumphed in all the provinces, and the 4,070,398 votes it received assured the party not only of all the provincial governorships and the majority in all provincial legislatures, but, in accordance with the Sáenz Peña Law, 70 per cent of the seats in the Chamber of Deputies(133) and all the 42 senators – as Babini described it with hindsight, 'an anti-republican majority of totally addicted Congress and governorships'.[1] The contradictory reactions sparked off by the news of the results of the elections held on 23 February provided an indication of the ambiguity of the UCRI victory. While Frondizi and the UCRI may have believed that they had been the winners, the chanting of Perón's name in the industrial suburbs of Buenos Aires in defiance of the ban still in force, coupled with the disquiet and unrest that such celebrations prompted in more central quarters, indicated that for a wide section of the population, the victor had been Peronism. This was not the prevailing feeling amongst UCRI members who reacted 'as if they had won the lottery'.[2] Frigerio has always insisted that the two million extra votes that the UCRI had obtained since July 1957, had been genuinely won over by the belief that Frondizi represented the continuation of the historic line represented by Yrigoyen and Perón. But in the streets the view predominated that Frondizi had won with 'Perón's votes' and would now implement the promised 'national and popular programme' heralded in the pages of *Qué*[3]. The British ambassador could be forgiven for forecasting that only the UCRP would have guaranteed 'a continuance of the economic and social policies' of the *Libertadora*.[4] This would prove a delusion soon to be dispelled. But if *frondicistas*, *frigeristas* and *peronistas* may argue as to whose triumph it really was, there was no doubt as to the identity of the losers. The results were a clear rebuff to the Provisional Government and the UCRP, united in their rejection of Peronism and Peronists alike.

2 FROM 23 FEBRUARY TO 1 MAY 1958

Robert Potash has recorded military unrest in the immediate aftermath of Frondizi's triumph.[5] Dr Laureano Landaburu even interpreted the 1962 coup 'as a settling of the 1958 accounts, so deep had the anger been at the time' against the man who had led the opposition to the *Libertadora*.[6] Many years later Frondizi said he should never have accepted the presidency in such conditions, since 'effective power lay with the military'.[7] But do the divisions, rivalries and widespread indiscipline rife in the armed forces at the time justify such *ex post facto* assessment? Generals de Nevares, Lanusse and Sánchez de Bustamante recalled that in the factious state of the military in 1955–63, no one person, political view or ideology had enough clout to sway the forces one way or another. Remarking that General Bonnetti, then commander of the 1st Army Division based in the City of Buenos Aires, had wanted to stop Aramburu handing over power to Frondizi on 1 May, once Aramburu thwarted this attempt the army was ready to obey President Fronizi, its new commander-in-chief, if he 'had had the courage and vision to use the power the Constitution invested on him'.[8] Sir John Ward was dismissive of the possibility of a coup after the elections, but added with foresight that 'the testing time is likely to be much later after Frondizi has shown his hand in office'.[9] Foreign Office records also corroborate the view that sympathy for Frondizi grew after his victory:

> [There has been] a marked swing in Dr Frondizi's favour of elements hitherto bitterly opposed to him. Officers of the armed forces and leading business men, who before the elections were loudly maintaining

that a victory for Dr Frondizi would spell the ruin of Argentina, now argue that Argentina has a new national leader of unquestioned ability who deserves the support of all men of goodwill.[10]

What seems indisputable is that the strength of Aramburu's resolution to respect the democratic process was decisive in ensuring that Frondizi took over the government on 1 May.[11] If the mood was changing in the military barracks, Perón was showing caution and remained unconvinced of Frondizi's real intentions. He wrote to Cooke:

> We must bear in mind that our agreements with Frondizi do not place us in the government . . . We are in the opposition, albeit collaborating, until Frondizi keeps his promise with the people and with us – then we shall unleash on him the whole weight of our political possibilities, greater every day. He is our ally against the *gorilas*. It is our common task to destroy them and subject the oligarchy and all traitors, but Frondizi must show that he shares our intentions.[12]

Perhaps it was Frigerio's wishful thinking, translated into the steamroller tactics grounded on sheer voluntarism – hallmarks of the *frigerista* style – that must be blamed for convincing Frondizi that the grand scheme of a 'national movement' could prove stronger than any man, whether armed or not. During the two months before Frondizi's formal investiture on 1 May, the president elect took every opportunity to emphasise the image of principled politician. One instance of misplaced determination was his refusal to exclude Raúl Damonte Taborda from his entourage during his visits to neighbouring countries. Damonte Taborda was editor of the vociferous periodical *Resistencia Popular*, where Frondizi had collaborated in the past.[13] 'A man of few political morals' and 'a rabble-rouser', Damonte Taborda was expelled from the UCRI on 23 March 1958 on the grounds that his paper had published Peronist propaganda. As Sir John Ward remarked, 'it was disingenuous [of the UCRI] to expel [Damonte] since, as everyone knows, without *peronista* support Frondizi's victory would not have been so complete'.[14]

Striving to appear to be taking a strong line *vis-à-vis* military pressures in the Damonte Taborda case, he was also disregarding the decision of the Disciplinary Tribunal of his own party. In the meantime he maintained his left-wing overtones during his visits abroad before 1 May,[15] while in his prandial encounters with businessmen he was careful to emphasise a very different aspect. On these occasions he repeatedly offered assurances that private investment and enterprise would receive wholehearted support from his future administration.[16] He was consistent in this during a private conversation he held on 23 December 1957 with the British ambassador who reported to London that 'as [Frondizi] was so much on his good behaviour, and we were on British ground, I refrained from teasing him directly about his speeches'. A Foreign Office official commented that

> [the conversation] presents Dr Frondizi in a less unfavourable light than that in which we have tended to regard him. If the 'real' Frondizi is the man who talked to Sir John Ward, there is nothing in his exposition of his views (except possibly on the multilateral trading point) which involves departure from the policies followed by the Provisional Government. But there is no certainty that his performance to Sir John Ward was not an 'act'.[17]

On the other hand, on 1 March 1958 *Pravda* 'noted with satisfaction that the American reaction to the election of a left-wing government in Argentina was distinctly cool', while a month earlier *Izvestia* had said that 'the Argentine people [were determined] to oppose the enslavement of Argentina by American capital'.[18] Thus on 1 May 1958 too many people were anticipating too many – and contradictory – things. Not surprisingly, many would be disappointed.

3 FRONDIZI'S INAUGURAL ADDRESS

Frondizi's speech on 1 May gave the first indication of what the country could expect from an UCRI government. Few voters could have known what they had voted for in terms of actual policies.[19] Amongst the two million non-Peronist voters, discounting those who voted for Frondizi because of his oppositionist stance against a military government which seemed to replace one form of arbitrariness with another, there were many who thought Frondizi offered a real alternative for the future: a politician able to sound as if he knew what he was talking about – in stark contrast with his principal opponent and one-time party colleague, Ricardo Balbín.[20]

The inaugural speech offered then the first opportunity to present to the country the intended policies of the newly-elected government. It opened with a promise to 'renew' national development – implying that it had been begun by Perón and abandoned by the *Revolución Libertadora* – stating that Argentina's fundamental problems were of an economic nature. In order to achieve progress and national greatness,

Frondizi stated that the past had to be left resolutely behind. In that spirit, he declared a comprehensive amnesty, and pledged that thereafter nobody in Argentina would be persecuted for his ideas nor for his political nor union activities. He announced that he was giving up all party-political responsibilities, placing himself above what he described as 'sectarian and intolerant' considerations, and anticipating that he would be seeking the collaboration of non-UCRI members in pursuit of 'the most capable men for each specific task'.

The most striking departure from the UCR tradition was to be found in the main body of Frondizi's speech. Perhaps in a token gesture to the structure of *Avellaneda*, he divided his speech into four 'bases' – political, economic, social and cultural. There was a further section on the armed forces and national development, and a final one on Argentina's role in the world. Where in 1947 *Avellaneda* had sought the subordination of the economy to 'national development and social welfare needs' rather than 'profit-making', in 1958 the emphasis would lie 'heavily on private activity', requiring 'an atmosphere of peace, security and stability'. The nationalisation of all public services and utilities was replaced by the statement that 'the Executive Power will not seek new nationalisations', and the role of the State would be to 'guarantee free competition in order to facilitate the creativity of private enterprise'. The 'immediate and profound agrarian reform' was dropped, replaced by the search for a solution 'to the problem of access to the land for all those interested in making it produce'. The fiscal reform promised in 1947 'to ensure that the heaviest burden would fall on larger incomes' was replaced by a reference to 'fiscal, monetary, credit and exchange policies' that would act as 'incentives to production'. Since the level of domestic savings was deemed 'insufficient to finance the rhythm of development' required, foreign investment would 'operate as an acceleration factor'. The exploitation of Argentina's 'potential oil wealth' was signalled as 'the shortest path to achieve the desired aim', and 'the cooperation of private capital would be accepted' 'insofar as official resources prove inadequate'. This did not mean 'the granting of concessions nor renouncing State authority over pre-existing oil and coal deposits'.

On the labour front, the 'workers' participation' promised in 1947 became a commitment to union democracy and non-State intervention in union matters, as well as the promise to lift all interventions and interdictions and to hand back the unions 'to their legitimate owners'. In the field of education 'the reinstatement of the 1918 University Reform' violated by Perón, was replaced by the principle of 'freedom to learn and to teach as prescribed by the Constitution' which in the context of the protracted battles between lay and Catholic elements for control of the education system in Argentina meant the sanctioning of both religious and private establishments: tantamount to sacrilege in middle class student eyes. The commitment that the Catholic Church had never managed to obtain from Perón was granted lock, stock and barrel by a Radical president. In the context of the UCR lay and anti-clerical tradition, this was a most remarkable success for the Catholic hierarchy.

In a tacit indictment of the Perón administration, 'administrative corruption' and the 'fracture of the ethical base of society' would not be allowed. The armed forces' respect for the democratic transference of power was acknowledged and they would be expected to play a role not just in the defence of the nation but in national development as well. Furthermore, the president declared 'the revolutionary period' completed, meaning that from that point onwards 'the armed forces [would] not take the decisions, but the representatives of the people would'.[21]

Hopes and desires, wishful thinking and declarations of intent that would inevitably be put to the test in the confrontation between the realm of the possible and of the real. Potash has written that the obstacles to the implementation of Frondizi's programme lay 'in the divisiveness and hostility that characterised the society as a whole'.[22] Rather than acknowledging such a predicament, Frondizi – and Frigerio – chose to ignore the depth of existing rifts and still open wounds that aflicted Argentine society since at least 1930 and which the events of the past fifteen years had only exacerbated. Nevertheless, as far as his style and manner of understanding the task of government were concerned, Frondizi promised something that it was his to deliver and he did not: a commitment to an open form of government, where transparency and accountability of actions would be guaranteed. He even pledged that 'leaders of political parties not represented in Congress' would have access 'to the most sensitive information' since he wanted to 'share the responsibility for the decisions taken'.[23] As it turned out such responsibilities did not include the oil contracts to be announced a few months later. As a Foreign Office official wrily noted when the UCRI issued a manifesto denouncing 'oil conspiracies', 'Dr Frondizi's public relations work on this issue [oil] does not seem to have extended to his party'.[24]

4 THE CABINET

When the Cabinet was announced everybody's misgivings about Frondizi seemed to be confirmed. The series of surprises that Frondizi had in store began with his choice of close collaborators and the assignation of responsibilities. Frondizi's announcement that he would not feel restricted by party allegiances when making his choice of ministers was in line with a traditional prerogative of the president in Argentina, where party government has been the exception rather than the rule. However, rather than complementing a partisan team with the inclusion of eminent extra-party men, Frondizi seemed to have in mind its substitution. On 6 May, Dardo Cúneo, the new Press Secretary,[25] announced the creation of four secretariats directly dependent on the Presidency: Colonel Juan Enrique Guglialmelli would head the Secretariat for Liaison and Coordination; the Executive Secretariat would be presided by Samuel Schmukler, who had been active during the campaign securing financial contributions in exchange for future favours; Architect Nicolás Babini was rewarded with the Technical Secretariat, and lastly – but certainly far from least – Rogelio Frigerio would become the new Secretary for Socio-Economic Relations. With the exception of Babini, none of the newly created Secretaries was a member of the UCRI. The appointment of the ministers themselves, if more predictable, also harboured a few surprises. Gabriel del Mazo, who was widely expected to hold the Education portfolio, went instead to the newly created Ministry of Defence, to be headed by a civilian, while Intransigent Luis MacKay, of Irish Catholic stock and noted for his religious devotion, went to the Ministry of Education and Justice.[26] The Church was duly rewarded: besides having one of 'their men' leading Education, divorce and abortion were obliterated from public debate, and the ecclesiastical hierarchy could once more expect to play a prominent role in all public functions and ceremonies.[27] Almost inevitably, the insistence on the importance of the Church was seen as part of a manipulative scheme which, precisely because it dealt with religious matters, received moral reprobation.[28]

The other senior members of the Cabinet were Alfredo Vítolo, a respected former Unionist and deputy from the Province of Mendoza who went to Interior; Emilio Donato del Carril, UCR National Deputy for the Province of Buenos Aires in 1946–50 who had been appointed Ambassador in Moscow in 1955 by the *Libertadora*, and whose hapless task would be to preside only nominally – and not for long – over the Finance Ministry (renamed Economy Ministry in June 1958); Dr Héctor Noblía, appointed Minister of Health, who had been Provincial Senator for Buenos Aires in 1948–52 and who once at the ministry surrounded himself with young, enthusiastic doctors with various degrees of commitment to the Communist Party, and Alfredo Allende, at 28 the youngest member in the Cabinet, placed at the head of the Ministry for Labour and Social

Security in June 1958. Allende was to become one of the close-circle *frigeristas*, although at the time he led the insurance workers' union.[29] The *Alem* group had hoped Ricardo Rojo would be appointed Labour minister but Frondizi did not send him to what was considered Rojo's 'natural destination' for the same reasons he did not send Del Mazo to Education – in short, that the policies he wished to implement were anathema to each men in his field.[30] But arguably the biggest shock of all for the UCRI was the appointment as Minister for Foreign and Religious Affairs of Carlos Florit, twenty-nine at the time and from a renowned Catholic nationalist family.[31] Frondizi's first choice had been Luis de Pablo Pardo whose appointment to the Interior Ministry by General Lonardi had been one of the reasons that prompted the latter's replacement by General Aramburu in November 1955. According to British records, de Pablo Pardo had helped to found *Qué*, and he became Frondizi's adviser on foreign affairs during the campaign. Frondizi presumably realised that de Pablo Pardo's track record as a Catholic nationalist meant his appointment would have been too much of an irritant for the armed forces. Instead, he was named legal adviser at the Ministry, where he became 'the power behind the throne'.[32] Even if their appointments caused bewilderment in UCRI circles, the public at large could have no misgivings about men – Florit excepted – with long-standing reputations in the UCR.

They were a motley group of men who under close scrutiny could not be immediately seen as sharing any common purpose. This fact contributed to broaden the field of action of Frigerio and his men. Increasingly it appeared that Frondizi paid little heed to anybody but Frigerio. While every minister's influence was restricted to the boundaries of his own department, from his position as Secretary for Socio-Economic Relations Rogelio Frigerio became a kind of 'super minister' with apparently unchecked authority. It would be Frigerio who from his post and, after he was forced to resign, through his carefully placed *locum tenens,* took over the responsibility for ensuring consistency of purpose. It is not too far-fetched to speculate that this had been the intention all along. Frigerio was finally in a position to exercise direct control after his disappointing experience with Lonardi.[33] The above then, plus the understudies placed by Frigerio in an underlying intricate network, were the men[34] who presided over what have been described as the 'untidy' months of the developmentalist experiment, while *frondicistas* prefer to refer to them as the 'revolutionary' months.[35] These were the months from May to December 1958, ushered in by Frondizi's inaugural speech delivered in the presence of both Houses of Congress even though the UCRP deputies refused to stand up when the President entered the Chamber in an 'ungracious performance' that would worsen in each subsequent inauguration of congressional sessions, when they kept away altogether.[36] Such contempt between the constitutional Powers was reminiscent of newly-elected President Yrigoyen's refusal in 1916 to attend the inauguration of the new Congress. On that occasion the Radical president had wished to manifest the low esteem in which he held a Legislative Power with a Conservative majority. In 1958 the UCRP emulated a gesture so poignantly symbolic of the long-standing institutional fragility in Argentina.

5 A 'REVOLUTIONARY' 1958?

The Economic Background

From the beginning of the decade the economy had been fluctuating between short periods of prosperity and recession, and as a result per capita income had grown at a yearly rate of one per cent. Many authors have remarked on the restrictive role in Argentina's growth of a stagnant external sector, whose exportable surpluses were constantly reduced by a growing urban population and the increase – however small – in real wages.[37] During 1950–59, 78 per cent of the total output of the agricultural and livestock sector of Argentina was absorbed domestically, compared with 50 per cent in 1920–29.[38] In the words of one analyst, since exportables in Argentina are also considered wage goods, during this period governments at times limited by decree the exports of certain commodities 'to assure an adequate level of domestic absorption of exportables at "reasonable" prices, even at the expense of cutting back deliveries to traditional overseas markets'.[39] The dramatic difference between the 1956 US $210 million deficit in Argentina's balance of payments and the 1954 US $47 million surplus was the result of the world wheat surplus caused by the US decision to dump its agricultural surpluses. An immediate consequence was the loss for Argentina of the Brazil market, saturated with US wheat. This was compounded by a drop of 60 per cent in the maize crop in 1956, owing to unfavourable weather conditions. However, as *The Economist* remarked, even if Argentina had had a bumper crop of any agricultural product, 'there [was] not the transport to move the crop to the ports. Transport, capital goods for heavy industry, fuel and power; these are the bottlenecks of Argentina's economy'.[40] In the words of another analyst, although it is true that Argentina's terms of trade worsened throughout the 1950s, it was 'the internal conditions that accounted for the inefficient response to

Implementation of Developmentalist Economic Programme 117

the unfavourable external conditions [that] will provide the fundamental explanation' for such balance-of-payments difficulties.[41] Therefore the decline in the Argentine share of world exports in the aftermath of World War II suggests that internal supply difficulties, rather than world demand conditions, account for the secular decline of the quantum of exports.[42] Energy shortages, transport deficiency, the need for a basic iron and steel industry were recurring themes, as well as the growing feeling that domestic savings were just not adequate to meet the needs.

In 1955 Prebisch had recommended a devaluation both to stimulate agricultural production and to finance investment in the sector. However, whenever policies to promote agriculture and livestock raising via devaluation were adopted in Argentina, they were accompanied by policies aimed at restricting imports, limiting inflation and attracting foreign exchange, resulting in a shortage of supplies and credit. Thus whenever the share of agriculture and livestock in the national economy increased, gross domestic product fell, which meant that 'inevitably, in the popular mind, policies that set out to favour the agricultural sector were seen as having an anti-popular bias', accusation the *Libertadora* could not dispel.[43] Given that exportable commodities have such considerable weight in the expenditures of wage-earners, devaluations have a very quick and significant impact on the average price of the consumption basket of urban wage-earners.[44] Thus the share of wage income in GDP dropped from 47.0 per cent in 1955 to 46.4 per cent the following year, but in 1957 it was down to 44.8 per cent.[45]

By 1958, the heavily protected domestic industrial sector – which was contributing about one third of GDP – was working at full capacity with a deteriorating industrial equipment in desperate need of modernisation. To be able to pay for imports that had outstripped exports since 1955, the government of the *Libertadora* had resorted to foreign borrowing, a policy that would also be preferred by the *desarrollistas*, with the result that during the period 1955–62, the foreign debt was every year financing 16 per cent of imports.[46] It has also been noted that since the post-war years, a typical feature of Argentina's industrialisation was that rather than substitute real imports, newly established industries satisfied a 'repressed' demand, in so far as the importation of the goods produced had been restricted or forbidden.[47] Thus, although the average propensity to import goods has been on the decline in Argentina throughout this century, the remaining imports had such strategic importance in the production process that any fall in their levels caused severe dislocations in the economy.[48] When the new administration took over in May 1958, Prebisch's aim which had been to achieve a redistribution of income in favour of the rural sector at the expense of industrial profits – to offset the opposite trend during the Perón years – 'had met at best only with some very partial short-run success'.[49]

The Eight Developmentalist Months: May to December 1958

Some analysts have made a distinction between the set of economic policies followed from May to December 1958, and those introduced as part of the stabilisation plan in 1959,[50] while others have preferred to follow the protagonists' own depiction of the period 1958–62 as one whole.[51] Frigerio not only emphasised the continuity in policies, but his paternity over them, indicating that the plan responded to his analysis of the Argentine problems 'from long before [he] had the opportunity to apply those ideas from the government, in my capacity as President Frondizi's collaborator'.[52]

Frondizi had insisted throughout his campaign on the need to cut imports, thus it came as no surprise when on 3 May the Central Bank announced the suspension of the granting of any new import licences – a restriction that would be lifted on 1 August 1958. That first month also saw the appointment of Arturo Sábato as 'personal presidential delegate in YPF'[53] and the signing of agreements to increase trade with Poland, Romania and the USSR following a mission sent by the Provisional Government at the beginning of the year to the countries of the Soviet Bloc to spend credit balances held by Argentina in her bilateral accounts with Eastern European countries.

Yet the two decisions that had the biggest impact were on the one hand, the announcement on 13 May of a 60 per cent wage rise across the board on levels existing on 1 February 1956, and on the other hand, the *Batalla del Petróleo* proclaimed by Frondizi at the beginning of July.[54] While the announcement of the 60 per cent wage increase ought to have delighted those who were expecting the promised 'national and popular' economic programme, the fact that simultaneously no price controls were established was not unreasonably interpreted by Peronist trade unionists as a signal to press for further increases in their direct bargaining with employers, effectively inaugurating what one analyst has described as an 'inflationary free-for-all'.[55] The outcome was a series of strikes in which both Peronist and anti-Peronist 'democratic' unionists strove to appear as the most effective champions of workers' living standards.

What was the logic behind what has been described as a 'populist' 60 per cent increase?[56] As Manuel Ordóñez of Industrias Kaiser Argentina had anticipated on 18 April 1958 to State Department and Eximbank officials, Frondizi would 'try to buy internal peace with labour by granting an immediate wage increase' because 'he wanted a period of relative quiet on that front for about six to eight months until he could get his economic programme started'. Having secured this breathing space, Frondizi would move quickly 'to get the economy on sound footing', and to this end he would need external aid. In Ordóñez's words, the corollary was 'if you [the US] do not help, the plan will fail'. According to Ordóñez, the 'group of young economists' working on Frondizi's programme – he mentioned Aldo Ferrer and Julio Olivera – although they did not have 'a positive liking' of the US, they shared 'a positive dislike for Europe and the European way of doing business', and thus regarded the US as the least of all evils.[57] The calculation was that production would be stimulated through the increased demand – a consequence of the greater disposable income. The unforeseen setback was that the raised costs were immediately transferred to prices, making it necessary for the government to set price controls and giving the opposition in Congress an opportunity to accuse the government of pursuing 'policies of hunger'. By the end of May price controls were imposed on kerosene and sugar, but hoarding became so serious that Congress passed a law to repress speculation in foodstüffs (Law No 12,830), while in the month of December the Trade Secretary was still extending the list of goods with fixed maximum prices.

The 60 per cent wage increase represented in real terms a far from insignificant gain of 10–11 per cent in 1958 taking into account the rises of around 25 per cent granted by Aramburu in 1957. But the nominal rise was what provoked the ensuing uproar. The problem was one of timing. The augmentation in demand that did occur, given the existing conditions of industry working at full capacity, was to be satisfied by means of increased imports. Since in Argentina, as has been remarked above, incentives to the agricultural sector are not traditionally reflected in the short term in expanded exportable surpluses,[58] the only means left to finance the new requirements of imports was to seek loans abroad. Furthermore, the momentum of inflation had been building since 1956 (13 per cent in that year against 25 per cent in 1957) thus the wage rises gave it renewed impetus.[59]

Was Frondizi ill-intentioned or incompetent in determining the wage increase? Ascher seems to favour the interpretation of incompetence, or at least ignorance of the probable outcome of certain economic measures:

> Nothing in populist rhetoric prepares the initially buoyant pro-redistributionist for the humiliation of increased inflation, a seemingly uncontrollable budget, and the apparent ingratitude of workers who undermine the economic balance by demanding even higher wages than the populist had intended.[60]

US ambassador Beaulac for one was not convinced that Frigerio had a complete grasp of economic complexities, remarking that he [Frigerio] 'mixed politics with economics [defending] an unbalanced budget as unavoidable in manoeuvring against political pressures' and simultaneously indicated 'his support of the stabilisation programme'. Beaulac attributed the contradiction between both objectives to the fact that Frigerio was not 'a trained economist' and therefore the problem might be 'a semantic one'.[61] There seems to be enough evidence to indicate that the so-called 'revolutionary' policies were never intended to be such. Frigerio himself stated that the 60 per cent raise was necessary 'to create the conditions for social and national cohesion'; it was a way of 'building a bridge' in the direction of the working class with the aim of ensuring its 'integration in an incipient National Front.'[62] Mallon and Sourrouille are inclined towards the interpretation of intent rather than incompetence behind the 60 per cent increase explaining Frondizi's 'extravagant initial policies' as a need not just to fulfil campaign promises, but 'to produce an economic crisis of sufficient proportions to justify a clean break with past policies so that he [Frondizi] could introduce his own "developmentalist" strategy.'[63] This interpretation is borne out by Frigerio himself, when he said in April of 1959 that 'we tightened our belts after having established the conditions for the economy to take off in an accelerated process of expansion'.[64]

Mallon and Sourrouille recognise that paramount in Frondizi's decision to grant the 60 per cent raise may have been the need to satisfy if not directly Perón, at least a majority of his followers, in the process effecting a schism between Perón in exile and his followers in Argentina. Most likely, the answer is to be found in a combination of pre-electoral (and until then, secret) pledges to Perón, total reliance on Frigerio's blueprint – according to which foreign capital would fill any gaps, crevasses, etc. – and a degree of incompetence resulting from the belief that sheer voluntarism could press results. Thus Frondizi was not being especially devious (in the eyes of the Right), neither treacherous nor hypocritical (accusation hurled by the Left), but dogmatic.

6 THE STABILISATION PLAN OF 1959–60

On 4 December 1958 Economy Minister Del Carril sent a letter to the International Monetary Fund outlining a proposed stabilisation plan as the basis for a stand-by loan of US $75 million (by instalments), while additional loans amounting to US $254 million from US official and private sources were also made available at the time.[65] On 16 and 17

December the Paris Club countries virtually gave Argentina permission to convert freely into dollars currency earned from trade with Europe, thus concurring to the undertakings Argentina had to give the IMF. On 29 December 1958 Frondizi announced on a national broadcast a new 'austerity' plan, prompting a Foreign Office official to note that economic rather than political considerations were finally being taken into account and that the president had 'either because of his own convictions or as a result from pressure from the Armed Services and informed public opinion' decisively reorientated his policy.[66]

Frondizi's language was duly apocalyptic – it was 'the end of an era and the beginning of a new life for all the Nation', and the times called for 'heroic remedies'. Inflation was affecting 'the moral bases of the individual and society', and the stabilisation plan was 'a supreme effort to [impede] the unleashing of an economic, social and political crisis of painful consequences for the people'. The distortions of a protectionist economy that favoured 'errors, unnecessary delays, privileges and peculation' would be rectified by a return to 'authentic free enterprise', while monopolies would be 'fought implacably'. Argentina would have to learn to live according to her means, something that had not occurred 'for the past fifteen years', a comment that did not ingratiate the president in anti-Peronist circles, since he did not apportion the blame squarely on Peronist policies and made no distinction between these and the *Libertadora's*. It would therefore be necessary to cut public expenditure in order to eliminate the fiscal deficit, while state enterprises would be rationalised to make them efficient ('Public Administration cannot be the refuge for comfort and minimal effort'). But it was not just the modernisation of the country's economy that was made to depend upon the success of the stabilisation plan. The president went on to say that 'without economic stability there will not be material progress, nor will there be peace, tranquillity, nor authentic trade union activities. Without stability there will be neither freedom nor democracy in the country'.[67] The campaign slogan of legality, social peace and development was overrun by the absolute priority of stability.[68] The period of sacrifices and hard work would only last two years, after which the economic structure would have been transformed. On the base supplied by the untapped oil, coal, and iron resources, an expanded electricity industry, and a new steel industry, the foundation would have been laid for a 'boundless expansion of domestic industry' – 'chemicals, plastics, metallurgy, newsprint, automobiles and machinery'. Although it was explicitly anticipated that 'the level of income of the Argentine people will fall in the next twenty four months', beyond that date 'that level will be elevated to reach unprecedented heights'. And he concluded proclaiming:

> We shall not look back nor shall we permit that the discussion of facts that history must judge hinder the recovery task that we have undertaken. We have the certainty of triumph and we know that the harsh reality of today will be followed by tomorrow's infinite possibilities.[69]

The main steps announced were the following,

- The introduction of a single free rate of exchange for all imports and exports, although less essential imports would be surcharged (varying between 20 per cent and 40 per cent) according to lists published by the government. All goods not appearing on the lists, including luxury goods and machinery produced locally, were taxed at 300 per cent;
- The removal of the existing system of quotas, import permits, certificates of necessity and 'other steps subjecting economic activities to the decision of officials';[70]
- Export retentions: 10 per cent on the value of the export of most livestock products, and 20 per cent on the value of the export of most cereals, oilseed, quebracho and hides;[71]
- Banking credit and the money supply would be restricted; and finally,
- All direct and indirect subsidies to public transport would be removed to make it pay for itself; fees for all public services (transport, electricity, railroads, and postal services) would be substantially increased.

Although some writers have referred to the programme as an IMF imposition, others have underlined the developmentalist commitment to it.[72] Thus Díaz Alejandro noted that of several alternative stabilisation plans 'suggested by staff economists of the [IMF], President Frondizi personally chose the harshest and most austere one'.[73] Moreover, on 27 October 1958 Frigerio told a Bank of England representative in the presence of the British ambassador that 'over the next three years [Argentina] must have US $600 million' and that they would 'gladly accept any conditions on their budget and credit control which might be laid down by the [IMF]'.[74]

7 THE EVALUATION OF THE DEVELOPMENTALIST ECONOMIC POLICIES

The general sense of the policies was to set free economic activities from State intervention, in tune with the then world-wide trend towards elimination of controls over trade and capital inflows.[75] A month after its announcement some observers could be forgiven for doubting the conviction with which the measures were being implemented. The British ambassador noted that the ensuing decrees were approaching liberalisation 'at best, by a roundabout route', and the remaining controls – in some cases amounting in practice to prohibition of importation – meant that it was 'highly unlikely there will be any cut in the red tape previously involved'.[76] Notwithstanding the declared intention of encouraging exports and restraining imports, the remaining red tape meant that in practice it was difficult to talk of a general move towards liberalisation.

Although the plan was aimed at checking the rising inflation and to achieve both balance of payments equilibrium and a high rate of growth in total output with the collaboration of foreign capital, references to its allegedly 'national and popular' features were widespread in the president's speech and declarations of officials, misleadingly giving the impression that the maximisation of equity was being pursued at the same time as economic growth. In fact Frondizi's administration did succeed in achieving the latter but not surprisingly failed as far as income redistribution in favour of the 'popular classes' was concerned. Although foreign capital did arrive it did not – and could not – satisfy the developmentalists' expectations, according to whose blueprint foreign capital would flow into the building of 'highways, airports, hotels', all of which was necessary 'to arouse enthusiasm' as well as to absorb government employees displaced by the rationalisation of the public administration.[77]

'Conservative' or 'Progressive'? The Appointment of Alvaro Alsogaray as Economy Minister

How real and sincere was the alleged developmentalists' 'conversion' to free trade economics? It may be more appropriate to regard their approach as fundamentally eclectic: 'development' was another way of referring to 'the development of productive forces'. This was an essential prerequisite to achieve the superior stage of 'national emancipation'. The development of productive forces in turn required capital accumulation, and for this to take place, the 'law of surplus value' had to operate; the language used was far removed from liberal notions of a non-regulated economy as the guarantor of a free society. Thus tariff barriers were defended as a means of protecting 'the fulfilment of an elemental economic law: that of surplus value . . . which is the prerequisite for accumulation, because without it there is no capitalist accumulation'.[78] In so far as profit-making was placed above income redistribution, the developmentalists could be described as 'conservative'.

What undoubtedly contributed to the attribution of conservatism was the fact that on 24 June 1959 Alvaro Alsogaray was appointed Economy minister to oversee the implementation of the plan. The apparently incomprehensible decision to place the most outspoken and coherent critic of the developmentalist strategy at the head of the Economy Ministry led to the interpretation that Frondizi was bowing to almost relentless military pressures, first obvious at the time of Frigerio's forced resignation at the end of 1958.[79] Although the idea of Alsogaray's imposition is widespread and encouraged by Frondizi himself, there is enough evidence to prove that at best, the fact that the military were reassured by Alsogaray – at least in the first instance – seems to have been a fortunate coincidence.[80]

Frondizi therefore called Alsogaray to put into practice an economic programme that was anathema to Radical principles, secure in the belief that in time the unpopular features of the plan could be blamed on a man whom it was credible to describe as a military imposition. Frigerio has also insisted that Alsogaray was called in to calm the military with the explicit undertaking to carry out an agreed programme, but that once in government, he did an about turn and followed his own policies, for his own personal motives.[81] Not surprisingly, Alsogaray's account differs radically since he insists he had been exchanging working memoranda and ideas with Frondizi since 1957 and that he became minister to carry out the policies expounded by his Independent Civic Party (PCI), inspired in Ludwig Erhard's social market economy, ideas to which Frondizi had been 'converted'.[82] De Pablo Pardo had told US ambassador Beaulac that Alsogaray had entered the government 'as a result of influences exerted on the president by the Armed Forces . . . and also by Mr Frigerio', while Frigerio himself had anticipated to Beaulac that '"a Conservative" would enter the Cabinet in order to help carry out the stabilisation programme', and the ambassador added there was 'little doubt that he had Ing. Alsogaray in mind'.[83] Twenty years after the event Frigerio insisted that his – and Frondizi's – economic policies had remained the same throughout 1958–62, and that Alsogaray's appointment was precisely to allow 'for the continuation of the economic policies announced during the first six months of 1958', in the process giving the appearance that what was not more than 'a reshuffle' was indeed 'a concession to *golpismo* [the military]'.[84] Frigerio's account is consistent with his belief in 'objective forces', of which men are but mere instruments.

In a meeting held at the home of a prominent businessman, and where Frigerio, Alsogaray, Gelbard (president under Perón of the CGE, the business federation) and their host were the only ones present, it was practically understood that Frigerio and Gelbard would be proposing the

Implementation of Developmentalist Economic Programme 125

names of those who would become Alsogaray's economic cabinet.[85] Both Frigerio and Gelbard were disagreeably surprised to find out that after his appointment Alsogaray had made his own choice as to the men who would accompany him.[86] Archive reports bare out the claim that Alsogaray would 'select and have direct control over the secretaries of state in charge of agriculture, finance and treasury, commerce and industry, mines, power and fuel' and would thus be in a position 'to exert a great deal of influence on the Argentine economic scene'.[87] There are also several references to meetings between Alsogaray and Frigerio recorded by observers, although Alsogaray himself is reluctant to admit to their frequency.[88]

Inevitably, the president's 'real intentions' in naming Alsogaray became suspect. Had he been genuinely converted, forsaking the statist, interventionist, socialising policies embodied in *Avellaneda*?[89] Or was he 'using' Alsogaray to carry out unpopular policies that would prepare the scene for a subsequent 'populist' stage? Alsogaray himself is not sure to this day.[90] Convinced of the need to reduce the fiscal deficit, Frigerio had presumably thought Alsogaray was ideally suited to cut ruthlessly the inefficient state machine. Alsogaray would carry out the 'dirty work' and then be promptly replaced by a more sympathetic figure in time for the important 1962 elections. Indeed, Alsogaray was dismissed without much ado – and much to his bewilderment – on 26 April 1961.[91] Frigerio did not conceal his disappointment with Alsogaray's performance, accusing him of having 'distorted the priorities' and 'delayed the policy of development'.[92] It is true that economic policy was given a 'slightly different slant' after Alsogaray's dismissal, in the view of the new British Ambassador, Sir George Middleton, 'to conform to the ideas of Señor Rogelio Frigerio'.[93] The new policies which seemed 'to have combined about as well as oil and vinegar' were 'free rein for private enterprise combined with greater rights for labour, and a stable currency combined with rapid economic development'.[94]

In a letter addressed to Frigerio on 1 April 1958, Scalabrini Ortiz warned him of the dangers of pursuing a policy of contracts with foreign oil companies, pointing out that 'readers of *Qué* are somewhat frightened by a certain implicit praise of Alsogaray and a reference to his "constructive position"'.[95] Someone who was less impressed by Alsogaray was the British ambassador, who referred to 'that *enfant terrible* of free enterprise' as a man who was 'a bit of a zealot and arguably lacking in the human touch', with no sense of humour and who 'refused to recognise that there was anything fundamentally wrong in Argentina's economic structure'. Ward attributed this 'potential defect' in the new Economy minister to the fact that he had 'a strong strain of typically Argentine nationalism combined with a financial expert's conviction that everything will come right if finances are put right'. Moreover, he did not seem worried by the distortion of the economy whereby 'high cost industry battens on agriculture and the country's export trade is in danger'.[96]

Foreign Investment

On 21 July the government announced the creation of a Foreign Investments Department and an Advisory Commission on Foreign Investments, both to function within Frigerio's Secretariat for Socio-Economic Relations. Frigerio was thereby given the responsibility for the central element in the developmentalist strategy, the attraction of foreign capital to bridge the time lag between stabilisation and growth and to soften the social and political costs of stabilisation. Frigerio's *modus operandi* was characterised by sheer voluntarism, impatience and the use of 'somewhat unattractive characters' who more often than not 'appeared to trade on [their] relationship with Dr Frondizi in an endeavour to further [their] own commercial interests'.[97]

To the distinction that Frigerio liked to make between nationalism of ends and nationalism of means, he added that between good and bad foreign capital. The latter was invested in backward countries exclusively to finance 'primary exploitation geared towards exports', resulting in 'the perpetuation of traditional structures' and acting as 'a brake to the expansion and autonomy of the countries in question'. On the other hand, the former arrived 'to satisfy the needs of the domestic market and to replace imported goods with locally produced ones', thereby contributing to 'the autonomy of the country [and the radical alteration] of its economic structure'.[98] There was little doubt that in the days Frigerio was writing in *Qué*, 'good' capital was American, while 'bad' was British. In October 1958 his design was rather different. The British ambassador was approached by Miguel Angel Cárcano who said that Frigerio 'was most anxious to meet him [the ambassador] for a private talk', because, Cárcano said, 'reversing the recent trend [. . .] the government were convinced that their real interests lay with the British rather than the Americans'. During the meeting Frigerio put it less diplomatically – 'the conversation . . . took a rather less pleasant tone' – and said that

> the Argentine government would soon find out who were their real friends. Those who lent her money now would be the ones with whom Argentina would do business in the future and the others would be left out in the cold.[99]

When Sir John Ward interrupted to say that there were often 'better ways of helping than by giving direct loans', Frigerio retorted that he had in mind 'loans of "friendship"', prompting the ambassador to add the comment in his report that he probably meant 'it would be unsporting to insist on normal terms of repayment'.[100] Ward's conclusion was that Frigerio and his 'lunatic fringe' used tactics

> reminiscent of that which you and I [Hankey and Ward] used to know in Italy, i.e. a mixture of blackmail (as applied to the unfortunate *Times* correspondent) and, with regard to myself, the old Italian gambit of artificially creating bad relations in order to stimulate the intended victim into paying a price for putting them right.[101]

Besides Frigerio's and his entourage's 'mafia' tactics, in January 1959 the government promulgated a Foreign Capital Investments Law (No. 14,780) granting foreign capital the same rights – including tax exemptions where applicable – as domestic capital. This went hand in hand with the decision to put up for sale the firms included in DINIE (National Directorate of State Enterprises) a group of German plants confiscated by Perón in the last few days of World War II, plus some former British ones that had belonged to the railways. The government wished the sale of DINIE firms to be read as a sign of its favourable attitude towards private *and* foreign ownership.[102] Under the 1957 Consolidated Debt Agreements (Paris Club) the enterprises were put up to public auction with the former owners having the first option to repurchase. Repurchases were made in approximately half the firms but under such favourable conditions that 'in many cases [the Germans] got the plants back for practically nothing'.[103]

The first twelve months of the Frondizi administration were not very successful in attracting foreign investment, which totalled just under US $32 million, although approximately an equal amount was refused responding to pressures from Argentine industrialists to prevent foreign investments which would offer unwelcome competition.[104] The introduction of the system of surcharges made many ordinary commercial transactions impracticable and encouraged schemes which, albeit presented as capital investments from abroad, were little more than devices to enable importers to bring in capital goods free of surcharge.[105]

In the course of the four developmentalist years, the location of 254 foreign firms was authorised. Although they covered the whole of the industrial spectrum, 90 per cent were concentrated in the chemical, petrochemical, transport, metallurgy and machinery sectors. As to the type and size of plant being established, the 25 largest projects amounted to 67 per cent of all proposed investments. Amongst the 25, the three 'Detroit giants' accounted for 20 per cent of investment.[106] American firms represented 60 per cent of all foreign investment, followed in order of importance by the Swiss, British, Germans, Dutch, Italians and French.[107] But none of the new projects had been exclusively designed to exploit at an international scale Argentina's relative advantages in either natural or human resources.[108]

The way in which foreign firms dominated the production in each relevant industrial subgroup is illustrated by the following figures:

- In the automobile industry, the eight largest firms accounted for 86 per cent of production. Foreign-owned firms accounted for 95.1 per cent of the total number of firms in the subgroup;
- In meat-packing plants, 10 foreign-owned firms (out of a total of 29) accounted for 81.7 per cent of production;
- In oil refineries, 3 out of a total of 19 firms were foreign-owned and contributed 36.9 per cent to the total production of the subgroup;
- In the tobacco industry, 4 out of a total of 7 firms were foreign and they accounted for 74.4 per cent of production;
- In rubber, 3 foreign firms produced 78.7 per cent of the output of the sector;
- In agricultural machinery, out of a total of 447 firms, 9 were foreign-owned, and these accounted for 85.8 per cent of production;
- In electrical machinery and spare parts, 10 firms were foreign-owned out of a total of 302, accounting for 83.7 per cent of output.[109]

In contrast with their remarkable participation in industrial output, foreign firms made a modest impact on the labour market owing to their highly capital-intensive features. The firms set up since 1958 employed 60,000 people (more than 4 per cent of the total work force employed in industry), but between 1958 and 1963 total industrial employment fell by 250,000.[110] Thus Frigerio's hopes that foreign firms would offer employment to the people made redundant during the process of rationalisation of the State were thwarted. If 'autonomy' was a priority, then it is difficult to see how it could be the outcome of massive foreign ownership of the country's basic industries. Once again, Frigerio was entangled in the rhetorical web of his ideological detritus.

Furthermore, the inflow of short- or medium-term private capital meant that the external debt grew sharply. By the end of 1961, it was clear that Argentina faced a heavy repayment schedule to service not only the new debt accumulated since 1959 but also earlier debts the repayment of which had in many cases been postponed during 1959–61 as part of the foreign co-operation in the stabilisation plan.[111]

Conclusions

The liberalisation policies resulted in an increase in the import coefficient in industry, a trend that had been started by Perón in 1953, continued by the *Libertadora* and intensified by Frondizi. Since 1945 around 60 per cent of all imports were composed of a large variety of raw materials and intermediate products, while 30 per cent of all imports represented capital goods.[112] While imports could not be reduced given the high import coefficient of industrial production, the series of protective measures accorded to the new industries set up after 1959 meant that the internal price of their products was higher than the international one, ruling out all chances of diversifying the profile of exports. In support of the British ambassador's misgivings about the neglect of agricultural exports (see above) some analysts have concluded that the developmentalists in fact worsened the 'anti-export bias' of the economy which had been started by Perón. They see in this the most damaging long-term result of developmentalist policies.[113] For Díaz Alejandro, the main failure of the 1959–61 policies was in stimulating an increase in the output of exportable goods, primarily of rural origin. Roberto Alemann shares his view, underlining that Argentina had lost out during the Perón years, since by stressing an antagonistic stance Perón had – among other things – played into the hands of the powerful farming lobby in Washington, which succeeded in keeping Argentina's competitive agricultural production out of the US market. Alemann was aware that much more could be gained by conveying a friendly attitude towards the US – it was the first step to setting up an effective Argentine lobby.[114] For the ten years 1951–61 Argentine exports had remained almost static at about US $1,000 million per year, while it was estimated that by 1964 double that figure would have been necessary to service her debts and pay for capital goods imports. As an observer put it, if exports on a per capita basis could be at the same rate in 1964 as in 1935–9, the target would have been met.[115]

The problem of the restrictive import policies of the European Community Market, Canada and the United States which closed crucial markets to Argentina's agricultural exports was compounded by Argentine production problems which were chiefly of two kinds.[116] On the one hand there was the inefficiency and rundown state of railways and ports, which often meant that agricultural production could not reach its destination on time. On the other, governmental policies which effectively meant that agriculture was not only neglected but made to subsidise industrial development by means of buying highly protected materials and equipment while selling at world market prices.[117]

Díaz Alejandro's final indictment of developmentalist economic policies was to point out the 'minor achievements' of 1959–61, which he listed as being,

- A slight improvement in the efficiency and financial position of several public enterprises, excluding the railways;
- A rebirth of an effective domestic financial market;
- Gains in labour productivity in several branches of production and in national government because of more rational working rules, albeit these improvements were offset by a growing – open *and* disguised – urban unemployment and excess capacity in many industries.[118]

The 'two years' Frondizi had hoped would suffice to bring about the desired structural changes, were not enough: post-stabilisation there was no recovery. In the year from October 1958 to October 1959, the cost of living rose by 124.5 per cent, and if the period January 1958 to March is considered, the cost of living increased by 326 per cent – dramatic figures for the times, less so seen from the perspective of 1992. 'Development' therefore, proved a more slippery, more complex, more difficult objective than the developmentalists had hoped it would be. Although securing the good will of foreign investors, governments and financial organisations, the developmentalists failed in the domestic front. The other two campaign banners of 'legality' and 'social peace' proved equally difficult to attain.

6 The Developmentalist Strategy: the Internal Constraints. The Second Aim: 'Legality'

1 INTRODUCTION

Together with 'development' and 'social peace', 'legality' – the rule of law – had been Frondizi's rallying cry in his oppositionist campaign during the government of the *Revolución Libertadora*. With a two-thirds majority in the Chamber of Deputies and total control of the Senate, the opportunities either to respect the rule of law or to flout it were available. 'Legality' had been taken to refer as much to the lifting of all political proscriptions imposed by the *Libertadora* as to the indictment of Perón's style of leadership, tending to be neglectful of the rules of the political game. Much then was expected of the Frondizi administration on this count, and the UCRP opposition would relish its chances to remind the government of their promises as well as of the 'honourable' record of some of its members when they had all belonged to the UCR.

That common past membership of the UCR, compounded by the fact that both UCRI and UCRP members had belonged to the Intransigent movement within the UCR, is a crucial element to understand the strangeness of some of the debates in the Lower Chamber. Frequently the deputies of both government and opposition invoked the same antecedents and heroes: they shared the same demonology and hagiology (or rather one could talk of demonolatry in describing the common obsession with Perón). Peronist sympathisers could not but feel estranged from such an institution.

2 COMPOSITION OF THE LEGISLATIVE POWER

The shortcomings of Argentina's presidentialist tradition were highlighted during the Frondizi administration. When an entire political system is centred round the President, the party in government is left without a role of its own and congressmen merely enact into law those bills originated in the Executive.[1] The culminating point of such practices was the UCRI's national convention held in the Province of Buenos Aires town of Chascomús in December 1961 which rubber stamped, retroactively, all the President's policy decisions and actions. Still, as will be seen, there were times when Congress challenged Executive decisions, as on occasion of the resentment in UCRI circles at Alsogaray's appointment, when the Senate issued a sharp protest on the minister's announcement that State enterprises would be sold to private firms. This forced the president and his minister to undertake that 'basic entities of the economic structure' would not be sold.

The Argentine Congress is composed of two chambers: the Senate, where each province, plus the Federal Capital, is equally represented, and the Chamber of Deputies, elected on the basis of population – according to the system of the 'incomplete list' – thereby reflecting the uneven pattern of population distribution in the country. Thus while the Province of Buenos Aires elects 50 deputies and the Federal Capital 35, Santa Fe elects 20 and Córdoba 18. Excepting Entre Ríos with 9, Mendoza and Tucumán with 7 deputies each, Corrientes and Santiago del Estero with 6 each, and Chaco with 5, the rest of the federal provinces elect between 1 and 3 deputies. While senators serve a nine-year term, deputies are elected for four-year periods. The electoral timetable in fact dictates that there shall be a general election every two years for the renewal of half the Chamber of Deputies; in the next period of general elections the electorate must vote in provincial elections, for electors for President, and for the renewal of the other half of the Chamber of Deputies. But since some electoral districts have their own electoral calendar, and the renewal of their executive and legislative powers does not coincide with elections at the national level, there tends to be an excessive electoral frequency.

Although the period of ordinary sessions extends from 1 May to 30 September, the Executive Power can convene Congress for extra-ordinary sessions. Most constitutional powers are granted jointly to both cameras, but the Lower Chamber has the exclusive authority to initiate laws on taxes, and on the recruitment of troops, and it can impeach the president, vice-president, Cabinet ministers and members of the judiciary. On its part, the Senate is empowered to authorise the president to declare the state of siege. It shall be seen how both areas of exclusive legislative power were overridden by Frondizi in the course of his four years in office, aided by the tradition of strong executive government which effectively allows presidents to legislate by executive decree. Although such decrees are subject to review by Congress, in Frondizi's time, sometimes out of a sense of loyalty stretched to the limits, the government majority effectively accepted the Executive's decision.

The results of the February 1958 elections meant that the UCRI had total control of the Senate, – the monotony was only broken in March 1961, when Alfredo Palacios, the colourful Socialist,[2] was elected senator for the Federal Capital – a two-third majority in the chamber of Deputies, where the UCRP had the other third of the seats (excepting two independents), and the totality of provincial governorships. Perhaps it was this too comfortable majority that helps to understand Frondizi's insouciant attitude towards the legislative power.

3 FRONDIZI AND CONGRESS

Even though there were instances in which deputies spoke out in defence of provincial or regional interests (for example, in the debate on sugar prices and quotas for Tucumán, the case of the federal intervention of Salta, or the closure of railway stations in remoter areas in the unsuccessful drive for more efficient railways), they were mostly concerned with defending the 'national' interest, increasingly equated with partisan definitions of that same interest. This reflected the fact that representatives owed their seats to their parties, in which the national committees overwhelmingly dictated the line followed by their provincial counterparts. Still, on more than one occasion the UCRI governors came into conflict with the president.[3]

More than lawmakers, legislators acted either as allies of the Executive's position or as its relentless critics, with the result that some legislators ended up leaving the party or being expelled from it. Rather than 'opinion-makers', articulating 'the interests of their real and would-be followers',[4] they were selected by party bosses concerned and consumed by personal rivalries and ideological intransigence. There were three main areas in which the Executive Power either by-passed or manipulated Congress against constitutional precepts: the oil contracts with private foreign companies, financial decisions taken by the Executive which should have been the exclusive attribution of the Chamber of Deputies, and the state of siege legislation.

The Oil Contracts

(a) The Background
Frondizi's *volte face* in this area is indisputably the single most remembered issue of his whole administration. It was brandished both by opponents and supporters of his policies as an example of his duplicity and

Machiavellianism. The emotional overtones that tinged the subject of oil in Argentina can be traced back to *Yrigoyenista* deputies' decision in 1927 to nationalise oil resources and granting YPF a monopoly over future production. Indeed the campaign in favour of oil nationalisation was started in 1923 by President Alvear and his oil chief Colonel Enrique Mosconi. So bitter and divisive had the debate been in 1927 that many authors have subsequently written that Uriburu's coup of 6 September 1930 'smelt of oil' in reference to rumours that the foreign oil companies had 'employed bribery [. . .] to influence the military to move against Yrigoyen'.[5] The President had utilised so determinedly the nationalisation argument against the Conservative opposition, that his pledge to nationalisation became firmly rooted in Radical mythology.[6] Writing in 1956 Frondizi recalled the 'doctrinaire vigour . . . patriotic energy and political ability' shown by the UCR 'in the Chamber and on the streets' in defence of what he termed the 'absolute thesis' of oil nationalisation.[7] According to Solberg, Yrigoyen's decision to decree a series of provincial interventions to ensure Radical control of the up to then Conservative-dominated Senate, was motivated by 'his intransigence on the petroleum issue'.[8] Whatever the true motivations, the interventions became the primary reason behind a serious legitimacy crisis that led to the breakdown of the political system in 1930.[9]

It was this 'popular and national' tradition that UCR deputy Arturo Frondizi brandished against Perón's intention to sign a contract with the Standard Oil of California. Not only had Frondizi led brilliantly the Radical opposition in Congress, but in his famous 27 July 1955 speech he made the proposed contract with *la California* the pivot of his attack, turning it into a political issue.[10] And yet Perón seems to have been – in this case – more careful of constitutional detail than Frondizi would be a few years later.

Perón's decision to negotiate with Standard Oil had been prompted by the hope that Shell and Esso could be lured at a later stage without insisting on their own model contracts, something Perón could not grant without offending nationalist sensibilities. This was exactly the same strategy that Frigerio undertook in 1958.[11] When Perón sent the proposed Standard Oil contract to Congress, he expected this to be a very first step, since he thought Congress would reject the contract outrightly. His next move would have been to take the objections set by Congress to the oil company, using them as a further basis in the protracted process of negotiation.[12] This alleged strategy was of course thwarted by the events of September 1955. Since Perón's intention to make oil concessions to an American company was widely used at the time as one reason for his overthrow, given the fragile basis of support on which Aramburu's government rested, it did not find it easy to acknowledge that Perón had been right after all. Nevertheless, the first hint that oil nationalism was not going to be harnessed was provided by Vice-President Rojas on 13 December 1957, on the occasion of the 50th anniversary of the discovery of petroleum in Argentina. He said that though richly endowed in petroleum, Argentina was spending on oil imports US $280 million per year by 1957 – either the petroleum policy was wrong or, if it was right, it was being badly executed. The Trade and Industry minister, Dr Cueto Rúa continued with the same theme and went further, explaining the dramatic medium-term financial difficulties the country would be in if it went on importing oil to meet its needs. The solution was self-sufficiency, and this in turn meant an investment of approximately US $314 million per year in order to attain it by 1960. Until then, it was more undesirable to import petroleum than to obtain it from oilfields exploited by private firms. But he did not explain how such sums would be obtained. The omission did not escape the notice of the British ambassador, who analysing – and discarding – internal sources of finance, concluded that the only sources from which the capital necessary to develop Argentine oil might be forthcoming appeared to be the large international oil companies, especially Esso and Shell. He added that it was 'well known that these companies, and others, would be most ready to extend their operations and make large investments in exploration and exploitation provided these were on a concession basis'.[13] His conclusion, alas, was pessimistic:

> Any rational solution of Argentina's petroleum problem is, however, virtually precluded at present by the prejudice and sentiment, which have been built up into a national psychosis against allowing foreign companies to lay their hands in any way on Argentine oil. [. . .] Argentina has become a victim of her own unhealthy brand of nationalism. The granting of outright concessions to foreign oil companies [. . .] was, ironically enough, the belated conversion of Perón to [their need] that was given as a main reason for his overthrow.[14]

Less than two months later, and in the heat of the electoral campaign, the 'Yadarola Plan' launched by Aramburu's ambassador in Washington, and a close associate of UCRP's Ricardo Balbín, received ample coverage in the Argentine press. The plan offered a half-way solution between total state control and handing over the industry to free enterprise, based on the granting of leases rather than the former type of 99-year concessions. The UCRI denounced the plan, but Yadarola was unrepentant and his views, according to Sir John Ward – who thought the timing of the launching 'left something to be desired' – represented those of 'a growing sector of opinion'.[15] Cueto Rúa released the Yadarola plan so that the public might 'judge it for themselves' immediately after a fact-finding visit of President-elect Frondizi to his office which gave rise to rumours that Cueto Rúa might remain in office under the Frondizi administration. According to Babini, this meeting was the watershed that changed Frondizi's thinking on oil.[16] Four months after Sir John Ward remarked that, however much credit Frondizi was given for 'intelligence and "flexibility"' it remained to be seen 'whether he will – or can – perform an about-face on so politically critical a question as petroleum at the beginning of his term of office', the then President Frondizi launched his 'Petroleum Battle'.[17]

(b) The Batalla del Petróleo

The memory of Frondizi's passionate opposition to Perón's oil contract, his verve and persuasion reflected not only in his brilliant addresses in the Lower Chamber, but in the compactly argued 400 pages of his book *Petróleo y Política*, was too fresh in people's minds when on 24 July 1958, less than three months after taking office, he launched his *Batalla del Petróleo*.[18] Although he won the battle in the short-run (by 1962 Argentina had become almost self-sufficient in petroleum needs) one can argue that in the long run the passions surrounding the totally unexpected and secretive manner of the contracts, lay behind President Illia's UCRP administration decision in 1964 to annul the Frondizi contracts, in line with the party's oft-repeated pledges.[19]

The *Batalla del Petróleo* speech was an emotional address in standard rhetorical register. Amongst other things it castigated the 'agro-importing structure' not just for maintaining Argentina in a state of underdevelopment, but for reinforcing the country's dependence on the importation of petroleum, thereby threatening the country's 'ability for self-determination', as well as its sovereignty. 'Powerful interests' had in the past 'hindered [YPF's] efficiency'.[20] With government support YPF would achieve the planned target of a yearly production 'not inferior to almost 16 million cubic metres, or more than three times present production'.[21] The surprise came towards the end, when the president announced that YPF would resort to the 'co-operation of private capital'. Moreover, a series of contracts and letters of intent had already been signed, pride of place given to a 'general agreement' with a group of US firms which had undertaken to drill 4,000 wells in six years in areas 'selected by YPF'. Perhaps to soften the impact that the announcement was bound to have in left-wing circles where Frondizi had been regarded as the champion of anti-imperialism, he included a dramatic announcement that at 6:30 p.m. that evening the Soviet Ambassador had informed the Argentine government that the

Soviet Government was ready to sell to Argentina oil-drilling equipment in exchange for raw materials, 'on a long-term basis', implying that this barter would somehow cost Argentina nothing.[22]

Frondizi concluded his speech stating that in use of his presidential prerogatives, he had 'exceptionally' undertaken to sign direct contracts. The contracts themselves contradicted the passionate anti-imperialist plea made by Frondizi in *Petróleo y Política*, where he had denounced the imperialist *modus operandi*, without distinguishing between 'bad' and 'good' foreign capital as both he and Frigerio would do a year later.[23] YPF, whose experience had contributed to 'the formation of an emancipating national conscience', showed that the 'government of monopolies' could be replaced by 'non-capitalist organisations'.[24] If there was a role in the economic realm for private enterprise, this was in the 'non-nationalised sectors'.[25] All this was in direct contradiction to Intransigent thinking, so it was hardly surprising that Frondizi's 24 July speech caused a major upset within UCRI ranks.[26] The British ambassador on his part, found it 'difficult not to be disappointed and depressed by this much heralded "Frondizi solution"' given that Frondizi's calculations of immediate benefits that would accrue seemed to be based on a 'degree of statistical optimism too extreme to be attributed wholly to naiveté'.[27] He feared the 'dazzling prospective' presented by the president was 'bound to lull the Argentine people into further complacency'.[28]

The plan managed to upset all and sundry. Yadarola complained that Frondizi had 'stolen his ideas', Cueto Rúa did not think the agreements so far were either 'convenient or adequate', Alsogaray said he could have no confidence in a plan run by YPF, an 'outstanding example of State interference . . . characteristic of totalitarian regimes', Balbín made one of his habitual raving comments ('the scenery was superior to the contents, which needed to be concrete and basic'), and nobody failed to point out that Frondizi had acted unconstitutionally in allowing the signature of even such letters-of-intent as had been signed. In Congress, UCRP deputies asked the Executive to submit the contracts and all relevant background information for their analysis by the Legislative Power, in an attempt to restore constitutional procedure.[29] But Frondizi chose to ignore the opportunity for a public debate. Years after the event he was still defensive about his oil policies, simpling adducing 'the experience of government' as the reason for his change of mind.[30] There are ample testimonies – including Frigerio's – that the decision to grant concessions to foreign firms had been devised as early as January or February 1958, and possibly much earlier.[31]

The chief criticisms levelled at the contracts – setting aside the issue of Frondizi's ideological inconsistencies and accusations of 'selling-out national sovereignty' – were firstly, that they were negotiated secretively, and without the participation of either Congress or the relevant governmental agencies and secondly, that YPF was being financially 'suffocated' in favour of Shell and Esso. The technical matters were discussed at length by Arturo Sábato in his defence of the policies he was responsible for carrying out as the president's 'Personal Delegate in YPF'.[32] It was the secretiveness, the suspicion that there were ulterior motives behind the decision, that the plan was a smoke-screen for 'concessions' to the oil giants, that was at the start of the erosion of public confidence in Frondizi that eventually led to his overthrow.

(c) The Oil Contracts: Frigerio's integracionista style and Frondizi's 'Machiavellian' tactics
All violations of the UCRI platform were invariably blamed on Frigerio and his *integracionista* approach. In fact, *integracionista* became a stigma purporting to depict everything that was wrong with the government and its policies. The speech that had produced such wide disappointment at first was later reinterpreted – at least by the British, since the Argentine public would remain in the dark – in the light of what Señor Puricelli, the Shell representative in Argentina, described as 'a piece of window-dressing to prepare the Argentine public for the real business to come'.[33] Puricelli said that Frondizi knew that his 'plan' was unlikely to succeed and that when that became too apparent 'and the country is even nearer to ruin', he would be able to turn to the people and explain that although he had tried to avoid it, 'the sole and inevitable solution' was 'to bring in the big foreign oil companies'. Puricelli added that the latter would then only 'agree to this on what would for all practical purposes be a concession basis'.[34]

The drastic reversal of Radical thinking that the contracts entailed gave rise to widespread rumours and accusations of peculation.[35] Although a Congressional Commission of Enquiry set up in 1964 was unable to prove the existence of peculation, Frigerio's replies were ambiguous enough to reinforce the overall impression of an unorthodox style of wheeling-and-dealing.[36] Misgivings about what was really going on were widespread. On 3 September the British Commercial Counsellor in the Caracas Embassy quoted an Associated Press report indicating that the agreement concluded between YPF and Loeb Rhoades & Co. (one of the 'US group') apparently indicated that the Argentine State enterprise would retain ownership and the right to dispose of all oil produced, while the American company would provide all the capital required and shoulder all the risk involved: 'we can hardly believe that they would do this without some hidden benefits', and he added that the agreement also appeared to contain 'other unusual provisions'.[37]

Notwithstanding the insistence that 'only three people' had been involved in the negotiation of the contracts, it seems that at different times there were a score of unofficial 'representatives' or 'intermediaries' invested – either by Frondizi or Frigerio – with different tasks. Such were the cases of Víctor Madanes, Peronist entrepreneur exiled in Montevideo since 1955, and of freelance journalist Emilio Perina. Madanes had acted in representation of the 'US group' and although Frigerio admitted meeting Mr Madanes in Montevideo, he was adamant this was in 1957 and that oil was not the subject of discussion. The point that an inquisitive deputy was trying to make in 1964 was that the change in oil policy had occurred long before Frondizi was elected, and the tacit suggestion was that the presumably substantial monetary commissions derived from the oil contracts had been part of the lure utilised to bring Perón into signing the Pact.

Frigerio had no previous experience in the field of petroleum, and he did not deem it necessary to seek expert advise. Instead, at 'many different addresses in Buenos Aires [. . .] problems were analysed and solutions arrived at [. . .] with the cooperation of all citizens and men of the national movement'.[38] The latter did not include most technical experts of YPF, since the contracts were 'a matter of emergency and priority', implying that it would have taken far too much time to seek their opinion.[39] In a speech broadcast on the national network on 28 September 1958 Frondizi replied to criticisms about the haste with which the contracts were agreed, saying that an international tender 'would have entailed considerable delays', and the 'emergency situation' in which he had found the country warranted immediate action.[40] The centrality that the oil question had for Frigerio and Frondizi was offered as justification for the secrecy surrounding the negotiation of the contracts. A member of the inner *frigerista* circle explained that the contracts were never sent to Congress because 'the aspect of urgency indicated the need to avoid the Congressional instance, something that would have given rise to endless debates'.[41] The man who had so ferociously castigated Perón in Congress on the occasion of the California contract knew how paralysing an effective opposition could be. But by going over the head of Congress Frondizi did not stop public debate; rather, he encouraged the frequently slanderous character of some of that debate. While it is true that the UCRP's draft bills and resolutions on oil were sometimes vague and almost invariably populist and demagogic, it is no less true that they responded to a tradition spanning half a century, tradition which until 1957 had been eloquently upheld by Frondizi himself. Although Frondizi was right in recognising what Aramburu, Perón and Alvear had recognised before him, the upholding of the 'ends and means' argument had implicit in it that the means (concessions to foreign oil companies) were questionable, and therefore postponed a reasoned approach to petroleum exploitation for another thirty years. Whereas for Frigerio, Sábato and Frondizi the oil contracts had become the symbol of a 'revolution' achieved, for many UCRI congressmen, party members and voters, it stood regrettably as the hallmark of a revolution corrupted.

The Amnesty Law and State of Siege Legislation

An analysis of the themes, arguments, and symbols that congressmen used to construct and justify their support of, or opposition to, the government reveal much about the hierarchies of beliefs and attitudes that alternatively brought together or divided UCRP and UCRI deputies. The oil contracts provided one such theme, and on this occasion the UCRI chose to dodge the issue on procedural considerations, responding to Frondizi's reluctance to have the subject discussed in the Chamber – nor would the UCRI have gained anything by exposing itself to the kind of grilling they had been used to inflicting on the Peronist benches in the period 1946–55. But alas, there were other equally prickly subjects that had to be tackled, however unpalatable: freedom of education, the appointment of an acerbic critic of the UCRI as Economy minister, and the frequent resort to repressive legislation, were the most ostensible.

(a) The Amnesty Law
The banner of legality wielded during the presidential campaign entailed the abolition of the repressive – that is, anti-Peronist – legislation enforced by the *Libertadora*. Throughout the campaign Frondizi had repeatedly promised an ample amnesty to cover political and trade union prisoners. The text sent to Congress on 5 May 1958 proposed an amnesty to include 'all political crimes and related ordinary and military crimes'. The accompanying letter to Congress stated the 'urgent and essential' need to establish 'a national pacification policy' in accordance with Frondizi's electoral pledges, 'to lower the curtain on all that has happened until this precise moment'.[42] The law explicitly included the lifting of all proscriptions decreed by the *Libertadora*. While UCRP deputies immediately branded it as an unacceptable blanket pardon for the 'institutional violations of all sorts' incurred in by Peronism,[43] and claimed its terms were wide enough to include Perón himself, who could thus be free to return to Argentina, the Peronists were not satisfied, since they apparently had expected that

the sanctioning of the law would indeed mean the prompt return of Perón.[44] UCRP deputies remarked that the law betrayed the existence of the electoral pact, something their UCRI colleagues vehemently denied.[45] To quieten anti-Peronist hostility towards the amnesty, three weeks later the congressional National Defence Committee recommended the sanctioning of the Executive's draft project promoting General Aramburu and Admiral Rojas to the highest echelons in their respective forces, and proposing an homage to the Armed Forces.[46]

(b) The State of Siege
Frondizi's own background as defence counsel for political prisoners in the 1930s and 1940s had contributed considerably to his reputation as a left-wing politician. He had his own background in mind when he said that his government had not declared the state of siege 'out of a vocation for the use of force. My [Frondizi's] long-standing political struggle proves the opposite'.[47] During the Peronist decade the UCR had earnestly opposed all repressive legislation and its deputies – including Frondizi – had abandoned the Chamber when on 12 August 1948 the Peronist legislators sanctioned Law No 13,234 on 'Organisation of the nation in times of war'.[48] When by Decree No 9,764 of 11 November 1958 Frondizi declared the state of war in all the national territory in response to the oil-workers' strike in Mendoza Province, citing as legal antecedents Articles 27 and 28 of Law No 13,234, the UCRP opposition did not let the opportunity pass to point at yet another inconsistency between the President's past record and his present policies.

Decree No 9,764 – later approved by Congress as Law No 14,774 – established the state of siege for thirty days 'in all the territory of the Republic'. On 4 December, before the thirty days expired, a new draft bill was sent to Congress by the Executive declaring the state of siege in all the country as from the moment of the expiry of Law No 14,774, without specifying a time limit, and declaring that the Executive would lift the state of siege 'once the circumstances which had dictated its sanctioning' had disappeared. The state of siege – which remained in force throughout most Frondizi's administration – had never before been declared by a Radical government, respectful of the wording and spirit of article 23 of the Constitution.[49] According to the latter, the state of siege could only be declared in case of 'internal commotion or external attack' in the 'province or territory' where order had been upset, while its establishment and lifting were the exclusive prerogative of Congress. Neither the oil strike in Mendoza nor the dispersed cases of sabotage during the period warranted the imposition of the state of siege in all the country.

Although the Peronists resorted to sabotage and terrorism, especially after Perón's public denunciation in June 1959 of his Pact with Frondizi, the swiftness of the declaration of the state of siege and the subsequent CONINTES (Internal State Commotion)[50] Plan setting up military tribunals for those civilians who violated Law No 13,234 revealed a certain propensity in Frondizi to dictate repressive legislation, out of character with his past record, albeit in line with his sometimes paranoid vision of conspiracies – both external and internal.[51] On 30 November 1959 the UCRP submitted a draft resolution asking the Executive to include in the agenda of the current period of Extraordinary sessions the freedom of all detainees for trade union, political or social motives; the abolition of the state of siege; and the lifting of proscriptions of political parties and popular sectors [including the Communist and Peronist parties].[52]

A new wave of terrorist attacks had led the Executive on 31 July 1959 to ask Congress for the urgent consideration of a draft bill proposing the amendment of articles 211 and 212 of the Penal Code with a view to increasing the sentences on 'acts tending to public intimidation' and lifting the benefits of bail and conditional release in such cases.[53] Five months later Congress got around to the debate in which Carlos Perette said the UCRP opposed legislation that endeavoured to 'use the shield of terrorism to undertake repression, injustice . . . the detention to workers, or to cover up attitudes contrary to the interests of the country'.[54] The amendments were finally sanctioned on 16 December 1959.

(c) The CONINTES Plan
The most controversial piece of repressive legislation was the CONINTES Plan. On the occasion of his annual speech to Congress on 1 May 1960, Frondizi emphasised that the 'two great aims' of his government remained those of 'legality' and 'development'. But he acknowledged that the state of siege and the CONINTES Plan of 15 March 1960 were 'negative' albeit unavoidable aspects of the existing legality. The need for both was based on the will to 'preserve the Nation' threatened by anarchy and coups d'état; both Communists and Peronists were blamed.[55] During 1959 the government had in fact lived on the edge of disaster. To a seemingly endless series of strikes were added street disturbances, bomb throwing and organised terrorism. CONINTES sanctioned a state of emergency in which the Armed Forces were given direct control over the repression of terrorism, as well as subordinating the provincial police forces to the authority of the Army. The contentious element about CONINTES was the setting up of military tribunals, given that the Constitution established the prerequisite of the military mobilisation of the population before a civilian

could be subjected to military justice, and according to Law No 13,234 such mobilisation could only occur when it was dictated by the imperative of national defence, in cases of catastrophes or serious emergencies.

4 FRONDIZI AND THE JUDICIARY

While the issue of the independence of the three constitutional powers figured in all of Frondizi's major speeches whenever he mentioned the return to democracy, in practice the Executive tended to trespass into Legislative and Judicial jurisdictions. For a President for whom 'legality' was paramount, the predicament of the Judiciary thrown into disarray by Perón's interference received little attention. And when it did, it became the source of bitter contention. On taking the oath of the five members of the newly constituted Supreme Court of Justice, Frondizi had said : 'We shall have independent judges who will pass sentence according to the law, and over whom it will not be possible even to attempt to exert pressures or influences of any sort.' Frondizi promised that the rule of law 'must not constitute another means of upholding an economic and social "status" founded on injustice'. Towards the end of his speech, mention was made of the need for 'ethical assurances' stemming from 'the absolute trust that the people have in the moral integrity of the men it has chosen to administer justice'.[56] Two of the judges appointed by the *Libertadora* on 1 October 1955 were confirmed – they were Alfredo Orgaz, President of the Supreme Court, and Benjamín Villegas Basavilbaso. The new members of the tribunal were A. D. Aráoz de Lamadrid, long-standing member of the UCR and UCRI delegate to the 1957 Constituent Assembly; Luis María Boffi Boggero, an independent who had had been deprived of his Chair in Law at the University of Buenos Aires by the Peronist purge of 1946 (he was reinstated in 1955), and Julio César Oyhanarte, at 37 the youngest member, from a traditional UCR family, who had been elected deputy for the UCRI in February 1958 but did not take his seat in the expectation of his appointment to the Court.

At the beginning of July 1958, and for the first time in the history of the country, Frondizi declared the whole of the Judiciary to be *en comisión*, thus allowing him to remove from office countless magistrates named by the government of the *Libertadora*.[57] Not surprisingly, his decision caused a major uproar since in the light of his earlier speech the President was casting doubts on the integrity of the dismissed magistrates. On 8 July, Orgaz presented his resignation after a series of unruly demonstrations opposite the Palace of Justice to protest at the removal of the magistrates. In Oyhanarte's words, 'there were many who felt that Frondizi's behaviour [in dismissing the judges] was exhorbitant and lacking in respect [to the judiciary]. A sort of abuse of the law'.[58] *La Nación* published Orgaz's letter of resignation on 9 July in which the president of the Supreme Court declared that the chief motive for his resignation was

> the manifest impoverishment of the administration of justice produced by the current reorganisation which has resulted from [. . .] partisan interests and tactics being given predominance over the true interests of justice and of the Nation.

A week later Orgaz retracted his resignation when most of the redundancies in the federal justice as well as some of the new appointments had been withdrawn by the Executive.[59] But when twenty months later the Executive took the political decision of increasing the number of judges in the Supreme Court from six to seven, 'without taking into account the real needs of the tribunal', this time Orgaz submitted his irrevocable resignation.[60] The previous month he had requested leave for reasons of 'moral fatigue', and now he stated that the increase in the number of Supreme Court members 'brought to a peak a [personal] process of despondency that [it was at that point] useless to try to repress or prolong'.[61] Orgaz had been only the most prominent of the many judges to tender their resignations, thus on 8 July the total disintegration of one of the Powers of the State was only forestalled when the members of the Supreme Court declared an indefinite 'judiciary holiday'. Their 'manifest intention', according to Oyhanarte's account, had been to allow Frondizi time to reconsider. Ten days later normal activities were resumed, and all the former magistrates were at their respective benches. According to Oyhanarte, the president had had the courage to rectify his mistake, and from that moment onwards 'there was not even a hint of interference in the activities of the judges'.[62] Oyhanarte replaced Orgaz in the presidency of the supreme tribunal, and many years later the former learnt that the attempted removal of the magistrates had been part of the pre-electoral agreement with Perón.[63] The non-observance of the clause in the Pact requiring the elimination of magistrates who had been involved in acts of political persecution against Peronists was one more reason why Perón chose in June 1959 to publicise the existence of the secret agreement between himself and Frondizi.

5 CONCLUSIONS

Consistent with his belief in the 'scientific' and 'technical' basis of his analysis, Frigerio operated in the conviction that he knew best where the interests of the country lay and how to pursue them. Notwithstanding his long political and congressional career, in many instances Frondizi seemed to accept Frigerio's premise, thereby disregarding the need for debate, discussion and negotiation.[64]

A series of partial elections held in several provinces showed that early on in 1959 the government had lost the Peronist electorate, who had switched back to blank voting, and was only supported by about a fifth of the voting population. Elections held in the provinces of Catamarca, Corrientes, Santa Fe and Jujuy showed that voter preferences were on average divided between Peronists (that is, blank ballots) with approximately 25 per cent of votes, followed by the UCRI and the UCRP with about 20 per cent each, a small proportion of Communist and Socialist votes, and an array of small Right-wing parties which were gaining ground with a combined total of around 20 per cent. In the national Chamber of Deputies 102 seats were contested, and the UCRP saw its seats increased by 52, totalling 76, while the UCRI saw its number reduced to 110. What the results symbolised was the failure of Frigerio's integrationist approach. The abandonment of the UCRI by Perón's followers signalled the rupture of the 'national front'. Frigerio was not the type to accept facts that did not tally with his expectations, and he squarely placed the blame for the losses on UCRI shoulders. Analysing the election results of 27 March 1960, he wrote:

> There is no doubt that the lack of coherence and consequence of the official party contributed to the electoral defeat. It is also necessary to take into account the boastfulness and smugness of some of its leaders, their isolation previous to the elections, their practical inefficacy when faced with popular confusion, the inclination of the State apparatus to give in to anti-popular interests, a mixture of pride and contempt vis-à-vis the allies that took them to power . . . [65]

By the end of 1959 Frondizi had largely lost the support of those who had voted him into power and was effectively governing with the backing of those who, for the most part, had opposed him in 1958. This inevitably undermined the government's claims to be the embodiment of democratic and constitutional virtue, revealing it instead as a minority government operating under a state of siege and dependent for its life, as shall be seen, on the continued support of the armed forces. Further erosion of the claim of 'a full working democracy' came from the evidence that political parties exerted very little influence on the course of events in 1959, compared with organised labour and the military. Vested interests, plus the sub rosa exploits of many in the president's entourage, continually challenged democratic functioning. And without a properly functioning democratic political system there is little hope that democratic values will be promoted in society.

7 Frondizi's Relations with the Political Parties

1 FRONDIZI AND THE UCRI

Introduction

Frigerio and his *integracionistas* could arguably be regarded as rivals of the parliamentary leadership, often dictating to it through the president. All too frequently Frondizi followed the advise put forth by Frigerio rather than heed the voice of his own party colleagues. And yet, with a few notable exceptions, the party was at times the only prop for a government orphaned of support. It must be borne in mind that there had not been a UCR government for 28 years; the UCRI not only had to learn to act as government, it had not yet had time to redefine its own identity as a party. As it turned out, it would not achieve it under Frondizi and the UCR is still struggling to do so today. The UCRI missed its chance in a tacit struggle against a small group of men who had monopolised the president's ear, and who were bent on carrying out policies of their own, bearing no relation with any political tradition in the government's ranks, however convenient they found it to invoke *Yrigoyenismo* when it suited their purposes. For the most part, political considerations were overruled by 'technological' ones, reflecting Frigerio's undaunted belief in the allegedly scientific character of his analyses.

The split of the UCR had resulted in one party – the UCRP – regrouping the pre-existing factions: Intransigents, Unionists and *Sabattinistas* were still together in the UCRP. The other party – the UCRI – and its leader, Arturo Frondizi, never succeeded in renovating their aims and purposes before finding themselves with the responsibility of government. This lack of clarity and purpose resulted in a majority of party members and activists acting on the belief that the UCRI programme was the Avellaneda Charter of the old Intransigence, while Frondizi and Frigerio had been busy redefining the contours of future government policy. The UCRI did not seem to realise that reheated *Yrigoyenismo*, anti-imperialist rhetoric and big-State dogma were no longer enough. In its predicament as a party without an ideology, the UCRI found itself without the defences against intruders that an ideology provides, defining the frontiers of acceptable political beliefs and, by implication, acceptable political behaviour. This lack of ideology impeded the party's task of devising a coherent programme to link short-term policies and long-term goals. The UCRI's programme – as it would turn out – was industrialisation, its policy was (unbeknownst to party members, congressmen and voters) to allow massive foreign investment in industry, especially in oil, and all this under the never previously embraced banner of free-market capitalism, and openly incongruous in the context of the 'national, popular and anti-imperialist programme' that *Avellaneda* represented. UCRI congressmen thus found themselves loyally voting in Congress for policies that were anathema to the tradition of the old Intransigence. Cases in point were the amended Education Law and the economic policies first announced with the launching of the 1959 stabilisation plan, which would be implemented by the man who had hitherto embodied practically the whole of Radical demonology – Alvaro Alsogaray.

Since his first meeting with Frigerio in January 1956, Frondizi had been earnestly moving forward while allowing his party to go on looking backwards. The UCRI had inherited from the old Intransigence the lack of a comprehensive analysis of Peronism.[1] In the past, Frondizi had led accusations that the latter was insufficiently 'revolutionary', although what the revolution entailed was never defined. Frigerio, instead, had endeavoured to understand Peronism, even if such understanding was misused to justify his grand scheme, his utopian view. The UCRI, deprived of a leadership committed to its survival, was unable to transform the learning process of government into a new and coherent party philosophy. This was the result of Frondizi's neglect as much as of the party's own shortcomings. By failing to undertake its transformation, Frondizi 'destroyed' the UCRI, as several authors have accused him of doing,[2] and deprived the country of a viable, credible party that could provide a democratic alternative to Peronism and the military.

The Education Law

Of the policy reversals that characterised the year 1958, the Executive's decision to send to Congress at the end of August a draft proposal for the amendment of Article 28 of the Education Law in favour of 'freedom of education' was the least surprising. Subsequently to his 1957 *Qué* interview, Frondizi had stated that he was 'not in favour of the State monopoly' in education.[3] This statement was quoted by UCRI deputy Oscar López Serrot in an attempt to remind congressmen on both sides of the Chamber that freedom of education had become party policy, since on 24 August 1957 the UCRI National Committee had declared that 'all the statements of UCRI candidates are part of the party's commitment to the Argentine people'.[4] Frondizi's 21 February speech, upholding freedom of education in accordance with Article 14 of the Constitution, added that the State would 'keep its obligations, granting all the necessary support to official institutions, and investing large resources in its education and popular culture programmes'. But he adroitly evaded the controversial issue in the proposed amendment of Article 28 of the Education Law: the creation of private universities.

As soon as national newspapers published on 26 August the Executive's proposal to amend the Education Law, students started mobilising against it. The first street demonstrations and public meetings were in support of *laica* (lay) education, and against *libre* (free) education, equated with religious education. One of the president's brothers, Risieri Frondizi, Rector of the University of Buenos Aires, launched the campaign against the government at a public meeting organised by the University of Buenos Aires students' union (FUBA). Risieri Frondizi said that he was not against freedom of education but against the right of unqualified institutions to grant official degrees, adding that Argentine culture was 'threatened [. . .] by circumstantial political commitments. [. . .] Dark forces moved furtively while we were working quietly and peacefully. We were unprepared for this'.[5] On 15 September an editorial in *La Nación* reported that children and adolescents had declared themselves on strike and were taking part in acts of violence. On that day, the supporters of 'free' education gathered opposite the Congress building. Amongst other speakers, Juan Carrizo, introduced by the organisers as 'a worker', attacked the idea of the State monopoly of education as a 'dire instrument' that had 'prevented the consolidation of the working class given the individualist traits it imposed on the national soul'.[6] When the demonstrators marched to Plaza de Mayo they were rewarded by the appearance of Frondizi and other officials in the balcony of Government House, the *Casa Rosada*. During the counter-demonstration organised by FUBA four days later to denounce 'the pressures of the Church hierarchy, the oligarchy, imperialism, "fascists" [and] foreign capital [. . .] in order to shape our minds in accordance with their own interests', the main balcony of the Casa Rosada remained empty.[7] Most notable amongst the speakers criticising the government were José Luis Romero, who had been Rector of the University of Buenos Aires as a result of the Socialist drive in higher education encouraged by the *Libertadora*, and his Secretary at that institution, Ismael Viñas. Both speakers accused 'American capital', 'reactionary forces' and 'a clerical plan' to take over education and culture in Argentina.

The debate in Congress was no less passionate. The parliamentary Education Committee issued a majority report that went against the government's recommendation to amend Article 28 of Decree No 6403/55 favouring private education. The membership of parliamentary committees reflected partisan representation in Congress; thus, the recommendation meant that a majority of UCRI members sided with the UCRP opposition. None the less, the final vote would be in favour of the amendment, even though the depth of feeling within UCRI ranks was strong enough for the leader of the majority to acknowledge that 'we must respect the problems of conscience that the nature of the issue has provoked in some members on our benches'.[8] Still, the loyalty that the government commanded was remarkable in some cases, such as that of López Serrot who had represented Intransigence in the *Libertadora*'s *Junta Consultiva Nacional* and had on that occasion opposed Education minister Atilio Dell'Oro Maini's Article 28 stating that 'private initiative may create free universities'.[9] This time López Serrot said 'this is a transcendental [. . .] debate. Ours is an historical decision. The Republic advances as a new freedom is enshrined. This is a step with revolutionary resonances'.[10] For other UCRI congressmen, 'revolution' in educational matters was too closely equated with the 1918 Reformist movement – and its lay, statist, and anti-clerical traits – to allow them to vote in favour of what they regarded as a violation of its principles.[11] The writings of Gabriel del Mazo were often cited in the debate to oppose the government. The bewilderment of many when Frondizi did not appoint del Mazo to head the Education Ministry was now dispelled. Del Mazo would have been in an impossible situation had he been heading the Ministry of Education in September 1958.

It is arguable whether the government's timing was justified in bringing up an issue that would provoke such passionate opposition. At a time when the country had hardly digested the implications of the 'Oil Battle', to confront it with another issue charged with ingrained emotions and prejudices can only be justified in the light of Frondizi's and Frigerio's anxiety to be seen as keeping their promise to the various components of the 'national movement' – in this case the Catholic Church. Only this can explain their dogged determination to keep stirring unrest in the increasingly disappointed middle sectors.[12] From the nationalist ranks close to Frigerio, the uproar was attributed to the *Libertadora's* decision to hand the universities to a 'communist-liberal coterie' trying to 'disfigure the Christian physiognomy of our national being'.[13] The fact remains that however laudable the principles of freedom of education, the president was seen as manipulating principles and values in pursuit of political gains.

With hindsight, it is possible to state that the price paid for the support of the Church was too high in terms of the government's widespread loss of trust and credibility. The expected gains were measured not only in terms of the advisability of seeking the support of the Church in the light of Perón's experience, but also in terms of securing the support of Monsignor Antonio Plaza, Archbishop of La Plata, renowned for his Peronist sympathies. Monsignor Plaza was seen as performing a key role in the *integracionista* attempt to bring Peronist workers into the UCRI fold.[14]

Frondizi's Lack of Political Loyalties

While 'treachery', 'double-crossing', 'deceit', 'personal disloyalty', are words that spring immediately to most people's minds when talking of Frondizi, those who still consider themselves his friends tend to remark on his personal loyalty. Nevertheless, when asked to name specific cases in which such loyalty was demonstrated, Frigerio's name was the first and only one mentioned. It would seem more a matter of people who have themselves remained loyal to Frondizi regardless of his conduct towards them.[15] An analysis of the several crises where the question of personal loyalty was a consideration reveals that, true to Frondizi's and Frigerio's historicist approach, the 'objective forces of History' prevailed over personal loyalties. Vice-president Gómez was never a personal friend and his own behaviour was itself lacking in loyalty to his President, but Governor Zanichelli was a case in point. So was the UCRI, which Frondizi manipulated rather than nurtured to use as his true support base.

(a) The Resignation of the Vice-President
Alejandro Gómez, *el maestro de Beravebú*, as he was dismissively known in a reference to the small provincial town in Santa Fe where he had worked all his life as a primary school teacher, had emerged as a compromise candidate in the 1957 Tucumán Convention of the UCR to share the presidential ticket with Frondizi. As a small-town politician, he was loyal to his party's tradition, in this case, the Intransigence, and was widely regarded as a 'good man', devoid of the sophistication – not infrequently equated with an inclination for mischief – of his big-city colleagues.[16] During the presidential campaign Frondizi had placed him in charge of a Committee for Political Action, based at the UCRI Rio Bamba headquarters, and – ignorant of the role played by the Luis M.Campos headquarters – ostensibly to run the campaign stressing Frondizi's image as a family man instead of 'emphasising his intellectual and technical abilities'.[17]

Just as other UCRI members and supporters, the vice-president had been taken by surprise by some of the government's announcements, mainly those concerning the amnesty law and the law allowing the entry of foreign capital. But it was not until the issue of the oil contracts arose that his disquiet turned to hostility. Apparently there were a series of meetings at the Naval Centre in August 1958, attended amongst others by Socialists Alfredo Palacios and Américo Ghioldi, and UCRP members Carlos Perette and Miguel Angel Zavala Ortiz, in which the overthrow of the government was discussed and Gómez's name was mentioned as a replacement for Frondizi, given that he was 'easily controllable'.[18]

This conspiratorial climate had presumably rubbed off on the vice-president, who had been meeting socially his old friends Palacios, Ghioldi and Luciano Molinas. On 9 September Gómez sent a memorandum to Frondizi asking him to deliver a 'realist message to the Argentine people', stating that 'those praising directly or indirectly the runaway tyrant [Perón] and communists' should be denied constitutional guarantees.[19] There is no doubting the sincerity of the preoccupations of a man so close to the core of the government,[20] just as the naiveté of his actions, while the *frigerista* version preferred to portray Gómez's letter as another instance in which 'the oligarchy showed its hand'.[21] Had the president taken the trouble to bring his vice-president nearer to his confidence, it is arguable that the whole episode could have been averted. As it happened, Gómez could be excused for thinking that it was his duty to salvage the best of a tradition that was being irretrievably eroded by little-known men pursuing little-known aims.[22] The announcement of the state of siege on 11 November started the snowball that culminated in the vice-president's resignation.

At the time Frondizi was ill in bed, and Gómez saw it fit to approach Interior minister Vítolo to acquaint him with an impending military coup, suggesting that the way to avert it would be to name a cabinet of national unity headed by himself – Gómez – given the president's illness. Notified by his minister, a weak and feverish Frondizi went to the Casa Rosada where he met with the three military secretaries, Vítolo, and Gómez. In the course of that meeting the military dismissed the vice-president's denunciation of a coup and asked to be told the source of the information. Gómez refused to disclose the name of his informant[23] and that evening newspapers carried reports of the 'vice-president's plot'. The UCRI, appeased by Frigerio's resignation ten days earlier (see below), issued a communiqué via its National Committee declaring its solidarity with Frondizi, and denouncing 'the colonialist oligarchy linked to the imperialist interests of oil trusts and cartels which are trying, by any means, to prevent YPF from achieving for the Nation its energy solution applying the contracts . . . with independent companies'.[24] Simultaneously, the UCRI bloc of deputies declared its solidarity with Frondizi demanding the vice-president's immediate resignation. The next few days, which saw the vice-president's office in the Senate ransacked, and its luckless occupier heckled and physically abused by parliamentary and party colleagues, bore the 'pathetic traits of a small-town melodrama'.[25] The shameful behaviour of most UCRI representatives led Arturo Zanichelli, governor of Córdoba, and Fernando Pirágine Niveiro, governor of Corrientes, to mediate, obtaining an exchange of letters between Frondizi and Gómez, resulting in the latter tending his resignation on 18 November and Frondizi declaring that Gómez was not 'a traitor' but 'a man of honour and an honest collaborator',[26] and the UCRI issued a public statement 'reviewing its previous decision' and 'cancelling all party sanctions against Dr Gómez as well as the request for his resignation from the vice-presidency'.[27] According to Potash's account, following Gómez's own, the attacks on Gómez to force his resignation 'appear to have been orchestrated by Frondizi, or at least carried out with his knowledge and consent'.[28] Even though Frondizi had enough motivations to want to rid himself of Gómez – unarguably, the vice-president had become a thorn on the President's side – to attribute the sequence of events to an elaborate conspiracy to shed the vice-president while inflicting the minimum damage on the party, seems somewhat exaggerated. As Babini points out, Frondizi had too many worries at the time – starting with his own health – to give consideration to such a plan.[29]

The month of November had witnessed another resignation, even if it would prove a mere formality and did by no means entail the removal of the person concerned from the president's confidence. This was to be Frigerio's 'first resignation' – the second, and more dramatic one, would take place six months later, when Frigerio had to resign even as 'personal adviser' to the president.

(b) Frigerio, the Pact and the 'Parallel Government'

Accusations of a 'parallel administration' emerged as soon as Frondizi announced the names of his collaborators, and perhaps because they were not altogether fantastic, proved impossible to dispel, even after Frigerio's resignation on 10 November 1958. After all, the military were aware of Frigerio's nightly surreptitious visits to the presidential residence in Olivos.[30] In his capacity as Secretary for Socio-Economic Relations attached to the Presidency, Frigerio saw it as one of his tasks to persuade Peronist union leaders to collaborate with the government. This was part of the effort to 'integrate' Peronists back into mainstream politics as part of a 'national movement' to attain 'development'. To help bring about this aim, Frigerio placed his people strategically in second-rank governmental posts, while others had *de facto* rather than *de jure* posts, as was the case of Arnaldo Musich, Oscar Camilión and Marcos Merchensky.[31] Those in more visible positions were far from reassuring; they 'did not appear to have much ideological connexion with the Radical Party and they [seemed] to have mixed and somewhat disquieting backgrounds'.[32] They included Isidro Odena, a Communist sympathiser and Frondizi's Press Secretary, Elpidio Gonzalez who had 'run a successful racket in Chevrolet motorcars in Perón's days', and Dardo Cúneo, a 'Marxist Socialist'.[33] And there was the motley group of 'braintrusters' or presidential advisers, such as Jacobo Timerman and Gerardo Schamis (the only UCRI member) or de Pablo Pardo, and those part of a 'dark network of unofficial representatives', such as Nasti [sic] and Bereny.[34]

The mounting political tension in the month of November which had started with the Mendoza oil-workers' strike and culminated with the imposition of the state of siege, plus military pressures voiced by Aramburu (see below) against 'infiltrators' in the government, convinced Frigerio that he would best serve Frondizi and their common project by working in a less visible capacity. In his letter of resignation, addressed to Frondizi, he wrote:

> In the present circumstances, my withdrawal benefits more the cause we both serve than my permanence. Outside the government, dedicated fully to the national and popular policies that together we embraced, I shall continue to serve our common cause with renewed strength.[35]

Less than seven months since his emergence in public as Frondizi's closest collaborator, Frigerio had to leave his office at the Casa Rosada and instead work both from the Presidential residence in the Buenos Aires suburb of Olivos and from his own home in Avenida de los Incas. Frigerio's 'enemies' seemed to be everywhere. In a radio broadcast on 10 September 1958, General Aramburu had reflected an increasing distrust of Frigerio within the armed forces when he made a plea for the government 'to conduct the *res publica* with men of impeccable republican militancy who with their background and attitudes will offer solid guarantees'.[36] A month before Frigerio's resignation, the UCRI's Movement of Intransigent Affirmation had felt it necessary to issue a public statement vindicating the government's roots in Radicalism:

> The victory of 23 February . . . was a result of the party returning to its old sources . . . the party's standards are, and will continue to be

those of ... Alem, Yrigoyen and Lebensohn ... All sectors will have access to the government ... but the central executive core must be constituted by UCRI men.[37]

This looking backwards, reheating old Intransigent slogans, held a slim chance of winning the battle against Frigerio for Frondizi's ear since probably the battle had long been lost. Frigerio was not a party man, nor did he intend to become one. His belief in 'movements' rather than parties was part of his élitist and vanguardist conception of politics and history. When in 1977 he referred pejoratively to the *partidocracia* (the rule of parties), saying that the parties had no role to play in solving 'the Argentine crisis', he singled out their 'doctrinal void' that prevented them from representing 'the alliance of social classes and sectors' that constituted 'the national movement', while his own Movement for Integration and Development (MID) was 'geared to the change of structures, to the removal of old economic schemes and of the leadership of the traditional parties'.[38] This seems to support Babini's contention that 'it is probable that the UCRI's liquidation was a deliberate manœuvre',[39] and Rouquié's that 'the isolation of the party [UCRI] resulted from its condemnation by developmentalism'.[40] Oscar Alende, governor of Buenos Aires Province from 1 May 1958 until Frondizi decreed the federal intervention on 20 March 1962, and who throughout the period remained faithful to the tenets of Intransigence, maintains that 'that group [Frigerio's] of parvenus had set their minds on the destruction of the UCRI and on the taking over of the country'.[41] The *frigerista* version argues instead that Frondizi had no party he could rely on, except figureheads with little technical ability, although some of them concede that the 'parallel government' was a result of Frigerio's unfailing disdain for formalities.[42]

Each and every one of the policies pursued with *frigerista* zeal violated a central precept of Radicalism. The latter's long-standing anti-imperialism had been offended by the law on foreign investment; its cherished belief in oil nationalism had been challenged by the oil contracts; its proud defence of the lay, anti-clerical and statist principles of the 1918 University Reform quashed by the Education law. At the beginning of June 1959, shock waves once again shook the party when Radio Rivadavia broadcast what it asserted was the text of the Pact signed by Perón, Cooke, Frondizi and Frigerio, pact whose existence Perón had recently disclosed declaring that a year after the elections

> the people [had] been deceived and inflamed by the acts of a government which [had] increased and consolidated the depredation, violence and

sell-out of its predecessors, leading the country towards the most iniquitous political chaos, social anarchy, economic disaster and submission to foreigners.[43]

This time it was the party's staunch anti-political-agreements tradition that was threatened. In the course of a press conference on 12 June, Interior minister Vítolo declared that the allegations about the existence of a pact were part of 'a dark conspiracy', and that Perón was trying 'to lead the country to a civil war from his secure and far-away retirement'. The minister reminded the country of several occasions during January and February 1958 in which the President had denied explicitly the existence of pacts or having sent delegates to meet Perón in his Venezuelan exile. The same day newspapers carried a statement by Frigerio, who on 14 May had resigned as presidential advisor, tacitly acknowledging the reality of the pact:

> The attempt to reduce to a mere piece of paper the historic popular pact of 23 February 1958 [. . .] is but childish and ridiculous. [. . .] This pact was signed by the people with their blood, and sealed by almost five million decisions. [To discuss the pact is pointless.] I leave such task to those who dream of colonial schemes and to those who would like the people to be but an instrument in the achievement of Argentine grandeur . . .[44]

The self-righteous tone was typical of the man who an UCRP deputy described as 'the omnipotent individual in the government'.[45] It revealed once more the dogmatism of somebody who believed History was on his side, and that political realities – in this case the all too-pervasive abhorrence of Peronism in wide sections of the population – could be dismissed as irrelevant. Frondizi, who knew otherwise, repeatedly sent his Interior minister to deny that he had ever put his signature on any such piece of paper. When the debate was opened in the Chamber of Deputies, following Vítolo's statement, an UCRI deputy indignantly backed his minister and the president against the opposition's demand for a committee of enquiry:

> We are not the expression of a political pact conceived in the backrooms of dictators who shame and humiliate the democratic conscience of America. [. . .] We stress that even to conceive as possible a comparison between the statements of a man like Arturo Frondizi and a man like the former dictator [Perón] implies a total lack of control, the absence of all

common sense, to cast into total oblivion what it means to respect the hierarchy achieved in the course of a long political militancy.[46]

This rhetoric did not suffice to persuade the opposition, who harboured no doubts as to the existence of the Pact.[47] This time there were no desertions from the UCRI ranks, and a resolution was passed affirming that those 'false accusations' about the existence of an alleged Pact were part of a 'subversive plan to alter the constitutional order of the Republic and frustrate Argentina's economic development'.[48] The UCRI was once more on the defensive, barely a month after it had relished in Frigerio's resignation. An UCRI deputy had told a journalist off the record that 'from "integration" we have now moved on to liberation'.[49] But this had not been enough to quell the widespread unrest, as reflected in an editorial published by *La Nación* on 23 June, the day the whole cabinet resigned: 'The country is living at a time of confusion. The restlessness in some military garrisons . . . only reflects the prevailing widespread uncertainty . . . Our crisis is moral and political.'

In an apparent anticipation of Alsogaray's appointment, the newspaper defended the stabilisation plan, but criticised its implementation by officials of a dirigiste mentality. This was the same criticism Alsogaray had made to the plan six months earlier, predicting that if the government continued down that path, 'failure would inevitably lead to a people's republic modelled along Communist lines'.[50] When the new Cabinet was announced the next day, Alvaro Alsogaray emerged as the replacement for both the Labour and Economy ministers.

(c) Alsogaray's Appointment: the UCRI is Challenged

For UCRI deputies, Alsogaray's appointment was difficult to take, as Frondizi himself has acknowledged:

> [. . .] although the UCRI did not like Alsogaray's appointment, the party accepted it and defended it in Congress because it understood the role that Alsogaray played in the politico-military stabilisation, and also – it moves me to recall this because the party's solidarity with my government's actions always seemed admirable to me – the appointment was accepted as another proof of trust in their president.[51]

Nelly Casas, a loyal *frondicista*, recalls that

> when the news of Alsogaray's appointment reached the streets, nobody could believe it; neither friends nor enemies of the government. [. . .]

Frondizi's friends in the UCRI harboured no illusions, since they did not trust the man who had come to replace two party bulwarks: Bléjer and del Carril, but above all, because [Alsogaray's appointment] was the clear proof of a new reversal in the president's policies.[52]

On 25 June *La Nación* reported widespread displeasure amongst UCRI members at Alsogaray's appointment, and the decision of the UCRI bloc of deputies to name a committee to interview Frondizi to tell him about their 'anxieties'. According to the newspaper's report, the president said he understood the feelings of the deputies, but that he had taken the decision 'exercising the faculties given him by the Constitution'. In the end, the bloc issued a statement in which Alsogaray's name was not mentioned. It was approved by 40 votes in favour, 32 against, and four abstentions. UCRI solidarity with Frondizi seemed increasingly to be in inverse correlation with internal cohesion. Deputy Liceaga, who had offered to resign his seat over the DINIE controversy on a matter of principle, took a much less principled stance a year later. He concluded his speech in defence of the government's economic policies saying that the urgency was to 'save the Nation', and in pursuit of this 'if necessary, we shall go as far as hell's gates to make a pact with the devil, and enter hell and bring out the torch that will illuminate the Argentine future and provide the energy needed for the great national transformation'.[53]

Why was the UCRI so ineffective? Why had the majority of those men and women who had so decisively fought for the predominance of Intransigence within the old UCR, given up their traditionally principled position and agreed to become little more than the president's echo? Babini, who from his post as Under-secretary to Vítolo at the Interior Ministry attempted to refloat the UCRI to provide the President with strong partisan support to replace Frigerio's influence,[54] has a none-too charitable explanation. In his view, UCRI members in the spheres of the legislatures and government, at a central, provincial or municipal level, were too busy with their own 'personal projects' to be bothered with the fate of the party.[55] Rouquié provides a similar explanation. The UCRI backed Frondizi at every instance because its members 'needed the support of the government so as not to lose their posts'.[56] And yet, remarking that Frondizi's Government suffered 'from political schizophrenia', an American official concluded that the 'ultimate solution' for such a condition appeared to be 'either the conversion of UCRI members into conservatives, or the separation of Alsogaray from the Cabinet' with all that this might mean for the economic programme.[57] Permanence, rather than performance, seemed once more the overriding factor in the UCRI's decision to back the intervention of the Province of Córdoba, just as permanence rather than performance would become Frondizi's overwhelming concern by 1961.

(d) The Federal Intervention of the Province of Córdoba
An event that threatened yet again with splitting the UCRI was the Executive's draft bill to declare the federal intervention in the Province of Córdoba. By mid-1960 the political climate was at simmering point. The consequences of Alsogaray's harshly recessive implementation of the stabilisation plan were being felt and the labour movement had responded accordingly; the denunciation of the electoral pact with Perón had left its mark both amongst UCRI members and on the opposition. Furthermore, the developments in Cuba and the mounting momentum of the Cold War had sensitised the military to unprecedented levels. The emergence of rural guerrilla groups in the northern provinces of Tucumán and Salta in the wake of Castro's success did not help to allay fears within the armed forces that Argentina was headed down the slippery road towards communism. Their success in achieving Frigerio's 'second resignation" as well as in ridding the government of all acknowledged *frigeristas*, had highlighted their encroachment in the political sphere.

In February 1960 the War Secretary had accused Tucumán's governor, Celestino Gelsi, of not having acted decisively enough on the emergence of *Comandante Uturunco*'s guerrillas – the first Peronist emulators of the Sierra Maestra.[58] The governor replied that the army had not precisely made a show of efficiency when confronted with young, inexperienced 'fighters',[59] inaugurating with his statements what would become a political tradition in Argentina, whereby armed groups set to topple democratically-constituted governments were never explicitly and unambiguously condemned by politicians. In Gelsi's defence it must be said that in those early days the Cuban experience invested all such attempts with an aura of romanticism. While Gelsi rode the storm – including a parliamentary interpellation[60] – his colleague from the province of Córdoba was less fortunate.

The CONINTES Plan had begun to be implemented on 12 March 1960; on 2 April the War Secretary and the CONINTES military authorities denounced Perón as the mastermind behind a terrorist campaign. Throughout the months of April and May there was a series of bomb attacks on diverse targets (the offices of an anti-Peronist businessman, the Central Police Department, the UCRI headquarters in Rio Bamba Street), the most serious of which was in Córdoba, where six people died as a result of a bomb attack on oil deposits owned by SHELL. In open conflict with the military authorities of the province, who on 24 April had taken over control of all prison establishments in Córdoba, five days later the Supreme Court ordered the transfer to a civilian court of seven detainees held under military jurisdiction. On 12 May *La Nación* reported that General Toranzo Montero, who in his capacity as Army Commander-in-Chief, was also CONINTES supreme commander, had submitted to the president CONINTES Report No 3. The latter was directed against the civilian authorities of Córdoba, and mainly against the governor, Arturo Zanichelli, who was accused of collusion in 1958 with Peronists now responsible for the terrorist campaign in that province.[61] What the military were in fact doing was accusing Frondizi for the events in Córdoba, implying that Zanichelli's policy was a direct consequence of the President's pact with Perón and of the *integracionista* approach *vis-à-vis* the Peronists.[62]

La Nación reported on 4 June that on the previous day General Toranzo Montero and Army Secretary Larcher had met Frondizi for half an hour before Vítolo announced that the Executive had sent to Congress a draft bill proposing the federal intervention of Córdoba. According to Article 6 of the Constitution, the extreme resort to federal intervention should only be used 'to guarantee the republican form of government or to repel external invasion' and in response to 'a request by the provincial authorities to sustain or re-establish them in case they have been deposed by sedition or invasion by another province'. UCRI congressmen opposed the intervention on the grounds that there were no constitutional reasons that justified it, but most UCRP deputies were in favour of the extreme measure against the provincial executive authorities.[63] In fact, the Intransigent faction within the UCRP, led by Balbín, was against the intervention, although it demanded Zanichelli's resignation. Balbín's argument was that the only one truly responsible for the situation in Córdoba was Frondizi, and that it was the president who had to be impeached.

From his sick bed in a clinic in Buenos Aires, Zanichelli let it be known that he had no intention of resigning – *La Nación* reported that Frigerio had been among the visitors to the clinic who had tried to persuade the governor to resign – since 'there was no institutional conflict' and the CONINTES report 'made accusations but did not admit any defence'.[64] But in an editorial published the following day, the newspaper dismissed as 'innocuous' Zanichelli's 'apparent defence' when accused of 'connivance with activities or attitudes that were turning his province into a subversive focus', and added that links between the UCRI and Peronism in Córdoba were 'getting stronger all the time'.[65] In point of fact, and as Frondizi told a group of UCRI congressmen who went to see him to discuss the Córdoba situation, there was a threat of a military coup against the central authorities if the Córdoba intervention was not decreed. The British Embassy report for 1960 corroborated Frondizi's version, remarking that the Córdoba intervention was the first 'practical manifestation' of a growing feeling, especially in the army, that 'the Government must be saved from its own incapacity effectively to eradicate peronist and communist subversion and to put the country on its feet both economically and spiritually'.[66] Frondizi accepted then to sacrifice Zanichelli in order to save himself.

In a Chamber dominated by the UCRI – the UCRP deputies had left the room on a point of procedure, and thus avoided taking a vote that would have split them – the federal intervention was approved on 11 June: fourteen UCRI deputies voted against it, but the majority was 84 in favour, even though the debate left little doubt that deputies were voting out of loyalty to Frondizi rather than out of personal conviction as to the wisdom of, or indeed the need for the intervention.[67] Zanichelli had left his bed at the clinic and in a deplorable physical condition had been a silent spectator at the debate for an hour. Visibly moved, on leaving the building of Congress he had declared to reporters that he had 'come to see what proofs there were against me, and also to witness how my colleagues cut my throat'.[68]

The episode highlighted that secretive connexions of politicians, with the suspicion of politics they engendered, provoked the impatience with constitutional processes of those who wanted to continue with the 'cleansing operation' left unfinished by the *Libertadora*. In the words of the British Ambassador, it all revealed the 'moral crisis' that Vítolo often referred to and which the Ambassador believed was a symptom of the fact that 'behind a thin shell of a western type democratic state' there lurked 'a jungle of violence, intimidation and survival of the toughest'. He singled out the trade unions, the military, the administration and professional politics.[69]

The Zanichelli saga did little to enhance the President's tarnished image, revealing his weakness when confronted with military pressure, as well as his predisposition to forsake *integracionismo* in order to preserve an administration that relied increasingly on the hopes it had placed on an economic plan that was already behind schedule. Nor did the party come out unscathed, and its convention, meeting six months later, attested to its demise.

(e) The Chascomús Convention
The party statutes of the UCRI were the same as those of the old UCR. The statutes allowed for a considerable degree of independence of provincial federations, replicating the federal organisation established by the Constitution. The provinces and the Federal Capital of Buenos Aires

sent the same number of delegates to the National Convention as they did to the national Congress; the delegates were chosen for four years by the direct vote of all party members in their respective district, and they could not be national deputies. The aims of the National Convention were to set the party programme for each presidential period; to choose the presidential candidates, and to administer party funds. The maximum party body was the National Committee, constituted by four delegates per province, chosen for two years.

The National Convention meeting on 16–19 December 1960 in the town of Chascomús in Buenos Aires Province had the purpose of drawing a new manifesto since the fact that *Avellaneda* was still the official UCRI programme meant that UCRI deputies were vulnerable to the opposition's jibes on this matter, especially when the government was accused of 'treason' to *Avellaneda*'s principles. In the event, the Convention, instrument of policy-making as laid down in the party constitution, was shown as docile and impotent when it swiftly sanctioned *ex-post facto* all governmental decisions as constituting 'official party policies'. In his opening speech to the Convention, the president of the National Committee, Senator Alfredo García said that 'it is not a question of abandoning any of Radicalism's old banners – neither is it necessary – , nor is it a question of altering principles, but simply of adapting them'.[70] Eleven national deputies who insisted that both banners and principles had indeed been abandoned, were expelled from the party. Chascomús was but a low-key victory parade for Frondizi. The Steering Committee of the Convention was charged with preparing the final document 'which will express the UCRI's identity and solidarity with the government of Dr Arturo Frondizi'. Its main points were:

1. National development: 'as the expression of a national conscience, the aims of Radicalism are those of the Nation as a whole. Intransigence will be the tool for national liberation'.
2. The unity of national development, in the creation of sources of energy; intensification of the production of steel and iron; building of roads and railways; encouragement of investment and industry, 'private enterprise, be it national or foreign, must not be hindered by bureaucratic hurdles'.
3. Social policy: one labour federation and one business federation; labour and industry must harmonise their endeavours to achieve national objectives and increase production.
4. Cultural policy: freedom of education to prepare the men needed for the development of the country.
5. Foreign policy: ratification of the traditional policies of peace,

respect for national sovereignty and the principle of non-intervention.[71]

The Chascomús programme had not reformulated *Avellaneda*, but instead had enunciated a new programme which shared with Radicalism its pretension to interpret the national interest. As *La Nación* remarked in an editorial comment on Chascomús:

> It is a new step . . . a guarantee of the UCRI's path towards the Right . . . The UCRI cannot force those who believe in legality, in national union and in development, to adhere to the government. [. . .] The difference between the new and the old Right is that while the latter points at the ethical and moral roots of our crisis, the former focuses on the economy . . . a kind of upside down Marxism.[72]

Whether intentional or not, Frondizi's and Frigerio's insistence on the primacy of movement over party resulted in the destruction of the UCRI. In a letter to Alfredo García dated 6 June 1961 offering advice on the selection of candidates for the elections to be held in December of that same year, Frondizi said that it was not for him, as President of all Argentines, to give advice to the party, but that the UCRI should not feel constrained to name as candidates only those who were party members, since 'what [mattered was] their coincidence in the great national objectives'. The UCRI had to defend 'a national programme based on the collective consciousness of the needs of the Nation, over and above partisan sectarianisms, class interests or ideological stands'.[73] Even so, when seven months later Frondizi presented the UCRI with a list of *frigeristas* to be included in the list of candidates to Congress in the March 1962 elections, the UCRI resisted. *La Nación* reported on 1 February 1962 that in the UCRI's list of candidates to deputies for the Province of Buenos Aires

> there were one or two names suggestive of extreme Left-wing ideas, alien to the party, another who symbolises an extreme nationalist position of an opposite sign [while Frondizi had to desist of another candidate] since his ideological origin was considered an insult to the Governor of the province [Alende] and to the Radicalism of the province itself.[74]

But the UCRI was much less successful in negotiating the list of candidates for the Federal Capital: in this case Frondizi accepted only four of the thirty names proposed by the party. The split of the UCRI in 1963 led by former governor Oscar Alende could not come as a surprise.

While Alende kept the UCRI's name, Frondizi left to set up, together with Frigerio, their minuscule MID.

2 FRONDIZI AND THE LEGAL OPPOSITION

The UCRP

The change of image that all governments undergo (and which perhaps came too soon for the Frondizi administration) did not revitalise the official UCRP opposition, which was not seen as an effective alternative: this resulted partly from the anomaly of there being an official (UCRP) as well as an unofficial (Peronist) opposition, and partly from the UCRP's own limitations. The UCRP's victory over the UCRI in the March 1960 elections was more the result of the Peronists deserting the UCRI than of any electoral swing in the electorate. Increasingly anti-Peronist in its stand, the UCRP could offer no alternative to the government but the vague populism of *Avellaneda*. As one UCRI deputy cried out during a debate in the Lower Chamber: 'our programme is the same as yours, but the people did not vote for you'.[75] The UCRP was ambiguously dedicated to the concept of 'the moral and spiritual well-being of man', a definition not altogether helpful to someone hoping for an indication of a possible (even if not probable) set of policies.[76]

Interestingly, while proclaiming itself the true inheritor of Radicalism, the UCRP was also keen to dispel its image as a statist and economically interventionist party. Opening the debate on the stabilisation plan, UCRP bloc leader Anselmo Marini stated that his party was equally distanced from 'the laissez-faire of extreme liberals as from totalitarian dirigisme'.[77] Throughout the four years of the developmentalist experiment, the UCRP concentrated its attacks on the government centred around a few issues. These were: (a) the government's 'sell out' to foreign companies; (b) its poor record on citizens' rights, given the almost permanent state of siege; (c) the 'moral crisis' arising from the government's conduct, the climate of *affairisme*[78] and the existence of a 'parallel' government; (d) its secretive dealings with Peronism. The last two points were underlined especially during the UCRP's contacts with the military. In the case of contacts with Peronism, Balbín himself had secretly sent emissaries to Perón, and thus was less than frank in allowing his party to insist on the seriousness of the issue of contacts 'with the deposed dictator'.[79] That its attitude was *golpista* was revealed in the UCRP's constant demands for Frondizi's resignation, but it is also true that the government seemed almost paranoically obsessed with real or imagined *golpes*. Perette's statement in Congress – in the wake of the *pacto* revelations – in the sense that 'every month the government announces the existence of a *golpe*. [In fact] the first *golpista* in this country is the government itself', did not contribute to distend the atmosphere.[80] During a rally in Córdoba at the end of March 1959, former UCRP vice-presidential candidate Santiago del Castillo practically called for the government's overthrow, suggesting it was up to the armed forces 'to offer their services to the people for the sake of restoring national honour' in a renewed effort to save democratic institutions, 'even though it might mean shedding blood'. A US embassy official remarked that 'some leaders of the democratic opposition speak even more violently than the Communists'.[81]

The UCRP showed no moderation in its political behaviour since there was no deep abhorrence of the breakdown of politics and its replacement by military rule – unless the coup was against them, as it had been on 6 September 1930. The driving to extremes and exaggerated rhetoric had a specific audience, the military. Justifying a particularly virulent UCRP anti-government and anti-imperialist declaration, UCRP deputy Mario Bernasconi explained to a US embassy official that those were 'the things people want to hear and the UCRP is out to accommodate them'. He was referring to a motion to impeach Frondizi on his return from his trip to the United States, on the basis of his unconstitutional acts (oil contracts, imposition of the state of siege, labour legislation, etc.) and the 'sell-out of Argentina to imperialists'.[82] On the occasion of the debate of the government's bill to amend the Criminal Code to increase the penalties for acts of terrorism, UCRP Carlos Perette used a dangerously determinist argument against the government, one which was far from fair, blaming 'the actions of the Executive Power' that according to him, had 'provoked this serious social unrest, increasing political antagonisms, acute economic injustice and a divisive condition of national anguish'.[83] The past twenty-five years had not prepared Argentine politicians for the vicissitudes of political life. Remarking on Frondizi's 'calm, confident, clear, if unoriginal, statement of the case for his government' when opening congressional sessions on 1 May 1959, Sir John Ward remarked that it remained to be seen whether the speech would 'lift the level of discussion out of the murky world of rumour, gossip, and personal accusations in which so much of the political life of Argentina is carried on'.[84]

The Minority Parties

The incomplete list system sanctioned by the Sáenz Peña Law discriminated against small parties, since the party first past the post won two-thirds of the seats, while the first minority was awarded the other third. The government of the *Libertadora* had tried to balance the situation by imposing proportional representation. Although the July 1957 elections had been held according to this system, the Sáenz Peña Law was once more in force for the February 1958 general elections after repeated protests from both the UCRP and UCRI. Thus the only parties represented in Congress for the first two years of Frondizi's government were both versions of the old UCR plus the Liberal Party of Corrientes Province with two seats. True to his belief that his government should represent the national interest, Frondizi asked Interior minister Vítolo to organise a series of meetings with all opposition parties, whether represented in Congress or not. Representatives of the UCRP, Socialist Party, Progressive Democrats, Popular Conservative Democrats and Alsogaray's Independent Civic Party duly met Frondizi and Vítolo throughout the months of May to July 1958. Not unexpectedly, but to the president's disappointment, little came out of those meetings, since what Frondizi had wished for was an undertaking that the opposition would support his government's policies.[85] The only party that was not implacably opposed to the government was the relatively new Christian Democratic Party, pressing for 'worker-participation in capitalism's benefits' and urging a change in the government's 'methods, attitudes and procedures'.[86] Inspired by Pope John XXIII's renovating doctrine, an enlightened Catholicism had started to displace Catholic Nationalists from lay organisations.[87] The conservative Federation of Centre Parties was much less guarded in its language, demanding 'moral authority' from the government and charging it with being 'a main factor of disturbance and the one which more persistently and efficaciously attempts against its own stability'.[88]

Nevertheless, the bitterest attacks came from the Socialists, whose fortunes had been revitalised by the liberalising intentions of the government of the *Libertadora*. This could scarcely contribute to the party's hopes of gaining back some of the popular support they had lost to 'Perón's demagogy' which had so 'misled the masses'.[89] Dissenting voices had begun to be heard after 1955 – the voices of those who thought the Socialist Party would have to moderate its anti-Peronism as well as its pro-*Libertadora* stand if it was to recover popular appeal. Such voices were in the majority at the time of the Socialist Party Congress held in the city of Rosario in July 1958, when the 'reactionary' minority led by such socialist bulwarks as Ghioldi and Nicolás Repetto, were expelled from the party. By the end of 1959 there were two Socialist parties. Ghioldi's minority became the Socialist Democratic Party (PSD), while the majority constituted the Argentine Socialist Party (PSA). Paradoxically, the PSA would prove the frailer of the two,[90] since its ranks were divided between pro-Peronists, several brands of pro-Communists,[91] and a few pro-*frondicistas*, while the PSD retained its old ideology and thus its internal coherence. By 1961, the faction including Alfredo Palacios, Alicia Moreau de Justo and Carlos Sánchez Viamonte had managed to retain control of the PSA name, while a multiplicity of left-wing splinter groups had emerged.[92]

A constructive opposition was certainly needed and Frondizi would never have it. Yet there was also a need for the government to concede the benefit of the doubt to those who had a different view of the national interest, without constantly doubting their patriotism and good faith. Frondizi was unwilling to acknowledge that a destructive opposition is not by definition 'evil and anti-national', but intolerant and emotional. It was for the government to offer an example of tolerance and reasonableness towards its legal opposition, in particular when it was simultaneously confronted with an opposition beyond the realm of democratic politics.

8 Government and Society: the External Constraints. The Third Aim: 'Social Peace'

1 INTRODUCTION

Concentrating on the pressures on the government, this chapter will seek to analyse the external framework, that is, the extent to which the institutional fabric of the nation obstructed or assisted in Frondizi's plan. The focus will be on the government's opponents, having in mind the fallacy of the argument that maintains that the power of any group (or alliance of groups) is of fixed magnitude, since this power most often arises from specific conditions and situations. The fallacy is evident in arguments such as 'the entrepreneurs, the exporters – or whomever – were the main force behind such and such a government'.

To achieve 'social peace', class conflict would have to be replaced by harmony between the 'social classes and sectors' part of Frigerio's 'national movement'. Uppermost amongst those classes and sectors were the intellectuals, the entrepreneurs, the workers and the military.[1] As will be seen, the desired social peace was unforthcoming, and the national movement disintegrated long before it could even become more than a mere aspiration.

2 DEVELOPMENTALISM AND INTELLECTUALS

Introduction

While in 1955 the State was taken over by a group that did not know what to do with it – whether to dismantle the scaffolding put in place by Perón, as Alsogaray passionately desired, or keep it for their own ends, as in Lonardi's abortive attempt, or perhaps find a half-way solution, as the developmentalists wanted – in the cultural and artistic realms the late 1950s and early 1960s marked a period of remarkable expansion and creativity. While the struggle to appropriate the edifice of the State went on at one level, society was seeking to express itself via channels that had been barred during the Peronist decade.

Peronism had had no place nor respect for intellectuals. As a response to university students backing the anti-Peronist Democratic Union in 1946, the regime adopted the slogan: '*Alpargatas sí, libros no*' ('Espadrilles – footwear favoured by factory workers – in, books out'). Within Peronism's Manichean view of the world, intellectuals belonged to the camp of the anti-people. Thus, liberals on the right and left welcomed with differing degrees of relief the end of a system that at worst had persecuted them, at best had ignored them. While the politicians in the Socialist Party embraced the *Libertadora* uncritically, its intellectuals, led by the newly-appointed Rector of the University of Buenos Aires, José Luis Romero, took over that institution from the 'Right-wing obscurantism of Catholics and Nationalists' in control throughout the Peronist period. Grateful to the *Libertadora* for having opened a space for them in society, they remained discreet in their overt praise, mindful of the fact that 'the masses', albeit 'misguidedly', remained Peronist. And 'the masses' were the chief concern of both right and left-wing intellectuals who saw their personal quest for 'truth' and 'certainty' – rather pretentiously – as inseparable from the Nation's quest to find its 'soul'.

World War II, the ensuing Cold War and the decolonisation of Asia and Africa were all exceptional processes experienced vicariously by the intellectuals of Spanish America. While during the Peronist decade the grandchildren of Spanish immigrants looked towards a backward-looking Spain, first- and second-generation descendants of Italian and East European immigrants sought their opportunity to shape the destiny of their country of birth according to the premises – and promises – of socialism. The liberal words – if not deeds – of the *Libertadora* opened up a path that apparently could only be extended and widened by the candidate of the Intransigence. Typically uncomfortable when thinking about power, in the realm of morals the left-wing intellectuals were at ease. They believed that History was on their side, that it had an aim and direction. This idealisation gave rise to enthusiasm and excitement, to be followed by despondency and disillusionment when things did not turn out quite as expected. No such feelings overpowered the right-wing intellectuals, who did not expect anything from History and was therefore less prone to disenchantment.

The Right

The Right in Argentina was never more than a handful of coteries, of individuals who, beyond their embrace of nationalism, seemed to have very little else in common. There were Catholic and liberal, free-trade and interventionist, aristocratic and populist versions.[2] It has already been seen how those nationalists who had abandoned Perón as a result of the latter's confrontation with the Catholic Church, attempted a comeback with Lonardi – and failed.[3] Two of those same men who had so aroused the fear and anger of liberals such as General Aramburu, were to return to the limelight with Frondizi; they were Mario Amadeo and Luis María de Pablo Pardo, the former, UN ambassador, and the latter advisor at the Ministry of Foreign Affairs, while a young man close to them, Carlos Florit, was placed at the head of this same Ministry – only to resign on 22 May 1959 as part of the first retreat of *frigeristas* .

The need for 'realism' and 'pragmatism' expounded in the pages of *Qué* and translated into a policy of *rapprochement* with the Catholic Church, as well as the insistence on a 'national movement' which would include the workers – all couched in the language of 'national grandeur' dear to the nationalists – was bound to attract at least a certain style of nationalist for whom the premises of *Avellaneda* – and for that matter the tradition of Radicalism as a whole – were anathema. Yet as early as 1955 some nationalists recognised in Frondizi a different kind of Radical, and Matías Sánchez Sorondo, that renowned anti-Semite and anti-communist who had been Uriburu's Interior minister, sought a meeting with Frondizi, then president of the UCR's National Committee. Babini recalled that Frondizi came out of that meeting 'deeply impressed by the intellectual brilliance of the Right'.[4] But not all nationalists were attracted to Frondizi, and there remained those who, from the pages of two periodicals, *Azul y Blanco* and *Mayoría*, relentlessly denounced a government bent on imposing policies 'lacking in spiritual direction' and allegedly only interested in administering a country industrialised by and for US interests. Furthermore, the presence in government of Marxists did not escape the attention of this more extreme version of the Right. Right-wing liberals (the *gorilas*) shared this apprehension – if little else – with right-wing nationalists. Obsessed by both communism and Peronism, they found little comfort in Frondizi's apparent conversion to free-trade economics when Frigerio was simultaneously engaged in the 'integration' of Peronism. The denunciation of Marxists in the governmental ranks was not exclusive to the Right. *La Nación* of 11 July 1958 reported that during a public meeting organised by the UCRP in Plaza Constitución, Balbín had demanded that 'the Sovietised Marxists be removed', while Zavala Ortiz mocked the government's 'slogan' of the 'rule of law', demanding to know 'what kind of legality is this, protected by communists, nationalists and Peronists?'[5]

Attitudes on the Right towards Frondizi's government remained mixed throughout his period in office; the same cannot be said of the Left which shifted from guarded optimism to positive enthusiasm during the campaign, very soon to turn to bitter disappointment when confronted with what it described as the 'treason of the national bourgeoisie'.

The Left

Since 1952, a group of independent left-wing intellectuals (writers, university graduates and journalists most conspicuously represented by the brothers Ismael and David Viñas, León Rozitchner, Ramón Alcalde, Susana Fiorito, Tulio Halperín Donghi, Noé Jitrik, Osiris Troiani and Rodolfo Pandolfi) had been publishing a monthly journal, *Contorno*. Publication significantly stopped in 1958. Its first issue had eight pages and 300 copies were printed, but in its heyday *Contorno* became an ideological guide in intellectual circles selling 10,000 copies, chiefly in the bookshops of Corrientes Avenue in Buenos Aires, and among students of the Faculty of Philosophy and Letters.[6] Their position *vis-à-vis* Peronism, while endeavouring to maintain a critical detachment, was more critical than anything else. Once the *Libertadora* took over, they began a process of soul-searching to understand what had happened during the previous decade, ten years in which they had not been allowed to play any role, and to define what their attitude towards the future ought to be. Their conclusion was to support the UCRI and Frondizi. What follows is an analysis of their reasons for doing so and of their ensuing disenchantment.

(a) Contorno's Analysis of Peronism
In July 1956 the journal devoted a whole issue to analyse what Peronism had meant from a left-wing point of view, and in particular what it had meant to middle-class intellectuals committed to the idea of socialism. While generally concluding that Peronism had represented a stunted vernacular version of fascism, the massive support it had received from the working classes needed justification if the latter were to continue to be defined, according to Marxian thinking, as the 'agent of revolution'. In this the Left coincided with the Right, concluding that Perón had misguided, misled and deceived the working classes, which had thus

fallen into a state of 'alienation'. The proletariat 'had seen the repression of their strikes, their brothers persecuted', but they 'could not understand it, because they were truly alienated'.[7] But Peronism notwithstanding, the proletariat had acquired 'a consciousness of the oppressed', a 'new language'. Rozitchner's psycho-philosophical interpretation of the proletariat's adherence to Perón utilised Kantian categories:

> Revolution is . . . the free causality described by Kant when he confronted the realm of morals with that of natural phenomena. The bourgeoisie, capable of being free *vis-à-vis* what is natural, becomes natural and annihilates its freedom. The proletariat, being 'natural', . . . wishes to become free [. . .] 'free *vis-à-vis* the bourgeoisie'. What does it matter then to back Perón, or whoever, if through that submission liberation can be accomplished?[8]

But there was no such Peronist 'revolution' since there had been no 'transformation of the consciousness of men at the same time as the transformation of the forms of production', therefore Argentines were 'not socially mature for a revolution'.[9] Intellectuals had their share of guilt for that predicament. They had remained marginal to society: 'neither wholly bourgeois, and even less so proletarian, [they] lacked a place in the country'.[10] The present moment was similar to that experienced by 'some people at the end of the last war – we are living the transition from the ideal to the real'. Troiani also tried to convey the guilt feelings of the *Contorno* intellectuals. Noting that their generation had 'left no legacy', he lamented 'We are guilty, we know we are guilty' because Perón's fall had produced a collective 'feeling of relief' which was 'sinful, because we had left the tunnel behind, but the country had not'. Intellectuals had felt that 'Mankind was going somewhere, History had a meaning, and thus, so did [their] own existence . . . All that was individualistic . . . had something scandalous about it, something obscene. [. . .]. To what extent did we consider [Perón] harmful because we personally found him unbearable?'[11] The opportunity was now present to break away from the isolation of the intellectual, and it could be achieved by backing, if not a 'revolution', at least a 'national and popular programme' that would promote 'a regime of revolutionary and anti-imperialist' contents, including nationalisations, the foundation of heavy industry and protectionism.[12] The clue lay in finding 'the language that will allow us to communicate with the Peronist masses', since *'there is no other way out: without the working class there is no democracy'*.[13]

(b) Contorno and Frondicismo

The gap dividing the contributors of *Contorno* and the public statements of the UCRI's presidential candidate was increasingly narrow.[14] Pandolfi wrote of the need to achieve a 'national union', one which would include 'the government, those entrepreneurs interested in developing a domestic industry, workers, peasants, intellectuals, men from our armed forces' – add the Church, which one is inclined to think Pandolfi deliberately left out, and the 'national union' bears an uncanny similitude to Frigerio's 'national movement'. The need was dictated by the existing conditions; Pandolfi called for realism when he wrote:

> I am amongst those who aspire to the abolition of *capitalism*. But *here* and *today*, *in our country* – and in the whole of Latin America – the path of *social revolution* is through *national revolution*. That is why, *here* and *today*, *perhaps* even before being *revolutionary*, it is necessary to work so that our people will conquer the right to be revolutionary tomorrow.[15]

Accordingly, most of *Contorno*'s contributors joined the UCRI, the only party whose leader talked about modernisation and offered a vision of the future. Moreover, Radicalism offered to intellectuals keen to become 'integrated with the popular classes', the tradition of a 'popular' party. Explaining the decision to join the UCRI, Ismael Viñas wrote that it was 'indispensable to enter an effective and real political movement rather than to raise *entelechias*',[16] and the UCRI – albeit 'handicapped by the limitations and ambiguities of the middle class' – had been able to

1. Formulate a basic programme sufficient as a starting point for a change of structures,
2. Create a group of cadres who postulate vividly such a position and who believe in the active participation of the popular classes in the life of the nation;
3. Maintain the ease to *feel popular*, the tendency to understand popular reactions and to become one with them.[17]

Viñas identified within Intransigence a group he termed 'orthodox' – they were those men and women who shared the unmistakable leftist propositions expounded by Frondizi in *Petróleo y Política,* a logical sequitur to the ideas contained in *Avellaneda*. José Liceaga and his wife Marisa Muñoz, both to become UCRI deputies, had written about the need to hand political power to the people in order to change social structures, abolish private property and the social division in classes.[18] But they recognised that the country was not as yet ready for such drastic transformations, and that therefore it was necessary to undergo certain stages, the impending one being that of a 'capitalistic, bourgeois democracy'.[19] The link with developmentalist thinking was evident: the conditions were not ripe for a revolution, and the only alternative that would at least open the revolutionary path was that offered by Frondizi.[20] However, *Contorno* recognised that there were risks in supporting Frondizi, and these involved chiefly the growing influence of Frigerio and what Viñas defined as the *tecnólogos* – those for whom technical considerations were uppermost. The confrontation between the latter and the men of *Contorno* had first surfaced in June 1957, on occasion of Frondizi's declarations in *Qué* favouring freedom of education.

Qué wrote dismissively that 'it is not worth stooping to fight the small battle against the existentialists who think their personal problem is the problem of the whole country'.[21] In *Qué*'s interpretation, principles had to be replaced by pragmatism. For the Left, on the other hand, certain principles could not be replaced without in fact abandoning the path towards 'revolution'. When reminiscing about his relations with left-wing intellectuals, Frondizi criticised those 'principled ideologues' who supported him during the campaign, the 'idyllic stage', but then opposed him remorselessly: once again he suggested the need to distinguish between a 'morality of ends' and a 'morality of means', implicitly condemning the former to enhance the latter.[22] Perhaps a more useful distinction would have been that between the different roles and activities of an intellectual and of a politician. While intellectuals are needed in the phase of planning and projects, once this is followed by the phase of execution, men of action are in demand. Frigerio was a rare case of a left-wing, self-taught intellectual who combined the usual feature of the intellectual's idealisation of reality with a keen awareness of power. And it was the evidence of both Frondizi's and Frigerio's ease when thinking about power that produced so many misgivings in the Left.

(c) The Disillusionment

Throughout Frondizi's years in office, while the economic structure was altered radically, various intellectual groups endeavoured frantically to overcome the isolationism of the Peronist decade. The new momentum accorded to higher education and cultural activities in general by the *Libertadora*, was continued under Frondizi. A series of cultural, educational and technical institutions were created to offer public funding for cultural and technical research.²³ During these years the Rockefeller and Ford Foundations granted generous subsidies to, amongst others, the recently founded Department of Sociology at the University of Buenos Aires, and a series of grants and scholarships made it possible for young graduates to study at American universities.²⁴ After the stifling atmosphere of the Peronist years, science and technology appeared to offer a panacea. But the Left was suspicious, and soon a neologism began to be used as an indictment of the new trends: *cientificismo*. *Cientificismo* was wrong because it purported to be a-political, because it was funded by American (that is, imperialist) money, and because social research projects could only be of use to the CIA. It was all part and parcel of Frondizi's 'treason': if 'change' was what everybody seemed concerned about, Frondizi's volte face and Castro's triumph proved that a Marxian-style, violent revolution was the only choice.²⁵ In the singular political climate provided by events in Cuba, Algeria and the former Belgian Congo, intellectuals revived the Leninist notion of an enlightened vanguard – something Frigerio was actively putting into practice, even if in his case the 'light' came from a different source.

Although it remains true that while all this was happening in Argentina and in the world, the political parties remained stagnant, all the blame cannot be placed on the parties, since intellectuals and young people turned their backs on them, dazzled by the romantic, idealistic, self-sacrificing aura of armed struggle, which they contrasted with the duplicity, pragmatism and self-interest of everyday politics and politicians. Those intellectuals grouped in *Contorno* who had hoped to find an institutionalised political arena in which to develop their contained energies, conceded to their peers who had remained adamantly critical of such 'bourgeois institutions' that they had been right all along. 'Democracy', Rozitchner wrote, 'is a fiction, and a formal concession'.²⁶ Once Frondizi abandoned the principled component in his discourse, and appeared to move from the realm of extreme principles and almost self-righteous positions, to their exact opposite, that is, the world governed by winks and nudges, pragmatism and versatility, intellectuals abandoned him.²⁷ In a chest-beating exercise, they once again – as with Peronism – attributed their folly in supporting Frondizi to their own irredeemable condition as members of the middle classes.²⁸ Rozitchner wrote in November 1958:

> Credulity or betrayal, the political dilemma is, for many, shameful. Those who contributed to the electoral victory are leaving, with sorrow in their soul. [. . .] So great is the gap between the statements of the candidate and the actions of the ruler, so incredible

the feeling of frustration, that the awaited explanations are the touchstone for self-esteem that everyone has: to have been deceived as children, not to have seen the intentions behind the declarations. Each and everyone who voted for him feels guilty of the utmost foolishness.[29]

While intellectuals were disappointed by the oil contracts, the decision to back private education, the economic policies that favoured foreign investment, and the closure of Left-wing periodicals, and accused Frondizi of favouring 'capitalist, bourgeois interests', the alleged beneficiaries of such favouritism (the domestic entrepreneurs) felt betrayed by the importance attributed to foreign capital and the lack of policies geared to protect their interests, replaced instead by an espousal of free-trade economics.

3 DEVELOPMENTALISM AND ENTREPRENEURS

Introduction

As part of his grand scheme Frigerio had embarked in the pages of *Qué* on an indoctrination campaign to persuade industrial entrepreneurs of the urgency and unavoidable responsibility of taking up their leading role in bringing about the 'revolutionary' transformation of the Argentine economy.[30] The answer to Argentina's predicament as an underdeveloped country, based on technical solutions, efficiency, productivity and private enterprise, should have been naturally attractive to these sectors. Frigerio's defence of private enterprise went back to 1956, when he wrote in an editorial that 'profit-making is an incentive that mobilises resources and creates the unifying factor of those forces without which the country condemns itself to stagnation' and to this end private enterprise should be protected from the 'invasion by the State'.[31]

Protection for domestic industries was explicitly promised in *Qué*, and it was offered on a person to person basis by Frondizi's Secretary Schmukler in exchange for campaign funds.[32] Instead, frontiers were open widely to foreign investment under the aegis of free-trade economics.[33] But, was there a 'national bourgeoisie', or was its existence merely hypothetical? Were Frondizi and Frigerio trying to build an Argentine capitalism without Argentine capitalists? If they indeed existed, what was their role to be? And could Frigerio be said to 'represent' them?

Protectionism and the 'National Bourgeoisie'

On 1 May 1956 *Qué* carried an article entitled 'PROTECTION to ensure the existence of an industrial sector' and on 5 June an article included the sentence 'we must start now to defend domestic industries as they exist, without discrimination and with iron tenacity, given that they represent the bread of our workers and the unyielding possibility of being a Nation, against the sinister prospect of being carried back to colonial times'. By 1961 the structure of manufacturing in Argentina was quite different from that of thirty years earlier, the most significant changes prior to 1959–61 having occurred in the period 1937–9, since in the Perón years the growth of manufacturing had been little more than vegetative.[34] The protectionist system, the policy towards foreign capital, and the combined policies towards income distribution and employment have all influenced the pattern of industrialisation in Argentina since 1930. From 1931 to 1959 Argentina lived under exchange control, often reinforced by import restrictions, duties, exchange surcharges and prior deposits.[35] The protectionist system developed before 1948–50 was not well suited to stimulate a smooth transition from one stage of industrialisation to another since it created vested interests within manufacturing. Each new stage of import substitution was correctly seen as increasing the costs of existing business since domestically produced inputs were more expensive than imports.[36] Often, during those years, the output of a firm depended primarily on its luck and ability in obtaining permits to import raw materials.[37] José Gelbard, who at the time had presided over the CGE, the small and medium business federation banned by the *Libertadora* because of its corporatist overtones, and who since 1956 was working very closely with Frigerio, was presumably trying to re-establish the sort of relationship between the CGE and the government that had existed under Perón.[38] After all, *Qué* had been arguing consistently in favour of 'a sole and powerful business federation to defend the common interests of industrial entrepreneurs'.[39] But Gelbard failed to create with Frondizi a similar relationship to the one he had had with Perón. A close associate of Gelbard's pointed out how disappointed the latter had been.[40] The Argentine Industrial Union (UIA, gathering large firms) and the Argentine Agrarian Society (SRA) were critical of the government's populist economic policies of 1958, but welcomed the stabilisation plan of 1959. The CGE, true to its Peronist past, criticised the liberal features of the plan which did not respond 'to the needs and interests of the country at this stage of economic growth'.[41] What domestic entrepreneurs resented was having to compete with multinational corporations with their superior technology, better products and better organisation.[42] In the words of an Argentine entrepreneur, the developmentalist project was

> conceived by a political technocracy which preached its dogma more to attract foreign investors than to bring together the interests of domestic entrepreneurs, at that time divided between a liberal agro-exporting project and another one which defended the domestic market.[43]

Terragno appeared baffled by what he termed 'the Argentine bourgeoisie's lack of understanding of the most coherent project in half a century to stem from within it'.[44] The problem was that the project did not emerge from the bourgeoisie's bosom, but was being forced upon it by outsiders who believed firmly in the goodness of the programme they were fostering.[45] In the words of an entrepreneur who would become Technical Secretary to Frondizi in November 1961, and who was close to Frigerio and Gelbard, 'Frigerio did not represent any entrepreneurs, but rather he embodied the *will* to represent them'.[46]

Protectionism, then, was unforthcoming. Besides, the indiscriminate opening of the frontiers to foreign capital meant the collapse of scores of small, inefficient establishments that had proliferated under Perón[47] and bemused many who had believed in the defence of planning made by Frigerio in the pages of *Qué*. Instead, the list of official authorisations for foreign investment did not reveal any instance of a project designed for the exploitation at an international level of the relative advantages the country had in either natural or human resources, favouring instead capital intensive activities.[48] Not everybody agreed that such a dramatic change in the structure of manufacturing amounted to 'development'. What soon became apparent was that the developmentalist model, far from setting the foundations of a 'national movement', ended up disputed by all and sundry – with the possible exception of the military who still appeared singularly unconcerned by economic matters, overwhelmed by their obsession with Peronism and communism.

Entrepreneurs and Rational Expectations

Frigerio may have been influenced by current theories, endorsed by ECLA, in the sense that 'underdevelopment' could partly be explained by the lack of Schumpeterian entrepreneurs. But such entrepreneurs needed to act on the basis of rational expectations. In the light of arbitrary protection and mounting inflation, there was little scope for sound business planning.

The violent fluctuations in relative prices meant entrepreneurs did not respond to the price signals. With some prices going up by 40 per cent per year, and others by 30 per cent or 50 per cent, it was not always clear to many entrepreneurs caught in the inflationary spiral which relative prices were increasing or decreasing, much less which would fall or rise in the immediate future, a situation hardly conducive to rational planning for the future. Díaz Alejandro has written that 'uncertainty about future government actions has plagued Argentine entrepreneurs of all types since the war. This has led many to hope more for stable rules of the game than for favourable ones'.[49] The 'short-term mentality' that became a notable feature of Argentine entrepreneurs began to take roots during Frondizi's administration. The constant changes in the rules of the game which at first confused businessmen became part of a learning process pointing to the defence of short-term objectives. The December 1958 Industrial Promotion Law (No. 14,781), never implemented, provides an example. It gave the Executive a set of policies for the protection of the domestic manufacturing sector allowing: [a] withdrawal of tariffs for the importation of capital goods that domestic industry could not provide; [b] the raising of tariff and exchange barriers on the importation of goods that could compete with domestic production; [c] prohibition of competitive imports; [d] exchange advantages for the export of manufactured goods produced by domestic industries; [e] preferential credit facilities to domestic industry; [f] preferential treatment by public enterprises; [g] fiscal exemptions for domestic industries. But the law was never implemented much to the chagrin of domestic entrepreneurs.[50] Laura Randall has suggested that in the Argentine case the variable used to reflect market evaluations of risk should be 'the Argentine presidency' rather than interest rates since 'Argentines invest, or withhold investment, and raise prices and wages, or keep them level, based on their evaluation of the president, his programme, and his ability to enforce it'.[51] The military *planteos* and Peronist trade unionists pressures that plagued Frondizi's presidency, seriously affected the belief in such ability.

4 DEVELOPMENTALISM AND LABOUR

Introduction

No doubt with Aramburu's experience in 1956–7, when unanticipated wage increases were granted after a series of strikes, Alsogaray decided early in the stabilisation plan to make sure that the wage lag would be maintained at all costs if there were any hopes of reducing the fiscal deficit. It is for this reason that he demanded the control of the Labour Ministry together with the Economy Ministry.[52]

The possibility of a successful relationship with the unions was restricted by the existence of Peronism and the absence of Perón from Argentina. Perón's exile meant that those who swore loyalty to his person had to rely on his delegate's advise and on a constant flow of clandestine correspondence, sometimes apocryphal and/or contradictory. Cooke's influence was at its zenith during the *Libertadora*, a time when the gains that unionism could expect via negotiations with the State were at its lowest point. Political mobilisations with long-term objectives (Perón's return) that could unite the labour movement seemed the only way of guaranteeing the survival of the latter.[53] The radicalisation of their discourse found its climactic expression in the anti-bourgeois content of Cooke's messages, at a time when Frondizi had decided to deepen the 'bourgeois' character of the model of development he was trying to implement.

Workers and the National Movement

The aim of social peace demanded a disciplined work force organised in one labour federation with which entrepreneurs could negotiate. To this end, in the road to development, the workers had to be 'integrated' into the national movement.[54] The government's schizophrenia was once again evident in the contradiction between the requirements of the stabilisation plan to keep wages under control, and Frigerio's urge to integrate the working class into the national movement. With no representative in the government, trade unionists were not easily persuaded to show loyal support for a government bent on imposing wage policies that in labour's tradition were regarded as anathema. The Church hierarchy and UCRI governors (especially Gelsi and Alende) acted as mediators in 1959, seeking a compromise between the sternness the Government was showing towards labour through the then Labour minister David Bléjer, and the unions' insistence on making political as well as union demands as a condition of their cooperation.[55] While the governors' role was largely self-attributed, Frigerio's main allies in pushing 'integration' were the nationalists and the Church, who had not given up hopes of implementing the project of 'Peronism without Perón' that they had failed to achieve with Lonardi. In mid-February 1959 the press published a letter from Mario Amadeo, at the time Argentine Ambassador to the United Nations, to Frigerio urging steps for the establishment of an effective and centralised CGT, and a few days later the Catholic Bishops addressed a letter to Frondizi calling attention to the 'burdens being borne by the working class as a result of the austerity programme'.[56]

As early as 1956 Frigerio had begun to insist from the pages of *Qué* on the need to normalise union life, since 'industry requires agreements with authentic representatives of the workers' – implying that those *democráticos* who had taken over the unions under the *Libertadora* could not claim such representation.[57] In fact in 1957 membership of the '62' neo-Peronist and communist unions was less than one million, while the '32 democratic' unions had a membership of about one and a half million. Celebrating Frondizi's electoral victory, *Qué* referred to the workers as principal actors with an acute awareness of their 'historic mission' in achieving social peace.[58] Any negotiations with labour would be facilitated if there was only one body with which to contend. This was in open contradiction to Socialist stands, against a centralised body they would not be able to control. But there was another reason. At a time when Frigerio was still defending protectionism, the Socialists continued with their traditional support for free trade as the only guarantee of good and cheap products for the urban working force.[59] Frigerio wrote that only after making amends for the assault on the unions carried out by *'free labour* of Socialist inspiration' during the *Libertadora*, it would be possible for entrepreneurs and labour to reach a 'prolonged and firmly-based social peace' in order to achieve the 'material development' of Argentina on the basis of the 'integration of the labour force with a technical-economic management within the perspective of . . . national progress'.[60] The problem was that while in the case of entrepreneurs the dividends would be gathered in the foreseeable future, the role of the unions was to keep the rank and file at bay while economic development was taking place, with the promise of future prosperity and 'liberation'.[61]

During Perón's early years (1946–52), the unions had learnt to expect tangible gains in terms of wage increases and social benefits, but both were ruled out within the austere framework of the stabilisation plan. Frondizi – through Frigerio – tried a system of co-optation offering official advantages to friendly union leaders but the room for manoeuvre was limited by the need to defend the stabilisation plan.[62] Cooke wrote to Perón:

> Now that Frondizi is persuaded that social peace is no longer possible via Frigerio's path of 'top level' negotiations, he will try to achieve it through intensifying the two methods employed until now, bribery and stick [*el soborno y los palos*].[63]

That 'bribery' was proving efficacious was revealed by Cooke's comment in the sense that 'Peronism, . . . a revolutionary movement with a doctrine and a leader . . . cannot tolerate a corrupt nucleus directing it towards the "tolerated opposition" desired by the government'.[64] When neither *soborno* nor *palos* worked, Frondizi used blackmailing tactics.[65]

The State of the Unions

Facts seem to contradict myth as far as the *Libertadora's* 'anti-labour' features are concerned. If such a slant was true in the political field, as far as wages were concerned in 1956–8 manufacturing workers' real wages were higher than during any previous three-year period with the exception of the Peronist boom years 1948–50. The 1959 recession that resulted from the stabilisation plan produced a fall in real wages in all economic sectors with a simultaneous dramatic fall in the share of wage-earners in GDP. Real wages started falling at the end of 1958 and reached an historic low in the third quarter of 1959, when they started recovering, although they would not reach again the levels attained in 1957.[66] The share of all wage income in GDP fell from 46.3 per cent in 1958, to 40.4 per cent in 1959, rising slowly to 41.0 per cent in 1960 and to 43.1 per cent in 1961.[67] The conclusion is that, as far as income distribution was concerned, the deterioration of the relative position of wage-earners that had begun in 1953, worsened during the developmentalist period. Perceptions do not necessarily coincide with facts, especially so in the heavily charged atmosphere of post-Perón Argentina; it was as a consequence of Frondizi's stabilisation plan that real wages fell, and not of any 'social revenge' embarked upon by the oligarchy in 1955.

Analysing the effect of Frondizi's economic policies on wages with a view to understanding the reaction of labour, it must be said that although the rule of lagging wages in the face of accelerated inflation can explain the situation in 1959, it cannot account for the remaining years, given that in 1960 and 1961 inflation decelerated (the rates were 27 per cent and 14 per cent respectively). The explanation would lie in the increase in the prices of foodstuffs as well as in the large stocks held after the 1959 recession. These would account for the fact that entrepreneurs were not terribly worried by the threat of strikes which would have a beneficial effect by reducing stocks.[68] After the *Libertadora* began to give way to workers' pressure in 1957, the labour movement emerged in a confident mood – it was this confidence and ensuing militancy of the working class after the *Libertadora* experience that led them into the series of massive struggles that characterised 1959.

(a) The CGT Única

The existence of a sole labour confederation – the CGT *única* – had been regarded as one of the worst consequences of Peronism, not necessarily out of class hatred or mistrust, but as a result of understandable misgivings *vis-à-vis* a powerful corporate body that offered little in terms of democratic practices and values. In promising that there would only be one CGT Frondizi was consistent; it had been one of his rallying cries against the government of the *Libertadora*, and he went ahead with it, albeit belatedly, even when he was aware of the bitterness that such a decision would provoke in anti-Peronist circles. Frondizi had been very much alone in the UCR on the issue of a sole CGT, widely regarded within the party as a totalitarian instrument.[69] This was of course one aspect that made Frondizi less unpalatable in labour eyes than the rest of party politicians, regarded since Perón's days as totally hostile to labour. His insistence on the subject, notwithstanding the ill will that he knew it provoked in many circles, contributed to build Frondizi's image prior to May 1958 as a principled politician.

The Socialists had been at the forefront of the post-1955 anti-Peronist attacks on the unions, accusing Lonardi of having 'tolerated the union machinery prepared during the dictatorship'.[70] They controlled the '32 democratic unions', and the Communist Party was in control of the '19', which at this time became known as the Movement for Unity and Coordination (MUCS). In 1957 Frigerio had warned against the creation of 'combatant islands [. . .] however well-intentioned' since they could only contribute to 'the will of disintegration that inspires the oligarchy' and which would make possible 'the plans of foreign capitalism'.[71] As if on cue, Serafino Romualdi arrived in Argentina at the head of a 'joint international free labour mission to Buenos Aires', ostensibly to enquire about the plight of railwaymen who had been militarily mobilised at the end of 1958.[72]

North American unionists, with Serafino Romualdi at their head, had rallyied round anti-Peronist unions in Argentina throughout Perón's years in power. Foremost among such unions were those representing rail workers: *Unión Ferroviaria* and *La Fraternidad* (footplatemen). Therefore when these unions were at odds with the newly elected democratic regime, the defenders of 'free labour' saw it fit to mediate. In this they were successful: Romualdi recalls in his memoirs that the government acceded to their request to demobilise the railwaymen, thus creating a climate 'favourable to the initiation of a dialogue between the democratic unions and the government concerning the normalisation of the CGT'.[73] According to Romualdi, Frondizi told him that if the two rail unions managed to gather delegations 'representative of a majority of Argentine organised labour' to a CGT convention, then he, Frondizi, would 'hand the CGT to them'.[74] Romualdi records the enthusiasm with which General Toranzo Montero received the news, but that opposition politicians 'tempered their encouragement with doubts of Frondizi's sincerity'.[75] The belief that the 'democratic unionists' could have convened such an assembly had they not been 'hopelessly divided, still raked by jealousies', reveals much about Romualdi's naivety and Frondizi's astuteness in making the suggestion.[76] In the end, after July 1960 several discussions were held between the '32' (who had dropped their more *gorila* positions and preferred to be called the 'independents') and the '62' regarding the normalisation of the CGT. One of the first issues on which they agreed was to exclude the communist-controlled '19' from any future CGT. When Frondizi finally lifted the intervention of the CGT in March 1961, the Peronists were able to regain 'absolute unchallengeable control'.[77]

(b) The Trade Unions Law (Ley de Asociaciones Profesionales)
Decree-Law No. 9270/56 had encouraged the setting up of parallel unions, a central issue in liberal thinking, just as 'one union per branch of industry' and the *CGT única* were pivotal in the Peronist tradition. Great expectations had surrounded the promised labour legislation to govern the tripartite relationship between State, unions and business. Frondizi's labour law turned out to be very similar to Perón's, another source of disenchantment for liberals who had expected the dismantling of such abhorred corporatist instrument. No government since 1955 has been able to resist the temptation to exercise State control over the unions: the Labour minister could grant, suspend or withdraw a trade union's legal right to exist (*personería gremial*). For the developmentalists, this law was crucial in their strategy to bring the workers into the national movement. Alfredo Allende, Frondizi's first Labour minister, wrote that the law 'was and is the legal instrument of the working class in its struggle to affirm its national condition'.[78] And another *frigerista* has insisted that 'without a strong working class', development and economic growth 'can only contribute to increase the power of imperialism and reactionary forces'.[79]

This law ensured such a degree of government control over the unions that the politicisation of the latter was inevitable.[80] The dependent condition that linked the unions to the State was re-established by Frondizi after the *Libertadora* impasse, but in contrast to their position under Peronism, the unions now maintained the oppositionist stand they had developed during the military regime. The '32' and '62' groupings expected different things from the law; the former wished it would not sanction the need for extensive elections to renew union authorities, fearful they might lose the control over the unions they had gained in 1956;[81] the latter expected precisely the opposite, in the belief they would win any elections. Another issue was the electoral system under which the authorities would be renewed. The 'incomplete' list ensured the representation of the first minority, while the 'complete' list – favoured by the '62' – meant that all posts went to the winner. The law sanctioned by Congress fulfilled Peronist expectations, but the Trade Secretary's almost simultaneous announcement that collective wage agreements would be frozen for a year dampened any enthusiasm Peronist trade unionists might have felt. However, throughout the months of 1958 during which Frigerio remained in charge of relations with the unions, the '62' tried to keep labour conflicts under control, at a time when the '32' and the '19' were trying to extend the conflicts and generally make things as difficult as possible for the government. The '32' had denounced the Law on 13 January 1959, perhaps aware that it had been the result of long negotiations between Peronist leaders and *frigeristas*.[82]

On October 1958 the tone of the statements issued by the '62' became more demanding, until on the 10th of the month they launched a general strike against 'the cost of living', in favour of a price freeze and other specifically labour demands. Since all the union groupings took part in the strike, demands were heard both in favour of the application of the Law and of its repeal given its 'corporative-fascist' character.[83] By February 1959 the situation had changed on the labour front; the '19' were making overtures to the '62' while the '32' were showing a much more favourable attitude towards the government.[84] In a conversation with a US Embassy official – 'to keep the Embassy informed of the point of view of the Peronist sector of the Argentine labour movement' – in the home of Barrionuevo, former Undersecretary of Health under Perón, Augusto Vandor and Bernardo Cabo expressed that they had only wanted the Labour Law in order to regain control of the unions, but that they did not trust Frondizi, adding that the law was 'dangerous' because it gave the government the right to intervene in union affairs.[85] What the labour leaders really feared was legislation that would guarantee the right to strike after a secret vote of all members of the union, and it was to defend their position that they politicised industrial unrest.

The Main Confrontations

(a) The Mendoza Oil Workers Strike
The two major strikes of 1958 – doctors[86] and oil workers – were political. The Mendoza branch of the oil workers union (SUPE) decided single-handedly to present the government with an ultimatum; either the

oil contracts were annulled within 72 hours or they would go on strike. The administration's response was decisive; the state of siege was declared in all the national territory. In a message broadcast to the nation on 9 November 1958 to announce the imposition of the state of siege, Frondizi stated that the government was aware that the strike was 'part of a plan of insurrectional strikes . . . which hopes to open the path to new dictatorships'.[87] This was the first time that Frondizi made an elliptic reference to Peronism using the habitual language of the *gorilas* – the explanation must be that he was trying to dispel the opposition's accusations of what indeed were close contacts between men close to the president and the Peronists. The fact was that the Peronists within SUPE were unenthusiastic about launching a frontal attack on a government they still thought was their ally, while Radicals, Socialists and Communists were intent on discredit- ing the administration. On the same day of Frondizi's speech, Frigerio had managed to bring about an agreement between the SUPE leadership and the Labour Ministry, according to which the union would be invited to take part in the discussion and final shape of the oil contracts; however, pressures from within the government ranks made Frondizi veto such a compromise. His standing *vis-à-vis* the unions thus undermined, Frigerio thought it best to resign his post as Secretary for Socio-Economic Relations.

Although the strike was lifted after seventeen days and the '62' abandoned its intention to declare a 48-hour general strike, the state of siege was not lifted, a constant source of disquiet for the President's friends and supporters, especially since Frondizi had promised his cabinet that it would be lifted 'as soon as the danger [posed by the oil strike] is over'.[88] Dr Bléjer, who was deputy Interior minister at the time, recalled his shock when the head of the police force requested 'the list' of people to be detained. When Bléjer replied that there was no such list, the officer replied that in that case the police would use their own lists. Consequently, not only were trade union leaders who were against the oil strike jailed, but even friends of the government and officials of the administration in the provinces. The ensuing resentment was never quelled.[89]

The *Lisandro de la Torre* Strike

If in the labour front 1958 ended on the bitter note of the Mendoza- SUPE strike, 1959 began with the meat-packers' decision to strike in protest at the proposed privatisation of the *Lisandro de la Torre* municipal meat-packing plant (*frigorífico*) and turn it to the CAP (Argentine Corporation of Meat Producers).[90] Although technically a private organisation, the CAP would have some of the attributes of a State enterprise, and would always be regarded by Argentine governments as something of a 'sacred cow'.[91] But that was not how it was seen at the time, and the strike in fact was the first in what became the worst year in terms of number and extent of strikes.[92]

Workers at meat-packing plants had a tradition of union militancy. During a strike in October/November 1946 police forces had been used to break up union meetings and to guarantee access to the plants, while union leaders were jailed and their offices closed down.[93] As a result of government policies constantly favouring the unions, from 1943 until 1958 production of meat-packing houses fell 63 per cent while the number of employees increased 300 per cent.[94] On 12 January 1959 the workers had announced their opposition to the 'sell-out' of 'the national heritage' in a letter addressed to Frondizi, asking him to grant them an interview in which they would explain their position.[95] The request was not heeded until 15 January, when the union representatives were told by the president that the law was the law and could not be changed.[96] Meanwhile the union had voted in favour of a sit-in at the *Lisandro de la Torre* and in the early hours of 16 January police forces plus 22 trucks carrying soldiers and four tanks were positioned at the gates of the *frigorífico*. When the workers refused to leave the premises, a tank moved in knocking down the huge entrance gates: while the workers erected barricades inside the *frigorífico* compound, the local population of Mataderos started erecting barricades in the streets and attacking the security forces. The ensuing scenes of violence gave rise to rumours that workers had died during the military attack, and very soon the riots extended to other areas where *frigoríficos* were concentrated, La Plata, Berisso and Ensenada. In Prieto's account, when union delegates that had been conferring all night with Frigerio, went in front of a workers' assembly at the occupied *frigorífico* to inform that nine out of ten of their demands had been met, John William Cooke emerged 'brandishing a handkerchief soaked in bovine blood', claiming that 'twenty workers had been massacred' and demanding a vote in favour of a revolutionary strike.[97] That night several bombs exploded in the city – amongst their targets had been Frigerio's home, an UCRI committee, and offices of the US embassy – inaugurating a terrorist campaign led by Cooke that was maintained throughout 1959.

On 17 January the '62' declared a general strike 'for an indefinite time', demanding the repeal of the legislation affecting the *Lisandro de la Torre*, the lifting of the military mobilisation of rail-workers, an emergency wage increase across the board, and an end to the 'denationalisation plan'. While Frondizi was away on an official visit to the United States, Bléjer had ordered the mobilisation of three important unions, six interventions, the arrest of 600 union members and some docks and oil-processing areas had been declared military precincts.[98] The Communist Party's headquarters were closed down, in a series of searches of union headquarters hundreds of unionists were detained, other unions were intervened, and the CONINTES Plan was applied for the first time, declaring La Plata, Berisso and Ensenada 'military zones'. Although the general strike was lifted after four days, the meat-packers' strike went on for one month and twenty days. During that period hundreds of workers were laid off at all the *frigoríficos*: on 8 March *La Nación* reported that at the *Lisandro de la Torre* 3,800 men had gone back to work, while another 5,200 'never returned'. If Frigerio had been the casualty of the SUPE strike, Alfredo Allende resigned as a consequence of the *Lisandro de la Torre* events, blaming a 'sinister minority' [Cooke] that had wanted to 'torpedo Frondizi's trip to the United States'.[99] That the agitation was related to Frondizi's trip was confirmed by Cooke who wrote to Perón that he (Cooke) believed that Frondizi 'should not have a peaceful trip' and added that he was 'preparing a few things' for 23 January.[100]

In left-wing Peronist mythology, the *Lisandro de la Torre* became the foremost example of an insurrectional strike. On 27 February 1959 the '62' issued a statement declaring that they 'did not want to form a subversive front against the government' in confirmation of the growing gap between the union leadership and the more militant strategy devised by John William Cooke.[101] While in the case of the union leadership, radical slogans were instrumental in securing the cohesion and survival of the union movement, for Cooke such slogans and combative tactics reflected the ideals of a wider revolution.[102] Perón himself had tried to restrain his delegate when he had told him in a letter dated 7 June 1958, and referring to Frondizi:

There is no need for us to declare war against him and to start provoking a revolution. It will suffice to use the same simulation he uses to send us into a lull. If he cannot control the *gorilas*, why should we pretend we can control the People?[103]

Perón distanced himself progressively from Cooke. In a letter dated 24 July 1961, Cooke noted that he had received only two letters from Perón during 1960, and complained that the latter's 'penetrating appreciation of the historical development, both national and worldwide' lost its 'original progressive impetus' in the hands of Peronism's 'structures of leadership'.[104] Still trying to convince Perón a year later, Cooke regretted that the latter had 'chosen blind men' to lead the Movement, and pleaded with Perón to define the Peronist Movement as the only thing it could be, 'a movement of national liberation on the extreme left, in so far as it aims at substituting the capitalist regime by social forms'.[105]

Cooke's dominant position in Peronism reached its zenith at the time of the *Lisandro de la Torre* strike, and immediately after the violent scenes in which Cooke played a leading role, Peronism's Superior Coordinating Council declared that 'Cooke did not hold any function of trade union or political leadership within the movement'.[106] The insurgency tactics of Peronism were defeated, and would not be revived again until 1969, when the *Montoneros* erected Cooke posthumously as their mentor.

(c) The Rail-workers' Strike

The labour defeats of the *Lisandro de la Torre* strike and the general strike of January 1959 inaugurated a defensive phase in union tactics, at the core of which lay the corporate demands of the lifting of the interventions and the renewal of union elections. An exception was the rail strike of 1961 in which workers were determined to defend their privileged position faced with a government equally determined to put an end to labour practices that contributed to the inefficiency of an obsolete system. This puzzled many observers who believed railways were always inefficient or, as a UCRP deputy put it, 'the government's mistake is to think that the railways should not have a deficit'.[107] Answering questions in the Chamber of Deputies, Alsogaray, who would be replaced as Economy minister by Roberto Alemann on 26 April 1961, challenged the opposition to explain how to increase the revenue of the railways if fares could not be raised nor unnecessary personnel be made redundant.[108] Meanwhile, locomotives remained stationary for lack of funds to pay for needed spare parts.

The crux of the matter for the UCRP was that the rail-workers' union (UF), one of the first to be established in Argentina and the largest in terms of number of members, was controlled by Antonio Scipione, a UCRP member. The UF had managed to uphold its independence under Peronism. Several protracted strikes in 1950 and 1951 had needed Perón's personal intervention which included new salary increases and the military mobilisation of trains and rail-workers, while the union itself was intervened by the CGT.[109] On that occasion Perón emphasised his government's generosity *vis-à-vis* the rail-workers, 'to the extent of creating a rail deficit of one thousand million pesos'.[110] A new strike had begun in January 1951 to obtain the release of all jailed unionists and to stop the repressive policies of the interventor appointed by the government: the strike was declared illegal and workers mobilised into the army.[111] Nearly 2,000 workers were fired and 300 jailed, while the strike received the support of all the opposition parties. A decade later, Frondizi had to face a similar situation, and his response was not dissimilar to Perón's; he too ordered the military mobilisation of rail-workers, imprisoned hundreds of them, and ended up conceding salary increases the government had earlier dismissed as excessive.

Economy minister Alemann – who was appointed with the specific brief of reducing the budget deficit – proposed to Frondizi the name of an entrepreneur with a long-standing managerial record to head the Ministry of Public Works and Services.[112] Arturo Acevedo had presided ACINDAR, the steel-making plant, before resigning to take up his new job, which included the restructuring of the railways.[113] During a whole day session in the Chamber of Deputies to debate the situation in the railways, an occasion the UCRP used to accuse the Executive of 'an act of provocation' in putting forward a plan to rationalise the system, plan which included the privatisation of coffee shops at stations and of repairs workshops, Acevedo insisted he could see no need for 'the State selling sausages at rail stations'. The Interior minister, Vítolo, who was also present to defend the government's plan, claimed that what was depicted as a 'provocation' in fact meant that rail-workers would have to work four and a half hours instead of the customary three and a half.[114]

While the deplorable situation of the railways demanded drastic solutions it is also true that the developmentalists had a badly concealed bias towards road transportation as a means of putting the deficient transport infrastructure of Argentina up to date – in the eyes of the opposition, a reflection of the decision to allow the indiscriminate settlement of automobile and truck factories. It was with few qualms that the government put forward a plan that would have cut down the rail network almost by half and reduced its personnel by 75,000 men. On 8 March 1960 Frondizi announced that the cooperation of workers would be required to carry out 'the retrieval of the railways', and on 31 January 1961 Decree No. 853 made effective worker participation in discussions to that end. But on 20 May 1961 Decree No 4,061 established the restructuring of the rail system thereby annulling the commissions in which workers were taking part, even though in his message to Congress on 1 May the president had announced that the 'rationalisation of public service enterprises would be carried out with the active cooperation of their personnel'.[115] On 5 June Frondizi launched the Transport Battle, a step that in Alemann's words, demanded 'considerable political courage'.[116]

As from the month of August, rail-workers started a series of 24 and 48-hour strikes, culminating on 28 October with a strike for an indefinite period. On 7 November there was a 72-hour general strike in support of the rail-workers, and throughout November acts of sabotage against the railways were rife. While both Frondizi and his Economy minister carried on with their planned trips overseas, Scipione requested the mediation in the strike of the Archbishop of Buenos Aires. Following a series of meetings between the Archbishop, union representatives and acting-president Senator Guido, the strike was lifted on 10 December after 42 days. This time the two casualties of the strike were Acevedo, who resigned because he disagreed with the wage increases of 22 per cent conceded to end the strike, and Alemann, who resigned in solidarity with his colleague over what he considered to be a matter of principle. But the main casualty was the plan itself, although the 75,000 workers that had been made redundant were not reincorporated. The British ambassador noted the 'considerable economic losses' that resulted from the strike since the government had gained 'financially, practically nothing' and had agreed to a substantial wage increase, while the consequent increase in the railway deficit had not been budgeted for, increasing the need for borrowing and pushing the country to a further stage of inflation.[117]

Conclusions

The CGT intervened by the *Libertadora* was not given back to the Peronist union leadership until 16 March 1961, while the ban on the Peronist party was not lifted until March 1962. The defeated strikes of 1959–60 ended the cycle of intense mobilisation that had begun in 1956, and although by the end of 1961 Peronists were still noisy and commanded a large support especially amongst unskilled workers, the 'diehard subversive variety' no longer held the centre of the trade union stage. Unfortunately, a few months into 1962 the military would move decisively into the centre stage of the country as a whole.

The possibility of a successful relationship between the government and the unions – or the constitution of the 'national movement' – was hampered by the limited room for manoeuvre in terms of salary concessions that the stabilisation plan allowed, as well as by the Peronist dominance in the unions. But both factors demand caveats; as exemplified by the rail strike, as from 1961 the government gave in more readily than in the past to labour demands of pay increases. The electoral perspective – a series of provincial elections in 1961 and 1962, plus the renovation of half the Chamber of Deputies due in March 1962 – was surely an important consideration, just as it had been in the sacking of Alsogaray, too closely identified with the 'anti-popular' features of the economic policies.

As far as the Peronist dominance in the unions was concerned, on the one hand the defeat of the meat-packers' strike put an end to the insurrectional line, emphasised by the displacement of Cooke, and on the other Frigerio's attempts at co-optation proved successful in some cases (for instance, the head of the meat-packers union, Eleuterio Cardoso, favoured an 'integrationist' approach), paradoxically highlighting the deviousness of the wheeling-and-dealing of the developmentalist – or 'integrationist' – tactics. The Peronist labour movement became divided into *duros* (hardliners), *blandos* (softliners), and a middle-of-the-road embodied in *Vandorismo*, while the 'democratic' unionists progressively abandoned their *gorila* traits and preferred to be known as 'independents'. While the emergence of internal lines within Peronism offered the government leeway in their negotiations with labour, it also allowed *Vandorismo* (so named after Augusto Vandor, leader of UOM, the steelworkers' union) to present the military with a picture of a 'plural' labour movement from which the communists had been ostracised. Moreover, the continuing suspicion that Frondizi harboured 'communists' in the administration helped bring closer together those who thought the 'solution' lay in the revival of the trade unions-military alliance that Perón had thrived upon and which Vandor and General Onganía would try to revive in 1966.

The internal currents in Peronist unionism were distinguished by their tendency to a more or less conciliatory approach towards the government. *Vandorismo* showed a distinct tendency to compromise, simultaneously maintaining the threat to both the State and industry represented by worker mobilisation. Vandor's slogan was *negociar y golpear* (talk and hit), while it was he who invented the 'neither Yankees nor Marxists = we are Peronists' that became the slogan of practically every labour mobilisation from 1961 onwards. Therefore it was *Vandorismo* that underlined the effectiveness of Peronism in counteracting communist influence in the unions, at a time when this had become the main concern of the military, especially after the revolution in Cuba.

5 DEVELOPMENTALISM AND THE MILITARY

Introduction

The armed forces were also to form part of Frigerio's grand design for a 'national movement' considering 'their natural consubstantiation with the national being, which leads the armed forces to participate in, and promote, national development'.[118] Their specific function was not only to defend the sovereignty of the country, but 'to intervene in the democratic process to guarantee the rule of law'.[119] The armed forces, together with 'the unions and business associations', are 'the only guarantee for the realisation of the Argentine destiny'. Any attempts at dividing or antagonising these sectors 'have their origin in the tiny group of anti-national interests which prevail at the expense of the country'.[120]

An harmonious relationship between workers and employees was essential to secure 'social peace', and when such relationship proved elusive, the developmentalists were prompt in calling in the military to restore the broken 'peace', as in the case of the oil, rail, and meat-packers strikes, a role that the military resented because of its unpopularity on the one hand, and the risks of conscripts 'entering into contact with communists' on the other.[121] Given that their role was so prominent in developmentalism's ideological tenets, it is the more surprising that when in government developmentalists' relations with the military seemed thwarted by misunderstandings, drastically reducing the government's room for manoeuvre. After his overthrow, Frondizi stated on several occasions that he should not have accepted 'a conditioned presidency' in May 1958. Military men who were known as *legalistas* at the time have insisted that such conditionality did not exist in 1958, but that Frondizi's room for manoeuvre became restricted by the military only after what they regarded as the shameful episode of 3 September 1959 (see below).[122]

Until Frondizi's accession to power, the dominance of the armed forces had been a constant feature of Argentine politics partly because such role was never disputed. Now, for the first time in forty years a candidate who had led the opposition to the incumbent – and for that matter, military – administration, was to become president. True to his belief that the armed forces had to revert to a specifically professional role, in his inaugural speech Frondizi had declared that the armed forces would no longer take political decisions. But not many officers regarded the mere safeguarding of the Constitution as 'their beautiful destiny'. From his very first day as president, Frondizi addressed the officers in a manner they considered offensive. Such misgivings would increase with time when the military were bemused by what they saw on the one hand, as an attempt to 'dictate to them', and on the other what they regarded as appalling 'weakness, indecision and lack of courage'.[123]

The great challenge was 'to work out a viable relationship' but Frondizi never devoted any efforts in this direction.[124] This was never achieved, and both sides were to blame. If Frondizi was clumsy, and at times arrogant, and placed too much trust on men despiteful of the rules of democratic behaviour, the officers were distrustful, often obdurate and prone to messianic feelings.[125] None of the issues confronting the military and Frondizi were insurmountable were it not for the deep suspicion in which they held one another, compounded by the military belief – constantly fed by an often short-sighted and irresponsible political opposition – that they were 'the ultimate moral reserve of the nation'.[126] '*Golpismo*', or 'the desire to overthrow the Government by force', became 'an endemic disease' that acquired 'particular virulence during the winter season' and, what bemused a US Embassy official even more, was that 'scarcely any social opprobrium attaches to it . . . and some incurables occupy high positions in the community, being known even to schoolboys'.[127] What became even more endemic than the threat of *golpismo*, were the recurrent *planteos* (demands) the military would make on Frondizi. There were more than thirty, and more often than not their purpose was to create the appearance of a crisis, derived primarily 'from the desire of the Armed Services' to remind the electorate what they could do 'if trouble arose'.[128] On his part Frondizi would frequently, and irritatingly, put to the people that any opposition to the government's programme entailed an attack on the constitutional regime, as he did on his 23 November 1960 speech entitled 'The Government and Communism'. In it he denied that there were any communists in his government, that he himself was not one and had never been one, but that he would not admit unfounded accusations against people simply because they thought differently. The problem was that given Frondizi's 'quite unusual political dexterity' and the fact that he 'wooed and obtained the communist vote' on February 1958, led many to believe – mostly in the armed forces – that he was using his 'finesse to cover up intentions far further to the left than can be readily perceived'.[129]

The State of the Forces

Frondizi was well aware that his election had caused antagonism amidst the military. After all, his campaign had been openly oppositionist to the *Libertadora* and his victory had been achieved with the aid of 'two million Peronist votes'. To compensate for such tainted origins, as a sign of goodwill Frondizi offered reassurances that the amnesty decreed on 21 May 1958 would not entail the reincorporation of either Peronist or nationalist officers, while he extended 'a blank cheque' to General Aramburu to grant salary increases to the forces before 1 May 1958.[130] Presumably he believed that the extreme generosity of the salary increases awarded by the outgoing administration to their colleagues in the forces would suffice to keep them contented. Indeed, they had ample reason to feel financial satisfaction: the increases granted amounted to 300 per cent in many cases, at a time when inflation bordered on 25 per cent.[131]

Just as the 60 per cent salary increase to labour had not sufficed to achieve the desired 'social peace', in the case of the forces the rise was insufficient to allay military fears that Frondizi might be prepared to appoint Communists or Peronists to high positions in his administration. The confusion, internal bickering and general state of indiscipline rife in military circles since September 1955 was a factor that could have been used to Frondizi's advantage. Instead, the president's change of image when he donned the hat of economic liberalism in place of that of Left-wing revolutionary, caused bemusement among the officers for whom the president's intentions would remain forever suspect. Moreover, in the highly sensitive atmosphere resulting from such internal disarray, many of Frondizi's decisions with direct reference to the armed forces were interpreted as attempts at deepening internal divisions.[132]

It is necessary to recognise the difficulty for a constitutional government of having to deal with constant interforce rivalries and suspicions, as for example the Navy's announcement on 4 July 1958 of the purchase of the aircraft carrier *Warrior* – renamed *Independencia* – which sparked off a wave of displeasure in the other two forces.[133] The first direct clash with military men occurred when Frondizi cancelled his participation in the 9 July 'comradeship dinner' of the forces once he became aware of the contents of the speech to be delivered by rear Admiral Arturo Rial, head of the Naval Centre. Rial had proposed to criticise the president on his trade union policies as well as on the political leanings of some of his collaborators. Instead, Rial was forced to retire and on 28 July Frondizi broadcast a message to the armed forces 'appealing to sanity' and promising them the necessary funds so that they would be able 'to protect national development effectively'.[134]

The Krause Case and Frigerio's Resignation

Frondizi's decision to recall Commodore Krause from retirement to become his Air Force secretary sparked off a rebellion in the force that posed the first real threat of a coup.[135] The coup was averted, but in a manner that proved costly to the president in terms of prestige and image within the forces. The extent of the protest that the decision to recall Krause from retirement gave rise to within the Air Force obliged the president to relent, but not before a week elapsed during which every day more Air Force officers threatened with their resignations. The president finally had to sacrifice his Air Secretary, Commodore Huerta, emerging from the episode with his image further tarnished: the widespread impression in the services was that Frondizi had tried to exert control over the Air Force, and had failed. Furthermore, he proved to be pliable in the face of determined resistance, a fact other officers would subsequently take into account. What also became a precedent was the president's inclination to appeal to Aramburu every time he had problems with the military. And if the latter proved willing to help – until March 1962 – it was always for a price. Aramburu's broadcast on 9 September denouncing 'backroom dealings' unleashed the process that ended with Frigerio's resignation from his post as Secretary for Socio-Economic Relations.

The Krause episode and Frigerio's resignation revealed, from early days, a style of political behaviour based on a pattern of principled attitude that, once it provoked the reaction of one sector of society or another, was abandoned, to be tried again in a different manner. What at first sight would appear as a reasonable bargaining tactic, was in fact the attempt at imposing one side's will on the other – eventually, with the exception of his economic policies, Frondizi gave in to most pressures, especially those from military quarters.

The Impact in Military Circles of Perón's Revelation of the Existence of the *Pacto*

Although in the highest military circles – and their civilian allies – the existence of an agreement with Perón was known from its inception in 1957, these sectors did not miss the opportunity to express their indignation once the issue became public.[136] Those who did not know – the majority, and almost everybody in the UCRI – were shocked. Amongst them was Interior minister Vítolo, who in a press conference on 12 June 1959 'denied that the government had any kind of agreement with the former dictator'.[137] Vítolo acknowledged the gravity of the situation stemming from Perón's disclosure when he declared that Perón, through his statement, from his 'secure and distant retreat . . . pretends to drag the people to civil war'.[138] Vítolo was referring to Perón's letter dated May 1959, but which *La Nación* published on 12 June, which ended in what could be interpreted as an incitement to the armed forces to rebel:

> [I] cannot understand how the forces whose mission it [is] to protect the sacred and permanent interests of the motherland [can] back and obey a government leading the people and the Nation to the most absolute chaos . . . Our [Perón's] yearning is not for power nor revenge, but for the salvation of the Motherland.

It would seem that earlier in the year Frigerio had made a desperate attempt to stop Perón disclosing the pact. In a telegram to the Department of State in Washington sent by the US Ambassador to the Dominican Republic, the latter reported that Trujillo had told him Frigerio had made a recent call to Ciudad Trujillo seeking his [Trujillo's] cooperation to 'influence Perón to accept substantial "pay off" for cancellation Perón-Frondizi agreement and discontinuance internal agitation Argentina'. Still according to Trujillo's account, he had expressed his willingness on condition that Frondizi 'should immediately take steps against ominous growth Communism in Argentina'.[139]

A series of events unleashed by Perón's disclosure resulted in the resignation of Army Secretary Solanas Pacheco on 16 June (although it was only accepted by Frondizi on 1 July), his replacement by the 71-year old General Anaya, who, by appointing General Toranzo Montero as Army Commander-in-Chief placed in centre stage a man who would pose a constant challenge to Frondizi.[140] The revelation of the Pact was one more factor that exacerbated the simmering unrest in military circles provoked by (a) the presence of what they deemed 'undesirable' elements in the administration, (b) the use of military units to mobilise labour, and thus pitting the armed forces against the working class; (c) 'high-handed methods' used by Solanas and his undersecretary Reimúndez.[141] The first victim of the unrest was Colonel Reimúndez, known as the *Dragón Verde*, after a secret lodge he was alleged to have founded.[142] Information was circulated in military circles that Reimúndez was involved in secret deals with hardline Peronist union leaders, chiefly Andrés Framini, who was close to Cooke. Although Potash attributes this to Frondizi's attempt at defusing the revelation of the Pact, there is evidence that Army officers were right in suspecting that Reimúndez was using his Army position for political ends.[143]

The night of 15–16 June was the first in which a serious attempt at breaking the constitutional order was made by retired Army officers Ossorio Arana and Toranzo Calderón who went to the Córdoba barracks in the hope of leading an uprising.[144] Solanas asked Frondizi for permission to repress the rebels, even if it meant shedding blood, but Frondizi refused, and Solanas submitted his resignation. In the political arena the consequence was the Cabinet reshuffle that marked the entry of Alsogaray in the government, and in the military one, the appointment of Anaya and Toranzo Montero.

The Struggle for Survival: Toranzo Montero as Army Commander-in-Chief

Solanas had suggested to Frondizi the names of Generals Señorans or d'Andrea as possible replacements for himself. On 30 June Frondizi told Solanas he would talk with them, and on 1 July Solanas found out that the president had named Anaya instead.[145] 'Overestimating himself' and 'underestimating Toranzo', Anaya insisted on naming Army Commander-in-Chief the senior officer on the active list: General Carlos Severo Toranzo Montero. The president failed in his attempt to persuade Anaya gently that Toranzo would make both their lives difficult, and as a consequence Frondizi had to spend a lot of time and energy in the following two and a half years trying to counteract Toranzo's destabilising actions.[146]

On 2 September, barely a month after his appointment, Toranzo's decision to shake up the Army hierarchy placing officers close to him in all key positions, drew General Anaya, fearful of further splits in the force, to remove him from his post. Toranzo refused to accept his removal and entrenched himself in the Army Mechanics School from where he radioed all provincial garrisons seeking their support. Federico de Alzaga, Rodolfo Larcher and Alvaro Alsogaray went to talk with Toranzo.[147] In Alzaga's account, Alsogaray challenged Toranzo to say he wanted to depose Frondizi, thereby 'calling Toranzo's bluff'. Alzaga left that meeting convinced that Toranzo could be forced out 'just at the sight of a tank' and told Frondizi so, also explaining that Toranzo had showed signs of mental discomposure.[148] Frondizi gave the order to suppress the uprising and the regiment loyal to the president, under General Fonseca's and de Alzaga's command, took to the streets with their tanks. When they had reached the suburbs of Buenos Aires, they received Frondizi's order to halt the advance. The president had called Toranzo to a meeting.[149] The outcome of that meeting was the reinstatement of Toranzo and the removal of Anaya, replaced by General Larcher. This was a disturbing outcome for many officers. Alzaga, for one, had to retire, embittered at what he regarded as Frondizi's betrayal of him. The way he saw things, *he* was punished for remaining loyal and performing his duty, while the rebel general was rewarded for his indiscipline. Furthermore, insult was added to injury when Frondizi offered him 'a low-interest credit or an embassy' as compensation for the loss of his military career.[150] While those officers who had remained loyal to the president felt 'sold out' by him, in his turn Frondizi felt he had reacted with real statesmanship in averting a bloody confrontation.[151] What on the one hand was interpreted as weakness and self-interest, on the other was seen as willingness to sacrifice friends when the superior interests of the Nation were at stake. Although arguably what military men may perceive as weakness or lack of courage can be also interpreted as a deep-rooted belief in the powers of compromise, accommodation, moderation, flexibility and tolerance central in a democratic political culture – and opposed to the notion of 'intransigence' – at least in this case facts support the contention that Frondizi acted inadvisedly, thereby limiting his subsequent room for manoeuvre.[152]

By October 1960 Toranzo appeared to have opted for a policy of control over the government rather than mere vigilance. The shift in his – and the Army's – attitude could be explained by their increasing conviction that Frondizi, although apparently making constant concessions, was in fact adamant in maintaining policies and men that displeased the military.[153] On 10 October Toranzo Montero made his strongest *planteo* yet to Frondizi, in the belief that Army Secretary Larcher would back his complaints. These ranged from the alleged presence of Communists in educational and cultural institutions, of Integrationists allegedly conniving with Peronists in terrorist acts (a reference to Governor Zanichelli), to corrupt practices in the running of state enterprises. The Commander-in-Chief backed down when he realised he could not count on the Army Secretary's support and furthermore, that the president had enlisted – once more – General Aramburu's help in discouraging Army officers from embarking on any attempt at endangering the constitutional order. This time the victim was to be General Larcher, whose relations with Toranzo Montero and other Army chiefs were at a low ebb, and his post was to be filled on 16 October by General Rosendo Fraga who remained until Frondizi's overthrow in March 1962.

When a build-up of events convinced Toranzo Montero in March 1961 that the occasion was ripe for Frondizi's ouster, he discovered that not only was Fraga against him, but that the Army Secretary had been successful in eroding the loyalty that some generals formerly felt towards their Commander-in-Chief.[154] Toranzo resigned on 18 April, signalling for Frondizi the start of a period of great optimism. A series of electoral victories in provincial elections during 1961, his decision to remove Alsogaray, his trips abroad and meetings with President Kennedy all contributed to enhance the president's confidence. It appeared that the worst had been left behind and that the prospects for the all-important March 1962 elections were certainly promising. Furthermore, his renewed confidence led him to pursue a path in foreign policy that is still a cause for private satisfaction and vindication whenever he is accused of betraying the basic tenets of Intransigence.[155]

The Cuban Issue

(a) Introduction

What most people regarded as an unfortunate tendency to bend and concede when placed under pressure by the military, Frondizi regarded as a demonstration of his pragmatism. He described to Casas his decision in September 1959 to recall the tanks to avoid a bloody confrontation with Toranzo Montero as 'the best political decision of [his] life, because [he] needed to gain time to carry out [his] economic policies which were . . . the only hope to guarantee [his] stability'.156

If in the domestic arena the stabilisation plan was paramount, in foreign affairs the president struggled to maintain the principled aspect of his stand. In the event, this would prove his undoing. Frondizi's insistence on following a foreign policy which though 'pro-Western and Christian' at times seemed to relish the possibility of an independent stand *vis-à-vis* the United States, puzzled and confused the armed forces and was taken as another indication of the President's ploys. The suspicion was that Integrationists felt that severing relations with Cuba would 'limit their room for manoeuvre *vis-à-vis* the United States'.157 No other foreign policy issue highlighted more the dilemmas and contradictions of Frondizi's administration than the question of Cuba, where internally the conflict was not seen predominantly in terms of 'democracy versus communism' but as 'yankee imperialism versus *fidelismo*'. As a British observer accurately remarked, amongst those in Argentina who abhorred communism there was also a feeling of '*Schadenfreude* at set backs to US policies'.158

Frondizi had met President Kennedy and had come out not just favourably impressed, but believing that Kennedy had given him 'a blank cheque' to mediate with Castro.159 The reasoning behind Frondizi's attempt at mediation was that the Cuban regime could not be disposed of by force without risking a third world war – a diplomatic solution was the only viable one, and ideally it would have to be reached within the inter-American system, thus staving off any threat of a Soviet intervention in the American continent. True to the permanent Argentine defence of the principle of non-intervention, which implied the inalienable right of every country to choose its political and social institutions without pressure from outside, Argentina opposed any US unilateral action. According to Frondizi, the success of a diplomatic solution would mean the triumph of the reformist line represented by Kennedy, Quadros and Frondizi himself, in opposition to 'reactionaries as well as insurrectional-revolutionaries'.160 Frondizi was walking down a slippery slope when he endeavoured simultaneously to secure a generous flow of funds from the Alliance for Progress coffers and to repair his tarnished image if not of an anti-imperialist, then at least of a man who could not be described as a 'stooge of imperialism'.[161]

On 6 March 1961 the Argentine Government had made public an offer to Castro – which the latter rejected – to help bring Cuba and the United States together again and settle their differences. The initiative had come as a complete surprise and the British could find no one in the Political Department at the Foreign Affairs Ministry to elucidate the matter. But the explanations gathered were symptomatic. On the one hand there were those who believed 'the evil genius Rogelio Frigerio . . . [had been] responsible for the idea in the hope of putting pressure on the Americans for more aid while at the same time pleasing left wingers' while another reason was that Frondizi had tried 'to regain some of the limelight being stolen from him by President Quadros of Brazil'.[162] As usual, there were elements of truth in both assumptions. Two days later Quadros suggested a meeting with Frondizi, which eventually took place in Uruguayana on 18 April 1961, while there are several indications of *frigerista* tactics. Potash has cited evidence that Frondizi 'hoped to get a billion dollars in loans from President Kennedy for Argentine development projects', while on 31 July the *Chicago Tribune* published a scathing attack on Adlai Stevenson's (President Kennedy's personal fence-mending emissary) visit to Buenos Aires. In the newspaper's view the visit 'got nowhere with [Frondizi] on the Cuban problem and [Stevenson] was reported to have agreed with the latter's comment that there should be no military intervention' against Castro. The sole – regrettable – outcome was 'a petition for more than one billion dollars in hand-outs from the United States [delivered to Stevenson] by Foreign Minister Adolfo Mugica'.[163] A year earlier, in the course of an official visit to several European countries, Frondizi met Macmillan and told him that although Latin America was 'at present an integral part of the free world' it was not possible to 'count on this situation as permanent unless further help was forthcoming from the West to assist in the economic development of the area'. Replying to the British Prime Minister's question regarding Frondizi's views on Cuba, the latter said that there were 'two important new forces at work' in Latin America, one was 'the Argentine experiment and the other was the Cuban regime', and thus the fate of Argentina's economic policies 'would have a great effect on the whole sub-continent'.[164]

(b) Frondizi's Secret Meeting with Che Guevara
In this context, Frondizi thought that Che Guevara's presence at the Conference of the Interamerican Economic and Social Council of the Organisation of American States (OAS) being held in Uruguay was

a good occasion to arrange a meeting. A secret visit by Guevara to Argentina was organised, and on 18 August 1961 both men met at the presidential residence in Olivos.[165] Guevara had arrived on a private plane sent by Frondizi, who sent his Navy advisor Quijada to meet him at the airclub.[166] In Casas' account, it was a friendly conversation during which Frondizi reiterated his offer to act as mediator to arrive at a 'status quo' with the US. She adds, moreover, that it had been an 'easy conversation' since both men were, 'deep down, seeking the same thing: the projection of their countries towards development, justice and self-determination'.[167] Guevara told Ricardo Rojo in 1963 that the only thing Frondizi had wanted was an undertaking that Cuba would not become a member of the Warsaw Pact. Guevara retorted that the USSR was not demanding that, 'and yet you are part of TIAR' (Inter-American Reciprocal Assistance Treaty).[168]

When the meeting was revealed in *La Prensa* the following day, the newspaper remarked that the Argentine president maintained 'esoteric links with leaders of international communism' and implied that he acted as a kind of advisor to the latter. In an atmosphere charged with suspicions and misunderstandings, Guevara's presence in Argentina caused political tremors that shifted the attention from the domestic issues to foreign policy, and the Government's support swung from the right to left and centre groups. Echoing the deep malaise in the forces resulting from Guevara's visit, Fraga resigned, but Frondizi persuaded him to stay.[169]

(c) The Punta del Este Conference of the Organisation of American States
The outcome of the Uruguayana meeting between Frondizi and Quadros was an agreement of 'friendship and consultation' that vaguely committed the governments of Brazil and Argentina to seek help from the advanced world to further the economic development of their countries. Although the explicit aims could hardly be faulted, Quadros was considered a communist by the armed forces of Brazil and Argentina. In the latter country Frondizi's *rapprochement* with his Brazilian equal was seen as proof of a plan to seek the constitution of a 'front' that would offer an independent alternative to countries such as Mexico, Venezuela and Colombia. The belief was that unless an alternative was offered them, the latter countries would have to toe the line drawn by President Kennedy and his 'inexpert' handling of the Cuban situation. Given Quadros's former explicit support for Castro, the Argentine armed forces were suspicious that Quadros and Frondizi wanted to start an anti-US front in Latin America. The Canadian Ambassador felt that Frondizi's statements at the end of August 'gave grounds for the

assumption that Argentina might, with Brazil, be among those who favour the principle of "peaceful coexistence" in America, thus putting Cuba in the same category as Poland and Yugoslavia', position that 'it is felt the majority of Argentines would reject'.[170]

Partly to allay military fears and defuse the post-Guevara crisis atmosphere, Frondizi accepted the resignation of his Foreign Affairs minister, Adolfo Mugica and on 12 September 1961 appointed in his place a man that should have provided the much needed guarantees that the president was not veering the country towards communism. Miguel Angel Cárcano was a widely respected Conservative who had become close friends with President Kennedy's father while they both were ambassadors to London in the eve of World War II. Alas, the fact that he had headed the Argentine delegation to Punta del Este was seen as confirmation that the 'parallel government' of the *frigeristas* was in fact running the show and that Cárcano was being used as a mere figurehead.[171] Argentina's minority vote in Punta del Este, when the majority of the OAS countries voted in favour of Cuba's expulsion from the inter-American system, seemed to confirm the military's worst fears.[172] At the end of the month Frondizi went to Palm Beach in order to tell Kennedy that 'the Castro problem could not be met head-on, that Washington was obsessed with Cuba at the expense of the long-run needs of the hemisphere and that a public OAS fight over Cuba would only strengthen Castro'.[173] According to Schlesinger Kennedy did not want a hard line at Punta del Este that might set off 'a chain reaction of government crises across the continent', but the hardliners led by deLesseps Morrison (US Ambassador to the OAS) and Senator Hickenlooper went for 'a *very strong* action' against Castro.[174]

Misreading the atmosphere of near-panic that the Cuban situation had provoked in many quarters, in his instructions to his Foreign Affairs minister Frondizi wrote that the principal concern of the countries gathered in Punta del Este was not

> the fate of an extremist *caudillo* . . . but the future of a group of underdeveloped nations which have freely decided to accede to higher levels of social and economic development. [. . .] We want to protect the unity of the inter-American system and for this reason we shall abstain from voting for sanctions that may affect the principle of non-intervention . . . [175]

The president had been stalling his military secretaries who had been pressing him to reveal what Argentina's position was going to be at the

OAS Conference.[176] Back in Buenos Aires, Cárcano issued a statement declaring that 'the juridical reasons that prompted our vote in no way diminish our firm decision to confront communism . . . neither do they undermine our solidarity with the countries that . . . voted positively'.[177] In fact, the Argentine delegation had only abstained from voting two paragraphs in Resolution VI (out of nine) referring to Cuba's expulsion, a step not contemplated in the OAS statutes, but they had voted in favour of all the others. But the military chiefs were not prepared to see the Cuban question in 'technical' or 'legal' terms as Camilión and Musich pretended.[178]

The reports on the outcome of the meeting were not destined to calm the spirits. *La Nación* of 1 February reproduced an Associated Press cable which said that 'the obstinate bloc of six nations that demanded a compliant attitude *vis-à-vis* the Castroist problem, did not vote in favour of the amendment that the United States had trusted would materialise', and Dean Rusk was quoted as saying that Punta del Este represented 'an historic struggle with respect to the principles on which our society is founded'.[179] General Aramburu added his voice to those outraged by Argentina's stand at the OAS Conference: 'The Argentine delegation has strayed from the path of our people's tradition and has omitted the due respect to the Christian and democratic feelings that extol our history.'[180] The Americans were equally mystified. As they saw it, having originally floated the idea of excluding Castro from the OAS, the Frondizi Government had 'mysteriously glided away from its own formula', leading Schlesinger to wonder whether Frondizi, 'the artful dodger, may not have thrown out the idea in order to lure us away from sanctions without ever intending to support it himself', and he added 'so far as his own military were concerned, it was almost the last knot in an overtwisted rope'.[181]

On 2 February Frondizi met his military secretaries and according to a report in *La Nación* offered three things: (a) to recall the ambassador from Havana; (b) to dismiss Cárcano, and (c) to revise the foreign policy area with a new minister. An editorial in the 2 February edition of *La Nación* stated that:

> it is deplorable that the Argentine delegation was unable to comprehend its duty and its responsibility in this grave hour for America. [. . .] Perhaps there is still a chance of amending so much error, of lessening, at least, the effects of such inexplicable incomprehension.

Diplomatic relations with Cuba were broken on 9 February 1962.

(d) Frondizi's Paraná Speech

Frondizi took the opportunity of the opening of a new underwater tunnel in the city of Paraná in the Province of Entre Ríos, to announce he was recalling the Argentine ambassador in Cuba. But both the contents and tone of his Paraná speech were such that Casas, while describing it as his 'most moving message', at the same time described it as 'Frondizi's death sentence'.[182]

In an impassioned speech, Frondizi started by recalling that every child was taught in Argentina to venerate 'the heroes who in the battlefields conquered the self-determination of the Argentine people', and that both the states of the Union and the new American republics 'considered it essential to establish and preserve the rights to self-determination and non-intervention as indispensable bulwarks of hemispheric unity and of the freedom of its inhabitants'. Self-determination was not a means but an end; it was the reason behind national independence. He went on to defend Argentina's abstention in Punta del Este on juridical principles: 'the juridical tradition of human civilisation rests on the principle that there is no crime without a law' and to ignore this was to revert to 'the law of the jungle'.[183] He ended by denouncing those who were conspiring against his government as 'enemies of the unity and greatness of the country', allied with 'reactionary sectors' in the United States, in the mistaken belief that they were in fact 'serving the cause of world freedom'.[184]

La Nación reported the next day that the armed forces believed that Integrationists were behind the decisions taken in Punta del Este. On 6 February an editorial in the newspaper commented on the Paraná speech, describing it as 'unexpected', 'causing amazement' and containing 'offensive insinuations'. A week later an article on the political situation published in the same newspaper stated that 'the doubts in different sectors about the true nature of the government surrounds it with the dangerous hypersensitivity in which we are living'. The article reported that suspicions about the existence of a 'parallel government' and the 'communist leanings of the Integrationists' were rife once again.[185]

In his Paraná speech Frondizi appeared to have taken up again the mantle of the anti-imperialist leader. His insistence on the respect for the rule of law in dealing with Cuba's exclusion from the OAS caused irritation amidst those who saw the Cuban threat as too great to treat it according to the niceties of international law. The view was that however 'correct' his economic policies were, Frondizi remained his 'old left-wing self'.[186] The Catholic magazine *Criterio* wrote in this respect:

[. . .] the Paraná speech shows that if it is true that, with all its ambiguities, the economic policies of the national government can be defined as right-wing, the radical side of the UCRI continues to be revealed in foreign policy in a latent left-wing mysticism.[187]

In Paraná Frondizi emerged as a man striving to recover the lost image of integrity he had had during his years as leader of the opposition to Perón. That image had suffered its worst battering in the domestic field, and perhaps the president believed foreign policy was an area where he did not have to make any concessions. Such extreme positioning in the political spectrum according to which area of policy was concerned, was bewildering at best, widely regarded as hypocritical at worst.

Conclusions

The state of disarray of the armed forces could have been taken advantage of to overcome their pre-eminence in the political arena. But for this to occur it would have been essential to strengthen a party that could have filled the void created by Perón. Instead, the armed forces were strengthened in their belief that there was no political party that offered a viable, modern, political, alternative.

This was all the more to be regretted when one of the three original ideas that Frondizi had tried to introduce in the old UCR had been the need to establish links with the armed forces.[188] Since the 1930 coup, with the exception of those UCR members who had relatives in the forces, or Unionists like Zavala Ortiz who had conspired with the military against Perón since the early days, the party as such regarded the military with a mixture of horror and fear. The UCR was still 'licking its wounds from the 1930 coup', and so it came to pass that in UCR demonology the military ranked as high as 'electoral pacts' .[189]

The belief of the armed forces in the sense that foreign policy was an area of their specific concern meant that the military chiefs expected to be kept fully informed and have an opportunity to veto actions that in their view endangered national security. Frondizi's decision to run foreign affairs himself was indeed his right as constitutional president. Nevertheless, precedent indicated that at least to attempt to avoid unnecessarily alienating military opinion, he could have kept them informed. The lack of communication turned rumblings of discontent into a determination that Frondizi would have to leave. Ideologically, Frondizi rightly believed that in a democratic society the forces should concentrate on their professional activities. But to think that this could be achieved overnight after thirty years was wishful thinking at best, arrogance at worst, the more so when he showed his readiness to call on the army to enforce a 'social peace' that was not in the offing. Furthermore, Frondizi's decision to retain as his close collaborators men of life-long communist or Peronist militancy constantly questioned by the military meant that the army especially, resented increasingly the task of repressing the workers on strike, carrying out the 'dirty work' of a government they did not trust.

The *planteos* of the armed forces were real enough, but to say that Frondizi received a 'conditioned presidency' sounds like an *ex-post-facto* apologia for shortcomings that it is not unreasonable to suggest could have been avoided. Just like with everybody else, Frondizi did not feel it was necessary to explain and persuade: he thought the goodness of his actions would be self-evident once 'development' was achieved. Although he had been elected on a political platform that was in opposition to the incumbent administration, Frondizi was to implement the main ideals of the *Libertadora*: economic and political liberalism, and the exclusion of Peronism. That is to say, until – erroneous – political calculations, more than matters of principle, drove the president to authorise the participation of a Peronist party, *Unión Popular*, in the elections to be held in March 1962.

9 A Gamble Too Many: The Elections of March 1962 and the Fall of Frondizi

1 INTRODUCTION

The year 1961 was signalled by a series of national and provincial elections whose outcome all parties concerned would take as an indication of expected results in the March 1962 contest. The importance of this date lay in the fact that it would be the occasion for the renewal of half the Chamber of Deputies as well as fourteen governorships. Moreover, in the case of the UCRI the 1961 elections helped them assess their strength – or lack of it – now that the party could no longer count on the Peronist votes. When Frondizi normalised the CGT in March 1961 and allowed Peronism a partial legality in 1962, he did it less to fulfil old promises than to scare the anti-Peronist forces into supporting him: the strategy seems to have worked since the UCRI's victories in provincial elections throughout 1961 reflected the massive support of anti-Peronist voters, while Peronism either abstained or took part in the elections under the guise of neo-Peronist parties.

There seemed to be few if any chances of refloating the February 1958 'front'. If on the one hand the UCRI needed to gauge its electoral strength, on the other Peronism had yet to decide to tell its followers how to vote if the government did not lift its proscription. The hopes of the other main contestant, the UCRP, lay almost exclusively in its anti-Peronism. But without the certainty of the Peronist votes, the UCRI began to rely increasingly on its anti-Peronist credentials.

2 THE 1961 ELECTIONS

If the March 1960 elections rendered the expected mid-term disappointment, the 1961 results revealed that increasing numbers of voters were being attracted by the government's policies. Since these were of a kind unlikely to lure the labour vote, the official party's electoral triumphs could only be attributed to its success in persuading anti- and non-Peronist

Table 9.1 Election results in Santa Fe, Catamarca and San Luis, 17 December 1961

Party	Santa Fe	Catamarca	San Luis
UCRI	299,512 (29.86%)	28,568 (43.5%)	39,708 (46%)
Laborista*	233,332	–	–
Populista*	–	19,620	–
UCRP	136,269	12,083	3,356
Blank votes	28,891	939	2,072
Arg. Socialists	5,101	539	1,287
Dem. Socialists	4,567	–0	1,140

Source: La Nación, 25 December 1961.
* Neo-Peronist parties.

voters that it – rather than the UCRP – was the most effective alternative to Peronism. The exception were the elections held on 5 February 1961 in the Federal Capital for one senator and one deputy. The first non-UCRI senator would be the Socialist Alfredo Palacios, who received Peronist support, notwithstanding 200,000 blank ballots cast by die-hard Peronists. Palacios had led a virulently anti-government campaign denouncing the atmosphere of 'crude materialism' in which the country was submerged and the 'Machiavellian policies of little men . . . which disconcert and confound', and endorsing agrarian reform and the Cuban Revolution.[1] The seat in the Chamber of Deputies went to the UCRP candidate, Carlos Adrogué, a former Education minister in the government of the *Libertadora*.[2]

The first elections since 1958 to renew a provincial governor were held in Mendoza on 12 February 1961, where the candidate of the Democratic Party (conservative) won. Once again Peronism resorted to blank balloting (*votoblanquismo*) tactics. The '62' issued a statement recommending blank voting because the parties 'were totally lacking a programme identified with the real needs of the people and the Nation . . . blank voting will represent an action of revolutionary resistance by the working class'.[3] But the electoral fate of the UCRI began to change in Catamarca when on 5 March 1961 it won the eight seats being contested for the provincial Congress, and similar results followed in Santa Fe on 19 March and San Luis and Misiones, on 9 April. But the real boost for the incumbent administration was the outcome of the 17 December elections held in Santa Fe, Catamarca, and San Luis (see Table 9.1). *La Nación* was being less than fair when it wrote on 20 December that the UCRI 'retained the Peronist votes', while it proved somewhat premature in its remark that the other important conclusion was 'that Peronism, as such, was defeated', since there had been 'clear orders to vote for neo-Peronist parties' which did not do well. The results were encouraging for the official party since they indicated for the first time that the UCRI could stand on its own in provinces with substantial Peronist following, like in Santa Fe – and win. The outcome of the elections in Formosa on 14 January 1962 seemed to reinforce this impression.[4]

3 THE MARCH 1962 ELECTIONS

Frondizi and the UCRI: the Bill of Proportional Representation and the Preparation of Lists of Candidates

At the beginning of November 1961 the Executive sent to Congress a bill on proportional representation. The Senate passed it without much ado, but once in the Chamber of Deputies the treatment of the bill that was bound to antagonise UCRI deputies was delayed until the outcome of the December 1961 elections was known.[5] The aim of proportional representation was to reduce the number of representatives allocated to the party first past the post, which under the incomplete list system received two thirds of the seats. This was a clear step to curtail the UCRP which had the lead over the UCRI in the provinces of Buenos Aires and Córdoba as well as in the Federal Capital. The proposed law had a pre-set duration: 30 September 1964. On this date general elections would take place, and therefore the government felt that the D'Hondt proportional system, if it was to be introduced, could jeopardise the expected government majority.

When a group of UCRI parliamentarians met Frondizi to discuss the controversial bill, the president told them that he too was opposed to proportionality, but that he supported it 'to achieve the pacification of the country' and that 'on 2 May 1964 [he] would once again fight for the incomplete list'.[6] Such analysis of the situation was bound to be criticised; as *La Nación* commented, 'a law sanctioned towards the end of 1961 and which is to be opposed in 1964 is not strictly a law [but] a device, a circumstantial tool, a patch'.[7] Nevertheless, the December 1961 results proved favourable to the government, and the electoral reform which had smacked of political opportunism was abandoned. However, dropping the law proved fatal for Frondizi for other reasons. Former president Aramburu, with his eyes on the 1964 presidential elections, wanted the sanctioning of the law of proportional representation, but Frondizi decided to make the sanctioning by the Senate conditional to the March 1962 results. If, as he expected, the UCRI won and Peronism was defeated, the UCRI was almost guaranteed the 1964 elections, and there would be no need to agree to Aramburu's nomination, something the former provisional president wanted.[8]

The other issue of open disagreement between the president and his party was the preparation of lists of candidates for the forthcoming elections. Traditionally, such lists were put together by local *caudillos*, whose dealings were open to corrupt practices, and by the relevant party's national committees, open to caucus pressures. Writing to Senator Alfredo García, chairman of the UCRI's national committee who had sought the president's advice on the drawing of the lists for the December 1961 elections, Frondizi pledged non-interference with the decisions of party structures, but recommended the inclusion of extra-party candidates who should only be required to express their commitment to the 'national programme'. However, when the party handed Frondizi a list of thirty names to consider for the March 1962 elections, he only accepted four. In the end, after much bargaining, Frondizi agreed to name five candidates for the Buenos Aires provincial Congress, albeit sacrificing his first choices, all Integrationists. By including them in the lists, Frondizi had hoped, perhaps, to produce the 'modernisation' of the party he had deemed essential many years before, and at the same time legitimise their ubiquitous presence. Instead, he split the party in what *La Nación* described as 'two branches' which differed 'in their methods and aspirations'.[9] While the UCRI 'operated openly, under the restrictions imposed by the Constitution', Integrationism '[endeavoured] to influence the specific decisions of the government even if it [meant] moving along lateral paths, away from public scrutiny and constitutional procedure', since the power it aspired to was the 'effective and undisputed control of the Nation', a 'total power not submitted to the checks and balances of the constitution'.[10] This onslaught on Frigerio and friends came after Punta del Este, and when rumours were rife about the former's renewed visits to Perón, by then exiled in Madrid.

Frigerio and Perón: a New Pact?

The March 1962 elections were crucial on many counts. Of the fourteen provincial governorships at stake, the Province of Buenos Aires was the most coveted one, since it had held historically the key to the political control of the nation. The largest, wealthiest and most populous province, 39 per cent of Argentina's electorate was concentrated in it. The government regarded the elections as momentous, when the success of its policies would finally be gauged. The relevance that Frondizi attributed to them is illustrated by the argument he used to comfort 'disheartened' legislators after the 27 March 1960 elections. He had told them on that occasion that 'success can hardly be expected before four years have elapsed, the approximate time limit for the results of my economic policies to begin to be appreciated'.[11] Furthermore, the unprecedented sums being spent by the UCRI in the campaign – *La Nación* reported that 150,000,000 pesos, approximately US $1,500,000, had been spent in the Province of Buenos Aires alone – indicated its importance.[12] Nevertheless, in a personal interview Frondizi maintained that he 'knew all along' that they would lose.

If he knew he would lose the elections, and furthermore, that this would mean his downfall, why did he allow direct Peronist participation under the name of *Unión Popular*?[13] He has declared that he did so as a matter of principle.[14] Events seem to point to a medley of reasons behind Frondizi's decisions. If he was so certain of losing, then why agree to Frigerio's attempts at reaching an agreement with Perón? Why promise the military secretaries he would order the federal intervention in the case of a Peronist win and then maintain that the interventions had been a military imposition? In his account Frondizi may have been thinking more about History's verdict rather than wishing to convey a sincere assessment of events.

Faithful to Frondizi's interpretation, Casas wrote that while he expected defeat in the Province of Buenos Aires – believing 'thousands of *gorilas*' would vote for the Peronist candidate to create an atmosphere favourable to a coup – his friends thought that the UCRI could win there. The UCRI put forward a strong candidate for the governorship: Guillermo Acuña Anzorena, who had been Under-secretary at the Ministry of Interior and had been at the Labour Ministry at the time the government returned the CGT to the unions. It was hoped this would make him attractive in the eyes of the considerable labour electorate in the province. When in January 1962 at a mass rally in the industrial quarter of Avellaneda in Buenos Aires Province Peronism launched the names of Framini and Perón as candidates for the governorship and vice-governorship of the province, the military secretaries met with the Interior minister who assured them that 'legal mechanisms' would stop Perón's candidacy. In a press conference on 30 January Vítolo anticipated the Courts' ruling preventing Perón from becoming a candidate on the grounds that he had failed to register in 1957. It would appear that Perón's intention in putting forth his name was to force the government to proscribe, and thus be spared having to call for the self-proscription of his movement.

But at the same time, Frigerio was again actively seeking an agreement with Perón. He and his friends – journalists Emilio Perina and Jacobo Timerman were the two most prominent – were secretly visiting Perón to convince him that self-proscription was the best solution. Casas mentions a memorandum that had widespread circulation in government circles and which allegedly provided the basis for the negotiations with Perón.[15] It contained the reasons why Perón's withdrawal from the Buenos Aires ticket was deemed essential. These were that it would avert the threat of a coup, allow Peronists to gain seats in Congress and posts in provincial governments, and above all, Peronism would be able to take part in the presidential elections in 1964 with experienced cadres. Halperín also mentions the existence of such a plan, but he adds that it included the promise that in 1964 there would be a closer alliance between the UCRI and Peronism, possibly around a common candidate, Frigerio.[16] A cynical view held that Frondizi was hoping the lifting of the ban would provoke immediate outrage in the armed forces, forcing him to comply and order the proscription, ostensibly against his will, to save the constitutional order.

In fact, Perón was about to accept the self-proscription of his movement worried about the consequences of a possible coup, about the possibility of the unity of the movement being weakened by a limited presence in isolated areas of power, and his own hopes for the 1964 presidential elections.[17] He changed his mind when a strong delegation headed by Vandor arrived in Madrid and persuaded him otherwise, underlining the 'unanimous and determined will of the Peronist masses' to take part in the contest.[18] But in the lifting of the ban on Peronism other considerations besides those of principle may have weighed on the president's mind: the time had come to reap the fruits of those dramatic appeals in which the incumbent administration was presented as the sole alternative to chaos and social revolution. Once the Peronists started to act openly in the political arena in February 1962 (the campaign was formally launched with a massive act in Plaza Once on 21 February to proclaim the ticket Framini–Anglada, and there were further multitudinous and near-riotous acts in February and March) the scare factor, it was hoped, would begin to operate.

The Parties in March 1962

If on the one hand Frigerio was hoping he could arrive at a new agreement with Perón, on the other the UCRI – and Frondizi – were seeking to ensure that the substantial anti- and non-Peronist voters rallied around them. This was indeed a reasonable expectation since the UCRP, which had fulfilled that role in February 1958, had proved incapable of offering any real alternative to the government. The nearest that Crisólogo Larralde, the

UCRP's candidate for the governorship of Buenos Aires came to spelling out policy matters was to suggest that 'the country needs to place the workers in the control room of the economy'.[19] This limitation was of course impossible to overcome: it resulted from the UCR's political tradition. Furthermore, a group of *Sabattinistas* within the UCRP declared unexpectedly that they would vote for the Peronist *Unión Popular*, as a manifestation of their support

> for the working class as such, and not for its political ideology [since they] preferred to back the political mistake . . . of the historically revolutionary class, than the wisdom of those sectors which, under a democratic disguise, confront and attack Peronism.[20]

At the same time that the UCRP was losing votes to Peronism, the UCRI struggled to gain those of anti-Peronists. A few days before the elections Vítolo declared that it was 'evident that the intention of Framini's candidacy was the formation of a Castroist front'.[21] And three days later, Alsogaray's Civic Independent Party issued a statement supporting the UCRI, 'in order to oppose the totalitarian front of nationalists, Peronist extremists and communists' gathered in the *Unión Popular*.[22]

According to all reports, Interior minister Vítolo was convinced the UCRI would win, thus proving that Peronism was a thing of the past. It was this appealing prospect that weighed on Frondizi not to proscribe.[23] So sure was he of the government's victory that on 29 January he signed a secret document with the military secretaries vowing that should any Peronist win, he would not be allowed to take office.[24] He repeated at the 15 March Cabinet meeting that especially Framini would be prevented from taking office, and in that case the Buenos Aires Province would be intervened by the federal government.[25] Publicly, Vítolo's message was different: when asked what would happen if the Peronists won, the minister replied that the 'the will of the people shall be respected', but that the Republic's institutions would be defended 'if someone tries to install a government of totalitarian restoration', something that would provoke the federal intervention.[26]

At that same Cabinet meeting the military secretaries once again complained about Frigerio's influence. Frondizi's reply was unexpected and bewildering. He took the opportunity, in one of his 'Dialogues with the People' being broadcast as part of the electoral campaign, to say that those who denounced the 'parallel government' were against 'national development', since all the government's plans would have miscarried had it not been for 'the drive and determination of a team of competent and dynamic advisors'. Moreover, without naming Frigerio, the president compared him with President Roosevelt's friend and adviser, Harry Hopkins, saying that 'when everybody else' went to see the president to ask him for a favour, it was a comfort to have nearby somebody like Hopkins, who never asked for anything, 'only to serve the president'.[27] These comments could hardly result reassuring, either for the UCRI or the military. After the Guevara episode, the latter were not prepared to give Frondizi the benefit of the doubt any more.[28]

The elections took place as planned on 18 March, their smooth running guaranteed by the armed forces. The Peronists, united in a Justicialist Front, won ten of the fourteen governorships at stake, including Buenos Aires. But the results were not as disastrous for the government in the congressional elections. Although the UCRI lost in Buenos Aires, it came first in the Federal Capital with 233,204 votes, followed by *Unión Popular*'s 200,575, while the UCRP came third with 181,823. The UCRI also came first in Entre Ríos, La Pampa, Corrientes, Santa Cruz, and Tierra del Fuego. The conservatives had retained their stronghold in Mendoza, and the UCRP its perennial predominance in Córdoba. Yet what clouded all objective analyses of the results was that Andrés Framini, the outspoken and 'extremist' textile leader, was to become the next governor of Argentina's main province, the seat of its most important military bases. The sheer notion of having to stand on the same dais with Framini at official functions was one the military could not even contemplate.[29]

4 THE FALL

The Intervention of the Provinces of Buenos Aires, Chaco, Río Negro, Santiago del Estero and Tucumán

Having gambled and lost, Vítolo resigned on 19 March and Frondizi ordered the federal intervention of those provinces where the winning party was clearly Peronist (in other cases, independent provincial parties had won with Peronist support). He had hoped the military would come out publicly demanding the interventions. Instead, they sat back and waited for the president to come out of the imbroglio – if he could. Decree No. 2542 ordered the immediate intervention of 'all provincial and municipal authorities' in the above provinces, since they were 'incapable of preventing the widespread subversive process' that had its origins in those same victors of the 18 March elections, who 'ignored the essential values of democratic politics and of a civilised life'.[30] The UCRI governors were shocked: their president was throwing them out as an excuse to annul the 18 March elections.[31] Even Framini at first thought the decree did not apply to him: he said 'the problem is Alende's [the incumbent UCRI governor]. We are taking over on 1 May', and he went on to make reassuring statements about Peronism, backed by Antonio Cafiero, his choice for Economy minister, who underlined the 'humanist and Christian principles of Justicialism'.[32]

Ten Hectic Days

The interventions marked the first step in the frantic comings and goings of the next ten days. Between 19 and 29 March, Frondizi tried almost everything to avert a coup, accepting every suggestion that came from military quarters, except one: the demand that he resign, first put forward by the Navy.[33] The fact that ten days elapsed before Frondizi was taken prisoner by the armed forces and flown to the island of Martín García was an indication that the military were far from clear or united as to the path to follow. Not only did the three forces differ in their views, but within each one there were those who were adamant in the defence of the constitutional order, and those who insisted that Frondizi's continuation as president was intolerable. Furthermore, politicians did not help.

On 21 March the whole Cabinet resigned, and Frondizi invited the political parties to discuss the possibility of forming a cabinet of national unity. The only parties that accepted were the president's own, and Alsogaray's PCI, while the Christian Democrats conditioned their acceptance to the lifting of the federal interventions. Rodolfo Martínez, who knew the military well and feared chaos and a possible dictatorship if the ultra *gorilas* had their way, spoke with Aramburu and separately with admirals Palma and Sánchez Sañudo and explained how the constitutional order could be maintained and Aramburu could become the next consitutional president in 1964. Martínez believed Framini should be allowed to take over the governorship, while the military – especially the Navy – 'kept an eye on him'. Come 1964, and with the law of proportional representation in force, there would be two candidates for the presidency: a Peronist one and Aramburu. There was no doubt that Aramburu would have been elected by the Electoral College given the distribution of forces. Thus Martínez's advice to Aramburu was: 'back Frondizi now and in two years' time you are the president'. But Aramburu preferred to listen to other civilian advisers, and at the umpteenth hour agreed to Frondizi's overthrow.[34]

The UCRI national committee on its part declared it would do 'everything possible to secure the reunification of Radicalism'. The offer had

A Gamble Too Many: The Elections of March 1962

come five years too late.[35] On 24 March the UCRP's national committee demanded 'Frondizi's resignation', 'juridical continuity' and 'the lifting of provincial interventions'.[36] Frondizi's next step was to form a new cabinet out of lists put forward by the military secretaries, and to ask Aramburu for his mediation with the armed forces. In exchange for his good offices, Frondizi allegedly offered Aramburu to be the UCRI's presidential candidate in 1964.[37] Rodolfo Martínez was offered the Education or Defence portfolios, and he chose the latter, telling Frondizi that he could be much more useful to him in that capacity given his profound knowledge of the military and his close personal contacts. On 24 March Aramburu issued a statement saying he had asked Frondizi for 'time, to think and make the necessary consultations to find out whether [Aramburu] could be of any help'.[38] *La Nación* also reported the presence of Alsogaray and former *Libertadora* minister Landaburu in the Casa Rosada on that same day. The president had asked for their help. Alsogaray's suggestion was that Frigerio be offered as a 'scapegoat' to appease the military. This the president refused to do.[39]

The 'removal of the *frigerista* team' was also a requirement in Landaburu's plan, which included 'maintaining the constitutional order', 'respect for the people's will', request to the Peronists 'for specific guarantees that there would be no return to dictatorship', the 'neutralisation of *golpista* military', a 'fairer and redistributionist economic plan' and 'Aramburu's urgent mediation'.[40] But Aramburu, in whose hands the fate of the government and of the constitutional order seemed to lie, appeared very quickly to conclude that the president was beyond deliverance. On 25 March *La Nación* carried the news of Frigerio's sudden departure for Brazil and a report on Aramburu's broadcast to the nation the previous evening.

The former president had said that 'nobody could place his personal predicament above the superior interests of the Nation', in a clear reference to Frondizi's repeated insistence that he 'would not resign, would not leave the country, would not commit suicide'. Two days later Aramburu published a letter he sent to Frondizi on the 26th and which effectively sealed the latter's fate. In it he said he was 'sure the president would not make the mistake of identifying the salvation of the juridical order with his own permanence at its head'. The man so many people – including the president himself – believed was the last hope, was giving up and joining the expanding ranks of those demanding Frondizi's resignation. Aramburu had not followed Martínez's advice. It is still arguable whether Aramburu on his own could have changed the course of events. In the Argentine body politic there was a widespread feeling of fatigue and irritation in the face of a government whose actions were always open to too many interpretations. It was too late – and the main actors too unrepentant – to expect that henceforth transparency would be the dominant feature of policies, and of politicians' behaviour.

Martínez kept trying other solutions.⁴¹ *La Nación* published his *plan político* on 28 March. The plan proposed the reduction of the presidential prerogatives: all major acts of government would have to bear the signatures of both the Defence and Interior ministers, appointed by the armed forces, thereby guaranteeing military control while safeguarding constitutional legality. But it did not work: by then the *golpistas* had decided they wanted a military government, and the loyalists had concluded that Frondizi's permanence was not worth defending. Still, those who had expected that Frondizi would be replaced by a military government were thwarted by Martínez who, with the help of Oyhanarte, literally 'scrambled to get a reluctant José María Guido', president of the Senate, loyal to Frondizi and next in line since there was no vice-president, 'to the presidential armchair ahead of Army Commander-in-Chief General Poggi'.⁴²

General Rauch, loyalist to the last minute, has offered an interpretation of Frondizi's fall that provides the ultimate illustration of Machiavellian deceitfulness attributed to the president. In this version, the overthrow was

> a self-inflicted revolution to allow him to divide and confront the armed forces ... to come out of an untenable situation of his own doing, to appear as a victim and critic of the continuation of the process, ensuring the maintenance in his hands of a series of means and mechanisms that would allow him to exert a permanent influence in the areas of foreign affairs, the press, the economy, education, etc.⁴³

Analysing the election results, *La Nación*, albeit stopping short from accusing the president of stage-managing his overthrow, spelt out the raw feelings that permeated the political atmosphere, and that Frondizi – and Frigerio – seemed bent on ignoring:

> On Sunday the country threw overboard the pillars of the new order [inaugurated in September 1955] and placed everything on a senseless and reckless wager ... [The lifting of the proscription on Peronism] encouraged amidst its followers a fantastic and impossible hope, while it opened the path for disillusionment and scepticism, perplexity and profound indignation at the annulled elections ... The September [1955]

scheme is irreversible . . . Peronism cannot come back . . . To promise it legality and participation in elections was knowingly to deceive it.[44]

Democracy in Argentina was liable to produce the 'wrong' result. And public confidence on the integrity of the political process, institutions and its practitioners, was undermined.

Epilogue

In 1958 Frondizi embodied the politics of hope. Hope that somehow the darker aspects of Peronism would be left behind forever, that the country would finally face the future and join the modern world, that reason and reasonableness would replace prejudice and demagoguery. In post-Peronist Argentina, if people welcomed a 'visionary' approach to politics, they were perhaps keener to find correct attitudes rather than abstract ideas. The 'technocratic' or 'scientific' appearance of the developmentalists was well received – it was regarded not only as 'modern' but 'serious' as well. The UCR had not been a party of ideas but of moral principles. Frondizi and the UCRI seemed to promise a new era in party politics, but the renovating intentions did not materialise. The promised 'modernisation' of the party resulted in its split in late 1962, with Frondizi and Frigerio remaining at the head of the minuscule Movement for Integration and Development (MID) which had its most prominent role supporting General Onganía's thwarted 'Argentine Revolution', and later added its tiny voice to the many Peronist coalitions that were set up in the next thirty years.[1]

After the experience of the Peronist decade, marked by the relegation of politics – and principled politics at that – large sectors of society expected a more honest, more open, behaviour. In this respect, they would feel deceived by the developmentalist preference for secretive wheeling-and-dealing. As an autonomous group in a society where interest groups were deeply entrenched, the developmentalists were dependent on ephemeral pacts and fortuitous circumstances which, in the last instance, weakened their strategy. They wanted too much too soon, and they hoped to achieve it through sheer will power.

If the military, aware of Frondizi's contacts with the Peronists, and angry at the oppositionist tone of his 1957 electoral campaign, were suspicious from the start, in general the public attitude was one of hopeful expectation. The favourable image began to change – as happens in time with all governments – perhaps a bit too soon as a result of the 'shock' treatment favoured by Frigerio. Policy reversals such as those entailed by the oil contracts with foreign companies required extreme prudence and openness, instead, the public was faced with ruthlessness and secrecy.

The problem was that any mass enthusiasm that existed arose from the expected delivery of policies that had already been forsaken at the time of the election, even though very few people realised this. It was not surprising that such enthusiasm soon turned into bitterness and anger. The enthusiasm of some, based on a broad confidence that the government would carry out the general principles in the *Avellaneda* charter, would soon turn into antagonism when it became clear that it was to follow an uncharted path. When Frondizi lost the backing of the Peronists, with whose votes he had won in 1958, he seemed permanently uncomfortable dealing with those sectors which could provide an alternative source of support.

In the debate between 'equity' and 'growth', the developmentalists chose the latter as a necessary base for the former. Frigerio seemed to believe that obstinacy and determination were enough to bring about the desired changes. There was little time for persuasion if in any case once economic growth was achieved, everybody would unfailingly recognise the correctness of the developmentalist strategy.

Since there is no one-to-one relationship between the economy and politics, perhaps in a country such as post-Peronist Argentina, where the degree of political mobilisation and institutionalisation was high, the emphasis could have been placed in nurturing and contributing to establish on a firm basis a political system where the rules of competition and succession would be awarded prime importance in the context of the separation of powers established by the Constitution. By neglecting party politics and undermining the checks and balances embodied in the 1853 Constitution, Frigerio – and Frondizi – contributed to intensify the political instability that became the outstanding feature of a protracted period in post-war Argentina. Frigerio and his Integrationists generally, showed a low level of tolerance for the political game, tending to regard democratic procedures as an obstacle. In their eyes, 'development' would achieve the political aim they had set themselves – the need to overcome the identity crisis dividing the Argentine population between Peronists and anti-Peronists. However laudable the objective, events proved that the wound Peronism had inflicted in the fabric of society could not be healed by will power alone.

When the question is asked as to what were the developmentalist goals and projections, what type of society they hoped and expected to build, one can hardly go beyond the aim of industrialisation. But the way they behaved, their style of political behaviour, inevitably shaped things to come. Their quest for certainty neglected political virtues of prudence in favour of the pseudo-science of development. In their zeal to change the economy, the developmentalists disregarded the existing institutions of parliamentary democracy, badly battered by the Peronist corporatist experiment. Frigerio's politics were based upon an amoral recognition of reality, and an expectation that politics be bent to serve a doctrinaire objective – industrialisation. His economic determinism prevailed.

The initial coalition of 1958 was inevitably going to be broken by the pragmatic approach to economic policy favoured by Frondizi and Frigerio, but in the process their methods prevented them from conforming a new balance of power, a new coalition of forces. This became impossible once the secretive nature of governmental decisions enhanced the view that Frondizi could not be trusted. Democracy – albeit limited – was rapidly corroded by private deals among the great, the good and the not-so-good, quietly trading away the people's right to judge for themselves what was happening. Perhaps if Frondizi and the Integrationists had showed more respect for democratic institutions and open government, they would have achieved more in the long run.

If Perón had believed that his own presence was enough to occupy the whole of the political arena, the Integrationists sought to replace politicians with technicians – the political argument was replaced by a technical one. It was this difference that made Perón old and Frondizi modern. This was, too, where Frondizi was set apart from the *Libertadora* – for him, Peronism was not wrong, it was obsolete, and so were all political parties, none more so than the UCR. It was this that had made the split of the UCR in 1957 unavoidable. Developmentalism was not an ideology in transition, attempting to bridge the gap between the traditional spirit of the UCR and the new imperatives of a modern, industrial, society. It was a new ideology, seeking to fill the void of the transition from one form of society to another.

It could be argued that the most lasting damage was the developmentalist contribution to the existing ideological disorder (to use Halperín Donghi's expression). While endeavouring to create a new political imagery, and bring about the modernisation of the country, the developmentalists stuck to old words which they unsuccessfully tried to imbue with new meanings. The result was an increasing semantic confusion which left the way open for those determined to fill those words with their proper meaning. Thus 'liberation', 'revolution', 'national and popular' were 're-redefined', and Frondizi emerged as the embodiment of the 'perfidious' character of reformism.

Perón had continued the old Radical tradition of blurring distinctions in the political spectrum. Under Frondizi, political alignments in Argentina still could not be neatly fitted into a framework of 'left' and 'right'. The developmentalist discourse was presented as in opposition to 'the enemy', an ill-defined mixture of old-fashioned imperialists (the US was never mentioned in this context, since it was the source of the 'good' capital, as opposed to British 'colonial' pretensions), exporters of primary products, and left-wing intellectuals blinded by their own dogmatism. Meanwhile, the bogeyman of 'dark interests lurking against the nation' was the kind of rhetoric that was hardly designed to restore Argentina's tarnished image of a reliable associate in world affairs. It had become a frontier zone in constant danger of changing sides, and on this basis Frondizi negotiated wearisomely every instance of the country's support in regional and international fora, something totally unacceptable in the eyes of the military for whom the allegiance to the 'Western and Christian world' entailed something more than a mere declaration.

While hoping to be fair to Frondizi and Frigerio and judge them in their own terms, it is still advisable to look at the opportunities that were missed as well as the ones that were seized. The depiction of their government as a 'conditioned government' does not paint the whole picture. It is not unreasonable to argue that the conditions were present in 1958 both to transform Perón into an anachronism, and to ensure the return of the armed forces to their barracks. This was the opportunity that Frondizi missed.

It has often been said that Frondizi was doomed from the start, and moreover, that once he had the benefit of hindsight, he said that he should not have accepted the government under such constraints. During the Frondizi years Peronism had more a reactive capability than the ability of posing a real threat – it was too divided, deriving its strength from the even deeper divisions of its opponents. Moreover, Frondizi failed to mention that the military's mistrust of him stemmed from the awareness of the close contacts some of his close collaborators were actively establishing with Perón in exile. Indeed, having so often been accused of Machiavellianism, double-dealing and treacherous behaviour, Frondizi has consistently tried to restore his image of principled politician. But a seasoned politician such as he was could hardly expect the revolutionaries of 1955 to swallow the bitter pill of his constant condemnation and simultaneous emulation of Peronist rhetorics. His claim that he should not have accepted the government has a feeble ring to it. One could plausibly argue that it was precisely the novelty of the situation that should have been – and indeed was – the cause for optimism. After all, the transfer of power on 1 May 1958 to a victorious oppositionist candidate was unusual in the political history of Argentina since 1916. Perhaps a more truthful self-criticism would have entailed the repudiation of Frigerio's advise to seek Perón's support.

Had internal factors been better managed, the impact of external ones might have been softened. It is not far-fetched to suggest that scores of university students and young professionals who in the late 1960s and early 1970s uncritically embraced violence as a *Deus-ex-machina*, might have been diverted from that tragic course if they had felt the politico-institutional system was worthy of defence. Politics became a disreputable activity once again. It was no longer an activity aimed at the conciliation of existing diverse interests. Diversity was shunned. There could be but one interest, that of the people as a whole. And such interest, threatened by the dark and evil forces of foreign and oligarchical conspiracies, could only be furthered by violent means. The contaminated activity of politics – hypocrisy, cynicism, *affairisme* – was contrasted with the purity and selflessness of violence.

Notes

Preface

1. Dietz, James and Dilmus James (eds) (1990) p. 203.
2. *New Society*, 13 November 1975.
3. PRO FO 371/155836, 2 June 1961.

Chapter 1

1. British Foreign Office files held at the Public Record Office, Kew Gardens, London, catalogued as FO 371/114019, Wilde, 5 September 1955.
2. FO 371/114019, 18 August 1955.
3. del Carril (1959) p. 57.
4. On Yrigoyen's style see Ana M. Mustapic (1984) and on the continuity between Perón and the Argentine political tradition see T. Halperín (1991).
5. Presidencia de la Nación, *Memoria del Gobierno Provisional de la Revolución Libertadora, 1955–58*, where Perón and Peronism were described in an almost incomprehensible rhetoric, as, for example: 'The process aimed at equalising all in the face of one man's omnipotence, a process which strengthened its structure on the unattainable illusion of demagogical sands, and which had marched on, imperturbable, for more than ten years, managed to impose a juridical order saturated with abusive restrictions . . . '. *Ibid.*, p. 9.
6. Quoted in Torre (1990) p. 171.
7. Jorge Triacca, leader of the plastic-workers union, remarked that the 'demobilisation' reflected the distance between the rank and file and the 'smug' leadership [Triacca interview]. For an account of workers disaffection with Perón at the time, see Guillermo Makin, 'Political Crises in Argentina: 1955 and 1975–76' (unpublished Ph.D. thesis, University of Cambridge, 1984) chapter 3. Makin quotes Gómez Morales, one of Perón's Economy ministers, as saying that 'Perón himself was worried that his doctrinal message was not receiving the same enthusiastic hearing of earlier days'. Robert D.Crassweller (1987) chapter IV, section 10, makes a similar point. In chapter 9 he offers a lively account of 'the decadence of Peronism, 1950–55'. For an interpretation of the special identification existing between Perón and the workers see Juan Carlos Torre, 'Interpretando (una vez más) los

orígenes del peronismo', *Desarrollo Económico*, vol. 28, no. 112 and Torre (1990), where he traces the pre-Perón union leadership's defeat in seeking to ensure an autonomous role for the unionised workers *vis-à-vis* Perón.

8. Torre would disagree that such disaffection existed among the grassroots; *ibid.*
9. Taking 100 as index value of Australia's exports, in 1945–47 the value of Argentina's exports was 163, while it had fallen to 65 in 1949–51 and 54 in 1954–6 (the index value for Brazil in those same years was 132, 79 and 84). Figures provided by Díaz Alejandro at a seminar held at St Antony's College, Oxford, on 3 July 1981. For the UK and US attitudes see Rapoport (1981), Escudé (1988) and Newton (1992).
10. See below.
11. Díaz Alejandro (1970) p. 112. Although world demand for wheat had greatly expanded in the aftermath of World War II, Argentina's share in the world market had gone down from 19% to 9%. Prebisch pointed out that Argentina was thirty years behind in agricultural technology: cf. his otherwise self-critical 'Recollections' in Di Tella and Platt (eds) (1985).
12. Report by FIAT/OECEI, *Veinticinco años de la vida económica y financiera de la República Argentina*, Buenos Aires, FIAT, 1961. See also Zuvekas (1966). Prebisch's *Preliminary Report* of October 1955 seems to have underestimated the total Argentine foreign indebtedness, which it placed at US $757 million in 1955 (FO 371/114030).
13. Díaz Alejandro (1970) p. 269.
14. See for instance Pablo Gerchunoff, 'Peronist Economic Policies, 1946–55', in Di Tella and Dornbusch (eds) (1989) p. 59.
15. Taking 1950 as 100, industrial wages fell from 104 in 1949 to 82 in 1952, *ibid.* For economic indicators for the years 1950–55, see Pablo Gerchunoff, *op. cit.*, p. 76. Gerchunoff's indices for real wages are: 172.1 in 1950, 145 in 1951, 128.5 in 1952, 135.2 in 1953, 152.2 in 1954 and 151.9 in 1955. Although higher than in 1952, wages in 1955 had not achieved 1950 levels.
16. Memorandum from the Deputy Assistant Secretary of State for Inter-American Affairs (Lyon) to the Secretary of State, on the 'Motives of the Argentine Revolution'. Besides what he described as the 'Weakness of Controlled Labour Movement', the Assistant Secretary of State listed the following reasons for Perón's downfall: (1) Desire for a change ('any government becomes shop-worn ... the serious moral let-down during the latter period of Perón's rule ... a drive for more and more absolute power ... abolition of many civil liberties ... perversion of schools, and a growing belief of the existence of widespread corruption'); (2) Church-State conflict ('if there was any one immediate cause ... it was the Church matter'); (3) uneasiness in Armed Forces. Department of State, Central Files, 735.00/10–755, reproduced in

Foreign Relations of the United States, 1955–57, vol. VII, pp. 381–2, henceforth *Foreign Relations*.
17. Milton S. Eisenhower (1963) p. 64. See also Stephen G. Rabe (1988), chapters 4 and 5.
18. Moreover, Perón had indicated to the Americans his readiness to discuss bilateral military cooperation in the context of 'Argentina's contribution to hemispheric defense [. . .] in the event of a third world war', *Foreign Relations*, vol. VII, p. 358 (Nufer to Department of State, 23 March 1955). See also Newton (1992) chapter 17. By May the Americans were talking about the possible initiation of a military assistance programme to Argentina, *ibid.*, p. 360. In August the Joint Chiefs of Staff did not consider it 'judicious to make an unsupported estimate of the probable initial size . . . of a military aid programme' without first undertaking a military survey of Argentina. They insisted on such a survey at the end of November 1955, by the time the *Revolución Libertadora* had taken over (*ibid.*, p. 361).
19. Cf. Jesse H. Stiller (1987) p. 230. On Braden's role see Roger Gravil (1991); Rapoport (1980); Carlos Escudé (1983), and chapters by Escudé, Rapoport and Callum Macdonald in Guido di Tella and D. Cameron Watt (1989). Also Newton (1992) chapter 19.
20. *Foreign Relations*, volume VII, pp. 353–4. The agreement was finally signed in Washington on 27 February 1956.
21. *Ibid.*, p. 359.
22. After much insistence from the Americans that waiting until 1956 would 'not be satisfactory', especially in view of the agreement with the UK to start remittances in 1955, a reluctant Gómez Morales, who had been 'unhappy over enforced compliance [of] Perón's commitment [to Nufer]', finally agreed on 22 August to equalise 'in all other respects the treatment of United States investors with that accorded the British', *Foreign Relations*, vol. VII, pp. 369, 370 and 373.
23. Decree 637 of 19 January 1955 granted retroactive application of Law No. 14222 of 23 August 1954 on Foreign Capital Investment, to capital investments antedating that legislation. Ambassador Nufer wrote to Washington on 20 January that the provisions of the decree were 'extremely disappointing. About half American companies [in Argentina] not engaged in manufacturing or mining', *Foreign Relations* pp. 350 and 363.
24. Memorandum of conversation held at the Department of State in Washington on 28 July 1955, between Argentine Ambassador Hipólito J. Paz and Assistant Secretary Holland, *Foreign Relations*, p. 372.
25. Holland to Nufer, 6 September 1955, *Foreign Relations*, vol. VII, p. 375.
26. Memorandum of conversation between Holland and Paz, *ibid.*, p. 367.
27. See Jorge Fodor, 'Argentina's Nationalism: Myth or Reality?' and Pablo Gerchunoff, *op. cit.*, both in G. Di Tella and R. Dornbusch (1989).

28. FO 371/114021, confidential letter from D. F. Muirhead to Ivor Vincent at the American Department, Foreign Office, 25 June 1955: 'Before June 16, US-Argentine relations were pretty good in spite of Perón's unpopularity with the Americans generally'.
29. *Ibid.* Muirhead went on to report that in an official Press statement, the chairman of the Inter-American Sub-Committee of the House of Representatives Foreign Affairs Committee concluded that 'the revolt was the work of anti-Perón forces and "Communist planning"', thus echoing Perón's own statements at the time.
30. *The Wall Street Journal*, 27 June 1955.
31. FO 371/114022. The UK embassy in Buenos Aires reported that the Radical Party was endeavouring to represent Perón as a 'stooge of the United States': 'there is mounting resentment in opposition circles against the support afforded to Perón by US policy, which is partly blamed for enabling him to remain in power', FO 371/114019, 18 August 1955.
32. Cf. FO 371/114019, A1015/17, 1955.
33. See Philip (1982) and Solberg (1979) on Perón's oil policies.
34. *Foreign Relations*, vol. VII, p. 382.
35. *Ibid.*
36. Decree No. 18,411, 31 December 1943; on Perón's 'instrumental use' of the religious question, see Lila Caimari's 'El lugar del catolicismo en el primer peronismo', paper presented at the Instituto Universitario Ortega y Gasset, Madrid, 29–31 May 1991.
37. Caimari (*op. cit.*) traces Perón's anticlericalism to 1948, and in October 1950 the Israeli ambassador interpreted Perón and Evita's warm words read at the opening of a Congress of the Spiritualist Movement (held under the slogan 'Jesus is not God') as another sign of the worsening of relations between Perón and the Catholic Church. Israel State Archives, Jerusalem, Report 100, 20 October 1950. I am indebted to Ignacio Klich for bringing the Israeli documents to my attention. The British were less impressed by such matters and as late as 1955 the UK military attaché concluded that 'despite rumours that the Government's recent attacks on the Church have caused some disaffection among army officers and their wives, Gral.Perón can count on the solid backing of the army', FO 371/114051, 28 January 1955.
38. Furthermore, the Church was increasingly worried at the spread of the Evita cult, at times placed on an equal standing with the Virgin Mary. For a comprehensive description of all the reasons behind Perón's decision to confront the Church openly see Crassweller (1987) chapter 9.
39. The Christian Democratic Party was established in Argentina in 1956, having had its origin in the Unión Federal Demócrata Cristiana that had been meeting clandestinely since 1954.
40. The Archbishop in Córdoba province prohibited Catholic youth from affiliating to the Córdoba branch of UES. The Israeli Ambassador

reported all such instances to the Foreign Ministry in Jerusalem aware that any deepening of the conflict between the Catholic hierarchy and Perón provoked a new wave of anti-Semitism. Israel State Archives, B/1/4/122. Such worries were also transmitted to the Argentine Foreign minister, see Archivo del Ministerio de Relaciones Exteriores y Culto, Depto. de Europa Oriental y Cercano Oriente, Expediente Varios, Buenos Aires, 17/955, 27 June and 5 July 1955. I am indebted to Ignacio Klich for drawing my attention to this documenatation.

41. *Boletín del Ministerio de Justicia e Instrucción Pública*, July 1947, p. 2062, quoted in Caimari (1991).
42. When the possibility of divorce legislation began to be discussed in 1952, Monsignor De Andrea had publicly addressed the government and asked 'What are you trying to do? Do you wish to attack the Church and her priests? If this is so, kill us, confiscate our goods, expel us from the country, but I beg you not to attack the integrity and purity of the family: do not destroy the basis of Christian society', quoted by Jonathan Pratto, of the Israeli Legation in Buenos Aires, 27 June 1952, Israel State Archives, /6868. Throughout June 1955 the Israeli Ambassador in Argentina reported to Jerusalem the circulation of anti-Semitic pamphlets blaming the issue of separation on the Jews, amongst which they included Angel Borlenghi, Perón's Interior minister. Israel State Archives, Jerusalem, 10 June 1955, Ambassador Arieh Kubovy to Minister Moshe Tov.
43. See Rouquié (1981) vol. II, pp. 105–7.
44. It was one of the main accusations resulting in Perón's degradation from the rank of general, and a reason for his permanent civil disqualification. These decisions were reversed during Héctor Cámpora's brief presidency – May to July 1973 – which opened the way for Perón's comeback.
45. Perón's apparent inclination towards spiritist practices and rituals fed this image. See fn. 38 above.
46. The late Radical Party leader Miguel Angel Zavala Ortiz confirmed in a personal interview that he had been aboard one of the naval planes.
47. FO 371/114021, 12 July 1955. There was no love lost between Perón and the Foreign Office. Penciled in the margins of a report from the UK embassy in Montevideo on the strength of anti-Peronist feeling in Uruguay, one reads 'My liking for the Uruguayans grows', *ibid*.
48. On the issue of remittances Scarpati had remarked 'this is something Nufer has talked Perón into', *Foreign Relations*, vol. VII, p. 370.
49. Hoover to Nufer, 20 June 1955, *ibid.*, p. 366.
50. See chapter 2. The other politician was Vicente Solano Lima, Popular Conservative.
51. *The New York Times*, 10 April 1955.
52. The late Dr Laureano Landaburu, who would become Aramburu's Interior minister, remarked that he had been 'a revolutionary since day one, long before the military', in a reference to civilian impatience

with what they saw as military procrastination. Personal interview. For details of the psychological campaign to impress the opposition to Perón, see Potash (1981) (Spanish edition), p. 170, fn. 68 and also p. 179. There had been earlier attempts to overthrow Perón. The first had been led in September 1951 by General Benjamín Menéndez which resulted in the imposition of the state of war lasting until Perón's downfall. In February 1952 Colonel José Francisco Suárez had planned Perón's assassination. See Potash, pp. 199–201.
53. For the full text see *La Nación*, 1 September 1955. For an account of the day's events, see Potash (Spanish version), pp. 266–8. For the UK ambassador's reaction see FO 371/114019, AA 1015/20, 1955.
54. FO 371/114019, 13 September 1955.
55. del Carril, p. 54. Lonardi's chief credentials, besides his undisputed moral standing, was his participation in the failed June 1951 attempt, for which he was imprisoned for a year. Several others, amongst them Alejandro Lanusse, were still in prison.
56. General Lonardi's son, Luis Ernesto, said these were the reasons behind his father's decision to act; letter published in the magazine *Qué sucedió en siete días*, 2 July 1957; see also Marta Lonardi (1981) for a personal account of her father's role.
57. Lyon to Barnes, 7 October 1955, *Foreign Relations*, vol. VII, p. 380.
58. *La Nación*, 19 September 1955.
59. *La Nación*, 24 September 1955.
60. General Lanusse, a staunch anti-Peronist who was still in prison in 1955 for his participation in the 1951 coup attempt, remarked that although a majority of military personnel were loyalists, they showed 'no enthusiasm to defend what was indefensible'. In the course of a personal interview in 1988, he remarked that of all the coups from the one on 6 September 1930 to the one of 26 March 1976, including all those in which he had taken part, the only one that was not a mistake was the one of 16 September 1955.
61. General Alejandro A. Lanusse insisted on this point, regretting the widespread tendency to refer to 'the army' as an entity with a unified conception. Personal interview.
62. Personal interview.
63. Perón's efforts in this sense had been so successful that the UK military attaché remarked that 'the Argentine army is the best in South America, with the possible exception of the Brazilian. [Improvements in the barracks means that] conditions of living therein are now as good as any in the British army'; FO 371/114051, 28 January 1955.
64. Secret despatch from Nufer to the Department of State, *Foreign Relations*, 9 December 1955, p. 391.
65. *Ibid.*, p. 392; see also pp. 398–9 on the matter of military aid to Argentina. For the background to these negotiations see Newton (1992) chapters 16 and 17.

66. *La Nación*, 26 April 1956. On the ideological trends in military society see Rouquié (1982) chapter 3.
67. Huntington (1969) p. 226, has argued that the ideology of guardianship has a corrupting effect on the political system, establishing the divorce between responsibility and power. See also R. Potash (1980) and A. Rouquié (1978), Spanish edition, 1982.
68. *La Nación*, 23 November 1956.
69. In November 1955 the Córdoba parachute regiment that had arrived at the Casa Rosada (Government House) with Lonardi told Aramburu that they wanted to leave because 'indiscipline was rife amongst young officers hanging about the Casa Rosada all day, having the use of cars and in contact with young women', Colombo interview.
70. At the time Aramburu wishfully tried to see it otherwise when he said, in a speech he entitled 'Freedom won': 'A lot of Argentine blood was spilt in a few hours. Let that blood, that Argentine blood, even of those who were in the wrong, bring about, once and for all, the unity of nationhood so that, united and without deception, it will advance in an enlightened path towards its lofty ideals.' *La Nación*, 10 June 1956.
71. US observers reported the execution 'following trial by military court', of 16 active and retired military personnel and 18 civilians; *Foreign Relations*, vol. VII, p. 412. The British quote Rojas' figure of 'only 28 executed'. In his account to Selwyn Lloyd, Fordham stated that if the rebellion 'did not develop into something a great deal more serious it was because the Government were well aware that trouble was brewing and were deliberately waiting for the revolutionaries to show their hand', FO 118–858, AA1015/37, 23 June 1956. According to Colombo, when on 1st June he told Aramburu and the intelligence service chiefs that he had heard that a conspiracy was on the offing, they dismissed him as 'a crazy man, a *gorila*' (personal interview). The accounts are not necessarily contradictory, since what Aramburu dismissed on 1 June may have been taken more seriously by Rojas a few days later. Fordham reported that 'the authorities seem to have had a last minute warning on the evening of the 9th', *ibid*.
72. *The New York Times*, 21 September 1955, and *Foreign Relations*, vol. VII, p. 378.
73. Del Carril (1959) p. 132. Another who would be surprised was Rogelio Frigerio: see chapter 4.
74. *La Nación*, 24 September 1955.
75. This pamphlet is reproduced in Amadeo (1956). The British ambassador remarked that although 'General Lonardi seems to have been a fundamentally decent type of Argentine [. . .] he exposed himself too readily to the influence of his Nationalist advisers, who were completely out of touch with political reality', FO 118–850, AA1015/82 Evans to Foreign Office. Amadeo, who represented the extreme clerical Right, was during the 1930s and later in World War II closely identified with German interests; Newton (1992) p. 120.

76. Newton (1992) pp. 240–1. Newton also reveals that while in Germany Goyeneche had sent messages to '"Juan" (i.e. Perón)' through the German embassy in Buenos Aires; *ibid.*, fn. 83.
77. *La Nación*, 26 September 1955. None the less, Sir Francis Evans wrote that 'it is reported from several factories that there are strong undercurrents not only of resentment (which is natural) but of expectations that Perón's return is imminent', FO 371/114020, AA1015/45, 6 October 1955.
78. Cavarozzi (1979) p. 15, records the displeasure of 'democratic trade unionists' at the appointment of Cerrutti Costa. For an illuminating account of the role of labour in the rise of Perón see Torre (1990).
79. *La Nación*, 22 October 1955.
80. For an analysis of the different views, see Cavarozzi (1979).
81. After his displacement Bengoa attempted briefly to lead a neo-Peronist movement. A French correspondent described him as in favour of 'a social and national reformism, corporativist and authoritarian . . . a sort of Francoism with the masses being looked after by the Army in the name of anti-imperialism and social justice', *Le Monde*, 2 October 1956.
82. For an account of its features and demise, see Halperín Donghi (1964). For the events of 13 November see Potash (1980), Lonardi (1981), and Lanusse (1988).
83. The US ambassador did not make a distinction in his telegram referring to 'the provisional government which took over after September 16 . . . first headed by Lonardi and now by Aramburu', remarking that '[the provisional government] is the friendliest toward US which has existed here for many years [. . .] friendly disposition toward US and democratic orientation – have been relatively infrequent in Argentina history and do not have firm, deep roots. It [is important] to help nurture this tender plant and do what we can [to] ensure its continuance and further growth', *Foreign Relations*, vol. VII, pp. 396–7. But two days after Aramburu displaced Lonardi, Assistant Secretary of State Holland noted that 'the new group [i.e. Aramburu] was more acceptable to the US than the Lonardi régime', *ibid.*, p. 383, 15 November 1955.
84. Halperín (1964) p. 81. The *Libertadora* tried to overcome this contradiction by making a distinction between origins and intentions: 'The Provisional Government never mistook its origin and *de facto* character [. . .] with the profound and genuine democratic goals, directives and achievements that are its guide, and which it has loyally been putting into practice. The democratic essence does not lie in its origin and manner of accession to power, but in the ethical reasons that determined the latter, as well as in the means it employs to achieve the proposed ends.' *Memoria del Gobierno Provisional*, *op. cit.*, pp. 32–3.
85. Interview with Héctor Sandler. Sandler was a lieutenant in the Air Force and was active in the September movement. He retired from the

Air Force in 1963 to become Aramburu's close political collaborator in the setting up of a new party, the *Unión del Pueblo Adelante* (UDELPA).
86. *Directivas Básicas del Gobierno Revolucionario*, Presidencia de la Nación (Buenos Aires, 1955) p. 12.
87. *Le Monde*, 2 October 1956.
88. S. Sigal and E. Verón, in Rouquié (ed.) (1982) offer a lucid analysis of Perón's speeches to illustrate the way he implemented the 'emptying of the political space', pp. 180–5.
89. Quoted in Lonardi (1981) p. 214.
90. *La Nación*, 9 June 1956. This speech was delivered hours before General Valle's failed insurrection (see above).
91. Sir Francis Evans to Selwyn Lloyd, FO 118– 859, 30 October 1956.
92. 'Dr Frondizi is *persona non grata* with most of the Provisional Government (particularly with the Naval Ministers) as it is feared that his election as President would mean a return to *caudillismo*, or a personal form of government', *ibid*.
93. The divisions within the UCR will be analysed in the following chapter. The *unionistas* had favoured the UCR's participation in the *Unión Democrática* against Perón in 1946, while the *intransigentes* had opposed it.
94. In personal interviews, both Dr Laureano Landaburu and Dr Miguel Angel Zavala Ortiz, the latter of the *unionista* faction of the UCR, confirmed that the intelligence services were aware of such contacts as early as 1956. These will be analysed in chapter 3.
95. Landaburu interview.
96. For an analysis of the debate surrounding the sanctioning of the Sáenz Peña Law, see Botana (1979) chapter 9.
97. Junta Consultiva Nacional, 30 October 1956, p. 4.
98. *Intransigente* López Serrot during the debate on the electoral law, *ibid.*, p. 298.
99. Frondizi would try to introduce proportional representation again in December 1961: see chapter 9. The 28 July 1957 elections will be analysed in chapter 3.
100. Quoted in *La Nación*, 17 November 1955.
101. Carri (1967) p. 76.
102. Sir John Ward to Selwyn Lloyd, FO 371/131947, AA1011, 10 March 1958. Ward had taken over as ambassador from the departing Sir Francis Evans on 30 October 1957. For an account of Peronist violence at the time, see Samuel Amaral, 'El avión negro: retórica y práctica de la violencia', paper presented at the XVI International Congress of the *Latin American Studies Association*, Washington, D.C., 4–6 April 1991.
103. Personal interview. Speaking at a dinner held to celebrate the 24th anniversary of the *Libertadora*, Admiral Rojas regretted that the latter was 'unable to perform the surgical and disinfectant mission that the

health of the nation required. It allocated itself too short a time', *La Nación*, 26 September 1979.
104. For an analysis of the unions throughout this period, see Carri (1967), Cavarozzi (1979), and Torre (1980).
105. Still, as will be seen below, workers did not do at all badly during those years. See Díaz Alejandro (1970).
106. Torre (1980) p. 145.
107. The rest of the Cabinet was 'more conformist, more in favour of maintaining a kind of hybrid', Alvaro Alsogaray, personal interview. At the time a US newspaper reported 'considerable pessimism . . . among US and other foreign investors. Among the contributory causes was the persistent belief that the government was not proceeding rapidly enough in eliminating state controls over business and industry', *The New York Times*, 4 January 1957.
108. For a detailed analysis of Prebisch's report, see Díaz Alejandro (1965).
109. Address at a conference held in Oxford in 1981. The proceedings were published in Di Tella and Platt (eds) (1985). Privately he had recognised his mistake much earlier. In the course of a private interview, Ingeniero D'Adamo, who in 1956 was working at ECLA, recalled that in May 1958 Prebisch had told him that he had erred in his report; that having left the country in 1944, he did not personally know any industrial entrepreneurs, and that his judgement had been influenced by his friends, all in the agricultural sector.
110. 'Argentina: Annual Review for 1957', 10 March 1958, FO 371/131947.
111. *Ibid.*
112. *Ibid.*
113. *Foreign Relations*, vol. VII, pp. 400–403. A copy of the memorandum was sent to the Treasury, Commerce, and Defense Ministries and the Export-Import Bank on 9 February 1956.
114. *Ibid.*, p. 407, letter from Viron Vaky of the Office of South American Affairs to Henry Holland, 27 February 1956.
115. NAC Staff Document 784, NAC Files: Lot 60 D 137, Staff Documents, quoted in *Foreign Relations*, vol. VII, p. 407.
116. *Ibid.*
117. Summation of discussions with Coll Benegas mission on 20 July 1956. The stress was on the need for Argentina to make arrangements with 'European countries regarding convertibility', since her main export gains were in European currencies. *Foreign Relations*, vol. VII, p. 427.
118. *Ibid.*, pp. 421–4. On 16 July Henry Holland arranged a meeting attended by Eisenhower, Secretary of State Dulles and Treasury Secretary Humphrey, together with officials from the Eximbank prior to the president's trip to Panama, where he was bound to meet Aramburu. Holland wanted Eisenhower to convey to the Argentine Provisional

President the impression that the US 'will help out Argentina with some financing', and mentioned the figure of US $200 million (out of the US $500 million he said Argentina sought).

119. Holland expressed his worries about the 'current Soviet campaign for closer economic and diplomatic relations with Latin America', and said that if the ABC countries 'follow an anti-communist, pro-United States, pro-private enterprise road, then the course of the balance of Latin America is assured'. The opposite path would have 'calamitous' consequences, and thus it would stand to reason to 'exceed the volume of loans which can be justified by purely banking and economic considerations'. He reminded the Secretary of State of the 'huge grant aid programmes' elsewhere in the world, where non-economic grounds had justified them, since they were deemed 'necessary in order to produce the kind of attitude that we want in the countries concerned'. After all, aid programmes 'in this hemisphere [. . .] cost little, less than 1% of the global cost'. Holland's secret memo to Dulles, 11 July 1956, *ibid.*, pp. 416–20.

120. Memorandum of conversation held in Washington with Coll Benegas at the start of the latter's mission, 6 July 1956. *Foreign Relations*, vol. VII, pp. 413–15. Holland's secret memo to Dulles on 11 July. *Ibid.*, pp. 416–20.

121. *Ibid.*, p. 414. The German-owned CATE had become CHADE (*Compañía Hispano-Americana de Electricidad*) in 1920, although the capital, technology and work-force remained German. In 1929 it was absorbed by SOFINA, with a majority of British and Belgian capital, although 15 per cent remained German. CHADE became CADE (*Compañía Argentina de Electricidad*) in 1936, and majority control lay with Berlin banks. By 1939 CADE produced 61 per cent of Argentina's electrical energy; Newton (1992) pp. 14, 18 and 104. See also chapter 2 below.

122. *Foreign Relations*, vol. VII, p. 414.

123. Again raised at the Panama meeting between Rear Admiral Rial (Acting Foreign Minister), Ambassador Vicchi, Dulles, Holland and Bernbaum (Office of South American Affairs, OSA) (*Foreign Relations*, 23 July 1956, pp. 429–33) to discuss the on-going Coll Benegas mission.

124. *Ibid.*, pp. 441–4.

125. *Ibid.*, p. 443.

126. Dulles' meeting with Vicchi, 13 September 1956, *ibid.*, p. 448. Vicchi again raised the issue of Argentine disappointment a month later, on 23 October 1956 during a meeting at the State Department to discuss military equipment for Argentina. He said that 'it was difficult to explain to the man in the street how a $100 million out of a total amount of $1,800,000,000 loaned to Latin America by the Eximbank could be construed as very favorable consideration of Argentina by the US', *ibid.*, p. 451.

127. Reporting on the 'considerable pessimism' that flourished among

US and other foreign investors, *The New York Times* underlined as one of the 'contributory causes' the 'persistent belief that the government was not proceeding rapidly enough in eliminating state controls over business and industry'; *The New York Times*, 4 January 1957.
128. FO 371/126159, Annual Review for 1956.

Chapter 2

1. Personal interview with Héctor Sandler. A lieutenant in the Air Force, he was an active participant in the September 1955 movement. He retired from the Air Force to set up the *Unión del Pueblo Adelante* (UDELPA) party with Aramburu in 1963.
2. Cf. Ana María Mustapic (1984) for a revealing analysis of Yrigoyen's style of leadership. For a general discussion of leadership style and political culture see Diamond *et al.* (1989), Introduction.
3. Crick (1979) p. 55.
4. In the 1951 presidential elections Perón had obtained 64% of the vote and Ricardo Balbín, the UCR candidate, 32%.
5. PRO FO 371/131947, 1957.
6. Cf. Rose (1976) p. 327.
7. Factions are to be distinguished from tendencies insofar as they are 'self-consciously organised as a body, with a measure of discipline and cohesion'. A tendency, on the other hand, is 'a stable set of attitudes rather than a stable group of politicians [. . .]; the attitudes are held together by a more or less coherent political philosophy', in Rose (1976) pp. 313–14.
8. See, for instance, Hernández Arregui (1960); Ramos (1961); Jauretche (1960), and Ciria (1975).
9. Cf. Gallo and Sigal in Di Tella *et al.* (1966), pp. 130–41. They remark that during the formative years of the UCR the dominant issues were (a) the struggle for political participation; (b) the criticism of the corruption of previous governments and (c) the demand for provincial autonomy in opposition to the government's centralism.
10. *Ibid.*
11. Gallo, E., 'Argentina: society and politics, 1880–1916', in Leslie Bethell (ed.), *Cambridge History of Latin America*, vol. V, c. 1870 to 1930. See also Botana (1979) chapter 6.
12. Hipólito Yrigoyen was the first UCR president and the first Argentine president elected according to the Sáenz Peña Law of 1912 establishing universal, male suffrage. He was in office for a full term between 1916 and 1922; elected once again in 1928, he was deposed by the first military coup in seventy years. It was led by General Uriburu on 6 September 1930.
13. del Mazo (1955) p. 27.

14. See Rock (1975a) and (1975b).
15. For a characterisation of *Yrigoyenismo* from 1930–43 see Susana Brauner Rodgers (1990) pp. 79–98.
16. The fiscal austerity that Alvear tried to apply while he was president between 1922–8, was highly unpopular within the ranks of his own party, where high levels of State spending were not only a matter of career opportunities for the urban middle sectors, but a means of avoiding the effects of the economic depression of the first half of the 1920s. Alvear had managed to restore Congressional control over financial affairs and although he did not succeed in curbing the upward trend in government expenditure, he managed to balance the budget and slow down the growth of the debt.
17. Smith (1974) p. 79.
18. Díaz Alejandro (1975), for example table 66, p. 451, showing the steady increase in workers employed in industry throughout the decade.
19. Smith (1974) p. 44. Newton's book (1992) adds a new dimension to the 'infamy' of the 1930s.
20. In that year the UCR's National Convention lifted the party's previous electoral abstentionism. Ciria (1975) regrets this fact, implying that the loss of the UCR's revolutionary clout is to be understood as an historical catastrophe.
21. The Argentine Constitution does not allow the reelection of a president for a second consecutive term, this is why Yrigoyen had to await until 1928 to contest the presidency once again. Cf. del Mazo (1984) and del Mazo and Etchepareborda (1984).
22. Jauretche (1960) p. 15. In his biography of Alvear, Félix Luna wrote that Alvear's 'terrible mistake' was 'his unwillingness to infuse Radicalism with a clear anti-imperialist and anti-oligarchical – that is, emancipating – purpose', Luna (1958) p. 185.
23. del Mazo (1955) p. 277.
24. *Ibid.*
25. Personal interview with Eugenio Mondelli who was a member of FORJA, who remarked that 'FORJA's leftist taint' was a characterisation applied after it had ceased to exist.
26. Luciano Catalano wrote about the need for a plan for the 'hungry, the disinherited, the shirtless', a plan that would instal 'social welfare, basis and essence of social justice'; L. Catalano, *Plan Constructivo del Radicalismo*, Buenos Aires, 1933, quoted in Brauner (1990), while Arturo Frondizi had also insisted on social justice and land distribution.
27. Quoted in Jauretche (1960) p. 177.
28. Brauner (1990) pp. 88–9. The Bloc left the UCR in 1938, but rejoined it in 1940.
29. Quoted in Brauner, *ibid.*, p. 91.
30. See Torre (1990) for an account of politics in the 1930s, pp. 21–39.

Both Roberto Ortiz and Agustín Justo had been members of Alvear's cabinet during the latter's presidency (1922–28).
31. Cf. Félix Luna in Ferrari and Gallo (1980).
32. Torre (1990) pp. 31–2, has remarked that Argentine politics would have followed a very different path had it not been by the deaths in a short span of time of the three men committed to upholding democracy: Alvear, Ortiz and Justo.
33. Quoted in del Mazo (1955) p. 279.
34. For Perón's overtures towards Sabattini and the role of the UCR in blocking them, as well as an accord between Sabattini and General Avalos that could have stopped Perón in 1945, see Tcach (1988) and (1991) and Torre (1990). Some Radical members have since regretted the decision to reject an agreement with Perón, since it would have provided 'a chance to keep Perón under control'; personal interview with Jorge Wehbe. On the other hand, Miguel Angel Zavala Ortiz suspected Sabattini's espousal of democracy as 'argentinidad' rather than 'pluralism'; personal interview.
35. Quoted in del Mazo (1955) p. 293.
36. *Ibid.*, p. 300.
37. The full document is reproduced in the MIR periodical *Raíz*, Año 1, no. 1, December 1945, pp. 35–8.
38. Quoted in del Mazo (1955) pp. 324–5.
39. *Ibid.*, pp. 325–7.
40. The isolation had begun in 1942 when Argentina refused to declare the war on the Axis powers at the Rio Conference of Foreign Ministers and was not reversed when she belatedly did so on 26 January 1944. For these events, and those surrounding the signing of the Chapultepec Treaty on 4 April 1945 see Lanús (1984) pp. 18–26. Perón kept Argentina away from the IMF, World Bank and the GATT. The government of the *Revolución Libertadora* took Argentina into the IMF in 1956, and into GATT in 1957.
41. The Peronist coalition had obtained 1,486,866 votes against the Democratic Union's 1,208,880.
42. Rouquié (1975) p. 33 defined their position as 'ultra-Peronism – Perón plus one'.
43. Luna (1963) p. 50.
44. From *Profesión de Fe* . . . , quoted in del Mazo (1955) p. 324.
45. Quoted in del Mazo, *ibid.*, p. 331.
46. Ezequiel Gallo has remarked that the 'long-standing fashion' for intransigence has been one of the contributing factors to the recurring crises of Argentine political parties, in Beltrán (ed.) (1978) p. 128.
47. Halperín Donghi in *Contorno*, no. 9/10, April 1959, p. 76.
48. Quoted in the Intransigent periodical *Raíz*, July 1947, p. 29.
49. Quoted in *The Economist*, 25 May 1957.
50. See above.
51. Frondizi's speech, Cámara de Diputados, *Diario de Sesiones*, 1946,

vol. VII, 314, from now on, *Diputados*.
52. Quoted in del Mazo (1957) vol. II, pp. 362–3.
53. *Ibid.*, in italics in the original. Yrigoyen's alleged patriotic defence of Argentine oil was hardly motivated by 'pristine economic nationalism', as the MIR claimed, but rather by political opportunism. See Newton (1992) p. 92 and also Biddle (1991).
54. Perón's overthrow five months later meant that the contract was never implemented.
55. Reproduced in del Mazo (1957) vol. II, p. 371.
56. Years later, such dread had softened into a nearly patronising attitude. In a personal interview, leading *unionista* Miguel Angel Zavala Ortiz remarked that *Avellaneda* was 'very pompous, and pleasingly sentimental'.
57. Zavala Ortiz, prominent *unionista* took active part in the anti-Peronist conspiracy. He never denied widespread rumours in the sense that he had been on board one of the naval aeroplanes that bombarded Plaza de Mayo in June 1955. See chapter 1, pp. 5–6.
58. See chapter 1.
59. The *caudillos*', or *punteros*' style was 'to do favours obtaining jobs, getting somebody out of jail', that was their political activity and their livelihood. Wehbe interview. See Babini (1984) p. 19, for the role that he alleges Sabatino, Frondizi's local *caudillo*, played in launching Frondizi into a political career. For an account of the machine-politics tradition of the UCR, see Rock (1975a) pp. 110–14 and (1975b). The *caudillos* were part of a political tradition going back to the years of Conservative rule; their role was greatly expanded by Yrigoyen and remained a central feature of UCR style of politics until the phenomenon of mass affiliations in 1982. For the Conservative period see Botana (1979) pp. 186–9, and for the early years of Radicalism see Gallo in Bethell (ed.), *The Cambridge History of Latin America*, vol. V, chapter 10, p. 380.
60. The vice-presidents were Oscar Alende (future governor of Buenos Aires Province) and Celestino Gelsi (future governor of Tucumán Province). Two other members of the committee also became governors in 1958: Arturo Zanichelli (Córdoba) and Carlos Sylvestre Begnis (Santa Fe), all of them Intransigents.
61. Public address at a meeting organised by the *Junta Consultiva Nacional* on 10 January 1956. Typescript supplied by the author.
62. Personal interview.
63. Delivered on Radio *El Mundo* on 14 March 1956. Typescript supplied by the author.
64. Quoted in *Qué sucedió en siete días*, 25 April 1956.
65. *The New York Times*, 12 August 1956.
66. Gelsi interview.
67. *La Nación*, 6 November 1956. In a personal interview, Alconada Aramburú, an Intransigent from Buenos Aires who replaced Landaburu

as Aramburu's Interior minister, recalled that Balbín maintained that 'Frondizi [was] not really a Radical'.
68. *La Nación*, 6 November 1956.
69. Personal interview with Oyhanarte. Julio Oyhanarte became President of the Supreme Court of Justice in Frondizi's government.
70. For Perón's overtures to Sabattini and the conflicts within the UCR that prevented both an agreement with Perón or with General Avalos in 1945, see Tcach (1988) and (1991).
71. Personal interview with Gelsi.
72. Other members of *Unidad Radical* were Ernesto Sanmartino, Carlos Perette and Arturo Mathov; they stood on the right of the UCR.
73. *La Nación*, 10 November 1956.
74. Gelsi recalled that Frondizi proved so inept at canvassing support that a group of younger delegates, led by Gelsi himself, asked Frondizi 'to sit and wait' in a side room while they got on with the task of getting votes for Frondizi. Gelsi interview.
75. Gelsi was appointed interventor in the Province of Buenos Aires, a task which he, as a *tucumano*, understandably relished. Personal interview.
76. Quoted in del Mazo (1957) vol. II, p. 357.
77. Retired Brigadier Rojas Silveyra recalled his clandestine nocturnal meetings with Frondizi in cars to avoid the surveillance of Perón's secret services, with the purpose of discussing the latter's overthrow. Rojas Sylveira was the last of President Frondizi's Air Ministers. Personal interview.
78. del Mazo, *ibid.*
79. *Qué*, 29 April 1958.
80. Díaz (1977) p. 33.
81. Potash (1980) p. 236.

Chapter 3

1. del Mazo (1957) p. 313.
2. But he had raised the issue with the Navy minister and Rojas, cf.Potash (1980) p. 247. The resignations accepted, besides the two already mentioned, were those of Podestá Costa (Foreign Affairs), Carlos Adrogué (Education and Justice) and Luis Ygartúa (Communications). The Junta was constituted by the president, the vice-president and the ministers of the three forces.
3. PRO 371/ 126 161, 11 February 1957, Sir Francis Evans to Selwyn Lloyd.
4. *Ibid.* Sir Francis described Dr Blanco as 'a brusque and difficult person'. Sir Francis' successor as Ambassador to Buenos Aires was Sir John Ward, who arrived on 18 October 1957. In his annual report he remarked that although 'better exploitation of national oil resources'

was probably 'the only way in which the vicious circle of Argentina's economy can be broken', Aramburu's government 'would not face the political difficulties of granting any form of concession to foreign oil companies'. PRO FO 371/131947, 10 March 1958.
5. PRO FO 371/126161, 11 February 1957.
6. *La Nación*, 16 February 1957.
7. Frondizi (1957) p. 46.
8. *Ibid.*, p. 249.
9. Peronal interview with Dr Alconada Aramburú (not related to Aramburu).
10. PRO FO 371/126161, 1957.
11. The most renowned being former *forjista* Arturo Jauretche, and Raúl Scalabrini Ortiz. For the latter's connections with the German embassy during World War II see Newton (1992) p. 124.
12. *Qué*, 5 February 1957.
13. Cf. chapter 1.
14. The oil debate is discussed in chapter 5.
15. This was emphasised in personal interviews by Generals Lanusse, Solanas Pacheco and Sánchez de Bustamante, Brigadier Rojas Silveyra and Conservative politician Rodolfo Martínez.
16. *La Nación*, 21 November 1956. Newton estimates that during World War II about 10% of army officers were pro-Nazi; Newton (1992) p. 116.
17. See chapter 1. For an account of the events leading to the purge, see Potash (1980) pp. 241–3. A secret National Intelligence Estimate (NIE) Report pointed at 'inter-service rivalries and factionalism within the Army' as among the main factors threatening government stability, cf. *Foreign Relations of the United States, 1955–57*, vol. VII, p. 425.
18. Apocryphal Navy documents, purporting to show the latter's plans to establish its political dominance over the government of the *Libertadora*, were circulated amongst Army officers. See Potash, *ibid.*, p. 240.
19. Potash (1980) p. 239. The struggle over the political parties statute (see chapter 1) had left its scars in the Navy. Potash's account, based on Admiral Hartung's unpublished diaries, favours the Navy minister's view of the situation: '[Hartung] felt that the Navy's intentions had been deliberately misrepresented by elements sympathetic to Frondizi to make it appear that it was trying to veto a Frondizi candidacy, when its real objective was to assure the existence of a strong, well-organised centrist party capable of winning an election and taking over as a successor government.' *Ibid.*, p. 238. Notwithstanding, Dr Landaburu, who was responsible for the statute and thus at the centre of all pressures, did not think there was a 'deliberate misrepresentation', rather, a 'very accurate description of the situation'. Landaburu interview.
20. See chapter 1. Rodolfo Martínez, from a Conservative background, became one of the founders of the Christian Democratic Party.

21. PRO FO 371/126161, A1015, 22 March 1957.
22. *Ibid.*
23. *Qué*, 19 March 1957.
24. Sir Francis Evans reported to London that he had it 'on good authority that it was not merely a question of principle' which was the real point at issue, but Krause's and the Air Force officers' agreement with 'Frondizi Radicals, Solano Lima's Popular Democrats and the Right-Wing Unión Federal' that there should be no July elections prior to the presidential ones. PRO FO 371/126161, A1015/19, 8 April 1957.
25. PRO FO 371/126161, A1011/57, 30 May 1957. The ambassador noted that Ossorio had lost the confidence and respect of many of his officers because 'he drank too much, was living with somebody else's wife and had made enemies by his severe policy of retiring senior officers [in November 1956]', *ibid*. The dramatic purges carried out by Ossorio at the end of 1956 had eroded the fragile condition in which the September 1955 events had left the force. Moreover, the determination of younger officers to rid the force of suspected Peronist sympathisers had led to the setting of 'parallel commands' who took orders from die hard *gorilas* (that is, anti-Peronists) rather than from their own superior officers to maintain control of the garrisons.
26. Rubottom to Herter, Department of State, Central Files, 735.13 / 3–2557, 25 March 1957, reproduced in *Foreign Relations*, vol. VII, pp. 454–5.
27. *Ibid.*, p. 455. On 25 May 1957 *The Economist* noted that even if the government had – which it did not – the popular or political support to impose a systematic policy of austerity 'it would [. . .] have been extremely difficult to maintain because Argentinians are about the least austere people in the world'.
28. Krieger had become Secretary of the Economic and Social Council set up by the Provisional Government in 1955 and was a member of the 1956 Coll Benegas Financial Mission to the US.
29. *The Economist*, 26 March.
30. *Ibid.*, p. 461, 10 April 1957. On the subject of US financial assistance to Argentina see also *Foreign Relations*, pp. 456–95.
31. *Foreign Relations*, p. 493, 29 October 1957, memorandum of a conversation between Coll Benegas and Viron Vaky of the Office of South American Affairs.
32. *Ibid.*, pp. 456–60, 10 April 1957.
33. *Ibid.*, p. 503 and PRO FO 371/126161, Sir Francis Evans' valedictory despatch of 29 July 1957 where he wrote: 'Contact with its people shows how sensitive they are, and under what an inferiority complex they are labouring. Their acute nationalism is an expression of this psychological condition . . . Our approach to Argentina should be as tactful, as considerate of raw Argentine sensibilities, as our patience can make it . . . patience, endless patience, coupled with firm insistence on

our legitimate and particularly our financial claims, is now and will continue to be needed. [. . .] Above all, we should never hector and never condescend to this proud and hypersensitive people'.

34. See on this matter the lengthy documentation at the Public Record Office on protracted UK/Argentine negotiations on the issue of compensation for the pensioners of the expropriated Primitiva Gas Company.
35. *Foreign Relations*, p. 464, 16 April 1957.
36. *Ibid.*, p. 463.
37. In Department of State files 735.00/10–856 of 8 and 10 October 1956 it is alleged that US $50 million had been sent from Switzerland to Uruguay by a friend of Jorge Antonio's 'to bankroll the Peronist struggle with Aramburu', quoted in Roger Gravil, 'Perón's standing with the UK and USA after 1955', p. 12, paper presented at the XVI International Congress of the *Latin American Studies Association*, Washington D.C., 4–6 April 1991.
38. Cf. Senén González (1974) and Torre (1980).
39. Cavarozzi (1979) p. 40. John William Cooke's father, John Cooke, had been President Farrell's Foreign Minister in 1945 and a personal friend of Perón.
40. Perón-Cooke (1973) vol. I, p. 114.
41. Gómez Morales interview, quoted in Makin (1984); see chapter 1.
42. For a trade unionist's view of the novelty of the situation, see Domínguez (1977) pp. 47–58. Frigerio had denounced in *Qué* the government's attempt 'to hand over control of the unions to groups obedient to the Socialist Party', 21 May 1957.
43. *La Nación*, 30 June 1957.
44. Report from Wylie, labour attaché in Buenos Aires, FO 371/131988, 22 January 1958.
45. The '32' gathered the rail-workers, commerce, state and gastronomic employees, while the '62' included construction workers, food industry, oil, telephone, wood and wine workers. There was a further grouping of 'neutral' unions (membership: 344,000) comprising footplatemen, and workers in the sugar, power and electricity, paper and printing industries.
46. Cf. Samuel Amaral, 'El avión negro: retórica y práctica de la violencia', paper presented at the XVI LASA Conference, Washington D.C., 4–6 April 1991. The British ambassador reported the existence of 'alleged Peronista agents who try to create a climate of disorder by exploding small bombs all over the city', PRO 371/126161, Sir Francis Evans to Selwyn Lloyd, 10 July 1957.
47. Perón-Cooke (1973) vol. I, p. 100, 1 May 1957.
48. General Carlos Toranzo Montero, Argentine ambassador in Caracas, requested the Venezuelan authorities to expel Perón 'because he was directing from Caracas the subversive and terrorist campaign in Argentina' (*La Nación*, 4 July 1957). When the Venezuelan Government

refused, Argentina broke off diplomatic relations with Venezuela (*La Nación*, 6 July 1957).
49. Perón-Cooke, *op. cit.*, p. 115. On 29 April Cooke had written to Perón: 'the timing for the insurrection may be before, during or after the Constituent Assembly', *ibid.*, p. 94. For Cooke's subsequent career as 'revolutionary' Peronist see Gillespie (1982) pp. 32–46.
50. The *unionistas* in the UCR had opposed the 1949 assembly, cf. chapter 2. Previous amendments dated from 1860, 1866 and 1898.
51. *La Nación*, 25 April 1957. Thedy directed the main thrust of his speech against Frondizi, whom he accused of perpetuating the divisions drawn by Perón between 'the people' and 'the anti-people' and of resorting to 'an old-fashioned Anglophobia', *ibid*. The Progressive Democratic Party, an offshoot of the UCR, was founded by Lisandro de la Torre in 1914.
52. *La Nación*, 10 July 1957.
53. If judged according to the prescriptions of the 1853 Charter – and of the 1949 one, too – the Provisional Government was guilty of the crime of 'sedition' as defined in Articles 22 (1853) and 14 (1949), stating that 'any armed force or group of people taking the attributions of the people and petitioning in its name, will be guilty of the crime of sedition'.
54. *La Nación*, 30 April 1957.
55. On 30 March 1957 Aramburu had said that the amended constitution would become 'the tomb of tyrants'; quoted in *The New York Times*, 21 July 1957.
56. *La Nación*, 10 July 1957.
57. *Programa Popular*, June 1957.
58. For instance, Juan José Basualdo, of the Conservative Party, declared that his party was taking part in the elections 'not because we believe in either the urgency or need for the reforms but as an act of deference [to the government] of the September Revolution on the basis of jointly shared principles'. *La Nación*, 25 July 1957.
59. *La Nación*, 25 July 1957.
60. *Qué*, 21 May 1957.
61. *The Manchester Guardian*, 30 May 1957.
62. *Ibid*.
63. *La Nación*, 14 June 1957.
64. Perón-Cooke (1973) vol. I, p. 123.
65. *Ibid*. The main advocate of blank balloting was Jorge Antonio who had no clout within the Peronist movement but wanted to build for himself a power base. In the 'Leading Personalities in the Argentine Republic for 1959' Jorge Antonio was described as a former 'male nurse who in 1946 had a salary of 600 pesos a month when he became the right-hand man of Perón's brother-in-law, Juan Duarte'. When Duarte died Antonio took over the former's 'numerous interests, particularly in the automobile and agricultural machinery business [. . .] and [in 1955)

Notes to pp. 68–71

66. Personal interview with Ricardo Rojo, who in 1953 went into exile escaping Perón's Argentina and in August of that year met Ernesto Guevara in Bolivia. They travelled together 'to enter into contact with Latin American reality' up to Mexico. Rojo returned to Argentina after Perón's fall in 1955, when he got in touch with Frondizi and started planning a strategy for the elections they knew the government would sooner or later have to call.
67. They fled to Chile, where the authorities kept them in prison at first. The escape came as a blow to the prestige of the Provisional Government, already at a low after the Rial episode (see above).
68. The more colourful expression Perón used was 'ustedes querían quedarse con el santo y la limosna'; Rojo interview.
69. Rojo's impression of Frigerio was not good, and he resented the manner in which he took over the contacts with Peronism; personal interview.
70. Cooke complained that 'one of the worst ills affecting the [Peronist] Movement [was] the excess of often contradictory directives', *ibid.*, p. 192.
71. *Ibid.*, p. 54.
72. *Ibid.*, p. 82.
73. *Qué*, 16 July 1957.
74. Cooke lamented Jauretche's endorsement of Frondizi in a letter to Perón dated 11 May 1957, adding that with Jauretche there were others who, 'less honestly, are working for the "YPF" formula'. YPF, the acronym for the State oil enterprise, were the initials of Yrigoyen, Perón and Frondizi. Perón-Cooke (1973) vol. I, p. 108.
75. *Ibid.*, p. 124. The 'coincidence' was a reference to the fact that a blank ballot was one vote less for Frondizi.
76. *The New York Times*, 31 July 1957. The British noted with relief that 'the worst did not happen' that is, a Frondizi victory, and added that there was a 'reasonable chance that it [would] not happen. in February', PRO 371/126161, 12 August 1957, Tandy to Selwyn Lloyd.
77. *Ibid.*, 22 September 1957.
78. Except three important provinces in terms of population and/or wealth – Corrientes, Entre Ríos and La Pampa. The other provinces where the UCRI won were: Chubut, Formosa, La Rioja, Misiones, Neuquén, Río Negro, Salta and San Luis. Source: Zalduendo (1958) pp. 31–2.
79. Perón-Cooke (1973) vol. I, p. 225.
80. *Ibid.*, p. 227.
81. To the 2,080,121 blank ballots, Cooke added 35,956 annulled ones, 1,500,000 of people he alleged had been fraudulently erased from the electoral register, and 800,000 abstentions, arriving at a total of 4,451,817 '*votos peronistas*'. Adding UCRI votes and those cast for other small parties opposed to the government (1,600,000 in all), he arrived at a grand total of 6,051,817 *votos peronistas*; *ibid.*, p. 257.
82. *Ibid.*

83. *Ibid.*, p. 228.
84. *Ibid.*, pp. 320–1.
85. *Ibid.*, p. 260.
86. *Ibid.*, pp. 312–13.
87. Many Peronist leaders seem to have shared this analysis, and therefore pressed Perón to come to an agreement with Frondizi. See, for instance, Prieto (1963) pp. 113–17.
88. Interviews with Wehbe and Oyhanarte. The latter believes that Frondizi would have won anyway, since Peronists wanted to cast a positive ballot, and 'no Peronist would ever have voted for Balbín [and the UCRP]'. This view is shared by many *frondicistas* – as opposed to *frigeristas*. See for example, Babini (1984) pp. 202–3. *Frigeristas* insist that the pact was essential: interview with Blanca Stábile de Machinandiarena, Frigerio's friend and collaborator.
89. Frondizi interview.
90. Babini (1984) p. 203. Babini was at the time one of Frondizi's closest collaborators and speechwriters: for his role in the electoral campaign, see chapter 5.
91. Odena (1977) p. 85.
92. A trade union leader, Cavalli, arrived in Buenos Aires on 10 February 1958 carrying 'five or six original versions' of the order with Perón's signature, see Prieto (1963) p. 116 and Babini (1984) p. 202, where he records that Cavalli told him that he himself had typed the text of the pact in Caracas.
93. Guardo (1963) p. 112. Oyhanarte has said that the existence of the order, plus Frigerio's commitment and Cooke's notes on the meeting, amounted to a pact from a juridical point of view, adding that 'any discussion on this issue is irrelevant'. Typescript supplied by the author of a paper delivered to the Argentine Bar Association in September 1978.
94. 'The people is in the know, Frondizi to Government House goes'. Jacobo Timerman, who worked for France Presse in Argentina, was instrumental in arranging that a France Presse reporter interview Perón. Personal interview with Timerman.
95. The alleged text is found in Guardo (1963) pp. 109–11 and reproduced in Babini (1984) pp. 200–1. Rojo's version (see above) in the sense that the demand for the return of all expropriated assets was finally left out seems more credible.
96. Personal interview with Frigerio.
97. See chapter 8.

Chapter 4

1. Babini (1984) p. 25.
2. Zavala Ortiz interview. His view was that an industrialised Argentina

'could only be in the long-term interests of the USSR, certainly not in the interests of Great Britain'.
3. Babini's quotations are taken from his book, pp. 13–25.
4. Personal interviews.
5. 'He pursues his objectives quietly and tenaciously, often preferring a tortuous and indirect approach', PRO 371/138997, 24 April 1959.
6. Babini. In the course of interviews carried out with past and present *frondicistas*, there was ample evidence of that feeling of 'veneration'. Jorge Wehbe, David Bléjer, and Babini interviews.
7. Casas (1973) p. 223. Casas was at one time married to David Bléjer, who served at the Interior and Labour Ministries in Frondizi's administration.
8. Babini (1984) p. 22.
9. *Ibid.*, p. 20.
10. Babini and Whebe interviews. Babini, who had been president of Rosario University Students' Union, met Frondizi in 1945, when the latter invited him to join the UCR with the words 'come into the party to change it'. Babini and Frondizi were arrested while taking part in a meeting to celebrate the anniversary of the 1918 University Reform. In 1954 he organised the Press Office at the UCR headquarters in Rio Bamba Street and started editing a weekly, *Cara o Cruz*.
11. Frigerio (1963a) p. 23.
12. PRO 371/138997, Leading Personalities in the Argentine Republic for 1959.
13. His own words; personal interview. Albert Hirschman met Frigerio in 1960 and was struck by the latter's 'demonic view of the world'; personal interview with Hirschman.
14. Personal interview with Babini. Babini pinpoints these conversations as signalling the possible reversal of Frondizi's ideas about the role of foreign companies in oil.
15. Díaz (1977) p. 151.
16. 'Dirigiste dogma' was an expression coined by D. Lal. On the status and issues of development economics see Balasubramanyam and S. Lall (eds) (1991).
17. Frigerio (1963b) pp. 74–5.
18. Cf. Nkrumah (1961).
19. Cf. Limoeiro Cardoso (1975) for an analysis of the ideology of developmentalism in Brazil during the Kubitschek administration.
20. Cf. Hirschman (1961) pp. 3–42.
21. Limoeiro Cardoso, *op. cit.*, p. 91 quotes Kubitschek in 1956 stating his aims as 'the expansion, stimulation and establishment of the industries that Brazil needs for its total and truthful economic liberation'.
22. Nkrumah (1961) p. 117.
23. The pioneering efforts in this field were undertaken in 1946 by R. F. Harrod and E. D. Domar; see Bruton in Hoselitz *et al.* (1960) pp. 239–98, and also Robinson (1965) pp. xv–xvi.

24. Bruton, *ibid.*, p. 239.
25. For a view that prescriptions for growth cannot be based on the successful growths of the last two centuries, see Hartwell in Kindleberger and di Tella (eds) (1982) p. 92, and E. L. Jones (1981). For an analysis of the conditions that made possible in Europe the passage from an agrarian to an industrial society, see E. L. Jones and S. J. Woolf (1969).
26. For an approach that rejects the 'sameness' argument, see Gerschenkron (1968).
27. Cf. E. S. Mason in Kindleberger and di Tella, *op. cit.*, p. 117.
28. Mathias (1969) p. 5.
29. Cf. Rostow (1963), and for a critical appraisal see Mason, *op. cit.*, and Habakkuk in Robinson (1965) pp. 112–30.
30. Frigerio (1967) p. 22. The issue of the 'rhythm' of development is also posed in Frigerio (1962) and (1963a), in Frondizi (1964) and in Díaz (1977).
31. Cf. Prebisch (1950). For an exposition and critique of Prebisch's ideas as reflected in UNCTAD, see Bauer (1976), especially chapter 6. Michel Debrun (1964) has noted the decisive influence that ECLA had on Brazilian economists.
32. Cf. Germani (1962).
33. Graciarena (1983).
34. CEPAL (ECLA) (1964), especially Introduction and chapter 1.
35. Frondizi (1964) pp. 51–2.
36. Frigerio (1963a) p. 117.
37. *Ibid.*
38. Frigerio was opposed to continental integration describing it as 'a long-standing rhetorical aspiration of a pretended Latin American motherland, today imbued with pseudoscientific traits in regional integration schemes'; Frigerio (1967) p. 125.
39. First published in Montevideo in 1959.
40. Frigerio (1979) p. 12.
41. Frigerio (1963a) pp. 35–6, and repeated in his taped conversations with Díaz (1977) p. 109. Laclau and Mouffe (1985) chapter 1 offer a critique of orthodox Marxism which operates a reductionism of the concrete to the abstract, distinguishing between a 'superficial' or 'apparent' level of society and an underlying reality.
42. Frigerio, who never went to university, was then active in the left-wing *Insurrexit* directed towards spreading Marxist-Leninist principles amongst university students. There were many left-wing groups active in Argentina in those days, mostly organised by the Communist Party. Among those who gathered round *Insurrexit* in 1934 were men who would become prominent members of left-wing circles in the future: Héctor Agosti, Ernesto Giúdice, Ernesto Sábato, and Rodolfo Puiggrós.
43. For Frigerio's almost literal reproduction of Marx's theory of value,

see Frigerio (1967) p. 126; (1979) p. 20; and in Díaz (1977) p. 30.
44. Zavala Ortiz and Alsogaray interviews, while Wehbe recalled how Frigerio jumped at his comment during a meeting in 1981, in the sense that Marxism was 'obsolete'; Wehbe interview.
45. Interviews with Félix Luna and Natalio Botana.
46. For a comprehensive account of Marxian influences on Latin American intellectuals in the 1930s and 1940s, see José Aricó (1981).
47. Díaz (1977) p. 107.
48. Cf. Salvadori (1981) pp. 278–89.
49. Díaz (1977) pp. 132–3.
50. Frigerio (1979) p. 11.
51. Frondizi *et al.* (1965) pp. 46–7. For a critique of historicism see Berlin (1969) pp. 41–117 and Popper (1972) p. 128.
52. Rodolfo Terragno's typescript of his 1975 interview with Frondizi.
53. Frigerio in Díaz (1977) p. 130.
54. Giddens (1971) p. 64.
55. Díaz, *op. cit.*, p. 124.
56. Frigerio (1967) p. 23. In Frondizi's words, 'the demand for economic development is peremptory since it is an essential condition to satisfy other dimensions of nationhood'; Frondizi (1964) p. 76.
57. Díaz, *op. cit.*, p. 76. See also his indictment of Illia's constitutional government, 'emptied of all revolutionary content', *ibid.*, p. 137.
58. Laclau (1977) pp. 53–4. Thus Frigerio maintained that three Economy ministers under three very different governments represented the same – anti-national – policies. He was referring to Krieger Vasena, who served under Onganía in 1966, Gelbard, under Perón in 1974, and Martínez de Hoz, under General Videla in 1976. He wrote that 'those three men . . . are the objective expression of transnational economic interests – and I say 'objective expression', I am not making personal criticisms of a moral nature'; Díaz, *op. cit.*, p. 140; also pp. 141, 147, 148.
59. Frigerio (1967) p. 18.
60. Frigerio (1979) p. 24 and also (1963b) p. 8.
61. Díaz (1977) pp. 112 and 116. See also Frondizi (1964) p. 51.
62. Frondizi, *ibid.*, pp. 51–2.
63. Popper (1972) p. 47.
64. Frigerio (1967) p. 16.
65. *El Príncipe*, March 1962. Years later a general asked 'what can be expected of a president who maintains that we are an underdeveloped country?' Rauch (1971) p. 94.
66. Frondizi (1964) p. 64.
67. US embassy to State Department, Central Files 735.00/42459, 6 May 1959. Counselor Nugent wrote that 'in the early days [of the Frondizi administration] . . . the concept of national integration had very suggestive overtones' since together with 'national and popular movement' it signified 'a carload of the most diverse political elements

(Peronists, Communists, Radicals *et al.*) travelling at a fast rate toward some vague objective'; *ibid.*
68. Frigerio (1967) p. 125, and (1963a) pp. 181–2.
69. Gelsi remarked how disappointed he, and his colleagues in the neglected provinces had been, since they had believed and hoped Frondizi would revert the historical trend; Gelsi interview.
70. Frigerio (1963a) p. 9.
71. Frondizi (1964) p. 8.
72. Frigerio (1963a) p. 110. The notion of class alliance bore resonances of the Popular Fronts endorsed by the Third International, as well as of Perón's 'organised community' with its corporatist connotations.
73. *Ibid.*, p. 101.
74. *Ibid.*, p. 171.
75. *Ibid.*, p. 157.
76. Frigerio (1963a) p. 154.
77. The trip took place at the beginning of 1955 and Swiss bankers gave Frigerio 'a lot more money than he had expected' as a contribution to the struggle against Perón. In exchange Frigerio had given the undertaking that a future government would lift the prohibition imposed by Perón to import textile machinery, mostly of Swiss origin. Frigerio himself had a small textile business making shirts. Interview with Juan Lozano, who accompanied Frigerio to Switzerland. According to Lozano, Frigerio remained in control of the Swiss funds. References to Swiss impatience with Perón are to be found in *Foreign Relations*, vol. VII, 8 June 1955, p. 364 and in Foreign Office records. The FO sent a report to the embassy in Buenos Aires noting that the Swiss 'have apparently been trying for a long while to start new negotiations on trade and payments . . . but no progress has been made because Argentina still refuses to transfer Swiss invisibles and while this situation continues the Swiss refuse to have discussions', PRO FO 371/108803, AA1151/41, 4 March 1954.
78. Furet (1981) p. 55 described the 'aristocratic plot' that revolutionaries were constantly denouncing: 'The "aristocratic plot" . . . became the lever of an egalitarian ideology that was both exclusionary and highly integrative. Two complementary systems of symbols came into play: the nation was constituted by the patriots only in reaction to its adversaries, who were secretly manipulated by the aristocrats. The potential applications of that basic proposition were practically unlimited, since equality, being a value more than a state of society, could never be taken for granted, and its enemies were not real, identifiable and circumscribed forces, but constantly renewed incarnations of its anti-values.'
79. Frigerio (1963a) p. 67.
80. *Ibid.*
81. *Ibid.*
82. Frigerio (1963a) p. 111. This book was written to serve the purpose

of 'systematising' the needed doctrine: 'We intend . . . this work to contribute to sytematising a national and popular doctrine. We hope to explain clearly the dialectical elements that will contribute to the understanding and the critique of a programme whose success is entirely dependent on the collaboration of all active sectors in the population. [. . .] Only the total communion between the Argentine people and the principles herein will make possible, and ensure, our victory. We shall have thus built a nation.' *Ibid.*, pp. 45–6.

83. For an analysis of the Calvinists' introduction in the sixteenth century of the then novel view of politics as a kind of conscientious and continuous labour, see Walzer (1966) especially chapters 1 and 2.
84. Reproduced in *Informativo Radical*, October/November 1957; the speech was delivered on 27 October 1957.
85. Cf. Babini (1984) pp. 174–7. Ismael Viñas acknowledged that Frondizi's only interest in them was 'because we controlled FUBA'; personal interview. Ismael's brother, David, was FUBA's president.
86. Leandro Alem's radicalism had led one historian to label him '*el Robespierre de Balvanera*'. On Alem see Gallo, in Ferrari and Gallo (eds) (1980) p. 220, and Félix Luna's 'Alem, la terrible integridad' in *ibid.*, pp. 245–53. General Luis M. Campos, ironically, had been War and Navy minister in 1893 when he was in charge of the repressive measures against the rebellious *cívicos radicales*; see Goyret in *ibid.*, pp. 291–303.
87. Quoted in Casas (1973) p. 225.
88. They included Ismael Viñas, Ramón Alcalde, Noé Jitrik and Susana Fiorito. David Viñas refused to work with Frondizi because he had 'all the trappings of a bourgeois, not of a revolutionary'. Personal interview with Ismael Viñas.
89. In Díaz (1977) p. 40, Frigerio maintains disingenuously that there were no contacts with Peronism during the campaign. Babini recalled his dismay when he heard that Jorge Antonio (Perón's financier) had been seen in Luis M. Campos; Babini interview. But Ismael Viñas maintains the 'inner circle' at Alem knew of the contacts and they accepted that the 'ostracism of Peronism could not be permanent'; personal interview.
90. Wehbe interview. For an account of the machine-politics tradition in the UCR, see Rock (1975a) and (1975b). Frigerio had nothing but contempt for them; personal interview.
91. Interviews with Babini and Marta Madariaga.
92. Babini, *op. cit.*, p.17 recalls how Frondizi set up study workshops in 1953 to 'consolidate the UCR programmatic base', and agrarian reform was the first subject chosen for discussion, while in Díaz, *op. cit.*, pp. 28–9, Frigerio dismisses agrarian reform as an anachronistic concern.
93. *Qué*, 29 April 1958.
94. *Qué*, 2 July 1957.

95. Casas (1973) p. 268.
96. Odena (1977) p. 49.
97. Interview with Blanca Stábile. Babini, *op. cit.*, p. 14 quotes Frigerio as saying in 1956 that 'Frondizi has one million votes, and I have the ideas'. According to Félix Luna, the relationship can be explained partly as a result of Frondizi's tendency to depression and despondency (also remarked on by Babini: personal interview), Frigerio being his 'tower of strength'. Moreover, according to Luna, Frondizi was 'very lazy, and Frigerio, with his brutal capacity for work, used to solve all his problems: he handed him his speeches, pointed out the main issues, told him what to say or do'. Personal interview.
98. Blanca Stábile, a member of that group, remembered the 'great personal sacrifice, the total availability at all times that the task required' and described her husband's role as that of 'a peon of the national movement'. Amongst the members of the group were Arturo Sábato, Marcos Merchensky, Carlos Florit, Arnaldo Musich, Mariano Montemayor 'and many others'.
99. *País Unido*, 26 November 1957.
100. Referring to *País Unido*, on 3 December 1957 an editorial in *Qué* said that it would be a voice 'to break the blockade of silence imposed around Frondizi by the chained and semi-free press'.
101. According to Frigerio, 200,000 copies were printed of some issues, but this figure was increased by the fact that the magazine 'went from hand to hand'; Frigerio interview.
102. Arnaldo Torrents, a Communist doctor who had been in charge of the Public Health column in *Qué* and later worked under Frondizi's Health minister, Héctor Noblía, described how everybody writing in *Qué* in 1946 was a member of the CP, and how they had been divided on whether or not to support Perón. Interview with the late Torrents.
103. Jaramillo committed suicide that year. In an effort to conceal their early anti-Peronism, in the course of a personal interview Blanca Stábile maintained that *Qué* had not been published in 1951–6 'as a result of financial problems'. As from 1956 *Qué* was financed by the Machinandiarenas, whose fortune was mainly derived from their control of gambling activities.
104. *Qué*, 26 November 1957. According to Hirschman, Frigerio saw conspiracies everywhere and was 'incapable of seeing two sides to each question, and thus unable to judge a situation objectively'; personal interview.
105. *Qué*, 3 December 1957.
106. *Ibid.*
107. In Díaz (1977) pp. 27–8, Frigerio described his differences with the 'populist' Scalabrini and Jauretche, who believed that what the masses accepted enthusiastically was always 'good' while that was 'neither historically nor scientifically correct'. But he explained he trusted in the 'objective behaviour of social sectors and classes' and in any case

the editorial column provided the coherence between 'the theory and practice of the national movement'.
108. *Qué*, 18 December 1956.
109. *Qué*, 4 June 1957.
110. *Qué*, 18 December 1956.
111. *Qué*, 3 December 1957.
112. Pandolfi (1968) p. 29.
113. Pandolfi, *op. cit.*, p. 36, quotes *Clarinada*, an ultra-right wing pamphlet subsidised by the German embassy during Worl War II, which described Frondizi as a communist and 'defender of Jews' because in 1938 he had represented the Argentine League for the Rights of Man at the First Congress Against Racism and Anti-Semitism. Interestingly, the editor of *Clarinada* was Carlos Silveyra, brother of YPF president Ricardo Silveyra; Newton (1992) p. 118.
114. Pandolfi, *op. cit.*, p. 39.
115. The full text is reproduced in Casas (1973) pp. 391–400.
116. Babini (1984) p. 191.
117. *Tribuna Cívica*, 27 February 1958.
118. Babini, *op. cit.*, p. 179, has written that del Mazo had made of the 1918 Reform 'a claim of his own' ensuring its constant inclusion in all Intransigent documents.
119. *Raíz*, September 1947.
120. *Qué*, 8 January 1957.
121. *Ibid.*
122. *Ibid.*
123. *Qué*, 8 January 1957.
124. Babini (1984) p. 178.
125. Rojo, Viñas and Babini interviews.
126. Sir Francis Evans noted that Aramburu's Education minister, Atilio Dell'Oro Maini, although a man of the Church himself, 'was criticised in clerical circles for allowing Left-wing elements to infiltrate into positions of importance in the Universities after the Peronista professors had been expelled'; PRO FO 118–850, AA 1015/82, 26 November 1955.
127. *Qué*, 16 July 1957, where the Left was accused of insensitivity towards popular culture represented in the 'semi-cult of the Mother Mary or Pancho Sierra, in the popular lithurgy that followed the memory of Evita'.
128. Blanca Stábile emphasised the importance attached to gaining the support of the Church to avoid Perón's mistakes; personal interview.
129. In a personal interview José A. Martínez de Hoz, one of its founders, recalled how the party had been 'a party of ideals, not of interests'.
130. Snow (1979) chapter 5. The Christian Democrats obtained 420,606 votes in July 1957; it was their first, and would remain their best election ever.
131. Frigerio (1963a) p. 170.

132. Perón was well aware of the importance of Catholics in the US. Amabassador Hipólito Paz expressed his concern that the Archbishop of New York might 'refer to the Argentine situation' but Holland regretted the US government's hands were tied given their policy of nonintervention in Argentine affairs; *Foreign Relations*, vol. VII, pp. 367–8, 27 June 1955. Noting that Perón's position after the failed 16 June revolution seemed 'strong', Henry Holland signaled the 'profound satisfaction' of the US at the improvement in relationships between the two countries, and adding in a postscript 'if by great fortune we were able to work out the *La Prensa* problem we could then consider the possibility of an attack on the church problem'; *ibid.* p. 376, 6 September 1955.
133. Quoted in Casas (1973) p. 237. 'Frondizi's record and publicly-stated views [...] stamp him as no particular friend of the United States or of US interests'; Buenos Aires embassy to Department of State, 16 January 1957, Washington Archives 611.35/1–1657.
134. Key (1966).
135. Full text of speech in Casas (1973) pp. 391–400.
136. Casas, *op. cit.*, pp. 44–5, has praised Frondizi's 'civil courage' which was the consequence of 'a particular Frondicista conception of ethics and morality, able to confront truth on a daily and even hourly basis, and in consequence go back on everything he had said'. Pandolfi, (1968) pp. 74–5, another panegyrist, contrasted Frondizi's pragmatism with what he described as typical 'petty-bourgeois morality of ... principled ideologues' who are not strong enough 'to tread in the mud'. Newton (1992) pp. 293–4 points that in 1943 both Britain and the US felt that Argentina was moving towards recognising the need for foreign participation in oil extraction to reduce the need for oil imports. Notwithstanding Frondizi's efforts, fifty years would have to elapse before that recognition gained wide enough acceptance as to allow President Menem to commit himself to the privatisation of YPF in 1993.
137. Philip (1982) p. 410, maintains that Aramburu's hesitant oil policies had worsened the situation of YPF.
138. *Informativo Radical*, May 1957 and *Programa Popular*, June 1957.
139. The crowds welcoming Lonardi in September 1955 when he arrived at the Casa Rosada were chanting '¡Petróleo sí! ¡California no!' Philip, *op. cit.*, p. 409.
140. *País Unido*, December 1957.
141. 1 January 1957.
142. *Ibid.* The following are some of the headings of articles on oil published in *Qué*: 'They are organising the failure of YPF', 11 December 1956; 'Sovereignty is at stake in the battle of YPF', 18 December 1956; 'We have all the oil we need and we can extract it: favourable exploitation circumstances explain why international consortia are pressing for concessions', 18 June 1957; 'A false alternative: popular misery or

foreign concessions', 16 July 1957.
143. *Qué*, 31 December 1957.
144. *Qué*, 7 May 1957. The first issue of *Tribuna Cívica* was published on 12 February 1957.
145. *Qué*, 23 April 1957. Hirschman remembers how Frigerio, who 'seemed quite paranoid', overwhelmed him with a list of people being on one or other oil company's payroll; personal interview.
146. *Qué*, 23 April 1957.
147. *Qué*, 5 March 1957.
148. *Ibid.*
149. Personal interviews with Frigerio and Alsogaray.
150. *The New York Times* correspondent shared this view. On 9 February 1958, covering the election campaign, the newspaper described Argentina's parties as out-dated: 'Their political slogans are the same as in 1946. Their programs for restoring the nation to economic and social prosperity are vague. With the exception of two new parties, the Christian Democrats and the *Cívico Independiente*, their programs are basically against the free enterprise system for Argentina'.
151. *Tribuna Cívica*, 12 Sept. 1957.
152. *Tribuna Cívica*, 12 February 1957.
153. In the course of a personal interview Alsogaray pointed out that he had met Frondizi privately on a couple of occasions in December 1957 'to exchange opinions', and after having discussed the situation, Frondizi had asked Alsogaray to prepare a memorandum including the 'twenty basic economic measures' that in Alsogaray's opinion were most urgent. This Alsogaray did, 'omitting to mention oil, since our positions were so opposed that I did not think there would be any point in including it'.
154. *Tribuna Cívica,* 27 February 1958.
155. *Tribuna Cívica*, 1 May 1958. Newton (1992) pp. 70 and 118 reveals that in 1934 Walter Leupold, advertising manager of YPF, was in control of the Nazi labour organisation in Argentina (DAF). Other known Nazis in YPF were the chief of geological exploration and local administrators in Salta, Mendoza, Comodoro Rivadavia and Plaza Huincul. Throughout the years references to corruption in YPF were rife in British archival documentation.
156. *Tribuna Cívica*, 1 May 1958.
157. *Tribuna Cívica*, 8 May 1958.
158. *The New York Times*, 3 March 1958.
159. *Ibid.*

Chapter 5

1. Babini (1984) p. 208 in a keen attempt at damping 'Frigerio's triumph', adds to and subtracts from the 1958 results, concluding that even

without the Peronist votes, the UCRI could have obtained a comfortable majority with 'at least 2,680,000' votes.
2. Babini, *op cit.*, p. 208.
3. Perón wrote that Frondizi had to talk 'like a Peronist' to make himself heard, Perón-Cooke (1973) vol. I, p. 82 and the British ambassador remarked that Frondizi's success 'must be attributed to the cunning with which he pandered to the egoism and nationalism of the average Argentine', but he also noted that the Provisional Government 'contrived to give the impression that Dr Balbín was their favourite candidate, while [. . .] they failed to do anything effective to help him'. PRO FO 371/131949, 8 April 1958.
4. PRO FO 371/138996, Annual Review for 1958.
5. Potash (1980) pp. 273–9.
6. Personal interview.
7. Personal interview.
8. Personal interviews. The quote is from General Lanusse who had been chief of the Grenadiers Regiment in 1955 under Lonardi and was military attaché in Mexico in 1958 when David Bléjer, Frondizi's close friend, was ambassador. General de Nevares (Frondizi's aide-de-camp in 1958–60) remarked that although Frondizi's supporters within the army were a minority, they had 'decisive clout'. Lanusse became sub-Director at the Army Academy in 1960, the year Sánchez de Bustamante began to teach Military History at that institution.
9. PRO FO 371/131949, A1015/12, 25 February 1958.
10. PRO FO 371/131949, 8 April 1958. The UK Secretary of State for Air, who led the UK delegation to Frondizi's inauguration, reported to the Foreign Secretary that 'it is clear that he [Frondizi] starts with a great deal of good will', PRO FO 371/131950, A1015/46, 8 May 1958.
11. Dr Alconada Aramburú, Interior minister at the time, remembered Aramburu's distress on the night of 23 February 1958. Babini, *op cit.*, p. 209 and Potash, *op. cit.*, p. 275. The British described Damonte as 'a man of few political morals [who] expected high rewards for his electoral services', since he had campaigned for Peronist support of Frondizi; PRO FO 371/138997, 24 April 1959. Damonte's unpalatable trajectory is followed in Newton (1992), fn. 61, pp. 436–7 and in Botana (1985) pp. 279, 297.
12. Perón-Cooke (1973) vol. II, p. 54.
13. Babini, *op. cit.*, pp. 216–17 and also Potash, *op. cit.*, p. 275. The British described Damonte as 'a man of few political morals [who] expected high rewards for his electoral services', since he had campaigned for Peronist support of Frondizi; PRO FO 371/138997, 24 April 1959. Damonte's unpalatable trajectory is followed in Newton (1992), fn. 61, pp. 436–7 and in Botana (1985) pp. 279, 297.
14. PRO FO 371/131950, A1015/38, 16 April 1958.
15. The tone was guaranteed by the fact that Babini was his speech-writer.
16. Personal interviews with Manuel Madanes, José A. Martínez de Hoz, Alvaro Alsogaray, and Isak Radunsky. These lunches were organised by Samuel Schmukler, who promised entrepreneurs favoured treatment once in government, in exchange for financial contributions to the campaign. Schmukler became Frondizi's Executive Secretary, and very

17. PRO FO 371/131949, 30 December 1957. Also present at the meeting were Aldo Ferrer and Rex Johnston-Smith. There is a handwritten remark by Hildyard: 'This rings fairly true to me. Dr Frondizi sounds very much the sort of person we must expect in the Argentine: nationalist, exigent, perhaps plausible and superficial but fundamentally quite intelligent. We may delude ourselves if we think that Dr Balbín would be much more reasonable in practice.'
18. UK embassy in Moscow to FO, PRO FO 371/131949, A1015/18, 5 March 1958.
19. University students who had followed the Communist Party's advice to vote for Frondizi, believed they were voting 'for heavy industry', and thus for the 'development of productive forces', a necessary 'stage of capitalist development' in the road to socialism. Personal interview with Silvia Sigal. The British ambassador had perceptively remarked a month before the elections that 'if there is any post-electoral recanting to be done, Frondizi may have a good deal more to do than Balbín, for he favours the election tactic of "promising" whatever he says "the people want"'; PRO FO 371/131949, A1015/6, 24 January 1958.
20. Halperín Donghi (1964) pp. 86–7, described Balbín's 'sentimental oratory' in whose paragraphs 'it would have been excessively cruel to try to find any sense . . . '. At the time when he still thought Balbín 'the least harmful of the alternatives', Sir John Ward added that he had heard that 'Balbín is very limited in intelligence . . . [but] wise enough to realise his limitations'; PRO FO 371/131949, A1015/7, 6 February 1958.
21. Frondizi (1978) vol. I, p. 50.
22. Potash, *op. cit.*, p. 281.
23. Frondizi, *op. cit.*, pp. 14–15.
24. PRO FO 371/131951, A 1015/74, 14 November 1958.
25. Cúneo had been a leading member of the Socialist Party until 1952 and had collaborated with Frigerio in *Qué* since 1946. In that year he had unsuccessfully stood as candidate for Congress for the Socialist Party.
26. MacKay had been one of the favourites to share the presidential ticket with Frondizi in 1956 before Alejandro Gómez, a schoolmaster who had taught himself law, was finally chosen as a compromise candidate to overcome the objections to MacKay, arising from his Church links.
27. A senior British diplomat in Argentina at the time remarked on the 'ostentatious Catholicism' of the president which was not necessarily seen as a sincere expression of deeply held religious beliefs; personal interview. In separate personal interviews, both Roberto Alemann and Alvaro Alsogaray remarked on Frondizi's 'almost fanatical' Catholicism in recent years. In contrast, Pandolfi (1968) p. 17, describes Frondizi as 'a mild theist', noting that 'not even as president

did he consider it necessary to go to mass, except in the case of Te Deums'.
28. Interview with Natalio Botana.
29. The British ambassador reported that del Carril was 'unfortunately lazy and not very well informed in economic matters' although 'reasonably intelligent'; PRO FO 371/131952, A1016/8, 16 May 1958, where Frigerio was described as Frondizi's *'eminence grise* in economic matters, definitely anti-British, and with certain simple preconceived ideas such as that by annoying the UK Argentina will gain the support of the US and Germany'; *ibid.* Dr Arnaldo Torrents was one of the young doctors working with Noblía; personal interview.
30. Frondizi told Rojo: 'I'm not sending you to Labour because after 24 hours you would resign making a scandal since I'm planning to do many things you would not tolerate'; personal interview with Rojo. Rojo had good relations with Augusto Vandor and the Peronist union leadership in general.
31. Florit's father, a retired admiral, had been notorious during World War II for his pro-German sentiments.
32. PRO FO 371/138997, 24 April 1959.
33. See chapter 1. During a private luncheon organised by Dr Miguel Angel Cárcano at Frigerio's bequest, since he 'was most anxious' to meet the British ambassador, Dr Cárcano told the ambassador that he was talking with 'the economic dictator of the country', while Frigerio 'nodded his head in a smug and self-satisfied way', PRO FO 371/131864, A1151/122, 31 October 1958.
34. There was a woman who was part of that carefully designed network of *frigeristas*: Blanca Stábile, Narciso Machinandiarena's widow and a member of the inner *frigerista* circle, who went briefly to the newly created post of Secretary for Women's Affairs before she was forced to resign as part of the purge of *frigeristas* from the government.
35. Petrecolla in di Tella and Dornbusch (eds) (1989) and Casas, *op. cit.*, pp. 31–63.
36. The comment was by the British ambassador, PRO FO 371/147756, 1 May 1960 who noted that the behaviour, not regarded as 'particularly reprehensible' in Argentina, revealed 'the absence in Argentina of any true Parliamentary feeling'; *ibid.*
37. Exports had fluctuated around the US $1,000 million since 1954, while Argentina's population had grown from 18,544,000 in 1954 to 19,979,000 in 1958 at a time when the share of urban over rural population was rising steadily; Díaz Alejandro (1975) table 3.
38. Díaz Alejandro (1965) p. 88.
39. *Ibid.*, p. 71.
40. 25 May 1957.
41. Díaz Alejandro (1965) p. 44.
42. *Ibid.*
43. Laura Randall (1978) p. 23.

44. Beef and bread accounted for about 20% of the expenditures of working-class families; Díaz Alejandro (1965) pp. 89–90.
45. *Ibid.*, p. 141.
46. Alieto Guadagni in Di Tella and Dornbusch (eds) (1989).
47. Alberto Petrecolla in *ibid*.
48. Díaz Alejandro (1965) p. 48. During the post-war period approximately 60% of all imports was composed of a large variety of raw materials and intermediate products such as oil, iron and steel, chemicals, paper pulp and rubber, while 30% of all imports represented capital goods, mainly destined to replace and repair the existing capital stock, *ibid.* pp. 48–9.
49. *Ibid.*, p. 144. A cursory look at data provided by Díaz Alejandro (1975) shows that the pace of 'development' of the Peronist years had in fact accelerated during the *Libertadora*. The following index numbers show the growth in industrial production in the years 1945–58 (1960 = 100): 1945 = 51; 1946 = 56; 1947 = 64; 1948 = 67; 1949 = 67; 1950 = 69; 1951 = 70; 1952 = 69; 1953 = 69; 1954 = 75; 1955 = 84; 1956 = 89; 1957 = 95; 1958 = 102. *Source*: Díaz Alejandro (1975) table 9, p. 396.
50. Cf. William Ascher (1984) p. 216; also E. Eshag and R. Thorp in Ferrer *et al.* (1969).
51. A case in point is Alberto Petrecolla in Di Tella and Dornbusch (1989).
52. Lecture given by Frigerio in 1959 at Columbia University, New York, quoted in Frigerio (1962a) p. 59; and repeats this point in Juan Carlos de Pablo (1980) p. 54.
53. Arturo Sábato was a member of Frigerio's inner circle since the 1940s; personal interview.
54. Describing the decision as 'tragic' (and a reduction of provincial railway fares as 'ludicrous'), in his Annual Review for 1958 the British ambassador wrote that 'several months were to pass before political debts ceased to take precedence over economic necessities'; PRO FO 371/138996, 26 February 1959.
55. Díaz Alejandro (1965) p. 144.
56. See Ascher, *op. cit.*, p. 182; Villanueva (1966) p. 76, and Zuvekas (1966) p. 28–30.
57. Washington Archives, Department of State Central Files, 611.35 / 4–1858. Ordóñez mentioned an increase of '30%, or possibly more'. The Kaiser vehicle plant, together with various pharmaceutical plants, had been the most prominent private US investments in Argentina under Perón.
58. Traditionally, cattle owners in Argentina have reacted to a devaluation by withholding herds in the expectation of higher prices for their offspring. The actual number of animals slaughtered decreases, and thus the anticipated increase in exports never materialises; Laura Randall (1978) p. 23.

59. Ascher, *op. cit.*, p. 182.
60. Ascher, *ibid.*, pp. 183–4.
61. Washington Archives, 611.35/6–459, 4 June 1959. The conversation took place on 21 May, on Frigerio's return from his unofficial trip to the United States.
62. Quoted in de Pablo (1980) p. 53.
63. R. Mallon and J. V. Sourrouille (1975) p. 19.
64. In de Pablo, *op. cit.*, p. 64.
65. The US $254 million was broken down thus: the United States Treasury, US $50 million; Export-Import Bank, US $125 million; United States Development Loan Fund US $25 million; finally, ten private US banks and one Canadian bank lent a total of US $54 million; Díaz Alejandro (1965) fn. 19. p. 148.
66. PRO FO 371/138996, Annual Review for 1958, 26 February 1959.
67. Frondizi (1978), where the whole text of the speech is reproduced.
68. Twenty years later Frigerio reversed the priorities saying that 1958 had meant that 'the process of development was irreversible' and only then did they apply the second – 'stabilisation' – plan; in de Pablo (1980) p. 64. For a detailed and critical analysis of the measures announced on 29 December 1958 see Díaz Alejandro, *op. cit.*, pp. 146–8, also Eshag and Thorp, in Ferrer *et al.* (1969) p. 93–7.
69. Frondizi (1978).
70. Report from Ward to Selwyn Lloyd, PRO FO 371/139015, 30 January 1959.
71. Most export taxes were removed during 1960–1.
72. For instance Eshag and Thorp in Ferrer *et al.* (1969) p. 66 and Ascher (1984) p. 185.
73. Díaz Alejandro, *op. cit.*, fn. 16, p. 145. Frigerio confirmed this years later, saying 'we had to win the battle with the IMF; we had to insist with all our energies to be allowed the total and simultaneous opening up of the economy. They could not accept it. They said: "You do not know what will happen to your currency"'; in de Pablo (1980) p. 57.
74. PRO FO 371/131864, 1958.
75. Díaz Alejandro, *op. cit.*, p. 186.
76. PRO FO 371/139015, 30 January 1959.
77. Report on 21 May 1959 conversation between Beaulac and Frigerio, Washington Archives 611.35/6–459.
78. Frigerio in de Pablo, *op. cit.*, pp. 61–2.
79. See chapter 7.
80. Ascher (1984) p. 180, supports the idea of the 'imposition' of Alsogaray. General Julio Alsogaray confirmed that his brother's appointment was a reassurance at a time when accusations of harbouring communists in the administration were rife. But Alsogaray was far from universally liked within the forces, where 'extreme nationalists' suspected him; PRO FO 371/139000, 26 June 1959. But it was not just nationalists that disliked him. According to Casas (1973) p. 87, every

time that Frondizi met Aramburu 'for a friendly exchange of ideas', the latter said 'Alsogaray must go'. In the course of a personal interview Frondizi stated that General Solanas Pacheco, Commander-in-Chief of the Army, warned him that 'there was a coup d'état atmosphere which could be stopped by producing a change in the economic leadership: in this context Alsogaray's name was mentioned. His appointment lowered the conspiratorial temperature'.

81. D'Adamo, Technical Secretary to Frondizi, declared that 'Alsogaray's and Alemann's appointments were not proof of Frondizi's contradictions or double-crossing, but rather a reflection of Frigerio's style: he demanded agreement on two or three general points, sat them in the respective ministerial chair [*el sillón*] and then concluded that they would be forever faithful and loyal to his person. And it was here that he was mistaken'; personal interview. Ward remarked that Alsogaray, who was 'reasonable and responsible in opposition', less than a fortnight after his appointment 'had already begun to show signs of demagogy [which] perhaps reflects his alleged high political ambitions'; PRO FO 371/139000, 3 July 1959.

82. Personal interview. On Erhard's thinking, see Volker Berghahn in R. J. Bullen, H. Pogge von Strandmann and A. B. Polonsky (eds) (1984). A US Intelligence report corroborates Alsogaray's claims of contacts with Frondizi and Frigerio 'in the early fall of 1958', when Alsogaray's sustained campaign in favour of liberalisation of the economy and the need for foreign capital was 'undertaken with the tacit approval of President Frondizi, if not at his request'; the report, dated 1 July 1959, was received at the Foreign Office on 29 July. For Alsogaray's single-minded insistence on these issues, see *Tribuna Cívica*, 11 April 1957, 9 May 1957, 7 November 1957.

83. Washington Archives, 735.00/8–459, 4 August 1959; the conversation between Frigerio and Beaulac had taken place on 27 May 1959; Beaulac to Department of State.

84. Published in J. C. de Pablo (1980); typescript of notes supplied by Frigerio in 1979.

85. Jacobo Timerman had described Gelbard to Irving Salert, Labour attaché at the US embassy in Buenos Aires, as 'a special advisor to President Frondizi' who would be joining Frigerio, Orfila and Galarce in New York and Washington for talks with US businessmen; Washington Archives, Central Files, 735.00/1–1959, XR611.35, 12 March 1959. Timerman went on to say that Frondizi would achieve for Argentina 'a sound economy and a conservative, pro-Capitalist regime patterned along [. . .] the United States'; *ibid*. Timerman was a feature writer for *Clarín* and 'braintruster and confidant' of Frigerio's; *ibid*.

86. Interview with Manuel Madanes. From personal recollections, there was at least one dinner in which Frigerio, Alsogaray, and Gelbard were the sole guests at Madanes' house. Although Frigerio did not deny the possibility, Alsogaray rejected having met Gelbard on such

an occasion. Madanes remarked that 'Frigerio and Gelbard shared a feeling of omnipotence'. Without mentioning Madanes' name, the MID document quoted in fn. 88 makes an explicit reference to this meeting. In Casas' account the meeting took place in Gelbard's house; *op. cit.*, p. 87. Ten years later Gelbard told General Sánchez de Bustamante that 'Frondizi and Frigerio had given him three million dollars, returning to him the assests that the *Libertadora* had taken away from him'; personal interview with General Sánchez de Bustamante.

87. PRO FO 371/13900, AA1015/42, 29 July 1959. On Alsogaray's background the report noted that he had built up 'a sizeable personal fortune' starting in 1941 with a small cooking oil manufacturing company and branching into newsprint and alcoholic products and in mining operations. He had taken voluntary retirement from the Air Force in 1947.

88. Prieto (1963) pp. 176–7, claims that Alsogaray was a frequent visitor to Frigerio's house after February 1958. Babini quotes an article in *Clarín* where it was reported that Alsogaray met Frigerio in November 1958, days before the latter's resignation as Secretary for Socio-Economic Relations, and that there had been a previous meeting a week earlier; Babini, *op. cit.,* p. 249. The *Movimiento de Integración y Desarrollo* (MID) published a paid advertisement in *La Nación* on 8 April 1983, repeating these claims. In a personal interview, Alsogaray remarked that he had met Frigerio 'occasionally' and only at Frondizi's request, since Frigerio was the latter's 'secretary, intermediary' and meeting him was a way of reducing the working pressures on Frondizi. In an interview published in the weekly *Somos* on 15 April 1983, Frigerio remarked that 'Alsogaray was a frequent visitor to my house in 1959, before his appointment as minister in June 1959. [. . .] The relationship resulted from Alsogaray's expressed wish to become Economy minister'.

89. During a meeting with Richard Ewbank, from the Bank of England, Roberto Alemann, who at the time was personal advisor to Economy minister Del Carril, stated that 'his advice was virtually never sought' given that in the current 'political and other circumstances the sort of advice which Alemann would be likely to give would not be acceptable to the Government'. His British interlocutors deduced that Alemann was saying that 'the sowing of multilateral and liberalising ideas' would fall 'on barren ground' given the 'bilateral and dirigiste tendencies of the more influential people round Frondizi'; PRO FO 371/131959, 17 October 1958.

90. Personal interview.

91. He has consistently claimed that his dismissal came as a total surprise since things were going as planned; personal interview. For Alsogaray's dismissal, see chapter 8.

92. Frigerio, *ibid.*, pp. 215–16. Alemann (Alsogaray's successor) supported this interpretation of the disillusionment with Alsogaray, stating that

Frondizi named Alemann in his place because the president believed that Alsogaray 'was not solving the problems that he [Frondizi] wanted solved, like the reduction of the public sector deficit, and the privatisation of State firms, especially the railways'. Alemann succeeded in cutting the number of people employed in the administration by 100,000 in eight months. Personal interview with Alemann.
93. PRO FO 371/155836, 15 December 1961.
94. *Ibid*. In support of Sir George's opinion, Alsogaray has claimed that after his dismissal, 'the main decrees on economic policy were prepared at Frigerio's home'; personal interview.
95. Quoted in Montemayor, *op. cit.*, p. 173.
96. PRO FO 371/139000, 26 June 1959. The report prompted a Foreign Office official to comment 'this removes some of the glamour which we have tended to attach to Señor Alsogaray'.
97. In this case, the British official was referring to Francisco Nasti [sic] who travelled to London without the knowledge of the Argentine embassy there, but carrying a letter from 'Frondizi's Economic Secretary' [Frigerio] to 'look at ways of broadening Argentine trade'. The impression he made at the Board of Trade in London was 'most unfavourable'; PRO FO 371/131963, 10 and 21 July 1958. The array of unpalatable characters was such that at one point Ward sent a secret report to the FO describing 'the mentality of the lunatic fringe around the President' whose dealings were increasingly becoming 'more ridiculous than sinister'. He was referring specifically to 'strange manoeuvres of certain members of the local Shell administration [Sr Puricelli]' as well as 'attempts to persuade *The Times* and *Daily Express* correspondents to root for Frondizi'; PRO FO 371/131957, 31 October 1958. *The Times* correspondent duly sent a report to the ambassador, referring to the 'anti-climax' of his visit to Colonel Guglialmelli after a month of 'persistent molestation by the intermediary Dr Bereny'. Guglialmelli offered any help he could give to the British correspondents, who were not impressed.
98. Frigerio (1963b) pp. 83–4.
99. PRO FO 371/131864, AA1151/122, 31 October 1958. Cárcano had been Argentine ambassador to Britain durging the Conservative government, up to the 1943 military coup.
100. *Ibid*.
101. Letter marked Secret from Ward to Henry Hankey, at the American Desk of the Foreign Office; PRO FO 371/131957, 31 October 1958. The British themselves were not unwilling to use the press, as in the case of the conflict with 'the odious' Governor Alende over the expropriation of a British-owned estancia, when an embassy official told the Foreign Office that 'a rather sad governessy piece on standard *Economist* lines could do good'; PRO FO 371/131977, 21 August 1958.
102. Frigerio (1962a) p. 68. There were 44 firms in the group, and the

privatisation of 40 of them was only achieved in six months during 1961, when Alemann became Economy minister in place of Alsogaray.
103. Since the patents and trademarks had already been handed back to them, 'they were able to put virtually what figure they liked on the use of these patents and trademarks'; PRO FO 371/139019, 22 May 1959.
104. PRO FO 371/139019, 22 May 1959.
105. Instances were 'investments' by the UK firm International Combustion importing £50,000 worth of boilers for Mellor Goodwin of Argentina, and Westinghouse's 'investment' in SIAM Di Tella; PRO *ibid*.
106. 'Argentina made great efforts to secure [Ford investment totalling US $15 million in 1959) under the impression that what Detroit does today the rest of the United States will do tomorrow'. The British were 'told that a third of the total "investment" . . . would be in the form of complete vehicles imported CKD. These will be sold when assembled at prices which may well give a profit of over 200 per cent, thus enabling the greater part of the "investment" to be repatriated through the free market without much delay'; *ibid*.
107. Sourrouille (1976) p. 17.
108. *Ibid*.
109. Data extracted from Sourrouille, *ibid*., chapter 2, tables 4 and 5, pp. 57–8.
110. *Ibid*., p. 18.
111. Díaz Alejandro, *op. cit*., p. 180.
112. *Ibid*., pp. 48–9.
113. Petrecolla in Di Tella and Dornbusch (1989).
114. This is what he had sought to do while in the Washington embassy, where Donato del Carril had taken him as adviser; personal interview. Donato del Carril was appointed ambassador in Washington as a compensation for being removed from the Economy Ministry, where he was replaced by Alsogaray.
115. Report from the Canadian ambassador in Buenos Aires to the Secretary of State for External Affairs, Ottawa; PRO FO 371/155840, 16 October 1961.
116. Before becoming Economy minister in April 1961 Alemann had won a considerable reputation in Europe for his activities over the Paris Club and in the United States as economic attaché at the Argentine Embassy; PRO FO 371/155823, 5 May 1961.
117. A tractor in Argentina in 1961 cost twice as much as a British import would have cost, and it was equivalent to '110 good steers whereas in the United States [the cost would be] 17 steers, and in France about 10'; *ibid*.
118. *Ibid*., p. 187. In January 1959, Mariano Wainfeld, a former member of the UCRI National Committee and at the time one of Frondizi's political advisors, explained to US embassy officials that income

tax could not be used as a tool to spread the burden of austerity more equally because the system was largely ineffective, adding 'half jokingly' that the Argentine government had enforced austerity 'in democratic fashion by starting at the bottom and working toward the top'.

Chapter 6

1. A. A. Marini (UCRP, Buenos Aires province) despondently remarked in September 1961 that 'not one of the bills submitted by the UCRP has been considered by the Chamber'; Diputados, Diario de Sesiones, 27 September 1961, p. 3346.
2. Palacios, 'Combining Socialism with anti-Semitism and nationalism' was 'an agreeable and entertaining companion' despite his 'vanity and tendency to exhibitionism'; PRO FO 371/138997, 24 April 1959.
3. One instance was the expropriation of the Norton Estate by Governor Alende, provoking Frondizi's 'great rage' at what he considered 'a stab in the back' from Alende, in Cárcano's account to Ward; PRO FO 371/131977, 22 August 1958. Another was the conflict with Governor Gelsi when the Tucumán Governor sided with sugar-cane workers in their protest against the cuts in sugar subsidies announced by Alsogaray. The feeling was that the strike would not have been successful were it not for the interference of Gelsi, 'a left-wing demagogue with considerable political ambitions'; PRO FO 371/139002, 11 September 1959. Gelsi's account, not surprisingly, delved on Frondizi's 'neglect of the smaller provinces and their needs'; personal interview.
4. Peter H. Smith (1974) p. xviii.
5. See Solberg (1979) p. 154, who accepts Yrigoyen's commitment to oil nationalism, while George Philip (1982) questions such commitment to nationalisation, and considers 'highly implausible' the alleged involvement of Standard Oil of New Jersey in the 1930 coup pointing out that 'the oil policies of the incoming government [...] did not represent any sharp reversal of earlier ones' (p. 178).
6. Nicholas Biddle throws new light on the manipulation of the oil issue by *Yrigoyenistas*, which he places at the crossroads of the struggle between Buenos Aires and the interior, the *Yrigoyenistas* of Buenos Aires and the Conservatives of Salta, both for political control as monetary advantage, since the nationalisation of oil meant that control over resources and benefits went to the central government; 'Oil and the Right in the 1928 Election', paper presented at the XVI LASA meeting, Washington, 4–6 April 1991.
7. Frondizi (1956) p. 198.
8. Solberg, *op. cit.*, p. 151.
9. Institutional crises had also abounded during Yrigoyen's first period in the presidency. For an illuminating account see Mustapic (1984).

10. Cf. Makin (1984) ; *La Nación*, 28 July 1955, *The Times*, 29 July 1955, and *The New York Times* 28 July 1955. For an account of the vicissitudes surrounding the California contract, see Makin, *op. cit.*, Laura Randall (1978) pp. 192–234, and Potash (1980) p. 162. On opposition to the California contract, see PRO FO 371/114059, 5 August 1955, where Fordham in Buenos Aires remarked that 'the moral of the story is that thanks to Argentina's past treatment of foreign capital . . . foreign companies are reluctant to operate in Argentina except on terms which are more favourable than they would be prepared to accept elsewhere'.
11. Ricardo Rojo maintains that Perón demanded that contracts with foreign oil companies be part of the developmentalist undertakings in the pact before agreeing to support Frondizi in 1958; personal interview. In the light of Newton's revelations, it is possible that Perón's decision to grant concessions to Standard Oil was motivated partly by his wish to build an arms industry in Argentina. For this, after Germany's defeat in World War II, he would have to turn to the US for help. The latter, in turn, would not be forthcoming unless foreign participation was allowed in the oil business. See Newton (1992) chapter 16.
12. Makin, *op. cit.*
13. PRO FO 371/131978, 10 January 1958. This file contains valuable information on the oil situation in Argentina, the position of H.M.G. and UK oil companies, as well as the Ministry of Power's worry that a decision to cut Argentine meat exports to the UK would adversely affect the oil companies.
14. *Ibid.*
15. PRO FO 371/131978, 5 March 1958. At the time Ward had thought that the way for the big oil companies to cooperate in the extraction of oil in Argentina 'might become easier if the moderate, Balbín, faction of the Radicals won the elections'; *ibid.*
16. Babini interview. The meeting was one of a series with government ministers suggested by Aramburu as a way of familiarising Frondizi with the affairs of State.
17. PRO FO 371/131978, 5 March 1958.
18. The 'oil battle' had resonances of Mussolini's preference for military imagery, cf. C. Hibbert (1965) p. 70.
19. Argentine domestic production of petroleum peaked in 1963, satisfying 90% of the country's needs, in contrast with 41.4% in 1950, while during Illia's presidency (1963–66) the proportion of domestic production to petroleum imports fell to 75.4%. Only during the military administrations of Onganía (1968: 90.1%) and Lanusse (1972: 93.3%) did domestic production reach levels that surpassed the Frondizi years, see Solberg, *op. cit.*, p. 173.
20. Frondizi did not mention that YPF's most dramatic process of decline and bureaucratisation had taken place during the Peronist administration; see Philip, *op. cit.*, pp. 403–4.

21. Total domestic production of oil in 1958 was 5,669,000 m³ (or 87.6% of the total) while in 1961 it reached 13,428,000 m³, the State fields accounting for 68% or 9,134,00 m³, the rest having been extracted by private contractors, inexistent in 1958; data in Solberg, *op. cit.*, tables 6.2. and 6.3., pp. 174–5.
22. It is interesting to note that in 1952 Argentina had signed a trade agreement with the USSR which included the provision of oil equipment, but Argentine technicians found it clumsy and not interchangeable with the US oil rigs in use; Philip, *op. cit.*, p. 407. On British reaction – not altogether unfavourable – to Argentina taking oil from the Soviet Bloc, see PRO FO 371/131978 and 979, 11 April 1958. Shell was less enthusiastic and wrote to the Treasury on 18 July 1958 seeking H.M.G.'s support to put the case that purchases of oil from the USSR or elsewhere were a breach of contract. Weston was not sympathetic and told Shell representatives that 'Shell had less to complain [in the Argentine context] than other United Kingdom exporters'; PRO FO 371/131979, 28 July 1958. An agreement was signed in Moscow on 27 October 1958; details can be found in PRO FO 371/131979, 19 November 1958.
23. Frondizi (1956) pp. xli–xliii.
24. Sir John Ward noted despondently that Frondizi's 'rhetorical support of that rickety organisation [YPF] belied earlier rumours that he would lay bare the long history of incompetence and sloth which has marked its fifty years'; PRO FO 371/131979, 25 July 1958.
25. Frondizi (1956) p. xliv.
26. Nelly Casas (1973) p. 42, records that on 30 July a group of UCRI 'notables' went to see Frondizi and asked him not to make his speech on the following day. According to Casas, he considered whether it was worthwhile to try to explain 'the lesson' but decided against it, thinking that it would be 'useless' and a waste of time. Instead, he told them that '[his] position was unchangeable. If [they] so wished, [they] could impeach [him]'. Earlier, as a response to the 1 May speech anticipating the cooperation of private capital, a group of UCRI deputies headed by José Liceaga had hoped to preempt any moves in this direction at least as far as oil was concerned by submitting to the Chamber a draft bill advocating the 'State monopoly of the oil industry in all its phases', the expiry of 'all exploration and drilling permits', and the expropriation of all equipment and plants belonging to private firms, 'be they national or foreign'; Diputados, 7 May 1958, p. 108. Twenty days later Liceaga submitted his resignation as deputy (unanimously rejected), depressed about the DINIE outcome since he had unsuccessfully pleaded for financial help so that a workers' cooperative could be formed to bid in the auction of OSRAM (one of the DINIE group).
27. PRO FO 371/131979, 25 July 1958.
28. *Ibid*.
29. Diputados, 31 July 1958, pp. 2118–19. The UCRI benches avoided the

	debate by indicating that it would interfere with the established agenda; *ibid.*, p. 2131.
30.	Cf. Luna (1963); Pandolfi (1968), Nelly Casas (1973) and Odena (1977).
31.	Arturo Sábato, personal interview; J. A. Martínez de Hoz, in a personal interview, recalled that Frondizi anticipated in his pre-election lunches with businessmen that the collaboration of foreign capital in the oil business would be sought. Prieto, a Peronist turned *frigerista*, argues in his book (1963) pp. 122–6, that soon after 23 February Frigerio and 'a group of people' got together in a flat in Quintana Avenue, where the decision to negotiate the contracts was taken.
32.	See Sábato (1974). Sábato said that Frigerio had offered him the job at YPF in 'January or February 1958, explaining in great detail what had to be done'; personal interview.
33.	PRO FO 371/131979, 8 and 22 August 1958. Eyebrows had been raised in London at the advisability of placing for the first time an Argentine citizen in charge of Shell interests in that country. Hildyard had perceptively anticipated that this might be the case in a comment to Ward's pessimistic report on Frondizi's 24 July speech. He noted then that 'a lot of the initial work in Argentina will consist in developing proven resources and tapping wells already sunk, but sealed and unexploited for lack of equipment. If small firms are successful in this, and the Argentine public becomes accustomed to the idea of foreign exploitation along these lines, they may later be inclined to accept the large companies who alone can undertake the more ambitious task of exploration on a large scale'; PRO FO 371/131979, 11 August 1958.
34.	PRO FO 371/131979, 8 August 1958. On October Puricelli repeated the same arguments during a luncheon in London with Fred Emery (Shell), Weston (Treasury), Whitehouse (Board of Trade) and Crick (Bank of England), adding that Frondizi was then 'far to the right of Balbín'; *ibid.* For a description of the kinds of contracts and results obtained, see Philip, *op. cit.*, pp. 411–13; Sábato (1974) pp. 55–64; Frigerio (1979) pp. 35–49.
35.	Diputados, 30 July 1964.
36.	Several people interviewed in Buenos Aires said they believed money had indeed exchanged hands, and that at best it had gone to fill the UCRI coffers. The party did spend unprecedented amounts of money in propaganda, and the source of that money is not known. Opposition parties that could not compete with such resources accused the government of financing UCRI expenses from public funds.
37.	PRO FO 371/131979, 1535/58, 3 September 1958. The worry in Caracas was that if 'distorted or inaccurate accounts' should start circulating, they might 'influence the Venezuelans in their attitude towards the oil companies here, more especially towards new concessions; [. . .] Betancourt hinted as much to the [UK] Ambassador a few days ago'; *ibid.*

38. Frigerio (1979) p. 111.
39. *Ibid.*, p. 123.
40. Reproduced in Frondizi (1978) vol. I, p. 171.
41. Odena, *op. cit.*, p. 224.
42. Diputados, 21 May 1958. All quotations from the text of the law and comments of deputies are from this same source.
43. Two months later, on 2 July, UCRP deputy Carlos Perette presented a draft bill in which any political grouping wishing to 'take part in civic activities' should have (a) 'an impersonal content'; and (b) a democratic structure. Diputados, 2 July 1958, p. 1463. The Peronist party had neither.
44. Casas, *op. cit.*, p. 62.
45. In her book published in 1973 Casas acknowledged that this had been the case; p. 61. See also Guardo (1963) p. 110.
46. Diputados, 16 June 1958.
47. On the occasion of opening Congress sessions on 1 May 1959; reproduced in Frondizi (1978) vol. II, p. 134.
48. The Senate, presided by Héctor Cámpora, voted law No. 13,234 article by article, without reading their content. The law established military jurisdiction in the national territory in cases of internal commotion. On 10 September 1948, the UCR's National Committee declared that 'all our freedoms capsize in the face of police arbitrariness and presidential absolutism', UCR, *Boletín*, 18 September 1948.
49. The state of siege was the norm rather than the exception in Argentina in 1930–83, with the UCRP administration of President Arturo Illia providing the exception.
50. Decree No. 2,639 of 15 March 1960 established the CONINTES Plan. Oyhanarte (a member of the Supreme Court under Frondizi) said that a secret decree setting the dispositions for the CONINTES plan was drawn in 1958. Personal interview.
51. Babini recalled that when challenged by close friends or supporters on the advisability of a policy decision, Frondizi would swiftly put an end to the subject invoking secret knowledge of 'impending catastrophes and apocalyptic conspiracies'. Babini interview.
52. Diputados, 30 November 1959, p. 6022.
53. Diputados, 10 December 1959, p. 6097.
54. This and the following quotations are taken from the debate of 10 December 1959, pp. 6117–20.
55. Frondizi (1978) vol. III, p. 53. The Argentine Federation of Bar Associations branded CONINTES unconstitutional since it omitted the constitutional prerequisite of the mobilisation of civilians before they could be submitted to military justice; *La Nación*, 21 December 1960.
56. Speech of 12 May 1958, reproduced in Frondizi, vol. I. *ibid.*, p. 67.
57. In a lecture delivered in September 1978 to the Bar Association, Dr Oyhanarte said that Frondizi was entitled to do this, since the judges

were '*de facto*' ones, appointed by a '*de facto*' government. But he recognised that although Frondizi had been right from a 'juridico-formal level', his decision could be disputed from the 'politico-institutional level'. Typescript supplied by the author.
58. Oyhanarte typescript.
59. *La Nación*, 15 July 1958.
60. Text of Orgaz's resignation published in *La Nación*, 3 March 1960.
61. *Ibid*.
62. Oyhanarte typescript.
63. Personal interview with Oyhanarte.
64. Smulovitz (1988) vol. 1, p. 23, makes a similar point.
65. Frigerio, 'A Balance of the 27 March Elections', quoted in Rouquié (1975) p. 131.

Chapter 7

1. The decision of *Sabattinismo*, part of Intransigence which had stayed on in the UCRP, to vote for Peronism in the March 1962 elections, provides an illustration of such ideological ambivalence.
2. See for instance, Babini, *op. cit.*, p. 295; Rouquié (1975) p. 127; Corbière (1978) p. 83.
3. *La Nación*, 16 January 1958.
4. Diputados, 26 Sept. 1958, p. 4401.
5. *La Nación*, 5 September 1958.
6. *La Nación*, 15 September 1958.
7. *La Nación*, 20 September 1958.
8. Gómez Machado, Diputados, 24 September 1958, p. 4193.
9. The JCN 29 February 1956 debate is reproduced in the 25 September 1958 issue of the *Diario de Sesiones*.
10. This and all quotations from the Education debate were taken from Diputados, 25 September 1958.
11. Nélida Baigorria and Angel Caggiano were two of the UCRI deputies who spoke against the proposed amendment. Nélida Baigorria was expelled from the UCRI in 1960 and joined the UCRP benches in Congress.
12. The unrest extended to secondary and even primary school children. While the former joined university students in setting up barricades, the latter took to wearing distinctive ribbons (green for '*libre*', purple for '*laica*').
13. Mariano Montemayor (1963) pp. 216–17. Montemayor was a nationalist journalist close to Frigerio who replaced the latter as editor of *Qué*.
14. Plaza was part of the *frigerista* circle; interview with Blanca Stábile, corroborated in Washington Archives, 735.00/10–1559, 15 October 1959. For the controversy surrounding Plaza's pro-Peronist activities

see Washington Archives, Central Files, 755.00/10–2959, 20 October 1959, American Embassy in Buenos Aires to Department of State.
15. A case in point is David Bléjer, who Frondizi placed first as Under-Secretary at Interior and then as head of the Ministry for Labour at a very difficult time, to remove him when Alsogaray became simultaneously Economy minister and interim Labour minister. Personal interview with Bléjer.
16. Admiral Hartung, at the time ambassador in London, considered Gómez 'a bore', while for the British he was 'generally regarded as a victim of his own vanity and ingenuousness'; PRO FO 371/138997, 27 April 1959.
17. Nelly Casas (1973) p. 66.
18. Cf. Montemayor (1963) pp. 183–5. Casas, *ibid.*, also refers to those meetings.
19. Casas, *op. cit.*, p. 68.
20. Babini, *op. cit.*, p. 250 wrote that Gómez was 'deeply dissatisfied with the direction the government was taking'.
21. Montemayor, *op. cit.*, p. 223.
22. Babini writes that Gómez believed he was speaking in the name of 'YPF's unyielding defenders, supporters of agrarian reform and party colleagues bearing a personal grudge against Frondizi', although he blames Gómez's actions on Palacios; *op. cit.*, p. 250. It seems that Palacios encouraged the vice-president to stay in the country and to refuse Frondizi's offer of a trip to Europe, stressing that in 'important circles' much was said about Gómez's 'presidential possibilities'; *ibid.*, p. 251.
23. In his book, Gómez (1963) pp. 361–5, states that it was Frondizi who asked him not to reveal the name, as a pledge of honour.
24. *La Nación*, 13 November 1958.
25. Babini, *op. cit.*, p. 252.
26. Casas (1973) p. 70.
27. *La Nación*, 18 November 1958.
28. Potash (1980) p. 296.
29. Babini, *op. cit.*, p. 254.
30. So great was the animosity towards Frigerio, that his visits to Olivos had to be made at night and during weekends, when they were least likely to be noticed. Personal interview. General Solanas Pacheco, Frondizi's Army Secretary until his resignation on 1 July 1959, confirmed how indignant the military felt at what they thought was 'a childish ploy to fool them'; personal interview.
31. Stábile and Musich interviews.
32. Secret report from the British Ambassador to the Foreign Office, PRO FO 371/131949, A1015/19, 7 March 1958.
33. *Ibid.* The list included Frigerio, 'considered to be a Communist sympathiser'. On 6 February 1958 Sir John Ward had reported to Selwyn Lloyd that 'Frondizi's known extreme Left tendencies in youth,

and the fact that one of his brothers [Risieri] and some of his closest advisers are Communists, are ground for doubt whether his cultivation of these dubious elements is purely opportunist'; PRO FO 371/131949, A1015/7.
34. PRO FO 371/131963, July 1958, British embassy to Foreign Office. It would seem that *frigerista* inner loyalty was far from strong, since during a private conversation between de Pablo Pardo and the American Ambassador the former explained that the June 1959 military unrest was a consequence of disquiet within the Armed Forces against the president 'because of persons such as Cúneo, Odena and Frigerio who had had Communist backgrounds and the Argentine military [had] become very Communist conscious and [regarded the three men mentioned] as sinister and as serving Communist causes'; Washington Archives, memorandum of conversation between Beaulac and de Pablo Pardo, 30 June 1959. Four months later Schamis (at the time Argentine Ambassador to Guatemala) explained to Beaulac that the presence of such a mixture of people responded to Frigerio's integrationist approach, aimed at including not just Peronists but 'as many other elements in the Argentine political picture as possible'; Memorandum of conversation, 735.00/10–1559, 15 October 1959.
35. Quoted in Montemayor, *op. cit.*, pp. 218–19.
36. *La Nación*, 11 September 1958.
37. *La Nación*, 2 October 1958.
38. Díaz (1977) p. 153. When the UCRI split in 1963, Frondizi and Frigerio formed the MID which became a pressure group ready to 'sell' its policies to whoever – especially the military – was prepared to 'buy' them.
39. Babini, *op. cit.*, p. 295.
40. Rouquié (1975) p. 127.
41. Corbière (1978) p. 83.
42. Musich interview.
43. *La Nación*, 12 June 1959. The letter was dated May 1959.
44. *La Nación*, 12 June 1959.
45. Conrado Storani, UCRP deputy for the province of Córdoba; see Diputados, 17 June 1959, p. 809. Frigerio's resignation was followed by that of all *frigeristas* in the government, including the Foreign Relations minister and the Secretary for Agriculture. The wave of resignations came after the denunciations of a 'parallel government'. For a defence of *paralelismo* see Ramón Prieto (1963) pp. 199–215, who wrote that 'parallelism' rescued the UCRI from 'utopia and the cheap demagogy of *Avellaneda*' and substituted its 'partisan passion' for 'national passion'; *ibid*, p. 201.
46. Diputados, *ibid.*, p. 843.
47. Diputados, *op. cit.*, p. 847. The *frondicistas* refused to believe the allegations. Babini has told of his personal quest in 1960 seeking confirmation of the Pact's existence. When it arrived, it only con-

tributed to deepen his disenchantment with Frondizi. Babini had resigned as Interior Under-Secretary in April 1959 after Frondizi gave in to military pressures not to appoint Babini's father to head the Department of Culture at the Ministry of Education. The military accused José Babini, a prestigious engineer, of being a Communist. For an account of this episode, see Babini, *op. cit.*, pp. 276–9.

48. Diputados, *ibid.*, p. 860.
49. *La Nación*, 14 May 1959.
50. Quoted in Washington Archives, 735.00/4–759, 7 April 1959.
51. In Luna (1963) pp. 46–7.
52. Casas, *op. cit.*, pp. 86–7.
53. Diputados, 13 August 1959, p. 2104.
54. Cf. extracts from the memorandum Babini sent Vítolo outlining his ideas, reproduced in Babini, *op. cit.*, pp. 274–5. Babini wrote that the UCRI could still be rescued if it were provided with 'leadership, organisation and a concrete programme for action'.
55. *Ibid.*, p. 274.
56. Rouquié (1975) p. 132.
57. Rabenold to Department of State, 735.00/10–3059, 30 October 1959.
58. The *Uturuncos*, of Peronist extraction, and the *Ejército Guerrillero del Pueblo* (EGP) of Trotskyist provenance, were short-lived experiences, easily wiped out by the army. While the first was based in Tucumán, the second chose the province of Salta. See Gillespie (1982) p. 38. Their impact would only be felt in student and intellectual circles. When the newspapers reported the discovery of 'another group of Peronist guerrillas in Tucumán' they had one revolver, 100 hand-grenades (only three were charged), a case with military boots and another with military blankets, food and medicines; *La Nación*, 11 March 1960.
59. *La Nación*, 19 February 1960.
60. In a personal interview Gelsi remarked that he survived the storm 'because I was defended by my friends among the military, especially General Sueldo'.
61. Soon after becoming governor in 1958, Zanichelli had tried to rid the local police force of its *gorila* elements. When the police force responded with a strike, the governor organised armed militias in which Peronists were included. This happened, it must be borne in mind, in the province that took especial pride in being 'the cradle of democracy', since it was from there that General Lonardi launched the anti-Peronist revolution in 1955. *La Nación* of 12 May 1960 published the main accusations included in the report.
62. Héctor Panzeri, who had presided the Córdoba Senate dominated by the UCRI until March 1960 and was then appointed by Zanichelli president of the Bank of Córdoba, remarked that the UCRI could never have won the 1958 elections in that province without Peronist support, and that Zanichelli had been of all the governors, the one 'to take

up the *integracionista* approach with the greatest fervour'. Personal interview.
63. The UCRP held the majority in the Córdoba provincial legislature since the March 1960 elections, and a resolution had been submitted to the Córdoba Senate demanding the resignation of Zanichelli, who, it was alleged, 'no longer fulfilled the qualities of behaviour inherent to his condition as governor', *La Nación*, 4 June 1960.
64. *La Nación*, 5 June.
65. Córdoba was the first province where a petition of the *Partido Justicialista* (Peronist) for legal recognition had been successful. On 29 December 1958 Federal Judge Carlos Chechi had said that 'any group of persons, regardless of their prior political activities, may today participate freely in the political life of the nation . . . '.
66. PRO FO 371/155822, 3 February 1961. See also Rouquié, *op. cit.*, p. 491, Potash, *op. cit.*, p. 323 and Frondizi in Luna, *op. cit.*, p. 124. Both Héctor Panzeri and Gelsi were very bitter about the episode twenty years later. The latter said that Frondizi sacrificed Zanichelli 'on the request of the insignificant General Lamas' while the former seemed to accept that Frondizi 'had to sacrifice Zanichelli to save his own skin'.
67. Diputados, 10 June 1960.
68. *La Nación*, 11 June 1960.
69. PRO FO 371/147756, 3 June 1960.
70. *La Nación*, 17 December 1960.
71. Quoted in Rouquié, *op. cit.*, pp. 135–6.
72. *La Nación*, 26 December 1960.
73. *La Nación*, 7 June 1961.
74. This was Marcos Merchensky, Frigerio's closest collaborator.
75. Diputados, 14 May 1959, p. 310.
76. The British Ambassador described them as 'fatuously impotent', criticising everything 'without any hint that they had a working alternative', PRO FO 371/147756, 11 February 1960.
77. Diputados, 13 August 1959, p. 2053. Earlier, Carlos Perette had sought to distinguish between a liberal economy, which he considered a good thing, and a free-enterprise economy, which he considered to be bad. Diputados, 16 July 1959, p. 1282.
78. The UCRP submitted several draft proposals demanding that the government include in the legislative agenda the discussion on the 'illicit enrichment of public officials'; cf. Diputados, 16 and 24 November 1960. The whiff of corruption accompanied the whole of Frondizi's period in office.
79. Interview with a UCRP member and close friend of Balbín's, who added that 'everybody sent emissaries to see Perón'.
80. Diputados, 18 June 1959, p. 924. UCRP deputy Verdaguer resigned his seat declaring that 'the people of the Republic have the right to declare themselves in a state of rebellion *vis-à-vis* those who, without

a mandate, are prepared to carry out such a cruel and wretched fate.', referring to the oil contracts and trade union detainees; Diputados, 14 May 1959, p. 304.
81. Washington Archives, 735–00/4–759, Nugent to Department of State, 7 April 1959. Nugent described Zavala Ortiz as a 'fire-eating "golpista"'. In a personal interview, Ernesto Laclau recalled how his father, a UCRP member, was General Toranzo Montero's 'permanent candidate to head the Interior Ministry in a military government'. Dr Laclau (senior) became Illia's ambassador to Denmark in 1963.
82. Bernasconi disingenuously told the Second Secretary at the US embassy Guy Ferri that the 'imperialists' were the Soviet Union, in a reference to the oil-extracting equipment contracts Argentina had signed with that country; Ferri was not impressed. Washington Archives, 735.00/1–157, 15 January 1959.
83. Diputados, 10 December 1959, p. 6118.
84. PRO FO 371/138998, 7 May 1959.
85. Personal interview with Frondizi.
86. *La Nación*, 19 December 1960.
87. José Alfredo Martínez de Hoz and Guido Di Tella were amongst the founding members of the PDC; personal interview with Martínez de Hoz.
88. *La Nación*, 22 December 1960.
89. The virulence of their anti-Peronism was illustrated by Américo Ghioldi's comment following the extra-judicial shootings of 9 June 1956: 'The milk of mercy has been exhausted.'
90. Although not in terms of electoral support. In March 1960 the PSD received 3.5% of the votes (309,462 in the whole country) and the PSA 4.8% (or 383,610 votes).
91. There were Castroits, pro Moscow Communists, Trotskyists, Titoists and Maoists.
92. Including the short-lived Popular Vanguard party, Communist Vanguard, Workers's Party and Socialist Party of the National Left. Palacios, who in 1904 had been elected the first Socialist member of Congress in the Americas, was elected Senator for Buenos Aires City in 1961.

Chapter 8

1. The support of the Church had been guaranteed with the Education Law and the commitment to oppose a divorce law.
2. Ismael Viñas described thus the most notable right-wing intellectuals of the time: Mario Amadeo (Frondizi's UN Ambassador) had an Olympian outlook; Castellani was a baroque figure with boorish proclivities; Jauretche was an atheist, materialist, economicist and statist; Marcelo Sánchez Sorondo was a Catholic, Cesarist and statist;

Meinvielle was Catholic but non-intervionist; Olmedo, a fossilised old man of an ultramontane anti-liberalism; in Viñas (1960) pp. 114–15.
3. For a nationalist indictment of Peronism, see Mariano Etchecopar, 'Esquema de la Argentina', in *Azul y Blanco*, 28 November 1956.
4. Personal interview. Federico Pinedo, the former Socialist responsible for the enlightened economic policies of the politically fraudulent regime of the 1930s, and thus high in UCR demonology, was also present at the meeting. Babini remarked that Frondizi was constantly 'dazzled' by the Right. In 1937 the then senator Sánchez Sorondo was warmly welcomed by Hitler and the Nazi hierarchy while on a visit to Germany; Newton (1992) pp. 183–4.
5. Towards the end of his life Zavala Ortiz remained convinced that the developmentalists were, consciously or unconsciously, furthering Soviet designs on Argentina; personal interview.
6. Personal interview with Ismael Viñas whose idea *Contorno* originally was, together with his brother's, David. On the role of intellectuals in Argentina in the 1960s see Sigal (1991), on *Contorno*, especially chapter III; cf. also Katra (1988).
7. León Rozitchner, 'Experiencia proletaria y experiencia burguesa', in *Contorno*, no. 7–8, July 1956.
8. *Ibid.*, p. 3.
9. *Ibid.*, p. 5.
10. *Ibid.*, p. 8.
11. Osiris Troiani, 'Examen de conciencia', *ibid.*, p. 9.
12. *Ibid.*, p. 10.
13. Rodolfo Pandolfi, '17 de octubre, trampa y salida', *Contorno, op. cit.*, p. 22. In italics in the original.
14. The *Contorno* group had been in contact with Frondizi since before 1955; I. Viñas interview.
15. Pandolfi, *op. cit.*, p. 28. In italics in the original.
16. For Viñas' criticism of the Left see Viñas (1960) p. 278, and also pp. 160–5, where he describes the thinking of the extreme Left. Chief amongst those Trotskyites who relentlessly opposed Frondizi and the Communist Party's decision to back him, was the President's own brother, Silvio Frondizi, who twenty years later was dragged from his flat in Buenos Aires and shot in the street by a paramilitary group.
17. *Cuadernos de Contorno*, July 1957, no. 1, p. 3.
18. Ismael Viñas recalled how they 'imposed Marisa Liceaga' on the list against the will of the UCRI *caudillos* in the City of Buenos Aires; personal interview.
19. For a summary of their views, see Viñas (1960) pp. 172–4.
20. Viñas was caustic about the Marxists who expounded what he described as 'Left-wing Machiavellianism': they remained loyal to Frondizi after 1958, dismissing the 'sell-out to American imperialism' since after all 'the capitalist world was in crisis and near collapse', so why worry

about compromising with 'a world that can be of no use to us and whose disappearance is certain'? Viñas, *ibid.*, p. 245.
21. Quoted in *Cuadernos de Contorno*, July 1957, no. 1.
22. In Pandolfi (1968) p. 74.
23. For instance, the National Endowment for the Arts, the National Council for Technical and Scientific Research (CONACYT) and the National Institute of Industrial Technology (INTI).
24. John King (1985), especially pp. 15–42 for an analysis of cultural developments in the sixties imbued with mythical status after the censorship, and cultural and ideological terrorism of 1966–82.
25. Frondizi lacked both the teluric attraction of populism and the romantic appeal of revolution. Writing in *Les Temps Modernes* in 1981, in an issue dedicated 'à ceux qui on fait *Contorno*, à ceux qui *Contorno* a fait', David Viñas remarked that Che Guevara provided the link between Sartre and *Contorno*'s contributors, marking the passage from the imaginary to the real. After the semantic confusion surrounding the word 'revolution' which everybody, from Perón to the *Libertadora* and Frondizi used, the generations that experienced the passions of the *laica* versus *libre* confrontations found a more satisfactory meaning for the word in the model proposed by Fidel. Halperín Donghi (1964) has remarked that the election of the Socialist Alfredo Palacios to the Senate in 1961 was 'Fidel's victory'.
26. *Contorno*, no. 9–10, April 1959, p. 4.
27. For the intellectuals' shock, dismay, bewilderment and disillusionment at Frondizi's volte face see Tulio Halperín Donghi (1964) p.93.
28. Viñas (1960) p. 279, and Rozitchner: 'the idea that we have of reality is determined by our own origin and emotional set-up, in the midst of the bourgeoisie and Christian values', in *Contorno, op. cit.*, p. 10.
29. *Contorno*, no. 9–10, April 1959, pp. 1–2. The double issue, with articles by Ismael Viñas, León Rozitchner and Tulio Halperín Donghi, is devoted to an analysis of their disillusionment.
30. Esteban Rey (1959) p. 25 and p. 50, a dissident communist, wrote an indictment of Frigerio for expecting the 'national bourgeoisie to play an hegemonic role in a revolutionary process'. The immigrant origin of industrial entrepreneurs and the slow integration of immigrants to political life have been stressed as causes retarding the formation of a strong industry party. Frondizi and Frigerio set out to reverse this situation, while all the time saying they were doing something else. See Oscar Cornblit, 'Inmigrantes y empresarios en la política argentina' (mimeograph, Di Tella Institute) and Díaz Alejandro (1970) pp. 214–16.
31. *Qué*, 4 April 1956.
32. Interview with Isak Radunsky.
33. Some entrepreneurs had been given notice prior to 1 May 1958 of the intention to embrace free trade. Personal interview with José A. Martínez de Hoz.

34. Díaz Alejandro (1970) p. 255.
35. *Ibid.*
36. *Ibid.*, pp. 259–60.
37. *Ibid.*, p. 261.
38. In 1954 the Central Bank resolved to grant import permits for industrial machinery on the basis of plans prepared jointly by the government and the CGE. Díaz Alejandro, *ibid.*, p. 261.
39. *Qué*, 7 May 1957.
40. Interview with Manuel Madanes, head of the only Argentine tyre factory at the time. Madanes emphasised the high hopes he had had on Frondizi, and how disappointed he had been at the lack of protection for domestic industries. Another businessman who expressed his dissatisfaction with the Frondizi administration was Guido Di Tella, who remarked he had been '[. . .] one of those disappointed by Frondizi [. . . .] I remember the anger I felt, as well as the anger felt by many other Argentines, at having been so miserably deceived', *La Semana*, 27 December 1984. In Di Tella (1983) p. 24, he wrote that the emphasis given by Frondizi to the capital-intensive, foreign-owned sector alienated 'the local industrialists who had been so favourable to Frondizi' and who began 'to veer away, looking back with nostalgia to the old days prior to 1955 when no foreign capital had competed with them'.
41. CGE, *Memoria Anual 1960*, p. 6.
42. Interview with Jorge Garfunkel.
43. Quoted in 'Los empresarios argentinos', typescript, 2 vols, Buenos Aires, Instituto de Investigaciones Administrativas, Facultad de Ciencias Económicas, 1987.
44. Typescript of Terragno interview with Frondizi.
45. With the exception of Frigerio, who had started with the family textile concern of shirt-making, none of the *integracionistas* had any firm business grounding. They were mavericks (Bereny), intermediaries (Schmukler), or journalists-*cum*-businessmen (Perina).
46. D'Adamo interview.
47. Díaz Alejandro (1970) p. 241.
48. Sourrouille (1976) p. 17.
49. Díaz Alejandro (1970) p. 256.
50. UIA, *Memoria del Ejercicio 1958*, p. 19.
51. Randall (1978) p. 216.
52. Alsogaray took over from David Bléjer, who had been Labour minister since replacing *frigerista* Alfredo Allende, a white-collar union leader, on 10 February 1959.
53. Torre (1980) p. 145. Torre has noted that the defensiveness of unionism in the labour front was in contrast with its militancy in the political arena, highlighting the gap between 'the level of political expression and the social struggle', *ibid.*, p. 149.
54. The concept of 'integration' had first been used by Isidro Odena on 23 February 1958. Ambiguity of the concept had sent people speculating

whether it could not mean the replacement of the UCRI, and therefore 'an election victory might result in the demise of a party'; Washington Archives, 735.00/3–1059 referring to US Embassy dispatch of 23 May 1958.

55. The Labour minister claimed to follow three rules regarding labour relations: (a) the government would no longer order payment of wages to striking workers; (b) the government would no longer undertake to promote negotiations while a strike was in progress; and (c) union delegates would not be allowed to disturb the order within factories; Díaz Alejandro (1965) p. 154.
56. Washington Archives, 735.00/3–1059, 10 March 1959.
57. *Qué*, 25 April 1956.
58. *Qué*, 6 May 1958.
59. For the role of Socialists in the pre-Perón labour movement, see Torre (1990); Walter Little, 'La organización obrera y el estado peronista, 1943–1955', in *Desarrollo Económico* (1979), and Louise M. Doyon, 'Labour Conflicts During the Peronist Regime, 1946–1955', typescript October 1974, and 'El crecimiento sindical bajo el peronismo', in *Desarrollo Económico* (1975).
60. *Qué*, 12 February 1957. For a critical view from a left-wing perspective of Frigerio's thinking on the role of workers, see Esteban Rey, (1959) pp. 25–9.
61. When the British Ambassador met some 'democratic' union leaders just after Frondizi's triumph, they forecast that in nine months Frondizi would have organised labour against him; PRO FO 371/131949, 1958.
62. Frigerio is still adamant that stabilisation and growth ('development') were simultaneously compatible, and that Alsogaray was pursuing personal political gains by insisting on 'stabilisation' over 'development'; personal interview.
63. Perón-Cooke (1973) vol. II, p. 147, February 1959.
64. *Ibid.*, p. 149.
65. Perón wrote to Cooke '[Frondizi] tells us that the *gorilas* prevent him from doing things, and to the *gorilas* he talks of the dangers of a popular uprising led by us', Perón-Cooke, *ibid.*, p. 60 (letter dated 7 June 1958).
66. Petrecolla in Di Tella and Dornbusch (1989).
67. *Ibid.*, p. 156.
68. At the time the British Embassy recorded this fact noting that 'with current small turnovers and high stocks [strikes] afford little concern to either employers or the Government'; PRO FO 371/139003, 25 September 1959. Díaz Alejandro (1965) p. 170–1 has argued that in some cases management arranged the strikes with workers. To support this claim, Díaz Alejandro quotes from a report by the World Trade Information Service of the US Department of Commerce, as well as from the 21 January 1961 issue of the *Review of the River Plate*.

69. Babini, personal interview. In April 1957, the UCRI National Committee issued a statement reaffirming 'the need for the workers to recover their legitimate organisation' and that there should be only one CGT; *Informativo Radical*, April 1957.
70. *Declaración de la Comisión Gremial del Partido Socialista*, 7 November 1955, quoted in Cavarozzi (1979) p. 22.
71. *Qué*, 27 August 1957.
72. Serafino Romualdi (1967) p. 165. Romualdi was one of the best-known Bureau of Latin American Research anti-fascist operatives. BLAR was started in 1941 as a direct dependency of Rockefeller's Office of the Coordinator of Inter American Affairs in Washington, acting as an ancillary intelligence agency; Newton (1992) p. 351 and 466 fn. 41.
73. *Ibid.*, p. 166.
74. *Ibid.*
75. *Ibid.*, p. 167.
76. *Ibid.*, p. 166.
77. *Ibid.*, p. 167.
78. Alfredo Allende (1963) p. 11.
79. Ramón Prieto (1963) p. 150.
80. 'Union leaders had to be interested in the complexion of national government – its potential hostility or friendliness towards them – whether they liked it or not'; Daniel James, 'Power and Politics in Peronist Trade Unions', typescript.
81. The '32' had the backing of ORIT representative Serafino Romualdi who on 18 November 1958, after a meeting with Frondizi, told reporters that the purpose of his visit had been 'to voice the stand of the international labour movement against the Argentine Law of Professional Association which does not permit trade union pluralism even if the rank and file desire it', see Romualdi (1967) p. 166.
82. The '32' declared that Frondizi had become 'an arrogant and tyrannical manager'; *La Nación*, 3 January 1959. The '19' added that the government had begun a 'repressive policy' against the unions (*ibid.*). Nelly Casas (1973) pp. 58–9 recalls how the 'more combative union leaders' – Cardoso (meat-packers), Framini (textiles) and Cavalli (oil-workers) – worked in close contact with the *frigeristas*, led by Ramón Prieto. Ironically, Cardoso and Cavalli would lead two bitter strikes against the government, while Framini's election to the governorship of the Province of Buenos Aires in March 1962 was decisive in bringing about the coup that toppled Frondizi.
83. Juan José Real (1962) p. 221.
84. Peronist leaders reassured US officials of their anti-communism and said their *rapprochement* with the '19' was only for 'tactical reasons'; Washington Archives, 735.00/6–259, 2 June 1959.
85. *Ibid.*
86. The doctors' strike, which lasted for two months and nine days, was sparked off by the decision taken by the Tramways Union (UTA)

to sack the medical chief of its social services – named by the military government – and reinstate the former Peronist medical officer. This decision was backed by Dr Noblía, the Public Health minister, who favoured the reinstatement of all doctors sacked by the *Libertadora*.
87. Frondizi (1978) i, p. 208.
88. Casas, *op. cit.*, p. 76
89. Personal interview with Bléjer.
90. The Senate passed legislation on 14 January 1959 to sell the meat-packing house notwithstanding the 9,000 workers demonstrating outside the building of Congress.
91. While the workers complained that *Lisandro de la Torre* was being 'privatised', a year later British and US companies in the meat-packing and exporting business complained at the disadvantage they were in with respect to CAP which had pressed for, and was promised by Frondizi, a 'regular flow of funds' amounting to a subsidy. This was at a time when all meat-packing plants had been making losses, but the foreign-owned companies had to resort to bank loans, not subsidies; Vestey's, Bovril and Liebig's had all made representations to HMG. They suggested that 'a Parliamentary Question might serve to strengthen the Argentine Government's determination to abide by their assurances' [that they would not favour CAP], something Sir John Ward had wisely discouraged; PRO FO 371/147803, 14 December 1960. There are copious files on the meat trade with Argentina though regrettably the Foreign Office still feels some of the information should be withheld indefinitely from public scrutiny.
92. The most serious strikes were: in May, bank employees; in August, a six-week strike in engineering and steel-making industries, in turn followed by a month-long textile workers' strike. Furthermore, eight days were lost in the course of the year as a result of three general strikes: over 11 million working days were lost in the Federal Capital alone, with 2.5 million workers involved. Daniel James has remarked that 'every one of these major conflicts was either lost or at best resulted in a bad compromise for the unions'; James (1978) p. 23.
93. L. Doyon, 'Labour Conflicts During the Peronist Regime (1946–1955)', typescript, 1974, p. 10.
94. Allende (1963) p. 93.
95. *La Nación*, 13 January 1959.
96. *La Nación*, 16 January 1959.
97. Prieto (1963) p. 190.
98. Bléjer saw himself as 'the exponent' rather than proponent of the hard line; US observers appear to agree with this self-perception; Washington Archives, 735.00/3–1059, 10 March 1959; also Casas (who later became Bléjer's wife) wrote that Bléjer accepted the post out of loyalty to Frondizi, knowing that he would be used as a 'scapegoat'; Casas, *op. cit.*, p. 82. The intervened unions were the

metallurgical workers' union (UOM), the textile workers' (AOT) and the meat-workers' (FOTC) and among the detainees were the top brass of Peronist unionism: Vandor, Cardozo, Alonso and Olmos.

99. *Frigeristas* like Allende and Prieto considered these events as the rupture of the '23 February front'; Allende, *op. cit.*, p. 101 and Prieto, *op. cit.*, pp. 189–91.
100. He added that 'conditions were not favourable to improvise a mass mobilisation, but with a few Resistance activists we can cause a big scandal that will have international repercussions'; Perón-Cooke (1973) p. 138.
101. *La Nación*, 28 February 1959. Cooke complained to Perón repeatedly that those in favour of a less militant approach (*los blandos*) were trying to undermine his (Cooke's) standing within and without the Peronist Movement, and appealed to Perón to intervene; *op. cit.,* p. 143, letter dated 5 February 1959.
102. Torre (1980) p. 146.
103. Perón-Cooke, *op. cit.,* vol. II, p. 61.
104. *Ibid.*, p. 179.
105. *Ibid.*, p. 222.
106. *La Nación*, 26 February 1959.
107. Diputados, 9 November 1961, p. 4823.
108. Although Alsogaray still claims he does not understand why Frondizi chose to dismiss him, there were several reasons. Firstly he had lost favour with Army generals over his handling of labour disputes; secondly, the UCRI had never stopped demanding his head; thirdly, Frondizi was growing 'restive at being subordinated to his own Minister'; PRO FO 371/155823, 26 April 1961.
109. For the events of those years see W. Little (1979) p. 364.
110. *Ibid.*
111. Doyon (1974) p. 38.
112. Alemann saw as his priorities balancing the budget, maintain a stable currency and thus attract foreign capital; he saw the reorganisation of the railways as the key to economic progress; personal interview. Although praising Alemann's ideas as 'orthodox and hitherto sensible', Sir George Middleton worried that he was 'very inexperienced, particularly on the political side, for such a big and tough job'; PRO FO 371/155823, 5 May 1961.
113. Acevedo had worked together with D. Fernández Beschtedt, Director General of Railways, in the drawing of the railways plan during Yrigoyen's presidency.
114. Diputados, 9 November 1961, p. 4859. Ernesto Sammartino, UCRP deputy, rashly accused the government of 'encouraging chaos, and persecuting workers, driving them towards desperate extremist positions', *ibid.*, p. 4819. For a summary of the main points of the plan, see Isidro Odena (1977) pp. 254–6.
115. *Mensaje del Presidente de la República al Honorable Congreso de*

la Nación, 1º de mayo de 1961, page 29. The plan included he construction of 13,000 kilometres of roads as well as 40 airports.
116. Interview with Alemann. Alemann implied that Alsogaray lacked such courage, and thus never carried out the rationalisation of the railways. Casas alleges that the 'spirit of rebellion' that characterised the rail strike was encouraged by the Navy intelligence services, and this was the reason behind Alsogaray's constantly placing obstacles; Casas (1973) p. 91.
117. PRO FO 371/155836, 15 December 1961. Alemann's and Acevedo's resignations had a 'depressing effect on business sentiment'; *ibid*.
118. Frigerio (1963a) p. 89.
119. *Ibid*.
120. *Ibid*., pp. 95–6.
121. de Pablo Pardo referred to this resentment in a conversation with US Ambassador Beaulac on 4 August 1959; Washington Archives, 735.00/8–459.
122. Lanusse interview.
123. Potash (1980) p. 280. Casas (1973) p. 101, points out that Frondizi had been very pleased with that part of his speech referring to the armed forces, and only later did he find out that his phrase about the forces no longer being 'the Praetorian guard of the president' had caused so much offence that some officers had considered early retirement, and others thought 'we must get rid of that guy'.
124. Potash, *op. cit.*, p. 272. Lanusse remarked how he had met Bléjer when the latter became ambassador to Mexico in mid-1959 after resigning the Labour ministry, and Lanusse was military attaché, and how a friendship developed after the mutual intial mistrust. Bléjer had on many occasions wanted Frondizi to talk with Lanusse, whose legalist opinions he held in great esteem, but Frondizi never acquiesced; Lanusse interview.
125. Many people pointed out as a serious shortcoming Frondizi's apparent inability to relate to the military. Babini offered as an interpretation Frondizi's alleged rejection when he had sought to follow a military career(personal interview); Bléjer in turn remarked on how Frondizi did not know how to relate to military men, a fact also underlined by Oyhanarte and Lanusse. Caraballo recalled two incidents which had caused unnecessary irritation in Navy circles, one involving Frondizi's nephew Román, and the other his brother Risieri; personal interview. Alsogaray referred to Frondizi's 'peculiar relatives' whose acts were not always easy to comprehend; personal interview. General Lanusse confirmed the 'messianic feelings' prevalent in some Army men; personal interview.
126. Zavala Ortiz told Federico de Alzaga in February 1958, 'Do you realise what has happened? Can't you see there's a communist in power?', to which Alzaga replied, 'Don't come to me with old wives' tales'; personal interview with Colonel de Alzaga. Alzaga recalled how the

UCRP was constantly urging the military to intervene, through Labayru and Toranzo Montero, who was really a 'Radical plotter'. General Colombo also recalled how 'every week the Radicals [UCRP] would come to the Córdoba barracks and urge us to overthrow Frondizi'; personal interview.
127. Washington Archives, 735.00/7–759, 7 July 1959.
128. PRO FO 371/147756, 16 March 1960, Sir John Ward to the Foreign Office.
129. PRO FO 371/147757, 25 November 1960, reporting on such misgivings.
130. Potash, *op. cit.*, p. 274.
131. See Potash, *op. cit.*, table 6, p. 275. For instance, a colonel who had received $3,100 prior to November 1957, was entitled to $10,500 six months later.
132. Casas, *op. cit.*, pp. 104–7, recounts several instances of inter-force rivalries.
133. Potash remarks that even within the Navy anti-Frondizi officers interpreted it as the intention of ending the force's land-based planes, *op. cit.*, p. 288.
134. Frondizi (1978) vol. I, pp. 151–6.
135. Krause had been Air Force minister during the *Libertadora*, and was one of the few high-ranking officers to support Frondizi during his campaign.
136. The British Ambassador wrote on 18 June 1959 that 'it had long been supposed that some form of agreement had been reached between representatives of Perón and Doctor Frondizi, if not between the two men themselves'; PRO FO 371/13899.
137. *La Nación*, 12 June 1959.
138. *Ibid.*
139. Washington Archives, 735.00/1–559, US Ambassador Farland in Ciudad Trujillo to Department of State, 6 January 1959. Trujillo went on to say that if Argentina 'would actively combat Communism' he would do 'everything within his power to keep Perón from causing political unrest in Argentina'; *ibid.* When in mid-August Trujillo 'in friendly manner' asked Perón for the reasons for engaging in a propaganda campaign against Frondizi in violation of the principles of exile, Perón 'explained his position saying [that] if Trujillo desired him to leave the Dominican Republic he prepared to do inasmuch as Castro offered him US £1 million as inducement [to] come to Cuba and engage in propaganda effort against "gringo imperialism in Latin America"'; Perón showed Trujillo a letter from Castro which he also showed to Vice-President Balaguer; Washington Archives, Secret telegram from Farland to Department of State, Washington, 15 August 1959, 735.00/8–1559.
140. President Aramburu and his commander in chief Ossorio Arana had recommended Carlos Severo Toranzo Montero as Frondizi's Army

Secretary, but the newly-elected President named Héctor Solanas Pacheco whom he knew since 1953 when they used to get together to discuss ways of overthrowing Perón; personal interview with Solanas Pacheco. According to Potash, the argument against Solanas was that he was not firm enough and was 'easily manipulated'; Potash, *op. cit.*, pp. 372–5 (Spanish version).

141. *Correo de la Tarde,* edited by Naval Captain Francisco Manrique, former chief of Aramburu's military household, and an acerbic critic of the government while insisting on the need to maintain legality, had carried a vitriolic article on 20 June blaming the 'unhappy state in the forces' on the government's 'devious policies' and 'infamous alliances with agents of dictatorship [Perón] or Communists', and warning that the country could 'no longer tolerate political Machiavellianism and integrationist infamous alliances'; quoted in Washington Archives, 735.00/6–2259, 22 June 1959. The US Embassy described Manrique's publication as representing '*gorila* elements, affiliates to the UCRP and conservatives (known locally as oligarchs), all of whom support democracy in principle especially if their candidate wins'; *ibid.*

142. Reimúndez had briefly been attached to the Labour Ministry during Lonardi's presidency. The belief was that on that occasion he had been in the forefront of Lonardi's attempt at establishing a '*peronismo sin Perón*'.

143. Gerardo Schamis, Frondizi's ambassador to Guatemala, told the US Ambassador that Reimúndez was an 'integrationist' close to Frigerio; Washington Archives, memorandum of conversation, 14 October 1959, 735.00/10–1559.

144. A US Embassy official remarked that apparently some time would have to elapse before the military 'become educated concerning the finer points of constitutional procedure and discipline'; Washington Archives, 735.00/7–759, 7 July 1959. The US Embassy was sufficiently worried about the situation as to suggest to Washington that an article should appear in the US press stating clearly that 'a coup d'etat or revolution in Argentina is the sure road to chaos'; Washington Archives, 735.00/6–2459, 24 June 1959.

145. Solanas believes Anaya's appointment was Reimúndez's idea via Bernardo de Larroudé; personal interview. Larroudé was Under-Secretary at the Ministry of Defence. For an account of the vicissitudes leading to General Toranzo Montero's appointment as Army Commander-in-Chief, see Casas, *op. cit.*, pp. 110–11, and Potash, *op. cit.*, p. 314.

146. Toranzo, from a Radical family, was showing signs of mental unbalance and was easily manipulated by UCRP plotters; Lanusse and de Alzaga interviews. Toranzo's father, General Severo Toranzo, had led a Radical military uprising against Uriburu in February 1931, and his son had been tortured after the rebellion was crushed. This episode is recounted in Potash (1969) pp. 58–61, fn. 11 and 14.

147. Alzaga went because he knew Toranzo well; they had returned together from exile in Montevideo in September 1955 and had flown together to Córdoba to join Lonardi's forces; personal interview.
148. Moreover, about 60 to 70 men who had been with Toranzo took the chance to escape that night behind Alzaga, 'so fearful were they of the possibility of a repression'. Alzaga was not impressed by the valour of his colleagues in the force. Years later he still shuddered at the recollection of Fonseca's comment when Alzaga insisted that the rebels had to be repressed: 'Well, you're used to that kind of thing', implying that coming from a land-owning family, Alzaga was presumably used to 'going around whiplashing peons' and would relish repression; personal interview.
149. According to Sánchez de Bustamante, Frondizi was following de Larroudé's advice, who told the president that 'once the first shot is fired, the government will have ceased to exist'; Sánchez de Bustamante believes Larroudé's mistake arose from his 'lack of sensitivity for psychological reactions in the armed forces'; personal interview.
150. These, of course, he regarded as 'bribes'; personal interview. The offer was made via General de Nevares.
151. Cf. Casas (1973) pp. 113–16.
152. Solanas, Lanusse and Sánchez de Bustamante regard these events as 'marking the point of no return' since the President strengthened his opponents and displaced those loyal to him; personal interviews.
153. Frondizi's friends saw it differently. A case in point was his refusal to appoint José Babini as Secretary of Culture because the Army regarded him as a Communist. On 27 April 1959 the government had issued Decree No. 4965, banning all activities by the Communist Party, ordering the closure of its offices and suspension of its publications, even though Vítolo preferred the legalisation of both Peronist and Communist parties; 'if Peronists can vote Peronist, they won't vote communist' he told a US Embassy official on 7 August 1959; Washington Archives, 735.00/8–1159, 11 August 1959.
154. The events were the handing over of the CGT to a committee representing twenty trade unions of which half were hardline Peronists; the election of Socialist Alfredo Palacios as Senator for the Federal Capital on a pro-Castro platform, and the Foreign Ministry's public offer on 6 March to have Argentina mediate between the US and Cuba (see below).
155. Personal interview with Frondizi.
156. Casas, *op. cit.*, p. 116.
157. PRO FO 371/155825, n.d. but probably mid-1961. Peruvian Ambassador Hoyos Ozores, a friend of Camilión's and Florit's, stated that the latter believed an agreement with Brazil was the way to 'force the United States to negotiate with Brazil and Argentina' in devising a policy towards South America; personal interview.

158. PRO FO 371/155825.
159. Personal interview.
160. Quoted in Pandolfi (1968) p. 94.
161. Frondizi was against Kennedy's Food for Peace, insisting on investment in heavy industry. In a memorandum to Kennedy, Schlesinger warned that in Latin America 'the atmosphere is set for miracles' and of the real danger that 'the intensity of present expectations may lead to future disappointments'; in Schlesinger (1965) pp. 177 and 188.
162. British Embassy to Foreign Office, PRO FO 371/155823, 17 March 1961. On Frondizi and Quadros see Lanús (1984) chapter 6.
163. Cf. Potash, *op. cit.*, fn. 11, p. 337. The *Chicago Tribune* report was attached to a secret report from the British Embassy in Washington to the Foreign Office, PRO FO 371/155832, 30 November 1961.
164. Record of conversation, PRO FO 371/14771, 14 July 1960. In a memorandum on the purpose of Frondizi's visit, the Foreign Office noted that 'Argentina hopes for positive and immediate economic benefits'; PRO FO 371/147770. A year later the British Ambassador had come round to Frondizi's view when he wrote to the Foreign Office: 'It is in our obvious political as well as economic interest that the efforts of this on the whole friendly and pro-Western government should be successful [. . .]. It is no use Argentina's friends waiting until full economic recovery has been achieved before producing their capital, for clearly this attitude can only lead to Argentina's ruin.' PRO FO 371/155836, 2 June 1961.
165. Ricardo Rojo introduced Carretoni, Frondizi's emissary, to Guevara in Punta del Este and was present when Carretoni extended Frondizi's surprising invitation, which Rojo interpreted as 'a provocation to the armed forces'; personal interview.
166. Air Secretary Rojas Silveyra recalled how he was notified by a lieutenant at the Don Torcuato airclub that an unauthorised plane had landed. Rojas Silveyra's reply was 'shoot and then tell me what happened'. When the lieutenant replied that there was a marine there, Rojas Silveyra repeated the order. The lieutenant disobeyed, and next thing Rojas Silveyra knew he received a telephone call from Frondizi telling him that Che was with him. The Air Secretary was horrified and told the president: 'Why did you not tell me? I would have brought him safely to you. There was almost a catastrophe'. Rojas Silveyra had known Guevara from the time both had belonged to the same rugby club; personal interview. Sánchez de Bustamante recalled that at the time, he had wondered 'what on earth was Frondizi up to', and that it was the 'clandestine manner' in which the affair was conducted that bothered the military; personal interview. General Lanusse also emphasised the latter point.
167. Casas, *ibid.*, p. 144. According to Pandolfi, Frondizi tried to convince Guevara to abandon guerrilla warfare; Pandolfi, *op. cit.*, pp. 95–103.
168. Personal interview with Rojo.

169. Such was the impact of Guevara's secret visit that it clouded any other consideration. Roberto Alemann recalled that few entrepreneurs 'understood that Frondizi was the solution: the majority was scared by Che's visit. Even those who support Frondizi (myself included) believe that he went astray in the foreign relations area', personal interview. See also Potash, *op. cit.*, pp. 338–9 for the impact of the visit, and Lanús (1984) chapter 5.
170. PRO FO 371/155825, 1 September 1961.
171. Cárcano's daughter had married Lord Astor of Hever and he was highly regarded in British Embassy circles. It was Cárcano who had first introduced Frigerio to the British Ambassador at the request of the former. The last two *frigeristas* in the administration holding posts of responsibility in the areas of foreign and economic affairs, Oscar Camilión (Undersecretary at the Foreign Affairs Ministry) and Economic advisor, Ambassador Arnaldo Musich, presented their resignations on 16 February as a result of the Punta del Este uproar. *La Nación* (18 Feb.) interpreted their resignations as 'a general movement towrds the dissolution of the "parallel government"'.
172. The other countries that abstained were Brazil, Bolivia, Chile, Ecuador and Mexico.
173. Schlesinger (1965) p. 780.
174. *Ibid.*, p. 781.
175. Quoted in Casas (1973) p. 155.
176. Potash has written that Frondizi did more than 'keep the military in the dark, that he deliberately undertook to deceive them, is the inescapable conclusion', *op. cit.*, p. 343. For a detailed account of the events of 1–3 February see *ibid.*, pp. 342–50 and Rouquié, *op. cit.*, pp. 184–5. The opposition had attempted – and failed – to include a debate on foreign policy in the day's agenda. See Diputados, 31 January 1962, p. 6525.
177. *La Nación*, 2 February 1962.
178. Personal interview with Nicanor Costa Méndez who was a member of Cárcano's Cabinet at the Foreign Ministry. Hoyos Ozores, the Peruvian Ambassador at Punta del Este, underlines the problems arising from the fact of Argentina's 'ambiguity towards Cuba' which was not the case with Quadros, who was openly pro-Cuba. The mistake Argentina made at Punta del Este was not to vote with the majority when it realised that the vote was going to be in favour of Cuba's expulsion; personal interview.
179. *La Nación*, 1 February 1962.
180. *Ibid.* In his letter of resignation Arnaldo Musich declared himself a Catholic, and said that those who were waging a campaign against him were 'agnostics belonging to the international freemasonry and to lay, materialist and atheist liberalism', *La Nación*, 16 February 1962.
181. Schlesinger (1965) p. 784.
182. Casas (1973) p. 160.

183. He was referring to the fact that the statutes of the OAS made no provision for the expulsion of a member state.
184. The whole text of the speech is given in Casas, *op. cit.*, pp. 444–52.
185. *La Nación*, 14 February 1962. Camilión and Musich submitted their resignations on the following day: see above.
186 Personal interview with Alsogaray. Pandolfi quotes an article published by Frondizi in *Confirmado* on 3 November 1966 where he declared his 'solidarity with the Vietcong' in its 'national struggle against a servile minority and foreign armies of occupation', *op. cit.*, p. 65.
187. Quoted in Rouquié, *op. cit.*, p. 185. In the 1930s *Criterio* had been the voice of Catholic Nazism, see Newton (1992) p. 124.
188. The other two were the need to think about economic matters, and the importance of only one labour federation at the national level; personal interview with Babini.
189. Babini interview.

Chapter 9

1. *La Nación*, 11 March 1960.
2. The results were:

	Senator	*Deputy*
Socialista Argentino	321,778	284,972
UCRP	314,377	317,560
UCRI	249,012	252,604
Blank	219,046	230,991

   Source: *La Nación*, 14 February 1961.
3. *La Nación*, 1 February 1961.
4. The Formosa results were:

UCRI	15,678
UCRP	14,665
Christ. Democ.	10,076
Socialist	746
Blank	544

   Source: *La Nación*, 16 January 1962.
5. As has been seen, the old UCR had been doctrinairily opposed to the proportional system, and both the UCRP and UCRI attacked the *Libertadora*'s decision in 1957 to favour the minority parties. See chapter 1.
6. *La Nación*, 24 November 1961.
7. *Ibid.*
8. Personal interview with Rodolfo Martínez, Aramburu's former Trade and Industry minister.
9. *La Nación*, 2 March 1962.

10. *Ibid.*
11. Casas (1973) p. 161.
12. *La Nación*, 9 March 1962. Frondizi told Pandolfi, 'it is natural that politicians should seek contributions from those who can afford them as long as they are not ideological opponents'; implying that the money had come from the oil contracts, Pandolfi added 'a financial puritanism would have been contradictory since it would not have allowed him to strengthen his political position'; Pandolfi (1968) p. 71.
13. In a personal interview Frondizi said he had bade farewell to his daughter Elena who left in February 1962 for a trip to the Far East, saying 'I shan't be here when you return'. Potash also doubts Frondizi's account of his own pessimism: *op. cit.*, p. 360.
14. Personal interview.
15. She attributes its authorship to a 'group negotiating between the president and Peronism', *ibid.*, p. 166.
16. Halperín (1964) p. 118. Rodolfo Martínez also mentioned Frigerio and Alende as the candidates being discussed; personal interview.
17. See Guardo (1963) pp. 347–67 for an account of the Peronist stance *vis-à-vis* the March elections.
18. Casas, *op. cit.*, p. 165 and Caraballo interview, who said that the trade unionists 'forced' Perón to agree to the participation of *Unión Popular* in the elections. Caraballo recalled how Perón used to dread Frigerio's visits: he complained the latter talked too much. Guardo also emphasises the role played by the union leaders in changing Perón's mind, *op. cit.*, p. 356. None the less, Sánchez de Bustamante recalled that Gelbard told him ten years later that the main factor behind Perón's change of heart was that 'a cheque for US $300,000 he had received [from Frigerio?] had bounced'; personal interview.
19. *La Nación*, 3 February 1962. Larralde died on 22 February. His death made the proscription of Peronism almost impossible, since it would have meant the UCRI candidate was the only one left.
20. *La Nación*, 16 March 1962.
21. *La Nación*, 14 March 1962.
22. *La Nación*, 17 March 1962. On 2 February the PCI had said it would not take part in the elections since 'no essential issues' were at stake and although the government had taken 'positive steps'(amongst which were the replacement of *Avellaneda* and the appeal to extra-party men), 'today, the government and the UCRI experience the increasing and conspicuous influence of a group and a mentality that we consider dangerous for the country. That group is Integrationist at the political level, opportunist on the international scene, and is imbued, as far as the economy is concerned, of a theory of dirigiste development which leads to inflation and corruption'; *La Nación*, 2 February 1962.
23. Cooke acknowledged the wisdom of the gamble when he wrote to Perón that he 'had no doubts that if Frondizi had remained in power, he would have upset us': see his 15 June 1962 letter to Perón (who had

not been replying to any of Cooke's letters for more than a year) in which he analysed the dangers for Peronism of losing its 'revolutionary character', Perón-Cooke, vol. II, pp. 223–35.
24. Alsogaray interview.
25. Potash, *op. cit.*, p. 359.
26. *La Nación*, 14 March 1962.
27. *La Nación*, 16 March 1962.
28. Interviews with Lanusse, Rojas Silveyra, Sánchez de Bustamante, Alsogaray, Hoyos Ozores. The view was that it had been a pathetic speech. Lanusse, who has regretted his role in Illia's overthrow in 1966, has not expressed similar feelings at Frondizi's downfall (Lanusse was out of the country at the time); personal interview.
29. Alsogaray interview. See also Potash, *op. cit.*, pp. 353–4.
30. *Anales de Legislación Argentina*, vol. XXII, 1962, pp. 342–3.
31. Interviews with Gelsi, at the time governor of Tucumán, and with Oyhanarte. Alende, the controversial governor of Buenos Aires, wrote to Frondizi demanding 'respect for the people's decision', *La Nación*, 20 March 1962. Indeed, a year earlier the British embassy remarked that 'Alende [was] one of a group of integrationist governors who have been in difficulties with the armed forces and there have been rumours that Alende might be removed and the Province "intervened"'; PRO FO 371/155823, 17 March 1961.
32. *La Nación*, 20 March 1962.
33. Juan Lozano remarked that during those days, 'the country was not being governed. The only thing in everybody's mind was how to "stay on"'; personal interview.
34. Personal interview with Martínez.
35. A *New York Times* editorial dated 22 March remarked that 'there is no nation in the hemisphere where politics, in the worst sense of the word, was played for personal gains and vested interests more callously than in Argentina. Had the Radical Party not split, the Peronists would not have won in a single province'.
36. When asked about the UCRP's decision to refuse Frondizi's overtures Zavala Ortiz said Frondizi was not interested in a political alliance but in the manipulation of people who might prove useful to him and thus could not be trusted; personal interview.
37. Interview with Bruno Quijano, a personal friend of Aramburu's and Frondizi's. According to Quijano, in 1961 himself, Aramburu, Frondizi and the UCRP's Larralde used to meet to find solutions to the several crises. Quijano was charged with visiting Perón in Spain: according to the former, General Franco was aware of what was going on. The solution proposed was that Aramburu would become president for the UCRI, Perón would be given back all his goods and properties confiscated by the *Libertadora*, and Larralde would break the UCRP and join forces with the UCRI. Aramburu's presidential ambitions were recorded by the British as early as 1959, cf. PRO FO 371/139004,

9 October 1959 and again in 1961 they reported that rumours were circulating in Buenos Aires that Amadeo would resign his UN posting to 'devote his energies' on behalf of Aramburu's campaign for 1964; PRO FO 371/155823, 17 March 1961.

38. Martínez recalls Aramburu's constant dithering during those days, at the receiving end of contradictory advice. In the end, still according to Martínez, Aramburu followed the worst advice and turned against Frondizi. According to Martínez, Aramburu, who was 'politically naive' had trusted Labayru's advice, something Martínez only found out after Frondizi's deposition, when he also found out from the then president Guido that Labayru had suggested his own name for the presidency. Thus Aramburu's more trusted adviser had all the time been 'playing his own game', personal interview.
39. Alsogaray interview.
40. *La Nación*, 24 March, and personal interview.
41. He was not alone. Potash reveals that US Ambassador McClintock 'acting apparently in advance of specific instructions from Washington . . . made personal calls on top military leaders to warn them of the serious difficulties Argentina would face with the United States if President Frondizi fell', *op. cit.*, p. 368.
42. Oyhanarte interview. Hoyos Ozores happened to be sitting near Poggi at the gala dinner Frondizi attended with the Duke of Edinburgh and asked Poggi about the rumours of Frondizi's overthrow; 'less than 20 metres away from Frondizi, Poggi replied: "But of course, we've got to get rid of this one as soon as possible"'. Hoyos says everybody was expecting Frondizi would be overthrown after Prince Philip's departure from Argentina. It was not to be.
43. Rauch (1971) p. 94.
44. *La Nación*, 22 March 1962.

Epilogue

1. After splitting with Frigerio, in the 1980s Frondizi went about inciting retired military officers to depose President Alfonsín, whose UCR administration was allegedly infiltrated by subversives and communists; Lanusse interview. At the beginning of the 1990s Frondizi has felt vindicated by President Menem's espousal of neo-conservative economic policies. In 1992, in the course of a very public ceremony conducted by Menem himself, Frigerio's son and close political associate, Octavio, became a card-carrying member of the Justicialist Party.

Bibliography

PRIMARY SOURCES

1. Interviews

In Buenos Aires, in the months of October–December 1979 and in April 1983:

Alconada Aramburú, Carlos
Alemann, Roberto
Alsogaray, Alvaro
Alsogaray, Julio
Babini, Nicolás
Bléjer, David
Botana, Natalio
Caraballo, Gustavo
D'Adamo, Roberto
Fernández, Raúl
Ferrari, Gustavo
Frigerio, Rogelio
Frondizi, Arturo
Landaburu, Laureano
Luna, Félix
Madanes, Manuel
Madariaga, Marta
Musich, Arnaldo
O'Connell de Alurralde, Liliana
Oyhanarte, Julio
Panzeri, Héctor
Quijano, Bruno
Quijano, Hipólito
Stábile de Machinandiarena, Blanca
Taccone, Juan José
Torrents, Arnaldo
Zavala Ortiz, Miguel Angel

In London in 1983:

Middleton, Sir George
Sándler, Héctor
Viñas, Ismael (in 1988)

In Toledo, Spain, in May 1984:

Alemann, Roberto
Alsogaray, Alvaro
Guadagni, Alieto
Hirschman, Albert
Martínez de Hoz, José Alfredo
Solá, Alberto
Wehbe, Jorge

In Barcelona and London, 1984:

Lozano, Juan

In Oxford, 1986:

Klein, Guillermo Walter

In Buenos Aires in the months of April–July 1988:

Alemann, Roberto
Alessandro, Darío
de Alzaga, Federico
Colombo, Eneas
Corach, Juan Carlos
Cornblit, Oscar
Cortés Conde, Roberto
Di Tella, Guido
Doglioli, Juan Carlos
Fraga, Rosendo (h.)
Frondizi, Arturo
Gallo, Ezequiel
Garfunkel, Jorge
Hoyos Ozores, Guillermo
Lanusse, Alejandro Agustín
Madanes, Manuel
Martínez, Rodolfo
Mondelli, Eugenio
Mora y Araujo, Manuel
Musich, Arnaldo
de Nevares, Jorge
Rojas Silveyra, Jorge
Rojo, Ricardo
Salonia, Alberto
Sánchez de Bustamante, Tomás
Solanas Pacheco, Héctor
Timerman, Jacobo
Triacca, Jorge

2. Printed Documents

Laws and Decrees: *Anales de legislación argentina, 1955–62*
Glennon, John P. *et al.* (eds), *Foreign Relations of the United States, 1955–1957*, volume VII, American Republics: Central and South America (United States Government Printing Office, Washington DC, 1987).

3. Congressional debates

Congreso Nacional, *Diario de Sesiones de la Cámara de Diputados, 1958–62.*
Congreso Nacional, *Diario de Sesiones de la Cámara de Senadores, 1958–62.*
Junta Consultiva Nacional, *Bases para la confección de una nueva ley electoral*, Buenos Aires, 1956.

4. Government Reports

Presidencia de la Nación, *Directivas Básicas del Gobierno Revolucionario* (Buenos Aires, November 1955).
Prebisch, Raúl, *Informe preliminar acerca de la situación económica*, Buenos Aires, 26 October 1955.
Presidencia de la Nación, Secretaría de Prensa, *Moneda sana o inflación incontenible*, and *Plan de restablecimiento económico* (Buenos Aires, 26 February 1956).
Presidencia de la Nación, *La Revolución Libertadora en 12 meses de gobierno* (Buenos Aires, November 1956).
Presidencia de la Nación, *Memoria del Gobierno Provisional de la Revolución Libertadora, 1955–58* (Buenos Aires, 1958).
Presidencia de la Nación, *Programa de estabilización para la economía argentina* (Buenos Aires, 29 December 1958).

5. Archives

Foreign Office Files on Argentina, 1955–61, held at the Public Record Office, Kew Gardens, London.
Department of State, *Foreign Relations of the United States: Diplomatic Papers* on Argentina, 1954–59, Washington National Archives, Washington DC
Glennon, John P. *et al.* (eds), *Foreign Relations of the United States, 1955–1957*, volume VII, American Republics: Central and South America (United States Government Printing Office, Washington DC, 1987).

SECONDARY SOURCES

1. Newspapers and periodicals

Cara o Cruz
Contorno
Criterio
El Príncipe
Financial Times
Informativo Radical
La Nación, 1955–62
País Unido
Programa Popular
Qué sucedió en siete días, 1956–59
Raíz
The New York Times, 1955–62
The Times
Tribuna Cívica

2. Unpublished theses and typescripts

Amaral, Samuel, 'El avión negor: retórica y práctica de la violencia', paper presented at the XVI meeting of the *Latin American Studies* Association, Washington DC, 4–6 April 1991.

Biddle, Nicholas, 'Oil and the Right in the 1928 Election', paper presented at the XVI meeting of the *Latin American Studies Association,* Washington DC, 4–6 April 1991.

Caimari, Lilia, 'El lugar del catolicismo en el primer peronismo', paper presented at the Instituto Universitario Ortega y Gasset, Madrid, 29–31 May 1991.

Cornblit, Oscar, 'Inmigrantes y empresarios en la política argentina' (mimeograph, Institute Di Tella, Buenos Aires).

Doyon, Louise, 'Labour Conflicts During the Peronist Regime (1946–1955)', mimeograph, October 1974.

James, Daniel M., 'Unions and Politics: the Development of Peronist Trade Unions, 1955–66' (Ph.D. thesis, University of London, 1979).

Makin, Guillermo, 'Political Crises in Argentina: 1955 and 1975–76' (Ph.D. thesis, University of Cambridge, 1984).

Sourrouille, Juan V., 'El impacto de las empresas transnacionales sobre el empleo y los ingresos: el caso de la Argentina', August 1976, mimeo.

Terragno, Rodolfo, 'Interview with Arturo Frondizi', typescript, n.d.

Zuvekas, Clarence, 'Argentine Economic Policies under the Frondizi Government, 1958–62' (Doctoral Dissertation, Washington University, 1967).

3. Books and Articles

Agor, Weston H. (ed.), *Latin American Legislatures: Their Role and Influence* (New York: Praeger, 1971).
Almond, Gabriel A., and Sidney Verba (eds), *The Civic Culture Revisited* (Boston: Little, Brown, 1980).
Allende, Alfredo, *Historia de una Gran Ley* (Buenos Aires: Arayú, 1963).
Amadeo, Mario, *Ayer, Hoy y Mañana* (Buenos Aires: Ediciones Gure, 1956).
Arendt, Hannah, 'Truth and Politics', in Peter Laslett and W. G. Runciman (eds), *Philosophy, Politics and Society* (Basil Blackwell, 1969).
Aricó, José, 'Il marxismo latinoamericano negli anni della Terza Internazionale', in *Il marxismo nell'eta della Terza Internazionale*, 3 vols (Torino: Giulio Einaudi editore, 1981).
Ascher, William, *Scheming for the Poor. The Politics of Redistribution in Latin America* (Harvard University Press, 1984).
Baer, W. and Kerstenetzky, I., *Inflation and Growth in Latin America* (Illinois: R. D. Irwin, 1964).
Babini, Nicolás, *Frondizi: de la oposición al gobierno* (Buenos Aires: Celtia, 1984).
Balasubramanyam, V. N. and S. Lall (eds), *Current Issues in Development Economics* (Macmillan, 1991).
Bauer, Peter T., *Dissent on Development* (Weidenfeld and Nicolson, 1976).
Beltrán, Virgilio (ed.), *El futuro político de la Argentina* (Buenos Aires, Editorial del Instituto Di Tella, 1978).
Berghahn, V., 'Ideas into Politics: The Case of Ludwig Erhard', in Bullen *et al.*
Berlin, Sir Isaiah, *Four Essays on Liberty* (Oxford University Press, 3rd edition, 1975).
Botana, Helvio, *Memorias. Tras los dientes del perro* (Buenos Aires, 1985).
Botana, Natalio, *El orden conservador* (Buenos Aires: Sudamericana, 1979).
——, *La tradición republicana* (Buenos Aires: Sudamericana, 1984).
Brauner Rodgers, Susana, 'El nacionalismo yrigoyenista (1930–1943)', *Estudios Interdisciplinarios de América Latina y el Caribe*, Tel Aviv, vol. 1, no. 2, July–Dec. 1990, pp. 79–98.
Bullen, R. J., H. Pogge Von Strandmann and A. B. Polonsky, *Ideas into Politics. Aspects of European History, 1880–1950* (Croom Helm, 1984).
Bruton, Henry J., 'Contemporary Theorising on Economic Growth', in Hoselitz *et al.*
Cantón, Darío, *Materiales para el estudio de la sociología política en la Argentina* (Buenos Aires: Editorial del Instituto Di Tella, 1968).
——, *Elecciones y partidos políticos en la Argentina. Historia, interpretación y balance: 1910–1966* (Buenos Aires: Siglo XXI, 1973).
Carri, Roberto, *Sindicatos y poder* (Buenos Aires: Jorge Alvarez, 1967).
Casas, Nelly, *Frondizi: una historia de política y soledad* (Buenos Aires: La Bastilla, 1973).

Cavarozzi, Marcelo, 'Sindicatos y Política en Argentina, 1955–1958', *Estudios CEDES*, vol. 2, no. 1 (Buenos Aires, 1979).

——, 'Consolidación del sindicalismo peronista y emergencia de la fórmula política argentina durante el gobierno frondizista', *Estudios CEDES*, ii no. 8 (Buenos Aires, 1979).

——, *Autoritarismo y democracia (1955–1983)* (Buenos Aires: Cedal, 1983).

CEPAL (ECLA), *Problemas y perspectivas del desarrollo industrial latinoamericano* (Buenos Aires: Solar-Hachette, 1964).

Chenery, Hollis B. (ed.), *Studies in Development Planning* (Cambridge, Mass.: Harvard University Press, 1971).

Ciria, Alberto, *Partidos y poder en la Argentina moderna (1930–1946)*, (Buenos Aires: Jorge Alvarez, 1964).

Conil Paz, Alberto and Gustavo Ferrari, *La Política Exterior Argentina, 1930–62* (Buenos Aires: Huemul, 1962) (English version by Notre Dame University Press, 1966).

Corbière, Emilio, *Conversaciones con Osar Alende* (Buenos Aires: Hachette, 1978).

Crick, Bernard, *In Defence of Politics* (Penguin, 1979).

Crassweller, Robert, *Perón and the Enigmas of Argentina* (New York: Norton, 1987).

Debrun, Michel, 'Nationalisme et politiques du développement au Brésil', in *Sociologie du travail*, vol. vi, Paris, 1964.

Del Carril, Bonifacio, *Crónica Interna de la Revolución Libertadora* (Buenos Aires: del Plata, 1959).

Del Mazo, Gabriel, *La primera presidencia de Yrigoyen* (Buenos Aires: Centro Editor, 1984).

Del Mazo, G. and Etchepareborda, Roberto, *La segunda presidencia de Yrigoyen* (Buenos Aires: Centro Editor, 1984).

de Pablo, Juan Carlos, *La Economía Argentina* (Buenos Aires: Editorial de Belgrano, 1977).

——, *La economía que yo hice* (Buenos Aires: Ediciones El Cronista Comercial, 1980).

Diamond, L., J. Linz and S. M. Lipset (eds), *Democracy in Developing Countries*, vol. IV, *Latin America* (Lynne Rienner Publishers, 1989).

Díaz, Fanor, *Conversaciones con Rogelio Frigerio* (Buenos Aires: Hachette, 1977).

Díaz Alejandro, Carlos, *Exchange Rate Devaluation in a Semi-Industrialized Country. The experience of Argentina 1955–1961* (Cambridge, Mass.: The MIT Press, 1965).

——, *Essays on the Economic History of the Argentine Republic* (New Haven: Yale University Press, 1970).

Dietz, James and Dilmus James (eds), *Progress Towards Development in Latin America* (Lynne Rienner, 1990).

Di Tella, Torcuato, Germani, Gino, *et al.*, *Argentina, sociedad de masas* (Buenos Aires: Eudeba, 1966).

Di Tella, Guido and M. Zymelman, *Las etapas del desarrollo económico*

argentino (Buenos Aires: EUDEBA, 1967).
Di Tella, Guido, *Argentina under Perón* (St Antony's/ Macmillan Series, 1983).
Di Tella, Guido and D. C. M. Platt (eds), *The Political Economy of Argentina, 1880–1950* (St Antony's/Macmillan Series, 1985).
Di Tella, Guido and Rudiger Dornbusch (eds), *The Political Economy of Argentina, 1946–83* (St Antony's/Macmillan Series, 1989).
Di Tella, Guido and D. Cameron Watt (eds), *Argentina Between the Great Powers, 1939–46* (St Antony's/Macmillan Series, 1989).
Di Tella, Guido and C. Rodríguez Braun (eds), *Argentina 1946–83. The Economic Ministers Speak* (St Antony's/Macmillan Series, 1990).
Domínguez, Nelson, *Conversaciones con Juan J. Taccone* (Buenos Aires: Hachette, 1977).
Doyon, Louise, 'El crecimiento sindical bajo el peronismo', *Desarrollo Económico*, April–June (Buenos Aires, 1977).
Eisenhower, Milton S., *The Wine is Bitter. The United States and Latin America* (New York: Doubleday, 1963).
Escudé, Carlos, *Gran Bretaña, Estados Unidos y la declinación argentina, 1942–49* (Buenos Aires, 1983, 2nd. edition 1988).
Feith, Herbert, *The Decline of Constitutional Democracy in Indonesia* (New York: Cornell University Press, 1962).
Fennell, C., 'Congress in the Argentine Political System: An Appraisal', in W. H. Agor, 1971.
Ferrari, Gustavo and Ezequiel Gallo, *La Argentina del Ochenta al Centenario* (Buenos Aires: Editorial Sudamericana, 1980).
Ferrer, Aldo, M. Brodersohn, E. Eshag, and R. Thorp, *Los planes de estabilización en la Argentina* (Buenos Aires: Paidós, 1969).
FIAT/OECEI, *Veinticinco años de la vida económica y financiera de la República Argentina* (Buenos Aires, 1961).
Floria, Carlos (ed.), *Reflexiones sobre la Argentina política* (Buenos Aires: Editorial de Belgrano, 1981).
Floria, Carlos and César García Belsunce, *Historia política de la Argentina contemporánea, 1880–1983* (Madrid: Alianza Universidad, 1988).
Florit, Carlos A., *Las fuerzas armadas y la guerra psicológica* (Buenos Aires: Concordia, 1963).
Foxley, A., McPherson, M. and G. O'Donnell, *Development, Democracy and the Art of Trespassing* (University of Notre Dame Press, 1986).
Frigerio, R., *Desarrollo y bienestar o contracción, miseria y dictadura* (Buenos Aires: Concordia, 1962a).
——, *Los cuatro años(1958–1962). Política económica para argentinos* (Buenos Aires: Concordia, 1962b).
——, *Las condiciones de la victoria* (Montevideo: A.Monteverde, 1963a).
——, *Crecimiento económico y democracia* (Buenos Aires: Losada, 1963b).
——, *Estatuto del Subdesarrollo* (Buenos Aires: Jorge Alvarez, 1967).
——, *De acusado a acusador: vigencia de una política* (Buenos Aires: Plus Ultra, 1979a).

———, *Síntesis de la historia crítica de la economía argentina* (Buenos Aires: Hachette, 1979b).
Frondizi, A., *Petróleo y Política. Contribución al estudio de la historia económica argentina y de las relaciones entre el imperialismo y la vida política nacional* (Buenos Aires: Raigal, 1956).
———, *Petróleo y Nación. Prólogo y notas por Arturo Sábato* (Buenos Aires: Editorial Transición, 1963).
———, *La Argentina: ¿Es un país subdesarrollado?* (Buenos Aires: Ediciones CEN, n.d.).
———, *Estrategia y táctica del movimiento nacional* (Buenos Aires: Editorial Desarrollo, 1964).
———, and R. Frigerio *et al.*, *Introducción a los problemas nacionales* (Buenos Aires: Ediciones CEN, 1965).
———, *Mensajes Presidenciales*, 5 vols (Buenos Aires: Ediciones CEN, 1978).
Furet, François, *Interpreting the French Revolution* (Cambridge University Press, 1981).
Gallo, Ezequiel, 'Reflexiones sobre la crisis de la democracia argentina', in Floria (ed.).
———, 'Argentina: Society and Politics, 1880–1916', in Leslie Bethell (ed.), *Cambridge History of Latin America*, vol. V, c. 1870 to 1930 (Cambridge University Press, 1985).
Gerchunoff, Pablo, 'Peronist Economic Policies, 1946–55', in Di Tella and Dornbusch.
Germani, Gino, *Política y sociedad en una época de transición* (Buenos Aires: Paidós, 1962).
Gerschenkron, Alexander, *Continuity in History and Other Essays* (Cambridge, Mass.: The Belknap Press, 1968).
Giddens, Anthony, *Capitalism and Modern Social Theory* (Cambridge University Press, 1974).
Gillespie, Richard, *Soldiers of Perón. Argentina's Montoneros* (Clarendon Press, 1982).
Goldar, Ernesto, *Buenos Aires: vida cotidiana en la década del 50* (Buenos Aires: Plus Ultra, 1980).
Gómez, Alejandro, *Política de Entrega* (Buenos Aires: Lillo, 1963).
Graciarena, Jorge, 'La industrialización como desarrollo. Políticas industrializadoras, orden social y estilos neoliberales', *Trimestre Económico*, L.(3), July–Sept. (Mexico, 1983).
Grancelli Chá, Néstor, *De la crisis al desarrollo nacional* (Buenos Aires: Ediciones Desarrollo, 1961).
Gravil, Roger, 'Gran Bretaña y el ascenso político de Perón: un nuevo enfoque', *Ciclos*, Año I, vol. I, no. 1, Buenos Aires, 1991.
Guardo, R., *Horas difíciles, 1955–Septiembre-1962* (Buenos Aires: Peña Lillo, 1963).
Habakkuk, H. J., 'Historical Experience of Economic Development', in Robinson (ed.).

Hall, Peter A. (ed.), *The Political Power of Economic Ideas: Keynesianism across Nations* (New Jersey: Princeton University Press, 1989).
Halperín Donghi, Tulio, 'Del fascismo al peronismo', *Contorno*, no. 7/8 (July 1956).
——, *Argentina en el callejón* (Montevideo: Arca, 1964).
Hartwell, R. M., 'Progress and Dissimilarity in Historical Perspective', in Kindleberger and Di Tella (eds).
Hayek, F. A., 'The Confusion of Language in Political Thought', *Institute of Economic Affairs* (1968).
Hirschman, Albert O. (ed.), *Latin American Issues. Essays and Comments* (New York: Twentieth Century Fund, 1961).
——, 'La confesión de un disidente', *Trimestre Económico*, LI, Jan.–Mar., 3–31 (Mexico, 1984).
Hoselitz, Bert F. *et al.*, *Theories of Economic Growth* (Illinois: The Free Press of Glencoe, 1960).
Huntington, Samuel P., *Political Order in Changing Societies* (New Haven: Yale University Press, 1971).
James, Daniel, 'Power and Politics in Peronist Trade Unions', *Journal of Inter-American Studies and World Affairs*, vol. 20, no. 1 (February, 1978).
——, *Resistance and Integration: Peronism and the Argentine Working Class, 1946–1976* (Cambridge University Press, 1988).
Jauretche, Arturo, *FORJA y la década infame* (Buenos Aires: Coyoacán, 1960).
Jones, E. L. and S. J. Wolf (eds), *Agrarian Change and Economic Development. The Historical Problems* (Methuen and Co., 1969).
Jones, Trevor, *Ghana's First Republic, 1960–1966. The Pursuit of Political Freedom* (Methuen and Co., 1976).
Katra, William H., *Contorno. Literary Engagement in Post-Peronist Argentina* (London and Toronto: Associated University Presses, 1988).
Key, V. O., *The Responsible Electorate. Rationality in Presidential Voting, 1936–60* (Cambridge, Mass.: Harvard University Press, 1966).
Kindleberger, Charles P. and Guido Di Tella (eds), *Economics in the Long View. Essays in Honour of W. W. Rostow*, 3 vols (The Macmillan Press, 1982).
King, John, *El Di Tella y el desarrollo cultural argentino en la década del sesenta* (Buenos Aires: Ediciones de Arte Gaglianone, 1985).
Klich, Ignacio, 'Failure in Argentina: The Jewish Agency's Search of Congressional Backing for Zionist Aims in Palestine, 1946', in Amilat (ed.), *Judaica Latinoamericana II* (Jerusalem: Hebrew University Press, forthcoming).
Kvaternik, Eugenio, *Crisis sin salvataje: la crisis político militar de 1962–63* (Buenos Aires: Ediciones IDES, 1987).
Lal, D., *The Poverty of Development Economics* (Hobart Paperback 16 (London: Institute of Economic Affairs).
Lanús, Juan Archibaldo, *De Chapultepec al Beagle. Política exterior argen-*

tina 1945–1980 (Buenos Aires: Emecé, 1984).

Lanusse, Alejandro A., *Protagonista y Testigo* (Buenos Aires: Marcelo Lugones Editores, 1988).

Lewis, Paul H., *The Crisis of Argentine Capitalism* (University of North Carolina Press, Chapel Hill and London, 1990).

Limoeiro Cardoso, Miriam, *La ideología dominante* (México: Siglo XXI, 1975).

Little, Walter, 'La organización obrera y el estado peronista, 1943–1955', *Desarrollo Económico* (Buenos Aires, 1979).

Lonardi, Marta, *Mi padre y la Revolución del 55* (Buenos Aires: Cuenca del Plata, 1981).

Luna, Félix, *Diálogos con Frondizi* (Buenos Aires: Editorial Desarrollo, 1963).

——, 'Alem, la terrible integridad', in Ferrari and Gallo (1980).

Mathias, Peter, *The First Industrial Nation. An Economic History of Britain, 1700–1914* (New York: Charles Scribner's Sons, 1969).

Mazol, A., N. Habegger and A. Armada, *Los católicos posconciliares en Argentina* (Buenos Aires: Galerna, 1970).

Meier, Gerald M. and Dudley Seers (eds), *Pioneers in Development* (Oxford University Press/World Bank, 1984).

Montemayor, Mariano, *Claves para entender a un gobierno* (Buenos Aires: Concordia, 1963).

Musich, Arnaldo, *La política económica argentina y su proyección internacional* (Buenos Aires: Concordia, 1962).

Mustapic, A. M., 'Conflictos institucionales durante el primer gobierno radical: 1916–1922', *Desarrollo Económico*, vol. 24, no. 93, April–June (Buenos Aires, 1984).

Newton, Ronald C., *The 'Nazi Menace' in Argentina, 1931–1947* (California: Stanford University Press, 1992).

Nisbet, Robert, *History of the Idea of Progress* (New York: Basic Books, 1980).

Nkrumah, Kwame, *I Speak of Freedom. A Statement of African Ideology* (Heinemann, 1961).

Odena, Isidro, *Libertadores y Desarrollistas* (Buenos Aires: Astrea, 1977).

Oyhanarte, Julio, *Poder político y cambio estructural en la Argentina. Un estudio sobre el estado de desarrollo* (Buenos Aires: Paidós, 1969).

Pandolfi, Rodolfo, *Frondizi por él mismo* (Buenos Aires: Galerna, 1968).

Parera, R., *Los Demócrata Cristianos Argentinos* (Buenos Aires: Editorial Buschi, 1986).

Pavón Pereyra, Enrique, *Conversaciones con Juan D. Perón* (Buenos Aires: Hachette, 1978).

Perina, Emilio, *El presidente cautivo* (Buenos Aires: Editorial Directrices, 1962).

——, *Detrás de la crisis* (Buenos Aires: Periplo, 1963).

——, *La máquina de impedir* (Buenos Aires: Editorial Historia Contemporánea, 1981).

Perón, Juan D. and John W. Cooke, *Correspondencia Perón-Cooke*, 2 vols (Buenos Aires: Granica, 1973).
Philip, G., *Oil and Politics in Latin America. Nationalist Movements and State Companies* (Cambridge University Press, 1982).
Popper, Karl, *The Poverty of Historicism* (Routledge and Kegan Paul, 1972).
Pisarello Virasoro, Roberto G. and Emilia E. Menotti (eds), *Arturo Frondizi. Historia y problemática de un estadista*, 3 vols (Buenos Aires: Depalma, 1986).
Potash, R., *The Army and Politics in Argentina, 1928–45* (Stanford University Press, 1969).
Potash, R., *The Army and Politics in Argentina 1945–62: Perón to Frondizi* (The Athlone Press, 1980).
Prebisch, Raúl, *The Economic Development of Latin America and its Principal Problems* (United Nations, 1950).
——, 'Recollections', in di Tella and Platt.
Prieto, Ramón, *El Pacto* (Buenos Aires: En Marcha, 1963).
——, *Correspondencia Perón-Frigerio, 1958–1973* (Buenos Aires: Macacha Güemes, 1975).
Rabe, Stephen G. [1988] *Eisenhower and Latin America. The Foreign Policy of Anticommunism* (Chapel Hill: University of North Carolina Press, 1988).
Ramos, J. A., *Revolución y contrarrevolución en Argentina* (Buenos Aires: La Reja, 1961).
Randall, L., *An Economic History of Argentina in the Twentieth Century* (New York: Columbia University Press, 1978).
Ranis, P., 'Profile Variables among Argentine Legislators', in W. H. Agor.
Rapoport, Mario, *Gran Bretaña, Estados Unidos y las clases dirigentes argentinas, 1940–45* (Buenos Aires: Belgrano, 1980).
Rauch, Enrique, *Un juicio al proceso político argentino* (Buenos Aires: Editorial Moharra, 1971).
Real, Juan José, *30 años de historia argentina* (Buenos Aires: Actualidad, 1962).
Rey, Esteban, *Frigerio y la traición de la burguesía industrial* (Buenos Aires: La Siringa, 1959).
Robinson, E. A. G. (ed.), *Problems in Economic Development* (The Macmillan Press, 1965).
Rock, David, *Politics in Argentina 1890–1930* (Cambridge University Press, 1975a).
——, (ed.), *Argentina in the Twentieth Century* (Duckworth, 1975b).
Romualdi, Serafino, *Presidents and Peons. Recollections of a Labour Ambassador in Latin America* (New York: Funk and Wagnalls, 1967).
Rose, Richard, *The Problem of Party Government* (Penguin, 1974).
Rostow, W. W.(ed.), *The Economics of the Take-Off into Sustained Growth* (New York: St. Martin's Press, 1963).
Rouquié, Alain, *Radicales y desarrollistas* (Buenos Aires: Schapire, 1975).

———, *Poder militar y sociedad política en la Argentina*, 1943–1973, 2 vols (Buenos Aires: Emecé, 1982).
———, (ed.) *Argentina hoy* (Buenos Aires: Siglo XXI, 1982).
Rozitchner, León, 'Experiencia proletaria y experiencia burguesa', in *Contorno*, no. 7/8 (July, 1956).
Sábato, Arturo, *Petróleo. Dependencia o liberación* (Buenos Aires: Macacha Güemes, 1974).
Salvadori, Massimo, 'Kautsky fra ortodossia e revisionismo', in *Storia del Marxismo*, vol. 2 (1981).
Schlesinger, Arthur M. Jr., *A Thousand Days. John F. Kennedy in the White House* (Cambridge, Mass.: Houghton Mifflin Company, 1965).
Senén González, Santiago and J. C. Torre, *Ejército y sindicatos. Los 60 días de Lonardi* (Buenos Aires: Galerna, 1969).
Sigal, S. and E. Verón, 'Perón: Discurso político e ideología' in A. Rouquié (ed.).
Sigal, Silvia, *Intelectuales y poder en la década del sesenta* (Buenos Aires: Puntosur, 1991).
Smith, Peter H., *Politics and Beef in Argentina. Patterns of Conflict and Change* (New York and London: Columbia University Press, 1969).
———, *Argentina and the Failure of Democracy. Conflict among Political Elites, 1904–1955* (Madison: University of Wisconsin Press, 1974).
Smith, William C., *Authoritarianism and the Crisis of the Argentine Political Economy* (California: Stanford University Press, 1989).
Smulovitz, Catalina, *Oposición y gobierno: los años de Frondizi* (Buenos Aires: Centro Editor, 1988).
Snow, Peter G., *Political Forces in Argentina* (New York: Praeger, 1979).
Solberg, Carl, *Oil and Nationalism in Argentina. A History* (California: Stanford University Press, 1979).
Stiller, Jesse H., *George S. Messersmith., Diplomat of Democracy* (University of North Carolina Press, 1987).
Tcach, César, 'Sabattinismo: identidad radical y oposición disruptiva', *Desarrollo Económico*, July–Sept. 1988, vol. 28, no. 110.
———, *Sabattinismo y Peronismo. Partidos políticos en Córdoba 1943–1955* (Buenos Aires: Sudamericana, 1991).
Terán, Oscar, *En busca de la ideología argentina* (Buenos Aires: Catálogos, 1986).
Torre, Juan Carlos, *Sindicatos y trabajadores en la Argentina, 1955–1976* (Buenos Aires: Cedal, 1980).
———, *La Vieja Guardia Sindical y Perón. Sobre los orígenes del peronismo* (Buenos Aires: Sudamericana, 1990).
Tosco, Agustín, *La lucha debe continuar* (Buenos Aires: Libros para el Tercer Mundo, 1975).
Troiani, Osiris, 'Examen de conciencia', in *Contorno*, no. 7/8 (July, 1956).
Vacs, Aldo César, *Discreet Partners. Argentina and the USSR since 1917* (University of Pittsburgh Press, 1984).
Villanueva, Javier, 'Argentina's Inflationary Experience (1943–62)' in Baer

and Kerstenetzky.
Viñas, David, 'Une chronologie et quatorze notes à propos de l'Argentine', in *Les Temps Modernes*, no. 420–421 (Paris, July–Aug. 1981).
Viñas, Ismael, *Orden y Progreso (La Era del Frondizismo)* (Buenos Aires: Palestra, 1960).
Waissman, Carlos H., *Reversal of Development in Argentina . Postwar Counterrevolutionary Policies and their Structural Consequences* (New Jersey: Princeton University Press, 1987).
Walzer, Michael, *The Revolution of the Saints. A Study in the Origins of Radical Politics* (Weidenfeld and Nicolson, 1966).
Youngson, A. J. (ed.), *Economic Development in the Long Run* (Allen and Unwin, 1972).
Zalduendo, Eduardo, *Geografía electoral de la República Argentina* (Buenos Aires: Hachette, 1958).
Zuvekas, Clarence, 'Economic Growth and Income Distribution in Post-War Argentina', *Inter-American Economic Affairs*, vol. 20, no. 3, 1966.

Index

Acevedo, Arturo, to restructure railways, 190, 191, 282n
agriculture
  agrarian question, 40, 98
  deprived of resources, 4
  exports neglected, 129
  fall in producer living standards, 27
  made to subsidise industrial development, 129–30
  reform, 43
agriculture/livestock programme, 28
Air Force, disassociated itself from Aramburu, 59
Alconada Aramburú, Carlos, 55, 56, 57
Alem headquarters, 93
  and *Avellaneda* principles, 94
Alemann, Roberto, Economy Minister, 129, 190, 191, 261n, 262n, 264n, 282n
Alende, Oscar, 155, 163–4
Allende, Alfredo, 114–15
  resignation of, 188
Alsogaray, Alvaro, 26, 99, 189, 217, 255n, 262n
  accused by *Qué*, 105
  dismissal of, 125, 262–3n, 282n
  as Economy Minister, 123–6, 260–1n; appointment of opposed by UCRI, 157–9; and Labour Minister, 179–80, 278n
  and Education Law, 148
  and *Partido Cívico Independiente* (PCI), 92, 105–6
Alvear, Marcelo T. de, 35–6, 237n
Alvearismo, 35
Alvearistas, 38
Alzaga, Colonel Federico de, 198, 283–4n, 286n
Amadeo, Mario, 17, 102, 170, 180, 231n
  urged an effective, centralised CGT, 180
Amnesty Law, 140–1, 152

anarco-sindicalists, 91
Anaya, General, 198
anti-Peronists, 15, 53, 213, 230n
antipersonalismo, 35
anti-Semitism, 229n
Aramburu, General Pedro Eugenio, 2, 12, 47, 78, 109, 110, 134–5, 141, 199
  asked for Frondizi's resignation, 217
  asked to mediate with armed forces, 217
  Cabinet: anti-Frondizi members, 56; reshuffle, 55
  a 'Democracy for Democrats', 19–30; economic issue, 26–7; electoral issue, 21–4; provisional character of new administration, 20; relations with labour, 24–6
  efforts to secure US financial aid, 27–30; turned down on matter of principle, 60–1
  establishing political rule, 32
  followed worst advice, 216–17, 292n
  government unable to form a coherent labour policy, 25
  outrage at Argentina's pro-Cuba stance, 204
  President: confrontation with armed forces, 57–9; and the economy, 59–61; Jan. 25th Government reorganisation, 54–7
  wanted proportional representation, 210
Argentina, 29
  as an underdeveloped country, 87
  bottlenecks in the economy, 116
  Britain blamed for state of, 90, 105
  dependence on world markets for primary products, 4
  isolation of, 43, 238n
  lacking dollar reserves, 30

Index

not socially mature for a revolution, 172
restrictive role of stagnant external sector, 116
satisfying British needs, 78–9
seen as nationalistic, 242–3n
voted against Cuban expulsion from inter-American system, 203
armed forces, 113
confrontation within the Aramburu government, 57–9
and CONINTES Plan, 142–3; applied in Córdoba Province, 159–61
and developmentalism, 192–207
distrust of Frigerio, 141–2, 152, 154
and foreign policy, 206
and Frondizi, suspicions concerning Frondizi-Quadros meeting, 202–3
and Frondizi: arrested, 216; exerting pressure on, 124; mistrust of, 223
and politics, 159
salary increase, 194–5
state of, 13–16, 194–5, 206
unrest in, 19, 109, 195, 197, 272n
army
a divided force, 14
indiscipline of, 15–16, 231n
intra-army confrontations, 57–8
political unrest continuing, 59
renewed intervention of, 16–17
army–navy confrontation, 58
austerity programme
Aramburu, 60
Frondizi, 121
Avellaneda Charter, 47, 53, 65, 82, 99, 112, 147, 173
main pronouncements, 39–44
remained official platform for UCRI, 91–2

Babini, José, 286n
Babini, Nicolás, 93, 114, 247n, 251n, 272–3n
Balbín, Ricardo, 22, 50, 56, 64–5, 160
Bases de acción política, 40–1
future path for Radicalism, 42–3
Batalla del Petróleo, 118, 136–8
Bengoa, General, 14, 19, 232n

Blanco, Dr Eugenio, 55, 240n
blank balloting, 67, 69, 209, 244n
Bléjer, Dr David, 186, 271n, 281–2n
moved against the unions, 187–8
Britain
Frigerio approached Ambassador for loan, 126–7
in Frigerio's thinking, 89
Buenos Aires Province, governorship elections, 211–12

cabinet of national unity, 216
Camilión, Oscar, 204, 286n, 288n
capital accumulation, 123
Cárcano, Miguel Angel, 258n, 288n
Foreign Affairs Minister, 203; explaining pro-Cuba vote, 204
Casa Rosada air-raid, 10
Castro, Fidel, 200–1
impact of triumph, 175
Catholic Church, 228–9n
backing needed by Frondizi, 100–2
price of support from, 150–1
retaliation against Perón, 9–10
rewarded by Frondizi, 114
Catholicism, enlightened, 166
caudillos' (*punteros*') style, 239n
la Causa, and the UCR, 34
Centro de Investigaciones Nacionales (CIN), 94, 95
Cerrutti Costa, Dr Luis, 18, 232n
CGE (small and medium business federation), 177
CGT (General Confederation of Labour), 10, 18, 68, 88–9, 208
CGT Unica, 183–4, 280n
intervention by Aramburu, 24
returned to Peronists, 191, 286n
seen as symbol of Peronist evils, 24–5
strike in support of Perón, 11–12
C(H)ADE (electricity company), 36, 45, 235n
expropriation of, 29
Chamber of Deputies, 132
Constitution (1853), 46
favoured by Constituent Assembly, 71
Chascomús Convention, 161–4
Che Guevara, 277n, 287n

Frondizi's secret meeting with, 201–2, 287–8n
Christian Democratic Party, 102, 108, 166, 216, 228n, 253n
churches attacked, 10–11
Cientificismo, seen as wrong by Left, 175
citizens' rights, 164
civilian/military links, 1
'cinco por uno' speech, 12
Concordancia, 36
Confederación General del Trabajo *see* CGT
Congress
  can be convened by Executive Power, 132
  composition of, 132
  and Frondizi, 133–43
CONINTES Plan, 142–3, 188, 269n
  applied in Córdoba Province, 159–61
conspiracy theory, 89
Constituent Assembly
  1957 July–Nov., 64–70; position of the parties, 64–7; position of Peronism, 67–70
  and Decree No 3838, 67
  elections for, 55
  party withdrawals led to end of, 70–1
Constitution, 1949, 64
  and state of siege, 141
Contorno (monthly journal), 171
  analysis of Peronism, 171–2
  and *Frondicismo*, 173–4
Cooke, John William, 67–8, 70, 180, 244n, 245n, 282n, 290–1n
  aimed to legalise Peronism, 71–2
  on Frondizi and social peace, 181–2
  participation in meatpackers' strike, 187
  and Perón–Frondizi alliance, 68
  and Peronism, 188–9
  Perón's personal representative, 62–4
  and the unions, 188
Córdoba Province, federal intervention of, 159–61
Córdoba rebellion, 12–13
Criterio (magazine), on Paraná speech, 205–6
Cuban Issue, 200–6

Damonte Taborda case, 110, 256n
de Pablo Pardo, Luis María, 102, 154, 170, 272n
  on Alsogaray's entry into government, 124
  as legal adviser, 115
del Carril, Bonifacio, 16
del Carril, Emilio Donato
  Economy Minister, 114, 264n
  proposed stabilisation plan to IMF, 120–1
del Castillo, Santiago, 165
del Mazo, Gabriel, 54, 99, 114
democracy
  devalued by private deals, 222
  institutions disregarded, 221
  restoration of, 54–5
democratic politics, to be restored, 19–20
democratic reorganisation, 55
de-nationalisation, 127
Depression, in Argentina, 35
devaluation, 27, 117
development, 108–30
  meanings of, 80
  priority zones, 88
  and underdevelopment, 86–7
developmentalism, 33, 76–7, 92, 220–4
  aims: development, 108–30; goals and projections, 221–2; legality, 131–46; social peace, 168–207
  as an ideology, 77–9; role of, 89–91, 222
  and the Catholic Church, 102
  developmentalists as Vanguard, 91
  economic programme, implementation of, 108–30; evaluation of policies, 122–30
  and entrepreneurs, 176–9
  and intellectuals, 168–76
  and labour, 179–82; main confrontations, 185–91; the state of the unions, 182–5; workers and the National Movement, 180–2
  and the military, 192–207
  as National Doctrine, 89–91
  preference for secretiveness, 220
  premises of, 83–9
  and science, 83
  'scientific' ('technological')

Index

approach well received, 220
and UCRI, 155
developmentalist months, May–Dec. 1958, 118–20
Díaz Alejandro, Carlos, 129
  on Argentina's economic performance, 4
  on industrial investment, 6–7
DINIE (National Directorate of State Enterprises), sale of companies, 127, 263–4n
di Pietro, Hugo, 13
divorce legislation, 229n
doctors' strike, 280–1n
drought, 4, 50

ECLA, 26, 178
  and industrialisation, 81–2
economic democracy, 42, 99
economic growth, 82
  transformation through, 79–80
economic modernisation, 121
economic policy
  and the electoral campaign, 92
  under Perón, 5
economic stability, priority of, 121
economy, centrally-planned, 42
education
  freedom of, 99, 148–9
  freedom to learn and to teach, 112–13
  Frondizi against State monopoly, 101
  private, 149, 150
Education Law, 112, 126–9, 148, 148–51, 155, 275n
Eisenhower, Milton, 5
election rigging, 1–2, 35
elections
  1961 elections, 208–10
  28 July, aftermath of, 70–3
  March 1962 elections, 210–15;
    Buenos Aires Province, 211–13
electoral abstentionism, 36, 69, 237n
electoral calendar/timetable, 55, 57
  and elections, 132
electoral campaign, and its organisation, 91–7
electoral issue, and the Aramburu government, 21–4

electoral law, 23–4
electoral systems, 185
  see also incomplete list system; proportional representation; Sáenz Peña Law
electricity, shortage of, 4
energy nationalisation, and UCR, 36
entrepreneurs
  and developmentalism, 176–9
  domestic, resented competition with multinationals, 177–8
  and rational expectations, 178–9
European Community, restrictive import policies, 129
Eximbank, 29, 30
exports, 129, 226n
  decline in, 117
  increase never materialised, 259n
  reduced, 4
external debt, 4, 128–9

factions, and tendencies, 236n
federal intervention, Córdoba Province, 159–61
Federation of Centre Parties, 166
fiscal policy, 112
Florit, Carlos, 115
foreign capital, 86, 103, 123, 152, 268n, 287n
  ECLA warning, 82
  good and bad, 126
  see also foreign investment
Foreign Capital Investment Law, 127
foreign debt, 117
foreign exchange, need to earn, 28
foreign firms, locating in Argentina, 127–8
foreign investment, 112, 126–9, 148, 155, 178
  Aramburu's government, 27–30
  pleas in favour of, 55, 99
foreign policy, 162–3, 200
foreign reserves, drop in, 26
FORJA (Fuerza de Orientación Radical de la Joven Argentina), 36–7, 38
Fraga, General Rosendo, Army Secretary, 199
Framini, Andrés, 214, 215
Framini–Perón ticket, Buenos

Aires governorship election, 212–13
La Fraternidad (footplatemen's union), 183
free trade, 123, 181
free-market economy, 26, 148
Frigerio, Rogelio, 73, 124–5, 145, 147, 220, 247n, 248n, 249n
  against Constituent Assembly elections, 66
  campaigned against blank ballots and abstentionism, 69
  Crecimiento económico y democracia, 79
  and development, 80, 279n
  dogmatism of, 155–7
  and ECLA, 82
  and economicism, 78, 85
  economic competence questioned, 120
  encouragement to industrial entrepreneurs, 176
  foreign investment, responsibility for, 126–9
  Frondizi's loyalty to, 151
  historical interpretations of, 84–5
  and petroleum, 139–40
  integracionista style, 138
  integrationist ideas, 88–9
  and *Luis M. Campos* headquarters, 93–4
  and Marxism, 248n; influencing thinking of, 84–5; Marxian readings, 78, 83
  and normalisation of union life, 181
  politics of, 221–2
  references to science, 83
  Secretary for Socio-Economic Relations, 114, 115, 153–4; resignation of, 154, 186, 196, 272n
  seeking agreement with Perón, 212–13
  The Statute of Underdevelopment, 85
Frondizi, Arturo, 1, 11, 36, 47, 78, 233n, 256n
  achievements of, 75–6
  agitation related to trip to USA, 187–8
  and the armed forces' role, 193–4, 283n

austerity programme, 121–1
  and *Avellaneda*, 40–2, 43, 173; role in drafting of, 40–1, *see also* *Avellaneda Charter*
  backed by Perón, 68–9
  and the business community, 110–11
  Cabinet of, 113–16
  campaigned against Constituent Assembly elections, 65–6
  and the Catholic Church, 100–2, 257n
  commitment to open government, 113
  and a 'conditioned Presidency', 207
  and Congress, 133–43; Amnesty Law, 140–1; CONINTES Plan, 142–3; oil contracts, 133–40; State of Siege, 141–2
  and the Cuban Issue, 200–6
  denial of Perón–Frondizi pact, 74
  distanced Radicalism from government, 49
  efforts to hinder candidacy, 22
  and elections, 56
  fall of, 208–19; Bill of Proportional Representation, 210–11
  from Radicalism to Developmentalism, 97–107; oil, 103–6
  growth in sympathy for, 109–10
  historical interpretations of, 85
  inaugural address, 111–13
  inept at canvassing, 240n
  intervened Provinces won by Peronists, 215–16
  and the judiciary, 143–4
  lack of political loyalties, 151–64, 198
  loss: of electoral support, 145–6; of Peronist backing, 221
  and the military, 192–207
  morality of ends and morality of means, 174
  Paraná Speech, 205–6
  and Perón, 72–3
  Petróleo y Política, 103–4, 136, 173
  as presidential candidate, 50–1
  on the Radical Party, 44–5
  recognised need for international finance, 86
  relations with the political parties,

Index

148–67; with minority parties, 165–7; with UCRI, 148–64; with UCRP, 164–5
  reminder to *Libertadora* on democratic rule, 48
  and the Right, 170–1
  secret meeting with Che Guevara, 201–2
  and a sole CGT, 183–4
  supportive publications, 95–6
  and the UCR split, 52–3
  writing in *País Libre*, 37
  see also Perón–Frondizi Pact
Frondizi, Risieri, 149
Frondizi–Quadros meeting, 202–3
FUBA (Buenos Aires University students' union), 149, 251n
  and *Alem* headquarters, 93–94

Gelbard, José, 124–5, 177, 261n, 262n
Gelsi, Celestino, 49, 50, 95, 159, 240n, 274n
general strike, against cost of living, 185
Golpismo, 194
Gómez, Vice-President Alejandro, 51, 257n, 271n
  resignation of, 151–3
Gómez Morales, 6
government expenditure, reduction in, 60
government/unions relationship, 191
governors, in conflict with President, 133, 265n
governorships, Buenos Aires Province, 211–12
Goyeneche, Juan Carlos, 17, 232n
guardianship, 15, 231n
guerrilla groups, 159
Guglialmelli, Colonel Juan Enrique, 114
Guido, José María, as President, 218

Holland, Henry, acting as go-between, 14–15, 27–8, 29, 234–5n

Illia, Arturo, 49, 51
  President, annulled Frondizi contracts, 136
impeachment, 132
import permits, 278n
import policies, restrictive, 129

import substitution, 4, 5, 26, 77, 177
imports
  and foreign debt, 117
  increased, 119
  need to cut, 118
  of raw materials, 177, 259n
income redistribution, 5
income tax, 264–5n
incomplete list electoral system, 23, 132, 185, 210
  discriminated against smaller parties, 165–6
Independent Civic Party *see Partido Cívico Independiente* (PCI)
industrial base, new, 121–2
industrial democratisation, 43
industrial development, 41
Industrial Promotion Law, never implemented, 179
industrialisation, 76, 77, 79, 87, 221
  and ECLA, 81–2
  investment hampered, 6–7
  pace slowing, 4–5
  and repressed demand, 117
  UCRI programme, 148
industry
  entry of foreign firms, 127–8
  growth in production, 259n
  protected, 117, *see also* protectionism
'Infamous Decade', 35
inflation, 28, 60, 119, 121
  causes of, 26–7
  checking of, 123
  rampant, 4
Insurrexit, 83, 248n
integracionista style, 138
integration
  concept of, 180, 278–9n
  geographical, 88
  idea of, 87–9, 249–50n
  political, 88–9
  regional, 88
Integrationism *see Developmentalism*
Integrationists, 205, 221, 222, 290n
intellectuals
  abandoned Frondizi, 175
  and developmentalism, 168–76
  left-wing, 171, 174–5
Intransigence, 41, 147, 148, 151, 238n

orthodox group in, 173–4
Sabattinismo, 270n
true spirit of, 43–4
Intransigencia, 39, 39–40, 98, 131
  during the Peronist decade, 44–7
  and Perón, 43

Jaramillo, Baltazar, 96, 252n
Jitrik, Noé, 100
Jauretche, Arturo, 70, 97, 245n, 252–3n
judiciary, and Frondizi, 143–4
Junta Consultiva Nacional (JCN), 20–1, 150, 270n
  bickering in, 57
  minority parties over-represented, 24

Kennedy, President, 200–3
Krause, Commodore Julio, 59
  Krause case, 195–6, 284n
Krieger Vasena, Adalbert, 60
Kubitschek, Juscelino, 79–81

La Nación (newspaper)
  analysis of March 1962 election result, 218–19
  comment on Chascomús, 163
  on deputies for Buenos Aires Province, 163
  on pro-Cuba vote, 204
  published Perón's letter concerning the armed forces, 196
  on UCRI split, 211
La Prensa (newspaper)
  attacked Church interference, 9
  problem of, 6, 254n
labour, 279n
  Aramburu's relations with, 24–6
  and developmentalism, 179–82
  Lonardi's relations with, 18–19
labour conflicts, 25
lagging wages, rule of, 182
Landaburu, Laureano, 22, 55, 217, 229–30n
Lanusse, General Alejandro A., 109, 230n, 283n
Larcher, General, 160, 198, 199
Larralde, Crisólogo, 49, 51, 52, 213–14, 291n
Latin American Common Market, 82

Lebensohn, Moisés, 38–9, 41
Left, the, 171–6
  and *Qué*, 101, 253n
legality, 131–46
legislative power, composition of, 131–3
liberalisation
  move towards slow, 122–3
  results of policies, 129
Libertadora see Revolución Libertadora
Lisandro de la Torre strike, 186–9, 281n
Lonardi, General Eduardo, 2, 8, 47, 170, 230n, 231n, 273n
  consulted Prebisch, 26–7
  the foiled 'National Revolution', 16–19
  relations with labour, 18–19
  as head of provisional government, 13
Luis M. Campos headquarters, 93, 94
  concerned with the future, 94–5
Luna, Félix, 93
  on Frondizi, 252n

Machinandiarena, Narciso, 95, 258n
MacKay, Luis, 114, 257n
Madanes, Manuel, disappointment of, 256n, 278n
magistrates, removed from office, 143–4
The Manchester Guardian, on Perón's influence on Frondizi, 66–7
manufacturing, structural changes in, 177
Martínez, Rodolfo, 58, 216, 217, 218, 292n
Marxism, 175
  in Frigerio's thinking, 84–5
Marxists, in the government, 170–1
meat-packers' strike *see Lisandro de la Torre* strike
Mendoza oilworkers' strike, 154, 185–6
Menem, President, 1, 16, 292n
Menéndez, General, rebelled against Perón, 7, 230n
metal-workers union (UOM), 18
MID *see* Movement for Integration and Development
military Junta, 13
military tribunals, 142
minority parties, relationship with Frondizi, 165–7

MIR *see Movement for Intransigence and Renovation*
Molina, General, 13
Movement for Integration and Development (MID), 87–8, 155, 164, 220
Movement for Intransigence and Renovation (MIR), 39, 39–40, 47, 48, 51
see also Intransigencia
Movement for Unity and Coordination (MUCS), 183
Mugica, Adolfo, Foreign Affairs Minister, resignation of, 203

national development, 162
national movement, 88, 89, 95, 110, 150, 168
and the armed forces, 192–207
favoured by *Qué*, 96–7
and the workers, 180–2
national reconciliation, 1
national union, 173
nationalisation Bills, 45
nationalism of ends and nationalism of means (Frigerio), 86, 90, 94, 126
see also Revolución Libertadora
natural resources, nationalisation of, 41
Navy, 10, 241n, 283n
asked for Frondizi resignation, 216
discontent in, 58–9
proposal on party registers, 22
New York Times, 291n
on Argentine political parties, 255n
on Frondizi's victory, 107
'19' group unions, 185, 280n
non-intervention, 205
non-Peronist voters, 213

oil, 57
Frondizi, *Qué* and Alsogaray on, 103–6
imports, 60
nationalisation, 103
nationalism, 99
need for self-sufficiency, 79, 104, 135
oil contracts, 75, 103, 125, 152
under Frondizi, 133–40, 266–7n, 268n

oil resources
exploitation of, 112, 240–1n
and nationalism, 45
State monopoly defended, 45–6
oil workers' union (SUPE), 185–6
Onganía, General Juan Carlos, 85, 192
Organisation of American States (OAS), 289n
Punte del Este Conference, 201–4
Orgaz, Alfredo, 143–4
resignation of, 144
Ossorio Arana, Arturo, 284n
Colonel, 12, 19; dramatic army purge, 15
General: Army Minister, 57–8, 242n
resigned, 59
Oyhanarte, Julio, 144, 218, 269–70n

País Libre (weekly publication), and the UCR, 37–8
País Unido (weekly publication), 95
on *Petróleo y Politica*, 104
Palacios, Alfredo, 133, 152, 209
Pandolfi, Rodolfo, 171, 173, 253n
called for realism, 173
parallel government, 164, 205, 214
accusations of, 153–5
Partido Cívico Independiente (PCI), 92, 124, 166, 216, 290n
battle against totalitarian bureaucratism, 106
support for UCRI, 214
Tribuna Cívica, 105, 106
party registers, 22
Penal Code, amendments proposed, 142
Perette, Carlos, 152, 164–5, 269n, 274n
Perón, Juan Domingo, 225n, 254n
ambivalent attitude towards Catholic Church, 8–9, 11
anti-clericalism, 228n
and Cooke, 72, 110, 188, 279n
effect of continued absence, 180
in exile, 62–4
and Frondizi, 72–3, 246n
and the *Intransigencia*, 43
and the labour market, 5
liberalised his regime, 10–11
nationalisation of the working class, 88–9

negotiations with Standard Oil, 134
overthrow of, 2–3
overtures towards Americans, 5–6, 7–8, 77; to discuss bilateral military cooperation, 227n
and Peronist vote, 68–9, 73
revelation of Perón–Frondizi pact, 196–7
and Sabattini, 238n
and Standard Oil contracts, 134
and the unions, 181
withdrawal from Buenos Aires governorship election, 213
and the working classes, 171–2
Perón–Frondizi pact, 70–3, 75, 284n
impact of revelation, 196–7
a stumbling block, 155–7
Peronism, 3–4, 89, 96, 180, 223, 225n
and blank balloting, 209
Contorno's analysis, 171–2
no respect for intellectuals, 169
partial legality, 208
position of, Constituent Assembly (July–Nov.), 67–70
and *Qué* magazine, 56–7
and sole labour confederation, 183
survival of as a political force, 25–6
in the unions, 191–2
without Perón, 17
Peronist regime, 113
decline of, 3–11; economic context and relations with USA, 4–8; religious front, 8–11
Peronists, 164
efforts to reintegrate into mainstream politics, 153–4
labour movement divided, 192
not satisfied with Amnesty Law, 140–1
participation in 1962 elections, 212
voted for UCRI, 108
winning governorships, 215
petroleum *see* oil
Pinedo Plan, 35
political contributions, 290n
political integration, 88–9
political parties
Frigerio saw no role for, 155
in March 1962, 213–15

position of, Constituent Assembly (July–Nov.), 64–7
statute of, 22–3
see also individual parties
political repression, 25
political rule, 32
political stability, enhanced, 221
Prebisch, Raúl, 4, 81–2, 117, 234n
Preliminary Report on the Economic Situation in Argentina, 26–7
presidentialist tradition, shortcomings of, 131–2
Presidents, legislation by decree, 132–3
price controls, 119
private enterprise, 112
and oil contracts, 136, 137
privatisation, 127, 263–4n
proposal led to *Lisandro de la Torre* strike, 186–9, 281n
productive forces, development of, 123
productivity, expanded, 27
Profesión de Fe Doctrinaria, 40–1
Progressive Democrats, 166
proletariat/working class, 88, 171–2
militancy of, 182
proportional representation, 24, 57, 166, 210–11, 216, 289n
intended to curtail UCRP, 210
protectionism, 176
distortions of, 121
and the 'National Bourgeoisie', 177–8
Provisional Government, rebuffed, 109
public expenditure, to be cut, 121
public services, rationalisation of, 190

Qué magazine, 53, 56, 59, 69, 78, 170, 252n
articles on oil, 104, 254–5n
Frigerio: editorials anticipating developmentalism, 76–7; and normalisation of union life, 181
and Frondizi: and Alsogary on oil, 103–6; campaigned for, 95, 96; education and the Church, 99–103; role of in electoral campaign, 96–7; support for, 56, 71
principles and pragmatism, 174

reported Frigerio–Frondizi friendship, 94–5

Radical Bloc of the 44, 44
Radicalism, 94, 99–100
  central precepts violated, 155–7
  Frondizi's government rooted in, 154–5
  future path, 42–3
  and the intellectuals, 173
  and the oil contracts, 138–9
  and the Organic Charter, 47–8
  reunification of, 216–17
  in the UCR, 40–2
radicalismo, as an opposition, 23
Radicals,
  and Perón, 228n
  and the UCR, 33–4
railways, 28, 129, 189
rail-workers
  demobilisation of, 183, 190
  strike, 189–91
rail-workers' unions, 183
Ramírez, General, 102
  UF: independence of, 189; intervened by CGT, 189
rational expectations, and entrepreneurs, 178–9
realism/pragmatism, 170, 200, 254n
rebellion, in Córdoba, 12–13
recession, 182
Reforma Universitaria, 36, 99–101
Reimúndez, Colonel, 197, 285n
relative prices, fluctuations in, 179
religious education, 42
  legalised, 8–9
remittances of capital abroad, 6, 227n
La Resistencia, 25
  Peronism in, 62–4
Revolución del Parque, 1
Revolución Libertadora, 1–31, 48
  an account, 11–13
  caretaker or revolutionary, 54–61
  differentiating between origins and intentions, 232n
  failure of, 31
  punishment of dissent, 16
  Qué's views concerning, 96
  and the unions, 182

Rial, Rear-Admiral Arturo, 58, 195
The Right, 170–1
Rio Bamba headquarters, 93–4, 151
road transport, developmentalist bias towards, 190
Rojas, Admiral, 1, 13–15, 16, 47, 141
  chairman of the JCN, 23
  vice-president, 58
Rojas Silveyra, Jorge, 287n
Rojo, Ricardo, 68, 115, 245n, 258n
  on oil contracts, 266n
Romero, José Luis, 101
Romualdi, Serafino, 280n
  brought N. American support to anti-Peronist unions, 183–4
Rostow, W. W., sequential development model, 80–1
Rozitchner, León,
  on political dilemma of the intellectuals, 175–6
  on proletariat's adherence to Perón, 172

Sábato, Arturo, 259n
Sabattini, Amadeo, 37, 38, 50, 51, 52
Sabattinismo, 270n
Sabattinistas, 71, 147
  to vote for *Unión Popular*, 214
sabotage, 63, 142
  against the railways, 191
Sáenz Peña Law, 23–4, 57, 65, 108, 166, 236n
Sánchez de Bustamante, General Tomás, 109, 290n
Scalabrini Ortiz, Raúl, 97, 104–5, 241n, 252–3n
  on contracts with foreign oil companies, 125
Schmuckler, Samuel, 114, 176, 256–7n
science, role of, 83
secretariats, dependent on Presidency, 114–16
self-determination, 205
Senate, 132
short-termism, 179
sindicalistas libres, 18, 19
'62' group unions, 184–5, 243n
  indefinite general strike, 187–8
  recommended blank balloting, 209

social justice, 37, 82, 237n
social peace, 168–207
  use of armed forces, 192–4
social policy, 162
social resentment, 19
social unrest and sabotage, 25
social welfare, through Eva Perón Foundation, 9
socialism, 169
  and development of productive forces, 84
Socialist Party, attacked Frondizi, 166–7
Socialist Party Congress, 166
Socialists, 108, 183
  support for free trade, 181
Sociedad Rural Argentina (SRA), 177
Solanas Pacheco, Héctor, 59, 76, 197, 198, 285n
Stábile de Machinandiarena, Blanca, 95, 253n, 258n
stabilisation plan, 118, 120–2, 181, 200, 260n
  consequences of harsh implementation of, 159–61
  main steps, 122
stand-by loan requested from IMF, 120–1
Standard Oil Company contract, 8, 46, 77, 103, 134
State
  and growth, 86
  role of: and take-off, 81; under Frondizi, 112
State interventionism, caused Argentina's problems, 106
state of siege, 141–2, 152, 154, 186
  authorised by Senate, 132
strikes, 25, 43, 63, 142, 281n
  doctors, 280–1n
  oil-workers, 141, 154
  rail-workers, 189–91
Suárez, Colonel José Francisco, 230n
subsidies, 281n
  elimination of, 60
Supreme Court of Justice, 143

'take-off', 81
tariff barriers, 123
tax laws, 132

technology, and integration, 87
tecnólogos, 174
terms of trade,
  deterioration in, 82
  worsened in 1950s, 116–17
terrorism, 63, 142
  blamed on Perón, 159–60
  repression of, 142
'32' group unions, 184–5, 243n, 280n
Timerman, Jacobo, 213, 261n
Toranzo Montero, General Carlos Severo, 160, 284–5n, 285n
  as Army Commander-in-Chief, 198–9
  a challenge to Frondizi, 197
trade union leaders, and Peronism, 62, 63
trade union membership, 181
trade unions, 43
  development of, 62–3
  militancy, 187
  opposition to Frondizi government, 184–5
  Peronist unionism, reconstitution of, 25–6
  role of, contrasting views, 18–19
  state control over, 184
  state of, 182–5
  subdued mood of, 5
  to be handed back, 112
  and wage policies, 180
Trade Unions Law, 184–5
transport deficiencies, 116–17
Triacca, Jorge, 225n
Tribuna Cívica
  on future moves of Frondizi government, 106–7
  sought to distance PCI from old political parties, 105–6
Troiani, Osiris, 171, 172
Trujillo, 284n
  and Perón–Frondizi pact, 197

UCR, 1, 21, 98, 273n
  in the 1930s, 35–8
  in the 1940s, 38–44; the *Avellaneda Charter*, 39–44, 47
  in 1952 elections, 47
  1956 National Convention, Tucumán, 49–51

antiacuerdista principle, 43–4
dominant issues, 236n
internal structure of, 47–9
Intransigencia, 22, 38–44
Manifesto of Three, 44
minority groups in, 48
National Committee, 48; intervened rebel districts, 51–2
Organic Charter, 39, 47–8
presidential candidates, 50
Radicalism in, 40–2
split of, 23, 32–53, 222, 233n; background of internal strife, 33–5; birth of UCRI, 51–3
tendencies in, 34–5
and Unionists, 43
UCRI, 23, 54, 70, 71, 145, 208
ambiguity of election victory, 108
Chascomús Convention, 161–4
and the Constituent Assembly, 65
control of Senate, 133
displeasure at Alsogaray appointment, 157–9
fought election on its programme, 92–3
ineffectiveness of, 158–9
lacking clarity and purpose, 147
Movement of Intransigent Affirmation, 154–5
and Peronism, 73–4
position on the oil issue, 104–5
relationship with Frondizi, 148–64, 210–11; the Education Law, 148–51; Frondizi lacking political loyalty, 151–64
retained *Avellaneda*, 91–2, 147
split in, 163–4, 211
three headquarters, three programmes, three styles, 93–6
and UCR split, 51–3
upset by *Batallo del Petróleo* speech, 137
UCRP, 23, 71, 145, 147, 166, 208, 274n
amendments submitted to Assembly, 65
formation of, 53
found Amnesty Law unacceptable, 140
losing votes to Peronism, 214

National Convention, rejected 1949 Constitution, 64
no real alternative to government, 213–14
preference for, 55–6
relationship with Frondizi, 164–5, 274n
UES (Union of Secondary School Children), 9
UN Economic Commission for Latin America *see* ECLA
underdevelopment, and development, 86–7
unemployment, 80
Unión Cívica Radical *see* UCR
Unión Cívica Radical del Pueblo *see* UCRP
Unión Cívica Radical Intransigente *see* UCRI
Unión Democrática, 8
Unión Ferroviaria (UF), see also Railworkers' Unions
Unión Industrial Argentina (UIA), 177
Unión Popular, Peronist, 212, 290n
unionistas, 22–3, 39, 233n
Unionists, 147
concern among, 46–7
and UCR, 43
unions *see* trade unions
Universities
need for changes, 100
private, 149
university students, 169, 270n
voting for Frondizi, 257n
Uriburu, General, 102
USA, 204, 232n
Aramburu's efforts to secure financial aid from, 27–30, 235n
refused on matter of principle, 60–1
attitude to Menéndez rebellion, 7
cultural, educational and technical assistance, 174–5
dumping of agricultural surpluses, 116
Frondizi hoped for loans from, 201
investment in Argentina, 7–8, 259n
loan to Argentina, 120–1, 260n
'Motives of the Argentine Revolution', 226–7n
on national integration, 249–50

willingness to assist Argentina, 5–6
see also Holland, Henry
USSR
    campaign for closer relations with Latin America, 235n
    willing to aid Argentine oil industry, 136–7, 267n

Valle, General, execution of, 16
Vandor, Augusto, 192
Vandorismo, 192
Verrier, Roberto, 55, 60
'vice-president's plot', 152–3
Viñas, Ismael, 171
    achievements of UCRI, 173, 251n
    criticism of Right, 276n
    on Marxists, 276–7n
    on right-wing intellectuals, 275–6n
violence, 223–4
    Peronist, 233n
Vítolo, Alfredo, 114, 152, 196
    felt certain of UCRI victory, 214
    resignation, 215

wages, 182
    agreements frozen, 185
    extensive rises, 118–19
wheat, 116, 226n

workers
    and the national movement, 180–2

Yacimientos Petrolíferos Fiscales
    see YPF
Yadarola Plan on oil, 135–6
Youth Conferences, UCR, 38–9
YPF, 46, 104, 118, 134
    monopoly position did not reject collaboration, 104–5
    and private capital, 136
Yrigoyen, Hipólito, 32, 43, 101, 116, 236n
    commitment to oil nationalisation, 134, 265n
    President, 1–2
Yrigoyenismo, 35, 147
Yrigoyenista themes, 40–2
Yrigoyenistas, 38, 134

Zanichelli, Arturo, 151, 153, 160–1, 273n
Zavala Ortiz, Miguel Angel, 25, 48, 51, 52, 152, 206, 239n, 275n, 276n
    on internal divisions in the UCR, 50
    worried by failing support of *Libertadora*, 48–9